REGNUM EDINBURGH CENTENARY SERIES
Volume 1

Edinburgh 2010
Mission Then and Now

REGNUM EDINBURGH CENTENARY SERIES

The centenary of the World Missionary Conference of 1910, held in Edinburgh, was a suggestive moment for many people seeking direction for Christian mission in the 21st century. Several different constituencies within world Christianity held significant events around 2010. From 2005, an international group worked collaboratively to develop an intercontinental and multi-denominational project, known as Edinburgh 2010, and based at New College, University of Edinburgh. This initiative brought together representatives of twenty different global Christian bodies, representing all major Christian denominations and confessions, and many different strands of mission and church life, to mark the centenary.

Essential to the work of the Edinburgh 1910 Conference, and of abiding value, were the findings of the eight think-tanks or 'commissions'. These inspired the idea of a new round of collaborative reflection on Christian mission – but now focused on nine themes identified as being key to mission in the 21st century. The study process was polycentric, open-ended, and as inclusive as possible of the different genders, regions of the world, and theological and confessional perspectives in today's church. It was overseen by the Study Process Monitoring Group: Miss Maria Aranzazu Aguado (Spain, The Vatican), Dr Daryl Balia (South Africa, Edinburgh 2010), Mrs Rosemary Dowsett (UK, World Evangelical Alliance), Dr Knud Jørgensen (Norway, Areopagos), Rev John Kafwanka (Zambia, Anglican Communion), Rev Dr Jooseop Keum (Korea, World Council of Churches), Dr Wonsuk Ma (Korea, Oxford Centre for Mission Studies), Rev Dr Kenneth R. Ross (UK, Church of Scotland), Dr Petros Vassiliadis (Greece, Aristotle University of Thessalonikki), and co-ordinated by Dr Kirsteen Kim (UK, Edinburgh 2010).

These publications reflect the ethos of Edinburgh 2010 and will make a significant contribution to ongoing studies in mission. It should be clear that material published in this series will inevitably reflect a diverse range of views and positions. These will not necessarily represent those of the series' editors or of the Edinburgh 2010 General Council, but in publishing them the leadership of Edinburgh 2010 hopes to encourage conversation between Christians and collaboration in mission. All the series' volumes are commended for study and reflection in both church and academy.

Series Editors

Knud Jørgensen	Areopagos, Norway, MF Norwegian School of Theology & the Lutheran School of Theology, Hong Kong. Former Chair of Edinburgh 2010 Study Process Monitoring Group
Kirsteen Kim	Leeds Trinity University and former Edinburgh 2010 Research Co-ordinator, UK
Wonsuk Ma	Oxford Centre for Mission Studies, Oxford, UK
Tony Gray	Words by Design, Bicester, UK

REGNUM EDINBURGH CENTENARY SERIES
Volume 1

Edinburgh 2010
Mission Then and Now

Edited by David A. Kerr and Kenneth R. Ross

First published 2009 by Regnum Books International

Regnum is an imprint of the Oxford Centre for Mission Studies
St. Philip and St. James Church
Woodstock Road
Oxford OX2 6HR, UK
www.ocms.ac.uk/regnum

09 08 07 06 05 04 03 8 7 6 5 4 3 2 1

British Library Cataloguing in Publication Data
A catalogue record for this book is available from the British Library

ISBN: 978-1-506476-68-1

Typeset by Words by Design Ltd

Distributed by 1517 Media in the US and Canada

EDINBURGH 2010 COMMON CALL

The Edinburgh 2010 Common Call emerged from the Edinburgh 2010 study process and conference to mark the centenary of the World Missionary Conference, Edinburgh 1910. The Common Call was affirmed in the Church of Scotland Assembly Hall in Edinburgh on 6 June 2010 by representatives of world Christianity, including Catholic, Evangelical, Orthodox, Pentecostal, and Protestant churches.

As we gather for the centenary of the World Missionary Conference of Edinburgh 1910, we believe the church, as a sign and symbol of the reign of God, is called to witness to Christ today by sharing in God's mission of love through the transforming power of the Holy Spirit.

1. Trusting in the Triune God and with a renewed sense of urgency, we are called to incarnate and proclaim the good news of salvation, of forgiveness of sin, of life in abundance, and of liberation for all poor and oppressed. We are challenged to witness and evangelism in such a way that we are a living demonstration of the love, righteousness and justice that God intends for the whole world.

2. Remembering Christ's sacrifice on the Cross and his resurrection for the world's salvation, and empowered by the Holy Spirit, we are called to authentic dialogue, respectful engagement and humble witness among people of other faiths – and no faith – to the uniqueness of Christ. Our approach is marked with bold confidence in the gospel message; it builds friendship, seeks reconciliation and practises hospitality.

3. Knowing the Holy Spirit who blows over the world at will, reconnecting creation and bringing authentic life, we are called to become communities of compassion and healing, where young people are actively participating in mission, and women and men share power and responsibilities fairly, where there is a new zeal for justice, peace and the protection of the environment, and renewed liturgy reflecting the beauties of the Creator and creation.

4. Disturbed by the asymmetries and imbalances of power that divide and trouble us in church and world, we are called to repentance, to critical reflection on systems of power, and to accountable use of power structures. We are called to find practical ways to live as members of One Body in full awareness that God resists the proud, Christ welcomes and empowers the poor and afflicted, and the power of the Holy Spirit is manifested in our vulnerability.

5. Affirming the importance of the biblical foundations of our missional engagement and valuing the witness of the Apostles and martyrs, we are called to rejoice in the expressions of the gospel in many nations all over the world. We celebrate the renewal experienced through movements of migration and mission in all directions, the way all are equipped for mission by the gifts of the

Holy Spirit, and God's continual calling of children and young people to further the gospel.

6. Recognising the need to shape a new generation of leaders with authenticity for mission in a world of diversities in the twenty-first century, we are called to work together in new forms of theological education. Because we are all made in the image of God, these will draw on one another's unique charisms, challenge each other to grow in faith and understanding, share resources equitably worldwide, involve the entire human being and the whole family of God, and respect the wisdom of our elders while also fostering the participation of children.

7. Hearing the call of Jesus to make disciples of all people – poor, wealthy, marginalised, ignored, powerful, living with disability, young, and old – we are called as communities of faith to mission from everywhere to everywhere. In joy we hear the call to receive from one another in our witness by word and action, in streets, fields, offices, homes, and schools, offering reconciliation, showing love, demonstrating grace and speaking out truth.

8. Recalling Christ, the host at the banquet, and committed to that unity for which he lived and prayed, we are called to ongoing co-operation, to deal with controversial issues and to work towards a common vision. We are challenged to welcome one another in our diversity, affirm our membership through baptism in the One Body of Christ, and recognise our need for mutuality, partnership, collaboration and networking in mission, so that the world might believe.

9. Remembering Jesus' way of witness and service, we believe we are called by God to follow this way joyfully, inspired, anointed, sent and empowered by the Holy Spirit, and nurtured by Christian disciplines in community. As we look to Christ's coming in glory and judgment, we experience his presence with us in the Holy Spirit, and we invite all to join with us as we participate in God's transforming and reconciling mission of love to the whole creation.

Contents

Foreword

It is a particularly privileged honour to be invited to write a foreword to a volume developed in the process of travelling to the significant centenary of the Edinburgh Conference of 1910 which in its own way recaptured the ecumenical imperative of the gospel and which, in turn, gave birth to the World Council of Churches, that principal privileged instrument of the ecumenical movement.

Theology and Biography

Theology is a science whose mantra includes objectivity, rationality, fact and theory. In spite of that affirmation, it is also arguable that one's biography mediates and "writes" theology. Therefore, I crave indulgence to begin with something of my biography to fill readers in on whence I come and the impulses in what I say here.

I am an African, indeed a Ghanaian and a Christian, indeed an Anglican. I have dabbled in theology for decades and at the same time been unrepentantly inserted in the Church's womb. By formation, a student of New Testament, I also came into Mission Studies and Ecumenics. In the providence of God, the celebrated Archbishop Desmond Mpilo Tutu and the celebrated early African Ecumenist, Rev. Prof. Christian G. Baeta initiated me in the Ecumenical Movement, leading to my serving for some fifteen years as Senior Executive at the World Council of Churches' Programme on (Ecumenical) Theological Education in Geneva.

When in the Preface of the editors, my name is mentioned in connection with the origins of this volume, my biography and my theology are inextricably married. Theological scholarship may not be just Mandarin's art; it is and should be a rational Confession of experience made with God's word in historical context and world. The essays in this essay are in part, at any rate, an endeavour to model that commitment and affirmation.

Sense of History and More

Over the years I have been wedded to the profound insight of George Santayana that "a people without memory are condemned to repeat it". A sense of history is concomitant of vitality, vibrancy and viability, the three Vs. To celebrate the centenary of Edinburgh 1910 is a serious business in and of the three Vs of the Church's mission and ministry.

In that regard, recalling the service of the Ecumenical "Saints" like J. R. Mott and J.H. Oldman among others, is an aid to vibrancy. I could have wished for more on the ecumenical saints in this volume. Nevertheless, the facets in the

Commissions of the Edinburgh Conference 1910 and the precious little on the Ecumenical Saints are, so to speak, teething us to a vision of the ecumenical imperative as a catalyst in and of renewal. As such this volume is a worthy contribution to developing that sense of history which is important for vital, vibrant and viable ecumenical commitment.

A revisit to the Reports of the Commissions on the principles and methodologies of Edinburgh 1910 reveal a treasure-trove in discerning the meaning and direction of Christian mission and the dynamics at play in the drama of human history.

At Once Denominational and Ecumenical

In my sojourn at the WCC in Geneva, there was a tendency to a mentality that denominational commitment and ecumenical commitment were mutually exclusive of each other. I was very much actively inserted and engaged in the Anglican Communion, serving on Inter-Anglican Theological and Doctrinal Commission and one of the Anglican delegation at ARCIC II, while still on the staff of WCC. Some attempts were made to stop my going to the Anglican assignments. Finally, sanity prevailed. But here is enunciated a cardinal principle of the ecumenical agenda: if you do not know whence you come, you neither know whither you go. Perhaps I sat comfortably in denomination and ecumenical movement because of a certain freedom to dare, issuing from the Anglican principle of the *via media* which, on the ground, means talking round all issues with openness and sensitivity and affirming groups across the board. This is not necessarily spinelessness. It is openness rooted in the guiding hand of the Holy Spirit.

That is why I recall with gratitude the title of the publication of Dr Eugene Carson Blake, second General Secretary of WCC with the title "In One Boat" with the explanation that it is portraiture of "the ecumenical arena and the storms we face", a description of the ecumenical position in which we find ourselves. In 1910 the Roman Catholics were not present. In this volume significant Roman Catholics feel able to engage in the discussion - John Radano from the Vatican and Teresa Okure, a Nigerian Roman Catholic nun and academic. The participants in the ecumenical debate have widened. So it is a measure of some progress. To reflect this widening circle of participants in the ecumenical dialogue is a remarkable achievement to be captured by this volume. It means the process is not just backward looking, as some see history, but a search after a promised future.

"People of Every Tribe & Tongue" : The Humour of God

In 1910 Africa, the second largest continent, Pacific Islands and Latin America were hardly there at the table. If they were there, "native churches" were there through the delegations of Western Missionary Societies. In this volume as we move towards the centenary of 1910, non-Westerners are much in evidence – Teresa Okure and Ogbu Kalu both from Nigeria; Sam Kobia from Kenya, Kyo-Sung Ahn, M.P. Joseph, Vinoth Ramachandra from Asia; and Samuel Escobar and Adolfo Ham from Latin America give voice to the so-called Third World. This is a measure of the dramatic change in the demographical and cultural make-up of the Christian World. The consequential issue is whether we are seriously ready to take the consequences of this change. For full measure let me mention the important place of the Orthodox today.

The foregoing fact represents a sea-change in the ecumenical movement, issuing in new dynamics of ecumenical engagement. This accounts for some of the tensions in the ecumenical movement because cultures represent different epistemologies and ontologies to be held together in the "One Boat". It is the humour of God that through the polyglot of world, intelligent and coherent dialogue emerges. This volume may be a model for dialogue in a divided and polarized world.

Recapture of Two Particular Insights

In my Geneva years there was a wearisome simplistic tendency in some quarters to antipose mission and ecumenism. This volume in a decided focus on Commission I "Carrying the Gospel to all the Non-Christian World", so to speak, the heart of Edinburgh 1910, in not so many words recaptures the integral linking of mission and ecumenism. To put it another way, the quest after the unity of the Church and Mission enrich one another.

The second recall of Edinburgh 1910 is the emphasis on spirituality as the dynamo of both mission and ecumenism. In 1910 there was an important "midday intercession meeting" styled "United Intercession". The WCC has been lampooned as having been too politicized, almost abandoning the pulpit for the political platform. No doubt the statement on racism in South Africa and colonialism contributed to that impression. But the ecumenical movement, though annoying, was an attempt to capture and model ecumenical spirituality. Spirituality has been a non-negotiable part of the ecumenical quest. The big difference is the broadening of the horizons of spirituality to worship at "both the altar in the sanctuary and the altar in the Market place", if I may dare use the phrase of St John Chrysostom. That is why the revisit to Edinburgh 1910, more than historical memory is a search after vitality, vibrancy and viability which are impossible without encounter with the Holy Spirit.

It is my humble privilege to commend this volume for serious consideration.

John S. Pobee

Preface

The Centenary of the World Missionary Conference, held in Edinburgh 1910, is a suggestive moment for many people seeking direction for Christian mission in the 21st century. Several different constituencies within World Christianity are holding significant events around 2010. Since 2005 an international group has worked collaboratively to develop an intercontinental and multi-denominational project, now known as Edinburgh 2010, and based at New College, University of Edinburgh. This initiative brings together representatives of twenty different global Christian bodies, representing all major Christian denominations and confessions and many different strands of mission and church life, to prepare for the Centenary.

Essential to the work of the Edinburgh 1910 Conference, and of abiding value, were the findings of the eight think-tanks or 'commissions'. These inspired the idea of a new round of collaborative reflection on Christian mission – but now focussed on nine themes identified as being key to mission in the 21st century. The study process is polycentric, open-ended, and as inclusive as possible of the different genders, regions of the world, and theological and confessional perspectives in today's church.

This publication is recognised as reflecting the ethos of Edinburgh 2010 and making a significant contribution to its study process. Both Kenneth Ross and David Kerr worked over many months and years to bring this collection of essays to our attention. It is commended to churches, mission groups and students of mission for study and reflection throughout the Christian world. It should be clear that material published in this series will generally reflect the diversity of the views and positions which Christian writers are known to share and not necessarily represent those of the series' editors or the Edinburgh 2010 general council.

For this first particular volume, we wish to thank Wonsuk Ma (Regnum), Robin Parry (Paternoster), Tony Gray (Bound Biographies) and Anthony Kinahan for their help in making its publication possible. We also wish to acknowledge with appreciation the support received from The Drummond Trust, 3 Pitt Terrace, Stirling, The Hope Trust, and the Lund Missionary Society.

Daryl Balia, International Director
Kirsteen Kim, Research Coordinator
Edinburgh 2010

Acknowledgements

The origins of this book lie in a visit to Edinburgh which John Pobee of Ghana made in the year 2000 in order to give a millennial lecture. During his visit John raised the question of the centenary of the 'Edinburgh 1910' World Missionary Conference. He challenged Scottish-based churches, mission agencies and academic institutions to embark on a process of preparing for the centenary. The following year the Scottish Towards 2010 Council was formed for this very purpose, with representation from Action of Churches Together in Scotland, the Church of Scotland, the Roman Catholic Church, Scottish Churches World Exchange, the Mission Representatives Fellowship, Edinburgh University's Centre for the Study of Christianity in the Non-Western World, the International Christian College, SCIAF, Tearfund and Christian Aid.

A central feature of the Council's programme was an annual day conference focussed on the Commissions which reported to Edinburgh 1910. The conference convened each Spring at New College on the Mound in Edinburgh, the location evoking the fertile memory of 1910. Each conference began with worship led by international students. A summary of the Commission Report was offered by David Kerr. It was then addressed, in two full-length lectures, by mission scholars of international repute. The lectures had threefold content: (i) assessment of the Commission Report in its original context; (ii) analysis of key developments regarding the theme during the twentieth century; and (iii) consideration of future prospects in relation to the theme.

60-80 people gathered to participate in the annual conferences and together formed a community of memory and hope journeying through the eight Commissions, with some participants ever present and others joining to contribute to particular events. A considerable *esprit de corps* developed with each conference carrying a real sense of occasion. The lecturers usually remained in Scotland for a few days after the conference and offered further lectures and seminars, deepening the engagement. The chapters of this book reflect not only the careful preparation of the original lectures but also their further development in light of the discussion which they provoked. Without exception, the lecturers have committed wholeheartedly to this task and it is to their hard work and rigorous thought that we owe the book. Working with them has been a great joy as together we caught the inspiration of Edinburgh 1910. We always felt that we were part of something much greater than we could fully apprehend and the journey of discovery will surely continue.

We are grateful to our fellow members of the Scottish Towards 2010 Council: John McLean, John Wylie, Bobby Anderson, Sung-Jin Chang, Elizabeth Grant, Jack Thompson, Lindsey Sanderson, Martin Johnstone and especially its indefatigable secretary David Miller. Heartfelt thanks are also due to our editorial assistants: Tony McLean Foreman, who did invaluable early work on revision of the text, and Maurie Sween, who meticulously worked on it as it neared completion. The project was fortunate to receive grants from the Church of Scotland Board (later Council) of World Mission, the Pollock Trust, the Society in Scotland for the Propagation of Christian Knowledge and the Professor Alexander Duff Missionary Lectureship Trust. To each of them sincere thanks are recorded.

Our hope is that the book will serve to deepen and extend the reflection being stimulated by the upcoming centenary and help to provoke a moment of missionary imagination in 2010.

David A. Kerr, Lund

Kenneth. R. Ross, Edinburgh

October 2007

In Memoriam: Professor David Allan Kerr 1945-2008

One of the editors of this book, Professor David Kerr, died on 14 April 2008, soon after preparation of the manuscript was completed. He had been diagnosed in 2005 with amyotrophic lateral sclerosis (ALS or Lou Gehrig's disease). Even as he became physically very restricted, his commitment to the editorial task was unyielding. At the time of his death David Kerr was Professor of Missiology and Ecumenics at the University of Lund in Sweden, having earlier served as Professor of Christianity in the Non-Western World at the University of Edinburgh, Scotland (1996-2005), Director of the Duncan Black Macdonald Center for the Study of Islam and Christian-Muslim Relations at Hartford Seminary in Connecticut, USA (1988-1996), and founder Director of Centre for the Study of Islam and Christian-Muslim Relations at Selly Oak Colleges in Birmingham, UK (1976-1988).

He was distinguished for his sensitive and innovative work in Christian-Muslim relations, having co-authored the seminal Chambesy Statement (1976) on religious liberty entitled "Christian Mission and Islamic Da'wah". During a time when Christian approaches to Islam often tended to be polemical, David Kerr stood out for an approach which was marked equally by robust intellectual integrity and kindly mutual courtesy and affection. His commitment to his postgraduate students was legendary and to the very last he continued to give of himself unsparingly to ensure that they were able to fulfil their potential.

From early in his Edinburgh period, David Kerr sensed the momentous importance of the approaching centenary of the Edinburgh 1910 World Missionary Conference. As Director of the Centre for the Study of Christianity in the Non-Western World he hosted, at New College in Edinburgh, the series of conferences on which this book is based. His particular role in each conference was to offer a succinct summary of the Commission Report which was being considered, thus freeing the speakers to concentrate their efforts on analysis and interpretation. His infectious, though by no means uncritical, enthusiasm for the Conference drew dozens if not hundreds of scholars into the task of reflecting on Edinburgh 1910 in light of the challenges facing the mission of the church in today's world. The volumes of Commission Reports remained by his side throughout his final illness and he found them an inexhaustible source of insight and stimulus. It is my sincere hope that this book will go at least some way towards fulfilling David Kerr's passionately held ambition that the recollection of Edinburgh 1910 should be a springboard for the rediscovery of the true missionary and ecumenical character of the church.

Kenneth R. Ross
11 October 2008

INTRODUCTION

INTRODUCTION: THE EDINBURGH 1910 WORLD MISSIONARY CONFERENCE: ITS EIGHT COMMISSIONS IN HISTORICAL CONTEXT AND THEIR CONTINUING SIGNIFICANCE

David A. Kerr and Kenneth R. Ross

Introduction

A bright summer afternoon in Edinburgh's Old Town, 14 June 1910, was the occasion of a solemn yet joyous gathering that was to have a profound impact on the development of Christian mission and Christian ecumenism in the twentieth century. Into the Assembly Hall of the United Free Church of Scotland, high on the Mound just beneath the Castle, trooped some twelve hundred leaders of missionary societies and church mission boards for the inaugural session of a 'World Missionary Conference'. 'Edinburgh 1910', as the Conference is generally known, began its ten-day discussion of current and future trends of the missionary movement, based on eight Commission Reports – each a volume averaging 250 pages – that had previously been circulated to, and studied by, the Conference delegates.[1]

It proved to be an event of momentous significance for the Christian faith. John R. Mott, the Conference chairman, called it: 'the most notable gathering in the interest of the worldwide expansion of Christianity ever held, not only in missionary annals, but in all Christian annals'.[2] Over subsequent years many have recognized the significance of the 10-day event, perhaps none more eloquently than William Richey Hogg:

> Edinburgh, 1910, appears to be the non-Roman Christian world's ecumenical keystone. The keystone, specially cut, stands as the central stone at the crown of an arch. It holds together and strengthens all beneath that converges in it. The arch it crowns provides a foundation upon which a superstructure can be built. The keystone is neither arch nor wall, but it belongs to both. Remove it, and both will collapse. It is unique. Thus it is with Edinburgh, 1910. It belongs to the nineteenth and to the twentieth centuries. It is the keystone through which developments in mission and unity in the one century relate to those in the other and apart from which the full meaning of neither can be assayed.[3]

No one seeking an understanding of the changing demographic shape of Christianity over the past 200 years would fail to take account of Edinburgh 1910. Moreover, the ambitious scope and analytical approach of the Conference have ensured that many of the issues it discussed remain pertinent even in the vastly changed world of today.

For these reasons it is well worth returning to the eight Commission Reports around which the Conference was structured and which did much to endow it with depth and enduring value. The present volume revisits the eight Reports that Edinburgh 1910 received and debated. Each section is devoted to one of the Reports, comprising a summary of the published volume, and evaluative reflections on its content by leading mission scholars and practitioners of today. The purpose of this first chapter is to situate the eight Reports, and the Conference of which they were part, in their historical context, to introduce the main themes with which they dealt, and to suggest some of the reasons why Edinburgh 1910 continues to merit critical consideration as we approach its centenary in 2010.

The genesis of the Conference

Edinburgh 1910 is often acclaimed as the 'first' World Missionary Conference. It was, indeed, the first international missionary conference to meet under this title, and it initiated a sequence of World Missionary Conferences through the later twentieth century. Yet it was not without precursors. More than a century earlier William Carey, the pioneer Baptist missionary in India, had proposed a decennial interdenominational world missionary conference and had suggested that the first should be held in Cape Town in 1810.[4] Another Bengal missionary, Alexander Duff, who later would become Professor of Evangelistic Theology at New College in Edinburgh – the first Chair of mission studies in the English-speaking world, retrieved and promoted the idea during his celebrated lecture tour of the USA in 1854.[5] Large-scale conferences were held in Liverpool in 1860, London in 1878, London again in 1888, and New York in 1900. In preliminary ways each of these strove to cultivate co-operation among Protestant missionary societies.

Edinburgh 1910 stood in this line of succession. However in three respects it proved to be innovative. The twelve hundred missionaries and mission leaders who assembled in Edinburgh came not merely as individual enthusiasts for mission, intent on propagating and recruiting for its cause; they were official delegates of more than 170 missionary societies and church mission boards. These delegates had been appointed to represent their organizations in a conference formally constituted 'to receive and consider the Reports of the (eight) Commissions' that the international planning committee designed to prepare for the Conference. Consonant with such elaborate preparation, the Conference – unlike its predecessors – was aimed to promote 'co-operative study of the common outstanding problems in the common missionary enterprise, with a view to helping (the represented societies and boards) to solve them, and achieve together the evangelization of the world'.[6] Deliberative rather than merely demonstrative, the Conference drew a clear distinction between its freedom to recommend, and its lack of authority to regulate policy for its participant agencies. Its strength lay in its power to persuade, by consensus rather than command. Its only decision – but one that again distinguished it from previous conferences – was to recommend the formation of a Continuation Committee, 'international and representative in character...to maintain in prominence the idea of the World Missionary Conference as means of co-ordinating missionary work, of laying sound lines for future development, and of evoking and claiming by corporate action fresh stores of spiritual force for the evangelization of the world'.[7]

Why was Edinburgh chosen as the Conference venue? The answer was that Scotland had an importance in worldwide mission out of all proportion to its size. It had produced some of the most celebrated figures in the modern missionary movement: Robert Moffat, Alexander Duff, John Philip, David Livingstone, James Legge, Mary Slessor, to name but a few. It had established some of the most highly regarded centres of mission work, such as Lovedale in South Africa, Livingstonia in Malawi and the Scottish educational institutions in India. 'In the earlier missionary enterprise which evangelized Europe', acknowledged the official Conference records, 'no country was more prominent than Scotland, and no country has in proportion to its size contributed to the evangelization of the world during the last century so large a number of distinguished and devoted missionaries.'[8] Importantly this movement had built up a constituency of support in Scotland on the basis of which a large-scale international conference could be organized. It was no trifling inquiry, therefore, that Fairley Daly, the secretary of the Livingstonia Mission of the United Free Church of Scotland, made to Robert Speer of the Presbyterian Board of Missions in New York, in 1906, asking if there were plans to follow up the 1900 New York conference.[9] The answer came back that the Americans would welcome such a conference in Britain. A group of Scottish mission secretaries met in Glasgow, and issued a call for a larger consultation of Scottish missions to consider the possibility of convening a new conference. Twenty-seven missionary boards and societies met in Edinburgh in January of the following year, and decided to convene a World Missionary Conference, in Edinburgh, in 1910.[10]

The preparation of the Conference

The process that was thus set in motion accumulated momentum, initially under a UK General Committee and a US Committee on Reference and Council. These were quickly superseded by a full International Committee, comprising ten British, five North American and three Continental representatives. It met for the first time in Oxford in June 1907, and achieved the extraordinary feat of organising the first World Missionary Conference in exactly three years.[11]

Two figures quickly established their leadership in the preparatory process, and went on to play dominant roles in the Conference and its sequel, the International Missionary Council. John Raleigh Mott, the American Methodist layman, was a figure of growing international reputation among Protestant missions. He first became involved by joining the Student Volunteer Movement (SVM), committing himself 'if God permit, to become a foreign missionary'. He would later become the student secretary of the Young Men's Christian Association (YMCA), and General Secretary of the World's Student Christian Federation, and use his influence in these positions to recruit large numbers of young people for mission. He was also one of the co-founders of the Foreign Missions Conference in North America. His first publication, entitled *The Evangelisation of the World in this Generation* (1900), gave the North American missionary movement its watchword in the early twentieth century.[12]

If Mott generated the grand vision and energy of the preparatory process for Edinburgh 1910, it was his Scottish counterpart, Joseph Houldsworth Oldham, who handled the immensely complex details of planning the conference. He did so with an administrative flair that brought lustre to the event and established his own distinguished career in missionary and ecumenical circles. Nearly ten years Mott's junior, and still only in his mid-30s, Oldham was born of Scottish missionary parents in India. Following his graduation from Oxford he worked with the YMCA in India before returning to Europe for theological studies in Edinburgh and Germany. As the United Free Church of Scotland's Secretary for Mission Studies, he attended the inaugural meeting of the International Committee in Oxford, where he was appointed secretary to the Committee with full-time responsibility for the preparation of the Conference.[13]

The Committee swiftly decided the focus, nature and process of the World Missionary Conference. Mott's watchword – the evangelization of the whole world in this generation – expressed the vision to which most of the International Committee members could subscribe. But it was not, as sometimes supposed, adopted as an official motto of the Conference. Some Continental mission leaders were uneasy with it. Gustav Warneck, the German founder of the modern science of mission studies, made this clear in a letter to Mott. Warneck expressed anxiety that qualitative concerns for the consolidation of Christianity in Africa and Asia should not be subordinated to quantitative goals of expansion. 'A predilection for the watchword "the occupation of the whole world in this present generation"' – he wrote to Mott, slightly misquoting the watchword – 'can easily miss the most hopeful opportunities…The great lesson which the foreign missionary enterprise of our time has to learn from the history of the expansion of Christianity during the first three centuries is that the principal strength of missions lies in the native congregations…We are at present in that stage of modern missions when the watchword must be the self-propagation of Christianity.'[14] Sensitive to such criticism, the International Committee settled for a judiciously sober title for the Conference that signalled its reflective purpose: 'World Missionary Conference: to Consider Missionary Problems..'.

The second part of the watchword raised a different problem. 'The whole world' served to signify the universal scope of Christian mission upon which all were agreed. But given that the International Committee was concerned only with Protestant missions, such universalism begged the question about those regions of the world where the Roman Catholic Church was already established. To secure the participation of the Anglo-Catholic wing of the Church of England, and thus achieve a breadth of participation that had been impossible in previous mission conferences, the International Committee agreed to exclude any discussion of mission that encroached on Catholic presence and prerogative. Protestant-Catholic proselytism was to be avoided – as, in the Conference proceedings, sensitivity was also observed regarding the Orthodox churches. The Continuation Committee determined that it should be only 'in relation to the non-Christian world' that missionary problems would be considered. While providing the Conference with a huge geographical agenda, the limitation excluded consideration of any of the Americas (with the exception of indigenous religions) Europe and the Russian Empire. The full Conference title thus emerged: 'World Missionary Conference: to Consider Missionary Problems in Relation to the Non-Christian World'. Oldham's diplomatic skills were fully tested in formulating an approach that satisfied the low-church missionary movement while enabling the Anglo-Catholics also to participate. Looking back fifty years later, he commented: 'This was the turning point of the ecumenical movement.'[15]

To allay apprehensions among the societies and boards that were invited to participate, the International Committee imposed another limitation on the Conference agenda. It agreed 'to confine the purview of the Conference to work of the kind in which all were united ... No expression of opinion should be sought from the Conference on any matter involving any ecclesiastical or doctrinal question on which those taking part in the Conference differed among themselves.'[16] Respect for the self-identity of mission societies and boards as inviolate was the condition of their agreeing to confer together. This implicitly weighted the intended consideration of missionary problems in favour of practical issues of method, administration, and cooperation in 'urgent and vital' missionary tasks. The theological understanding of mission, and the missionary nature of the Church were issues of general acclaim, and considered – for purposes of the Conference – as beyond debate.

The International Committee took a similarly pragmatic approach to the question of participation. It decided that the only qualification for participation was that a missionary society or board was in the business of supporting foreign missionaries. 'It was resolved that representation ... should be confined to Societies having agents in the foreign field and expending on foreign missions not less that £2000 annually'. The size of delegation was calculated on a similar criterion: 'Societies should be entitled to an additional delegate for every additional £4000 of foreign missionary expenditure.'[17] On this basis 176 missionary societies and boards sent delegations – 59 from North America, 58 from the Continent, 47 from the United Kingdom, and 12 from South Africa and Australia.

The criteria of membership effectively excluded representation by churches in Africa, Asia and the Pacific since they were not 'missionary societies', and did not sustain 'foreign missions' as understood by the International Committee. This begged a question that was to become of central concern in the Conference itself: namely, the relationship between missionary societies and what were termed 'native churches'. The consequence of the International Committee's decision, however, was that members of these churches could only be included in the Conference within the delegations of Western missionary societies, or as specially invited delegates. Thus the number of non-Western Christians at the Conference was very small: the names of fifteen Asians appear in *The History and Records of the Conference*, representing China, Japan, India, Korea and Burma.[18] Not a single African, Latin American or Pacific islander appears in the lists.

In terms of subject matter, the International Committee received recommendations from both Britain and the United States that an 'earnest study of the missionary enterprise' was in order. Accordingly eight themes were selected, each being in the Committee's judgement 'of cardinal importance and special immediate urgency'.[19] The preparation of each topic was assigned to a 'Commission', or preparatory working group, mandated 'to gather up, and present in summary form, the results of the largest experience and best thoughts of missionaries in the field'.[20] Eight Commissions were thus created. Commission One was given the task of preparing, and presenting to the Conference, the Report on *Carrying the Gospel to all the Non-Christian World*; Commission Two was charged to report on *The Church in the Mission Field*; Commission Three, *Education in Relation to the Christianisation of National Life*; Commission Four, *The Missionary Message in Relation to Non-Christian Religions*; Commission Five, *The Preparation of Missionaries*; Commission Six, *The Home Base of Missions*; Commission Seven, *Relation of Missions to Government*; and Commission Eight, *Co-operation and the Promotion of Unity*. Each Commission comprised twenty specialists from both sides of the Atlantic, five having British conveners, with American and European vice-chairs, and three being chaired by Americans, with British and Continental vice-chairs. Among Oldham's chief tasks was to provide central support for the Commissions, a challenge to which he brought the skills of scholar-cum-organizer that had distinguished him as Study Secretary for the United Free Church. Under his leadership the International Committee constructed a questionnaire for each Commission, and in February 1909 these were sent to missionaries in different parts of the world. About one thousand replies were received, many written at considerable length. This 'raw material' provided the Commissions with the data on which to construct the eight Reports, each combining the views of missionaries, reflections of the commissioners, and recommendations of the commissions.

The Conference programme

For the ten days of the Conference – 14–23 June 1910 – the city of Edinburgh honoured the national and international delegates with symbols drawing on the civic, academic, and ecclesiastical traditions of Scotland's ancient capital. The Lord Provost threw a reception in the City Chambers and another was held at the National Museum; by special convocation the University conferred honorary degrees on fourteen of the most distinguished delegates; an opening service was held in St Giles, the High Kirk of Edinburgh, and a daily communion was celebrated for Anglican delegates at the Episcopal Church of St John the Evangelist on Princes Street. Families throughout the city also provided much domestic hospitality. This was but one of the ways in which the local population expressed an active interest in the Conference's affairs.

Another was through public participation in two events that paralleled the main Conference. A sequence of public meetings took place in the Synod Hall on Castle Street, just over the Royal Mile from the Assembly Hall where the delegates gathered. These broadly featured the subjects under discussion in the main Conference with the aim of sharing them with the home supporters of foreign missions. Open evening lectures were also held every day in the Tolbooth Church at the head of the Royal Mile. During the second half of the Conference selected national and international delegates spoke at another series of public meetings that were held at the St Andrew's Hall in Glasgow. At the instigation of the Edinburgh Medical Missionary Society a shorter specialist conference for medical missionaries was held in the Royal College of Physicians in Edinburgh.[21]

The main Conference convened on the afternoon of 14 June 1910. As a 'conference' it gathered under the chairmanship of one of Scotland's leading politicians and church leaders, Lord Balfour of Burleigh. Messages were received from the King and the former President of the United States, Theodore Roosevelt, who would have participated as a delegate of the Dutch Reformed Church in America but for the fact of being called back to his country. The first task of business was to agree on Standing Orders. These drew a distinction between the 'Conference' that was empowered to resolve recommendations, and the conference as 'Committee' in which the delegates would exercise their main duty of debating the eight Commission Reports. J. H. Oldham was nominated as Secretary for the entire Conference – that is, Conference and Committee – and John Mott as Chairman of the 'Conference in Committee'. Both nominations were upheld, and the following day the working sessions of the Conference began proceedings, which convened every morning and afternoon over the next nine days, with the exception of the weekend.

A Business Committee managed the Conference agenda. It determined the sequence in which the Commission Reports were taken, and the elements of each Report that were selected for debate (it being impossible in the time available to discuss every page of every Report), and provided the Chairman with the names of those delegates who had indicated a wish to contribute to the discussion of a particular topic. It remained at the Chairman's discretion to call speakers with 'regard to a fair representation of different countries and societies, and … an adequate expression of differences of view', but having been called, 'the time allocated to each speaker in the discussion upon the Reports (was) not (to) exceed seven minutes'.[22] By efficient scheme of conference management, the Business Committee undertook, and achieved, the remarkable feat of preparing minutes of each day's discussion by the end of day. These were published in the *Daily Paper* that was available for delegates by the following morning. At the beginning of each new day's business these minutes were taken as read, and approved without further discussion.

If the largest allocation of time was to be given to discussion of the Commission Reports, the Standing Orders decreed that 'the most important part of each day's proceedings' on which depends 'more than all else … the realisation of the blessing possible for the Conference' was to be 'united intercession'. Accordingly, at 12.00 pm. sharp, debate was suspended and one of the delegates would introduce 'the midday intercession meeting', leading the Conference in a brief reflection on a given theme and in general prayer. As Temple Gairdner recalled: 'Every day, at the very time of the day when the audience was at its freshest and most vigorous, this great Conference, which was daily finding its available time insufficient, deliberately suspended its discussion; for a full half-hour the voice of debate was hushed, and the Conference, as a Conference, fell to prayer.'[23] During these times of intercessions, delegates were forbidden to enter or leave the Assembly Hall, and the Standing Orders imposed a similar discipline on the prayers with which each morning's business began: 'all members should endeavour to be in their places by 9:40 each morning, so that all may take part in the opening act of worship and intercession (at 9:45 A.M.), and that there may be no disturbance nor distraction from members arriving late'.[24]

The focus on 'enquiry and study'[25] that characterized the Conference agenda was extended into the evening sessions when, every day including the weekend, the delegates listened to two, sometimes three lectures on theological, historical, and methodological dimensions of the missionary challenge.[26] While these sessions were not part of the formal debate of Commission Reports, they complemented the latter and are published in a separate volume together with the Minutes and other Records of the Conference.

The Commission Reports

Since the substantive work of the Conference was to debate the eight Commission Reports, any account of the Conference proceedings must address both the Reports themselves, and the debate they generated. Later sections of this book present summaries of each of the Reports, and each is subject to scholarly evaluation. To avoid superfluous repetition, the aim of the present review will focus on two aspects that do not feature in the following chapters: the remarkable synthesis of conviction and content that the eight Reports evince, and some of the most striking contributions from delegates in plenary discussion.

Without entering into fruitless speculation as to which Report was the most important, that is which most closely expressed the 'essence' of Edinburgh 1910, it can be said that Commission One's mandate for *Carrying the Gospel into all the Non-Christian World* merited its chronological priority in the Conference programme (15 June). It introduced the missionary goal of the whole Conference, and raised issues that anticipated the other Commissions to which it was 'bound by natural ligaments'.[27] Indeed its title came closer than those of other Commissions in serving as the Conference motto, expressing the sentiment of Mott's watchword but in language that avoided some of the latter's associations.

As the Report surveyed the non-Christian world the vastness and urgency of the task of evangelism are acknowledged time and again. With an unshakeable belief in providence, it identified the rapidly changing conditions in non-Christian societies as God-given opportunities for the Church to fulfil its missionary obligation. 'In our judgment', declared Mott in his capacity of Chairman of Commission One, 'the present time is the time of all times with reference to the evangelisation of the non-Christian world'.[28] Striking a second note of his characteristic repertoire, he emphasized the urgency of entering 'the so-called unoccupied fields'[29] of the world; in face of Warneck's warning, he fairly summarized the Commission as believing that 'many, if not all of these unoccupied regions might be entered by the Church as a result of wise, concerted, prayerful effort'.[30] For this to be achieved, however, there must also be 'united planning and concerted effort on the part of the missionary forces of the Church'[31] – a divided Christendom being no match for the challenge. Looking to the future, he expressed a central insight of the Report in emphasising that 'the evangelisation of the world ... is not chiefly a European and American enterprise, but an Asiatic and African enterprise'.[32] In tension with this, however, he concluded that 'The missionary enterprise after all is the projection abroad of the Church at home'.[33] Other tensions emerged in the discussion of the Report, although it is fair to acknowledge that the Business Committee in organizing the debate anticipated them. These included debate over questions such as: Should missionary priority concentrate on entering unoccupied fields or strengthening churches where they already existed? Where lay the balance between conversion of individuals and communities? Was the future of evangelism better secured through 'native' local churches or foreign missionary work, and what should the relationship be between the two? How could the legitimate independence of mission agencies be reconciled with the perceived need for unity of missionary action?

The Report of Commission Two examined one of the great themes of Commission One, focussing on *The Church in the Mission Field* – 'the young

Church which missions have founded, but which is itself now *the* great Mission to the non-Christian world'[34] – to quote the Commission Chairman, Campbell Gibson. With long missionary experience in Southern China, Gibson was an emphatic advocate of the right of 'native churches' – to use the language of the Report – for independence from missionary societies. He ardently argued that, 'the Church (in the mission field) is not (merely) a by-product of mission work, but is itself by far the most efficient element in Christian propaganda'. The cardinal principle of the Report was that of 'self-determination' for native churches, supported but not controlled by foreign missions. Though none disagreed with the principle, its practical implementation was contentious. The Report's metaphor of choice, likening the relationship of missions and churches to that of parent and child, produced some critical rejoinders from Asian delegates. As the child matures, the wise parent needs to stand aside, at least not stand in the way, quipped a Chinese delegate. A Japanese delegate illustrated the problem with examples of difficult relations between foreign missionaries and the Church of Christ in Japan.[35] V. S. Azariah from India struck a nerve in perhaps the most strident and best remembered speech of the entire Conference when he insisted: 'We have a new generation of Christians who do not wish to be treated like children ... True co-operation is possible only with a proper *spiritual* relationship'; and he appealed 'in one word, for *friendship*'.[36] The tensions served to underline the importance of finding a genuinely cooperative relationship between missions and churches in the future, on the ecclesiological basis articulated by the Chinese delegate, Cheng Ching Yi (London Missionary Society) that 'all Churches of Christ are dependent first upon God and then upon each other'.[37]

Complementing this focus on the missionary leadership in the churches of Africa and Asia, Commission Three engaged the broad agenda of *Education in Relation to the Christianisation of National Life*. Its primary concern was distinctly stated: 'inasmuch as the only way in which the native Church can bear its own proper witness, and move forward toward the position of independence and self-government in which it ought to stand, is through native leaders, teachers and officers, we believe that the most important of all ends which missionary education ought to set itself to serve, is that of training those who are to be the spiritual leaders and teachers of their own nation'.[38] Pressing the primacy of this task in his introductory speech to the Conference, the Commission Chairman, Bishop Gore of Birmingham, echoed the larger challenge of the Report: 'The greatest possible care will have to be taken to avoid the risk of denationalising those who are being trained. In particular, we desire to lay the greatest emphasis on the importance of giving religious teaching, not only of the elementary kind, but as far as possible throughout, in the vernacular.'[39] This marked a fundamental departure from the principle of English-language Christian education set by Alexander Duff in India, and opened the way for the development of indigenized forms of educational methods and material. But in continuity with Duff and other educational pioneers, the Report did not limit the scope of Christian education to the Christian community, but saw it as 'leavening' the general welfare of the people.[40] If Japan figured highly in Edinburgh 1910's hopes for the future, it was because of what missionary colleges had already achieved there: the evidence of four Japanese principals of Christian colleges among the Conference delegates spoke for itself.

As the only Commission to broach theological issues in a significant way, Commission Four's presentation of *The Missionary Message in Relation to Non-Christian Religions* merits the scholarly attention that it has received in recent years. In the context of the Conference, however, it should be read in relation to the educational interests of Commission Three and Commission Five's Report on *The Preparation of Missionaries*. In its consideration of the nature and priorities of missionary education, and by extension the education of native churches, Commission Five emphasized the importance of cultivating 'the spirit of courtesy' toward non-Christian cultures, and 'sympathy' towards their peoples. In like manner, Commission Four acknowledged that, in such spirit, Christians might discern traits of God-given goodness in non-Christian religions. Although not all delegates could agree on this, some Asians among them gave personal testimony of ways in which they continued to value religions to which they had once belonged: for example, the civic and moral order of Confucianism, or Buddhism's detachment from material desire. In much missionary literature, regretted K. C. Chatterji, ex-Moderator of the Presbyterian Church of India, 'there is a great deal of exposure of the evils of Hinduism, but not a word of recognition of that which is good in it',[41] and this produces only negativity toward the Gospel among Hindus. Building on such attitudinal concerns, many of the Western contributions to both the Report and the debate urged an irenic Christian encounter with non-Christian religions that would present the Gospel as the fulfilment of their own inner hopes and yearnings. The 'schoolmaster to Christ' replaced the 'soldier of the Cross' as the metaphor for the missionary in the theology of Commission Four.

If missionary education was properly concerned with national life as a whole, it was appropriate that the Conference should consider the relationship between missions and governments. This was the subject of Commission Seven. The fact of its being the shortest of the eight Commission Reports was due, perhaps, to its Chairman, Lord Balfour, and its principal drafter hailing from Scotland where they were habituated to the virtue of economy. Equally it reflected the difficulty of elaborating general principles that could be applied to the vast range of political situations in which missions worked. These were described and assessed on the criterion of the disposition of governments toward missions. On this count Japan was considered to have the most civilised of non-Christian governments, while on the other end of the scale was 'the absolutely independent savage chief'. However varied these contexts, the Report recommended that missions should, as a matter of principle, relate to governments wherever possible in 'a conciliatory and reasonable manner', since stable government is decreed by God. But governments, Lord Balfour emphasized in his remarks to the Conference plenary, should appreciate that they stand in the debt of missions even more than trade: 'trade provides revenue, but … does not need sympathy and pity. If you are going to elevate a people – and without elevating you can not do the best for the Government – it is the missionary, and the ideal of the missionary, you must give to that side of Government support.'[42] Few delegates disagreed with this judgment. But scarcely concealing his displeasure with the Report's acquiescence in the 'Unequal Treaties' imposed on China, a Chinese delegate, C. C. Wang (London Missionary Society), reminded the Conference that, 'every true Christian should carry the Cross and not the Dreadnoughts to spread the Gospel to all lands'.[43]

In his closing remarks Lord Balfour spoke strongly of the need for greater 'inter-communication' among missionary societies in matters of political representation. This echoed the unanimous opinion of the chairmen of all the other Commissions, co-operation being seen essential for the advance of every aspect of mission. Commission I raised the issue at the beginning of the Conference, and the Business Committee scheduled an earlier hearing of the Commission Eight Report on *Cooperation and the Promotion of Unity* – presumably in anticipation of its central recommendation: 'that a Continuation Committee of the World Missionary Conference be appointed, international and representative in character … to maintain in prominence the idea of the World Missionary Conference as a means of co-ordinating missionary work, of laying sound foundations for future development, and of evoking and claiming by corporate action fresh stores of spiritual force for the evangelisation of the world'.[44] The debate preceding the unanimous adoption of this motion demonstrated the delegates' ecumenical vision. If most contributions concentrated on the first element of the Commission title – 'co-operation' – the issue of 'unity' was by no means ignored. Some urged that ecclesiological issues be suborned to the imperative demands of practical co-operation in mission fields; others cautioned of the need to resolve ecclesial differences in order that joint action could be a genuine expression of unity. Some European delegates were surprised to discover how both dimensions were being combined in Australia. Others spoke of the urgent need for discussions with both the Roman Catholic and Orthodox Churches. In what must rate as among the most impressive speeches of the entire Conference – and merits consideration as a foundational contribution to the ecumenical movement – the Chinese delegate, Cheng Ching Yi (London Missionary Society) explained the pioneering role of the Christian federation movement in China, that had developed inter-Christian co-operation in educational and evangelistic work to the point where it was possible 'to see in the near future a united Christian Church without any denominational distinctions'.[45] This Conference thus reached its high point with the decision to create a Continuation Committee with thirty-five members, ten from the UK, North America and the Continent respectively, and one apiece from South Africa, Australasia, Japan, China and India.

The last two Commissions to report – Commission Five on *The Preparation of Missionaries*, and Commission Six on *The Home Base* – dealt with issues pertaining primarily to missionary societies and board in their own countries. The logic was clear: co-operation that was actually being achieved in the mission field often eluded missionary societies in their home countries. Furthermore, resources of provision and personnel that were so much needed by 'the Church in the mission field' were enjoyed in abundance by 'the home Church'. The latter – as the two Reports tirelessly re-iterated – needed mobilization for world mission as never before.

Commission Five, chaired by John MacKenzie of the Hartford Seminary Foundation, addressed the educational side of this task. Hartford Seminary was already pioneering the professional training of missionaries in the United States, combining theological and regional studies with character formation. The neighbouring Yale Divinity School had a similar programme. In Germany Gustav Warneck had been developing mission studies since the late nineteenth century. But the needs of the societies and boards far surpassed the provision of this field of study deemed to be 'yet in its infancy'. The Report challenged universities to take up the challenge of mission, and called especially on theological faculties to equip themselves to deal with the global dimensions of Christianity. Co-operation between missions and universities was envisaged as the way forward, with missions reserving to themselves the responsibility of 'special training' for their personnel.

Commission Six, chaired by the leader of the American Board for Commissioners for Foreign Missions, James Barton, broadened the question of missionary support to 'the home Church'. But the focus remained on what the Report termed 'missionary intelligence', meaning an effective understanding of 'the mission field' that would translate into active support among 'home churches'. The 'science of the missionary society' should be part of the 'science of mission' itself. The Report illustrated this concept with examples from the United States, especially the recently founded Laymen's Missionary Movement (1906) that was successfully propounding missionary ideas that attracted volunteers and financial giving among American churches.

Both these Reports recognized the growing contribution of women to mission both in the home churches and overseas. Whereas the nineteenth century had seen women confined to supporting roles, or 'Women's Work for Women' – to quote another of the missionary watchwords – it was now time to realize 'the vision of the place of women in the building up of the whole fabric of national life'.[46] The Commission Five Report contended that it was time to break down the artificial division between missionary men and women, and to include women in all levels of missionary society leadership and management. This said, the Report could only point to one example of provision for the professional training of women missionaries, the Women's Missionary College in Edinburgh, directed by Annie Small.

The great new fact

The only formal achievement of Edinburgh 1910 was the formation of the Continuation Committee under the leadership of John Mott as Chairman and J. H. Oldham as Secretary. Its responsibility was 'to confer with the Societies and Boards as to the best method of working toward the formation of such a permanent International Missionary Committee as is suggested by the Commissions of the Conference and by various missionary bodies apart from the Conference'.[47] Within two years the Continuation Committee helped form the Conference of British Missionary Societies (CBMS) with its membership of forty missionary societies.[48] The two bodies shared single premises in London, suitably named Edinburgh House. The First World War (1914–18) retarded the development of international missionary co-operation, but within three years of the war's end, in 1921, the International Missionary Council, with Oldham as its first General Secretary, succeeded the Continuing Committee. With headquarters in London (Edinburgh House) and New York, its membership included 14 interdenominational missionary associations (e.g. the CBMS) and 16 interdenominational field bodies (e.g. National Christian Council of India). The second great achievement was the launching of *The International Review of Missions*. The journal, edited by Oldham, was dedicated to continuing Edinburgh 1910's emphasis on the disciplined study of mission.

There can be little argument that Edinburgh 1910 achieved its central goal of developing missionary co-operation in an official, organic form. This transformed the *status quo ante*, and laid the foundations of the International Missionary Council, a Council that managed a series of international missionary conferences in Jerusalem (1928), Tambaram, India (1938), Whitby, Canada (1947), Willingen, Germany (1952) and Achimota, Ghana (1958) until it merged with the World Council of Churches at the New Delhi General Assembly, 1961, to form the Commission of World Mission and Evangelism. Under the latter's auspices, further great international mission conferences were held at Mexico City in 1963, Bangkok in 1973, Melbourne in 1980, San Antonio in 1989, Salvador de Bahia in 1996 and Athens in 2005. Meanwhile a stream of Evangelical mission engagement flowing from Edinburgh 1910, organized from 1974 as the Lausanne Committee for World Evangelization, also held a significant series of international missionary conferences. From 1974 the Committee held conferences at Lausanne in 1974, Pattaya in 1980, Manila in 1989 and Pattaya again in 2004. This movement understands itself to be maintaining the priority that the Edinburgh conference gave to evangelism when the WCC, in their view, has often been preoccupied with other concerns. While institutionally there is a direct line of continuity from the Edinburgh Conference to the World Council of Churches, there are mission movements outside the WCC that understand themselves to represent the spirit and focus of Edinburgh 1910.

The place of Edinburgh 1910 in the formation of the modern ecumenical movement has also been a matter of some debate. On the one hand, there is the judgement of Kenneth Scott Latourette that: 'The World Missionary Conference, Edinburgh 1910, was the birthplace of the modern ecumenical movement.'[49] On the other hand, Willem Visser t'Hooft – one the pioneers of the ecumenical movement, and the first General Secretary of the World Council of Churches on its formation in 1948 – makes only passing reference to Edinburgh 1910 in his account of the origins of the WCC.[50] The WCC website states that Edinburgh 1910 'cannot be considered 'ecumenical' in the actual sense of the word since there were no Catholic or Orthodox delegates present', and of the participants only '17 came from "the Third World".'[51] While both of these points are true, it is unclear what 'the actual sense of the word' ecumenism should be taken to mean. There were no Catholic, and very few Orthodox participants in either the Life and Work or Faith and Order Conference in Stockholm (1925) or Lausanne (1927) – and neither included so-called 'Third World' participation. Yet they qualify as ecumenical conferences out of which flowed the two streams of ecumenism that converged in the formation of the WCC in 1948.

If we describe Edinburgh 1910 as a 'proto-ecumenical' conference, concerned with advancing 'co-operation and unity' in the study and practice of mission, its most significant achievement was that it raised – arguably for the first time in European Christian history – the vision of the Church as a global reality. It was a vision, admittedly, that the Conference itself only partially glimpsed, and in one important respect wrongly in that its fascination with the anticipated growth of Christianity in East Asia blinded it to the actual growth of Christianity in Africa. These failings reflect the Conference's colonial assumptions and mindset. But the sense that Christianity was poised to transform itself by becoming truly global was evident in many of the Conference debates. It would be the task of the International Missionary Council to keep this vision before the ecumenical movement as, in its inter-war development, it focussed its the concerns mainly on co-operation among European churches – Protestant and Orthodox – with scant attention to the rest of the world.

Certainly so far as Protestantism is concerned, no event was more definitive for the emerging shape of Christianity in the twentieth century than Edinburgh 1910. It was the first clear glimpse of what William Temple would describe as 'the great new fact of our time' – a truly worldwide Christian church.[52] This epoch-making vision of the Church as a truly global missionary community has continued to inspire subsequent generations, making it an enduring point of reference for those who hear Christ's call to a mission that extends to the ends of the earth. It is therefore with a sense of how much is to be gained for our understanding of mission today that we turn to a fresh consideration of the eight Commission Reports.

Endnotes

[1] These volumes have been out of print for many years but in 2007 have been made available digitally by the University of Michigan and can be accessed at http://quod.lib.umich.edu/cgi/t/text/text-idx?c=genpub;idno=1936337
[2] John R. Mott, in C. Howard Hopkins, *John R. Mott 1865–1955: A Biography*, Geneva: World Council of Churches; Grand Rapids: Eerdmans, 1979, p. 342.
[3] William Richey Hogg, 'Edinburgh, 1910 – Ecumenical Keystone', *Religion in Life* 29 (1959–60), pp. 339–51.
[4] Ruth Rouse, 'William Carey's "Pleasing Dream"', *International Review of Mission* 38 (April 1949), pp. 181–92.
[5] A. A. Millar, *Alexander Duff of India*, Edinburgh: Canongate Press, 1992, pp. 169–76.
[6] World Missionary Conference, 1910, *The History and Records of the Conference*, Edinburgh & London: Oliphant, Anderson & Ferrier; New York, Chicago and Toronto: Fleming H. Revell, 1910, pp. 7–12.
[7] 'Minutes of the Conference', in *History and Records*, pp. 95–6.
[8] *History and Records*, p. 18.
[9] *History and Records*, pp. 5–6.
[10] *History and Records*, p. 6.
[11] *History and Records*, pp. 8–17.
[12] See John R. Mott, *The Evangelization of the World in This Generation*, London: Student Volunteer Missionary Union, 1900.
[13] Keith Clements, *Faith on the Frontier: A Life of J. H. Oldham*, Edinburgh: T. & T. Clark; Geneva: World Council of Churches, 1999, pp. 73–99.
[14] Gustav Warneck, 'Letter to Mr. Mott from Dr Gustav Warneck, Ex-Professor of Missions in the University of Halle', World Missionary Conference, 1910, *Carrying the Gospel to all the Non-Christian World*, Report of Commission I, Edinburgh & London: Oliphant, Anderson & Ferrier; New York, Chicago and Toronto: Fleming H. Revell, 1910, pp. 434–5.
[15] J. H. Oldham, 'Reflections on Edinburgh 1910', *Religion in Life* 29 (1959–60), p. 333.
[16] *History and Records*, p. 8.
[17] *History and Records*, p. 7.
[18] *History and Records*, pp. 39–71.
[19] W. H. T. Gairdner, *'Edinburgh 1910': An Account and Interpretation of the World Missionary Conference*, Edinburgh & London: Oliphant, Anderson & Ferrier; New York, Chicago and Toronto: Fleming H. Revell, 1910, p. 19.
[20] *History and Records*, p. 11.
[21] *History and Records*, pp. 28–31.
[22] *History and Records*, p. 74.
[23] Gairdner, *Edinburgh 1910*, p. 66.
[24] *History and Records*, p. 75.
[25] *History and Records*, pp. 141–351.
[26] These consisted of: 'Christianity, the Final and Universal Religion', 'The Missionary Enterprise in the Light of History', 'The Missionary Enterprise from the Standpoint of

Missionary Leaders on the Continent of Europe', 'Changes in the Character of the Missionary Problem in Recent Years', 'The Duty of Christian Races, and the Contribution of non-Christian Races to the Body of Christ', 'The Problem of Co-operation between Foreign and Native Workers', 'Demands on the Church made by the Missionary Enterprise', and 'The Sufficiency of God'. See *History and Records*, pp. 139–351.

[27] Gairdner, *Edinburgh 1910*, p. 84.

[28] *Carrying the Gospel*, p. 403.

[29] *Carrying the Gospel*, p. 403.

[30] *Carrying the Gospel*, p. 404.

[31] *Carrying the Gospel*, p. 404.

[32] *Carrying the Gospel*, p. 404.

[33] *Carrying the Gospel*, p. 405.

[34] World Missionary Conference, 1910, *The Church in the Mission Field*, Report of Commission II, Edinburgh & London: Oliphant, Anderson & Ferrier; New York, Chicago and Toronto: Fleming H. Revell, 1910, p. 341.

[35] K. Ibuka, 'The Problem of Cooperation between Foreign and Native Workers', *History and Records*, pp. 294–305.

[36] V. S. Azariah, 'The Problem of Cooperation between Foreign and Native Workers', *History and Records*, pp. 306–15.

[37] *The Church in the Mission Field*, p. 352.

[38] World Missionary Conference, 1910, *Education in Relation to the Christianisation of National Life*, Report of Commission III, Edinburgh & London: Oliphant, Anderson & Ferrier; New York, Chicago and Toronto: Fleming H. Revell, 1910, pp. 371–2.

[39] *Education in Relation to the Christianisation of National Life*, p. 373.

[40] *Education in Relation to the Christianisation of National Life*, pp. 369–70.

[41] World Missionary Conference, 1910, *The Missionary Message in Relation to Non-Christian Religions*, Report of Commission IV, Edinburgh & London: Oliphant, Anderson & Ferrier; New York, Chicago and Toronto: Fleming H. Revell, 1910, p. 315.

[42] World Missionary Conference, 1910, *Missions and Governments*, Report of Commission VII, Edinburgh & London: Oliphant, Anderson & Ferrier; New York, Chicago and Toronto: Fleming H. Revell, 1910, p. 184.

[43] *Missions and Governments*, p. 156.

[44] *History and Records*, pp. 95–6.

[45] World Missionary Conference, 1910, *Cooperation and the Promotion of Unity*, Report of Commission VIII, Edinburgh & London: Oliphant, Anderson & Ferrier; New York, Chicago and Toronto: Fleming H. Revell, 1910, pp. 195–7.

[46] World Missionary Conference, 1910, *The Training of Teachers: with Supplement*, Report of Commission V, Edinburgh & London: Oliphant, Anderson & Ferrier; New York, Chicago and Toronto: Fleming H. Revell, 1910, p. 153.

[47] *History and Records*, p. 96.

[48] The British Conference of Missionary Societies became a division of the British Council of Churches in 1977, and in 1990 was reorganized as the Churches' Commission on Mission. Since 2006 it has been known as the Global Mission Network.

[49] Kenneth Scott Latourette, 'Ecumenical Bearings of the Missionary Movement and the International Missionary Council', chapter 8 in Ruth Rouse and Stephen C. Neill, eds., *A History of the Ecumenical Movement, 1517–1948*, vol. I, 4th edn, Geneva: World Council of Churches, 1993 [1954], p. 362.

[50] See Willem Visser t'Hooft, *The Genesis and Formation of the WCC*, Geneva: World Council of Churches, 1987.
[51] See www.wcc-coe.org/wcc/what/mission/hist-e.html#1 (accessed July 2006)
[52] William Temple, *The Church Looks Forward*, London: Macmillan, 1944, pp. 2–3.

Commission One

Carrying the Gospel to all the Non-Christian World

Commission One
'Carrying the Gospel to all the Non-Christian World'

The Commission in Summary

Commission One was the flagship of the Edinburgh 1910 Conference. Its title, 'Carrying the Gospel to all the Non-Christian World', was the overarching theme of the Conference's eight Commissions – the term 'Non-Christian World' being intended to focus the Conference mainly on Africa, Asia and the Pacific Islands, to the exclusion of regions – notably Latin America – where Catholicism was established. The Commission's Chairman, John R Mott, was also the Chairman of the Conference sessions that discussed the eight Commission Reports. As General Secretary of the World's Student Christian Federation, Mott popularized the watchword of Anglo-Saxon Protestant missions: 'the evangelization of the world in this generation'.[1] Although the phrase is scarcely used in the Report of Commission One, or the rest of the Conference – seemingly out of respect for Continental criticism – its ambition imbued both. 'Carrying the Gospel' was envisioned as the 'occupation'[2] of the vast regions of the world from which Christianity was, at the beginning of the twentieth century, still absent.

Based on close to 600 responses to a questionnaire previously circulated to missionaries, and indigenous Christian leaders in Japan, Korea, China, Malaya and Oceania, Western and Central Asia, Africa, and Other Fields, the Report was compiled by 20 Commissioners under the guidance of Mott in the United States, and George Robson and Julius Richter in Scotland and Germany respectively. The Report comprises four parts: the first dealt with *The Opportunity and Urgency of Carrying the Gospel to all the Non-Christian World*; the second, containing the main body of the Report, presented a *Survey of the Non-Christian World* from the perspective of missionary challenge and opportunity; under the title *Factors in Carrying the Gospel to all the Non-Christian World*, the third part discussed issues of missionary strategy; and the fourth part, *Findings of the Commission*, published edited selections of the plenary discussion of the Report at the Conference itself.

The entire document exudes an optimistic expectation of opportunity. Communications, railway lines, treaties and trade made the non-Christian world accessible to the 'carrying of the Gospel' as never before. 'When in the history of our religion has the Christian Church been confronted with such a wide opportunity as the one now before her in the non-Christian world as a whole?'[3] With resources at its disposal, the Church was equipped to 'execute a campaign literally world-wide in scope'.[4]

Such opportunity should arouse great urgency. The non-Christian religions were deemed to be loosing their hold on the educated classes whose minds were open and favourable as never before to the Christian message. Even where non-Christian religions sought to adapt themselves to modern conditions, they were perceived as failing to satisfy the yearnings of their faithful, and thus resorted to aggressive methods of propaganda. As new leadership emerged in non-Christian nations they manifested the 'plastic condition'[5] of peoples who were caught up in the 'corrupting influences in Western civilization',[6] as represented by Western commercial and political interests, modern secular education, and the growing spirit of nationalism. Amidst such tumultuous change the Report sees evidence of a 'rising spiritual tide'[7] on an unprecedented scale. Pointing to 'the movement toward Christ in many parts of the non-Christian world', it was confident 'that there might be large harvests gathered' if the 'three great laws of God' are applied: the law of sowing and reaping, the law of intercession, and the law of sacrifice.[8] The application of these laws required the committed support of 'the home Church'[9] which itself must be renewed for mission, both at home and abroad, lest it succumb to 'the imminent perils of growing luxury and materialism'.[10]

Against such elaboration of the opportunity and urgency of Christian mission, Part Two – the *Survey of the Non-Christian World* – reviews conditions across Asia, Australasia and Oceania, Africa, and among non-Christians in the Western hemisphere (Indians and Orientals in the Americas and Artic regions, and Jews) as these conditions were perceived to relate to the missionary task. The *Survey* was to be read in conjunction with the *Statistical Atlas of Christian Mission*, prepared in New York and New Haven, that included a directory of Protestant missionary societies, statistics on the history of the missionary movement, maps of the distribution of Protestant mission throughout the world, and an index of mission stations 'occupied' by foreign missionaries.[11] Information about Roman Catholic and Orthodox missions is also included in a separate section of the *Atlas*.

It is neither possible nor fruitful to attempt to summarize the 238 pages of the *Survey*, or the *Atlas*. They contain an immense amount of information, and merit the reading of all who are interested in the history of Protestant missionary movement. As Mott emphasized when introducing the Report to the Conference: 'The work of studying how to make Christ known to all mankind (*sic*) has related us to the whole world problem.'[12] From a missiological point of view they represent a fascinating attempt, quoting Mott again, to comprehend 'the vastness, the variety, and the infinite difficulty of the task of carrying the Gospel to literally all the non-Christian world'.[13] By bringing together information provided by missionaries in so many different regions, they try to 'look(ing) at the world as a unit, as Christ did and does, and as all His true disciples should'.[14]

The *Survey* is candid in acknowledging that there were vast areas of the world that remained 'unoccupied'[15] in the sense of being untouched by the Gospel, or, if included in a missionary scheme, not yet 'occupied' by a missionary operation. These included 'what might be called the heart of each of the two great continents of Asia and Africa',[16] and represented more than '122,000,000 people without missionary provision'.[17] While a scientific survey and analysis of these regions and peoples was not yet possible, the Report offered some discussion of 'the causes of neglect': for example, the lack of accessibility, political obstacles created by both 'native' and Western governments, 'a lack of a comprehensive vision of the goal of missions,' and the tendency to assess the missionary movement 'from the standpoint of progress made and not sufficiently from that of the work to be done'.[18]

This opens the way for Part Three of the Report that considered 'the question of how best to utilize the comparatively insufficient yet valuable force at the disposal of the Church to make Christ known to the largest possible number of people, and to build up strong and enduring Churches'.[19] Following a brief survey of evangelistic methods reported by missionaries in Japan, China, India and Africa, the Report distinguished between methods that are 'indispensable' – 'the preaching and teaching of the revealed Gospel', 'the establishment and edification of the native Church' and 'the translation and circulation of the Bible in the vernacular'[20] – and methods that vary in usefulness according to the needs of specific mission field – education, medical work, literature, and industrial training.[21]

The relationship of foreign missions and native churches, and the relative value of each in the missionary enterprise was the focus of intense debate. Introducing the Report to the plenary, Mott clarified the two poles of the discussion: 'The evangelisation of the world ... is not chiefly a European and American enterprise, but an African and Asian enterprise';[22] on the other hand, 'the missionary enterprise after all is the projection abroad of the Church at home'.[23] The tension between these two postulates is refereed, if not resolved, in the Report's conclusion that 'it is essential ... on every mission field to seek to permeate the whole life of the Church from its beginning with the evangelistic spirit, and further, in proportion as the Church increases, to develop strongly a native evangelistic staff, working in cooperation with the foreign force'[24]

A second tension is evident in a related question: should the priority of mission be the 'occupying' of 'unoccupied' regions, or the empowerment of indigenous churches for leadership in mission? The Report's repeated emphasis on reaching *all* the non-Christian world as quickly as possible – and certainly by the next world missionary conference – echoed Mott's 'evangelization of the world in this generation'. The alternative view was stated most succinctly not the Report itself, but in an appended letter from Gustav Warneck, the pioneer of mission studies in Germany, who was not present at the Conference itself. Addressing himself to Mott he argued that 'a predilection for the watchword 'the occupation of the whole world in this present generation'...can easily miss the most hopeful opportunities'.[25] These lay, in his view, in strengthening local churches. He argued: 'The great lesson which the foreign missionary enterprise of our time has to learn from the history of the expansion of Christianity during the first three centuries is that the principal strength of missions lies in the native congregations…We are at present in that stage of modern missions when the watchword must be the self-propagation of Christianity.'[26]

Endnotes

[1] See John R. Mott, *The Evangelization of the World in This Generation*, London: Student Volunteer Missionary Union, 1900.
[2] World Missionary Conference, 1910, *Carrying the Gospel to all the Non-Christian World*, Report of Commission I, Edinburgh & London: Oliphant, Anderson & Ferrier; New York, Chicago and Toronto: Fleming H. Revell, 1910, p. 58.
[3] *Carrying the Gospel*, p. 10.
[4] *Carrying the Gospel*, p. 10.
[5] *Carrying the Gospel*, p. 25.
[6] *Carrying the Gospel*, p. 21.
[7] *Carrying the Gospel*, p. 35.
[8] *Carrying the Gospel*, pp. 43–4.
[9] *Carrying the Gospel*, p. 44.
[10] *Carrying the Gospel*, p. 46.
[11] World Missionary Conference, 1910, *Statistical Atlas of Christian Missions*, Edinburgh: World Missionary Conference, 1910.
[12] *Carrying the Gospel*, p. 402.
[13] *Carrying the Gospel*, p. 402.
[14] *Carrying the Gospel*, pp. 402–3.
[15] *Carrying the Gospel*, p. 279.
[16] *Carrying the Gospel*, p. 279.
[17] *Carrying the Gospel*, p. 283.
[18] *Carrying the Gospel*, pp. 284–6.
[19] *Carrying the Gospel*, p. 289.
[20] *Carrying the Gospel*, pp. 312–13.
[21] See *Carrying the Gospel*, pp. 313–16.
[22] *Carrying the Gospel*, p. 404.
[23] *Carrying the Gospel*, p. 405.
[24] *Carrying the Gospel*, pp. 368–9.
[25] *Carrying the Gospel*, p. 435.
[26] *Carrying the Gospel*, p. 434.

Commission One and the Church's Transforming Century[1]

Andrew F. Walls

The great migration

Around 1500, a development occurred with more significance for the future of Christianity than the Reformation itself. A great maritime migration began that was to shape the modern world and have complex effects upon the world's religions. Over the years it was in being, millions of people left Europe to make their homes or seek their fortunes in lands of which before 1500 Europeans had not known, or had not considered accessible. Whole nations, some with vast populations, came into being as a result of the movement, and the migrants and their descendants established hegemony over much of the world and control over much of its trade. The movement lasted for four and a half centuries, until the twentieth century during which the system which it produced imploded.[2]

When the process began, Europe was more Christian than it had ever previously been. It took many centuries for Europe to become Christian; by 1500 Europe was 'Christendom', Christianity territorially expressed, while Christianity had become eclipsed in many other parts of the world where once it had been strong. Western Europeans, holding a form of Christianity heavily acculturated by centuries of inter-action with the languages and cultures of Europe, became by default the representative Christians of their time. At first they essayed the crusading mode of propagating their faith, a method developed by long competition with their Muslim neighbours, the only non-Christian people (other than Jews), of whom they had much knowledge. The Spanish conquest of the Americas was the last of the Crusades. But in much of the rest of the world the crusading method was manifestly out of the question; especially when Portugal, a small power in the context of great empires like that of the Moghuls, or China, or Japan, was the agent. For the most part, the powers of Christendom, whether Catholic or Protestant, soon tired of official attempts to promote the spread of Christianity in the non-Western world outside the Americas.

The missionary movement emerged as an alternative to the crusading model of evangelization. Its origins lay not in the official policy of the European powers, but among radical Christians for whom the faith of Christ was more important than the economic, military and political advantages that derived from overseas activity. The missionary movement was based on dedicated people whose function was to offer and persuade, without the power to coerce. Such people frequently needed, as crusaders did not, to live on terms set by another society. Born in Catholic Europe, and fuelled by the new devotion of the Catholic Reformation, the missionary movement had by the seventeenth century entered into genuine interaction and engagement with the cultures of China, India, Japan and South East Asia.

The Protestant version of the movement took longer to blossom. Beginning in a small way in Puritan North America, it took new forms in the eighteenth century inspired by German and Central European Pietism. The Evangelical Revival gave it fresh impetus, and by the early nineteenth century its impress lay deep on European and American Protestantism as a whole.

The World Missionary Conference

The high point of the Protestant missionary movement is marked by the World Missionary Conference, held in Edinburgh in 1910.[3] The Conference was no triumphalist celebration of achievement; it was a serious attempt at a systematic and business-like analysis of what Protestant missions had already achieved and of what remained to be done. Immense labour went into preparatory documents, and notably into the *Statistical Atlas of Christian Missions*,[4] designed so that those attending the Conference could have all the available data about missions at their fingertips. Representation at the conference was carefully balanced to reflect the proportional involvement in missions of the main sources of missionaries, i.e. Britain, North America and Continental Europe, with a small place reserved for the 'colonies', that is the white populations of Australia, New Zealand and South Africa. Great pains were also directed to ensuring coverage of the entire theological spectrum represented in non-Catholic missions.

No conference was better prepared beforehand. Eight commissions toiled for months to produce book-length reports as a basis of discussion of major aspects of missions; discussion itself was kept crisp and pointed by limiting participants, mostly schooled in an age of pulpit eloquence, to seven minutes each. The report that has attracted most attention in later times is that of Commission Four,[5] entitled *The Missionary Message in Relation to Non-Christian Religions*, with its analysis of the replies received to a detailed questionnaire sent all over the world. But of all the volumes that contain the record of the conference, none stands closer to the focus of the meeting than the report of Commission One, published under the title *Carrying the Gospel to all the Non-Christian World.*

The Commission was chaired by John R Mott,[6] who was the dominating figure at the conference, and its twenty members – eight British, eight North Americans and four Continental Europeans – included some of the biggest names in the missionary movement at that time. Its report conveys its drift in the very title of its first section: 'The opportunity and the urgency of carrying the Gospel to all the non-Christian world', and in the opening statement: 'It is possible today to a degree far greater than at any time in the past to give the Gospel to all the non-Christian world.'[7]

For one thing, the report argues, the world was now known and explored. For another, it was largely open; open not only in the political sense of unimpeded access, but also in the more important sense of the attitudes of its peoples. The decision-making classes in countries such as Japan and Korea, long closed to outside ideas, were now ready to listen. In India the outcaste and lower caste groups were recognizing the advantages of Western civilization, and were taking the Christian message seriously as a result. Africa and the Pacific were at last open to mission enterprise, even if colonial governments still placed obstacles in the way of missions in areas where there was a Muslim presence.

If the Commission was impressed by the opportunities that the contemporary situation offered, it was also insistent that those opportunities might be merely transitory. While it was certainly true that the non-Christian religions were losing their hold on key groups in some countries, it did not necessarily follow that those classes would become Christian. They might turn elsewhere; or the old religions might re-form to meet the challenges of modern thought, or the modern secular education now spreading in Asia might create a climate unfavorable to Christianity. Islam, with the aid and protection of European colonial governments, might become the religion of Africa. Western influences were spreading on a global scale; but the net result might be that the worst, and not the best, features of Western civilization would take root in Asia and Africa. The worst face of the West was already displayed among European and American residents in the non-Western world. Though at present the winds were fair, the Commission saw the possibility of unsettled weather ahead. It was another incentive to immediate action.

The second, and by far the largest division of the report is a survey, continent by continent, of the non-Christian world, the *Statistical Atlas* acting as a companion to it. To the missionary situation in Asia 142 pages are devoted, followed by 42 to Africa and ten to Australasia and the Pacific. There is a short section on 'Non-Christians of the Western hemisphere', devoted entirely to the native peoples of the Americas, North and South, and to Asian immigrants there.

This last detail points to a major lacuna in the World Missionary Conference. The organizers had aimed at theological inclusiveness; the more 'catholic' expressions of Anglicanism, though to a significant degree involved in missions, had not been officially represented at earlier mission conferences, and the general theological climate of the time did not make such meeting easy. In the event – though this had required intense diplomacy on the part of the organizers – almost the whole spectrum of contemporary Anglicanism was represented at Edinburgh, making it important to avoid flashpoints where traditions might come into conflict. The greatest potential for such flashpoints lay in discussions of Latin America, bearing in mind the expressed concern of the conference for the unevangelized parts of the world. For many delegates, Latin America as a whole could be considered unevangelized; for others, only those mountain and forest peoples that had never been reached by Catholic missions could be properly so described. The effect of this was to make all reference to Latin America a sensitive matter; hence the marginal place it has in the report of Commission One.

After the section on the Western Hemisphere comes another on the Jews throughout the world, and there is a final statement about 'Unoccupied sections of the world' i.e. those with no missionary presence at all. This section first indicates areas of special difficulty of access or sparse population, such as Central Asia, and then resumes the theme of the position of Africa.

> To a far greater degree than even in the case of Asia, the heart of Africa constitutes a vast unoccupied field .... There are therefore to be found in Africa ... more than a third of the population of the entire continent without any existing agency having plans actually projected for their evangelisation. These figures are overwhelming, and they become more so when it is pointed out that the extent of the effective influence of existing missionary agencies has probably been greatly overestimated. The question can seriously be raised, Has the Church more than made a beginning in the evangelisation of the Dark Continent?[8]

The last division of the report concerns factors to be taken into account in planning for evangelization on the non-Christian world. It includes a substantial chapter on 'The Church in the mission field as an evangelistic agency', which includes in its summing up the statement:

> The small native Church, left to itself, is in danger within a generation or two of losing its tone under the influence of monotony, isolation, or ill-success. As a rule it needs the guidance and stimulus of the spiritual ideas, as well as the spiritual aids, which are supplied through contact by means of missionaries with the life of older Churches. While many noble leaders have arisen among the early converts in the field, it will take time to develop a sufficient number of men of knowledge, gifts, and character to enable the Church to stand with advantage, or even with safety, apart from foreign missionaries.[9]

The impression given by this whole division of the report is that the task of evangelization depends largely on Western missionaries. The factors to be taken account in carrying the Gospel to the non-Christian world are how missionaries should be deployed, how historical factors have skewed deployment, what methods missionaries should use, and missionary participation in the spiritual disciplines. The report addresses words to the 'Home Church' (that is, the church in the West) about the danger that increasing luxury and growing materialism may enervate it and quench the missionary spirit. Missionaries are represented as overstretched physically, mentally and spiritually, unable to get time for either the intellectual or the spiritual preparation for their demanding task. The thrust of the report is about the responsibility of the Home Church, that is, the Church of the fully evangelized world in Europe and North America. It must produce the missionaries and resources needed to tackle the unprecedented opportunities now being offered to evangelize the non-Christian world – before it was too late.

As we read the report almost a century later, it is at this point that the greatest difference appears between the conditions under which the older missionary movement sought to fulfil the Great Commission and the conditions of our own day. The best analysts and thinkers of 1910 could take for granted that there was a reasonably homogeneous fully evangelized world, and a world beyond it that was unevangelized or only partly evangelized. From the fully evangelized world of Europe and North America the Home Church must send forth it's choicest to carry the Gospel to the non-Christian world, where the Native Church, a tender young plant, stood as earnest of the future.

> How to multiply the number of Christians who, with truthful lives, and with clear, unshakable faith in the character and ability of God, will, individually and collectively or corporately as a Church, wield this force [intercessory prayer] for the conversion and transformation of men, for the inauguration and energising of spiritual movements, and for the breaking down of all that exalts itself against Christ and His purposes – that is the supreme question of foreign missions.[10]

We have seen that the analysts and the visionaries of 1910 realized that the hopeful signs they saw in Asia could quickly change to something much less hopeful for Christian progress. We have also seen that they recognized the possibility of the church of the West losing all missionary zeal under the influence of its rapidly rising standards of living. What they did not glimpse was how soon the West, and Europe in particular, would become part of the non-Christian world. Perhaps the military language of 'occupation' helped to disable them from remembering that Christian history, from the first century onwards, suggests that there are no permanently Christian lands. Christianity is serial in its growth, often decaying in its areas of apparent strength to start anew at or beyond its margins.

The analysts of 1910, living in an age of seaborne communications, held a maritime view of the Church and of the world. They saw the carriers of the Gospel as crossing the seas in order to fulfil their task.[11] Though they lived at the climactic period of the Great European Migration, and generally believed that the spread of Western culture was favorable to the Gospel, there is little sign in their report of triumphal rejoicing in the Western empires. When the report makes direct reference to those empires, it is usually to decry the obstructiveness of Western governments towards missions, and there are abundant references to the negative impact of certain aspects of Western culture. Further, while recognizing the difficulties that anti-foreign movements in Asia create for missionaries, the authors have no condemnation for nationalism:

> This national and racial spirit cannot and should not be crushed or checked. It is a matter of profound concern to the Christian Church. It will have much power to hinder or to facilitate the spread of Christ's Kingdom. Christ never by teaching or example resisted or withstood the spirit of true nationalism. Wherever His principles, including those pertaining to the supreme claims of His Kingdom on earth, have had the largest right of way, they have served to strengthen national spirit and not to weaken it.[12]

Even in India, the report goes on, where the national movement gave rise to strong anti-missionary feeling, it was important to note that the same national movement also denounced and discarded caste, hitherto the main obstacle to Christian preaching.[13] Nationalism should cause missionaries to take their work to a deeper level, and to realize in humility that they must decrease while the native church must increase.[14]

On mission theology, Edinburgh 1910 has little to say. The conference ground rules, of course, precluded the introduction of topics known to be controversial among the participants; even so, it seems remarkable today that so many people, representing such a wide range of theological views, could take for granted that they were agreed as to what the Gospel was. It seems equally remarkable that they could all accept that evangelism, translation, education, medicine, literature, industrial training and 'women's work' were simply different methods of carrying the Gospel.[15] The most notable questioning voice was that of the German missiologist Gustav Warneck. Warneck was not present at Edinburgh, but sent a long letter to Mott, reproduced as an appendix to the report of Commission One.[16] Edinburgh 1910 reflects a certain confidence that, whatever issues may divide Christendom, there is a consensual theological deposit that is the common heritage of Christians.

The conference was a time of dreams and visions; the excitement of delegates is palpable, even in the staid pages of the official record.[17] The accounts of such participants as W. H. Temple Gairdner[18] show it still more. Not for nothing are the origins of the modern ecumenical movement conventionally dated from this meeting. A mere handful of Asian delegates attended amid the hundreds from Europe and North America, and Africa and Latin America were essentially without indigenous representation; yet many who were present caught a first glimpse of what a truly World Church might be like. Yet the meeting was not solely visionary; most of it was severely practical, directed to systematic planning and co-operative effort.

Then and now

The apparatus planned at Edinburgh for international missionary co-operation came into being, but with much more difficulty than had been anticipated at the conference and against the background of international events then unforeseen. Within a few years of the meeting came the shock of the Great War that pitted the missionary-sending countries against one another and ushered in the most violent period in modern history. The whole basis of the secure worldview that underlies the analysis of the world made by the members of Commission One was swept away. Most surprisingly of all, the fundamental assumption on which Edinburgh thinking, and indeed the missionary thinking of the whole of the previous century was founded, was called into question. The Edinburgh delegates had thought of the 'Home Church' in Europe and North America, the old Christendom, as the base for the evangelization of the rest of the world, and had assumed that it would remain so. But in the course of the twentieth century, perhaps the largest and fastest recession in Christian history (far faster, for instance, than that which followed the first rise of Islam in the Middle East) fastened on that old Christendom. Its most obvious effect was in Europe, but it affected most of the lands newly settled by people of European origin in the course of the Great European Migration. The effect has been slowest in the United States, but not the less clear for that. The old Christendom had lasted many centuries; around 1500, as the West newly engaged with the non-Western world and the Great Migration began, Christianity could be identified with Europe. Five centuries later, Europe could best be described as post-Christian; and Western people were no longer the representative Christians.

All this might seem to invalidate the whole vision of the World Missionary Conference and the project it represented, were it not for another extraordinary aspect of twentieth century church history. This is the extent to which the dreams and visions of the conference about the evangelization of the non-Christian world were fulfilled, though not in the way, nor always by the means, nor even in the places that the delegates expected and planned. The fact remains that, by a huge reversal of the position in 1910, the majority of Christians now live in Africa, Asia, Latin America or the Pacific, and that the proportion is rising. Simultaneously with the retreat from Christianity in the West in the twentieth century went – just as the visionaries of Edinburgh hoped – a massive accession to the Christian faith in the non-Western world. The map of the Christian Church, its demographic and cultural make-up, changed more dramatically during the twentieth century than (probably) in any other since the first.

But it happened in ways that the analysts of 1910 could not have predicted. The most favourable signs about the future that they could observe lay in Asia. They saw multitudes in Japan, in China, in India turning to new ways of thought, and thus, as it seemed, becoming open to Christian ideas as never before. The great Asian cultures had long received the heaviest deployment of missionary personnel and effort. Medical missions (the most financially intensive branch of missions), and other specialisms had been developed largely with Asia in mind. Missions were significantly involved in higher education to university level in Asia, in addition to equipping entire medical faculties there. But the Christian growth that has taken place in Asia has not always followed the patterns of missionary investment. China has indeed seen substantial, if as yet unquantifiable, Christian growth; but that growth has come in the second half of the twentieth century, and in the teeth of official disfavor and often of outright hostility. And it has taken place in the period after missionaries were excluded from the country. Korea was somewhat cursorily treated in the Commission's report, since Protestant work there was then so new, and the country's long period of isolation from foreign influence was so recent. (North Korea's present isolation is in some ways a reversion to tradition.) But the twentieth century – a time of frequent and varied trauma for Korea – saw Korean Christianity becoming a major force in the land, taking shape in the national movement against Japanese colonialism, burgeoning in the times of the dreadful troubles that followed. In recent decades Korean Christianity, besides becoming a significant force in North America, has produced thousands of missionaries to serve in other parts of the world, including some of the most inhospitable, that the 1910 report called 'unoccupied', where Western missionaries never penetrated. If any country can be said to preserve the spirit of 1910, it is South Korea.

A whole chain of churches now stretches across the lands bordering the great mountain ranges from the Himalayas to the South East Asian peninsula. Most of these churches were tiny or non-existent in 1910. Then, and for long after, Nepal was considered a country wholly closed to the Christian message; now it has a thriving church. Vigorous churches have also arisen among the complex of peoples who live in North East India and South West China who are neither Indic nor Han Chinese, and for these the period of decisive growth was the twentieth century. There are states in North East India where Christianity is the majority religious profession. Across the frontier with Myanmar, among peoples of similar ethnic origin, Christian growth has accelerated since the expulsion of missionaries in the 1960s. In each of the countries mentioned – Nepal, India, China, Myanmar – Christians are a minority, and often a small one; but taken together (and with the related Christian communities in Thailand) they form a substantial Himalayan-Arakan Christian community of which there was little trace when the conference met in Edinburgh.

Latin America, which diplomacy led the World Missionary Conference to leave aside, has now become a theatre of Christian operations that no one can possibly ignore. The peculiar history of Latin America has given it an unusual Christian trajectory. The conquest was intended to bring it within the existing Christendom; thus Mexico became New Spain, with the expectation that its laws and customs would be those of old Spain. In the sixteenth century Latin

America received the church settlement adopted in Southern Europe, a settlement arising out of the conditions and controversies of sixteenth century Europe. It received the Catholicism of the Council of Trent without going through the processes and experiences that produced the Council of Trent. For several centuries there seemed no reason to doubt that Latin America had been successfully incorporated within the Christendom framework derived from medieval Europe. But Latin America, though in one sense a European artifact, was no mere extension of Europe; it was a union of diverse peoples with powerful indigenous religious influences. And in the twentieth century, with rapid urbanization and huge social ferment, the lid blew off the religious pressure cooker. A theological upheaval occurred as drastic as any that befell Europe in the sixteenth century, and Latin America's delayed Reformation era began. As in Europe, there was a pastoral revolution within the established church; as in Europe, reforming zeal took both conservative and radical ecclesiastical forms; as in Europe, popular religious movements burst the bounds of the old Church altogether. Outside immigrant communities, Protestantism had traditionally played no significant part in Latin America; at the time of the World Missionary Conference it was hardly visible there. By the end of the twentieth century, however, Protestants formed a significant proportion of the population; in some Central American countries perhaps actually forming a majority of the actively practising Christians among the population. But the movement took an indigenous form; the overwhelming majority of Latin American Protestants are Pentecostal, what in the West has been marginal has in Latin America become the mainstream. Latin America may be an artifact of the West, manifestly carrying the impress of European and North American influences; but its potent mixture of the cultures of three continents ensures that it has a religious dynamic of its own. Liberation theology and Pentecostal preaching and congregational life alike are examples of its effect; and the spread of a huge diaspora from Latin America, with the United States as its main focus, (a further effect of the twentieth century), will ensure that its influences spread far beyond Latin America itself.

We have seen that the analysts of 1910 saw inland Africa as 'a great unoccupied field', and questioned whether more than a beginning had been made of the evangelization of the continent. It is perhaps in Africa that the strongest contrast appears between the Church today and the Church as seen by the writers of the report of Commission One. The number of professing Christians in Africa has risen over the period from something like ten million to well over 300 million. Sub-Saharan Africa has become one of the Christian heartlands, and is quietly slipping into the place in the Christian world that was once occupied by Europe.

A transformed Church

The twentieth century saw transformation wrought in the Christian Church and opened a new chapter in Christian history. For several centuries the forces shaping Christian development were those emerging in the West. The Church now has a new shape, a new ethnic composition and a new cultural orientation. Christianity is in the process of becoming a non-Western religion again.

It is the fulfillment, the rich fulfillment, of the vision of the World Missionary Conference of 1910, although the processes that brought it about were far different from those the participants expected. The new shape of the Church provides the starting point for any contemporary consideration of the task of Commission One; 'Carrying the Gospel to all the Non-Christian World'.

At the time of the World Missionary Conference, the leaders and decision makers were overwhelmingly European and North American, and the primary step to the evangelization of the world appeared to be the mobilization of the Christian resources of Europe and North America to that end. A century later, it is not, as at Edinburgh in 1910, for North America and Europe to preside by right at the table. The representative Christians, those by whom the quality of twenty-first (and perhaps twenty-second) century Christianity will be judged, are now Africans, Asians and Latin Americans; Western Christians are a minority among Christians; if present trends continue, they will form a smaller and smaller proportion of the Church. Taking primacy and leadership for granted since the time the Great European Migration began, they will need to learn new skills as assistants and facilitators. Globalization is a fact of the modern world. The way that globalization works in many spheres leaves the West in charge, at least for the present. Globalization in the Church opens the West to new creative sources of life, energy and leadership elsewhere. And the mobilization of the Church's resources for mission on a worldwide scale, that in 1910 seemed inevitably to be a Western concern, now involves Christians on every continent.

The meeting in 1910 envisaged the 'Native Church', as the churches of Africa and Asia were then collectively designated, as a tender young plant in need of constant supervision. It is salutary to remember the fiery trials, the multiple testings that many of those churches have endured since then. Is there a parallel in Christian history to the story of the church in China over the past fifty years, in terms of what it has endured and how it has emerged? Over the same period, Christian faith in many parts of Africa has been honed on endemic disaster in places where the normal climate of the life of faith has been war, disruption, dispersal, disease and disappointment. The churches of South Africa were called to give moral leadership to their nation in ways the Western church has not known for many centuries. There are other countries where the churches, sometimes the only functioning forms of civil society when even the state has broken down, have become salt and light to nations in distress. If suffering, persecution, and faithful wrestling with impossible situations are marks of Christian authenticity, then perhaps God has been training some of the churches of Africa and Asia for leadership in mission, imparting to them accumulated knowledge of God's salvation.

More and more, events and developments in Africa, Asia and Latin America will shape the future of Christianity, for these are great modern theatres of Christian mission, the scene of crucial engagement between the Christian Gospel and what the Fourth Gospel calls 'the world'. Increasingly this engagement will raise issues for Christian faith and Christian service, and define the agenda for the Christian Church worldwide.

One pressing item on the agenda of the Church worldwide will be the re-evangelization of the West. This is the vista the analysts of the missionary situation had no reason to contemplate in 1910. Now the situation of the West has to be pondered, not in terms of Christian revival, but of cross-cultural primary evangelism, the penetration of a non-Christian culture. And here anyone attempting for our day the task that Commission One undertook for their's must take account of a feature of our world that was barely noticeable in 1910. The World Missionary Conference met – though this was hidden at the time – near the climax of the Great European Migration, the point from which its recession was about to begin. The world order that European migration had established was about to implode, as its internal rivalries were projected into a worldwide arena. With this implosion came the end of the Great Migration; and, from the middle years of the twentieth century, its reversal. Since that mid-century period, slowly at first, but with increasing momentum, multitudes of people from Africa, Asia and Latin America have migrated to Europe and North America. The process looks set to continue, for it has powerful drivers; falling population in the most developed nations requiring immigration to sustain their economic position, and intolerable pressures elsewhere forcing vast numbers of people to seek new homes. Those coming to the West include many Christians, who have transplanted their churches and congregational life. Their coming opens the possibility both of fuller realization of the Body of Christ within a multi-cultural church, and of new opportunities for bringing about the Christian penetration of Western culture from the outside.

The new shape of the Christian church may have significant effects on theology. Theology is about making Christian decisions. It is the effort to think about faith in a Christian way. The great doctrinal issues of the Trinity and Incarnation were forced on Christians because they had to explore their deepest convictions about Christ by thinking in Greek, asking Greek questions, using indigenous Greek vocabulary, categories of thought, and methods of debate. It was strenuous and painful – there is no 'safe' theology. But the process led to discoveries (genuine discoveries, though not necessarily the final ones) about who Christ is, that could never have been achieved using only the inherited categories, such as Messiah. The great creeds that resulted can still draw us out in worship and adoration as we recite them. The discoveries they enshrine came from the process of translation; by exploring the meaning of Christ in terms of the Greek heritage and identity. The process did not involve abandoning the venerable past rooted in the history of Israel; Messiah and the other traditional titles of the Divine Son continued to mean what they always did. Nor did it mean abandoning Scripture; the process made clear things that were in Scripture all the time, but were fully apprehended only when they were brought out through the process of cultural translation.

Analogous processes can be traced in other centuries as Christian faith has crossed cultural frontiers and required Christians to think in new categories and face issues never faced by Christians before. We could well be entering a time of theological creativity such as the Church knew in the third and fourth centuries. That earlier period of creativity arose from the interaction of the Gospel with Hellenistic culture and a firmly established Greek intellectual tradition. In our time the ongoing Christian interaction with the ancient cultures of Africa and Asia may open new developments in Christian thinking as events, conditions and traditions in Africa and Asia force themselves on the theological agenda because they require Christian decisions.

The Western theological academy is at present not well placed for leadership in the new situation. It has been too long immersed in its local concerns and is often unaware of the transformation that has taken place in the Church. It is often hugely ignorant of the world in which the majority of Christians live, their social and religious contexts, and the history and life of their churches. Its intellectual maps are pre-Columbian; there are vast areas of the Christian world of which they take no account. Nor are its products always readily transferable outside the West. Western theology is in general too small for Africa; it has been cut down to fit the small-scale universe demanded by the Enlightenment, which set and jealously guarded a frontier between the empirical world and the world of spirit. Much of humanity lives in a larger, more populated universe, in which the frontier is continually being crossed. It is a universe that comprehends what Paul calls the principalities and powers. Such is the background of the majority of the world's Christians, and it requires a theology that brings Christ to bear on every part of that universe. A theology that takes seriously what Paul calls the principalities and powers, and makes evident the victory over them that Paul ascribes to Christ's triumphal chariot of the Cross could enlarge and clarify the theology of evil. The new age of the Church could bring a theological renaissance, with new perspectives, new materials, new light on old problems, and a host of issues never faced theologically before.

In the Epistle to the Ephesians we have a vivid account of the place in the early Church of two sharply contrasting Christian lifestyles. On the one hand, the way of life of the first believers represented converted Judaism. They still rejoiced in Torah and circumcision, understanding Jesus wholly in terms of Jewish history and experience. On the other hand there was the new Hellenistic way of being Christian, without Torah or circumcision, that Paul's letters show in process of construction among Greek former pagans. Not for them the ordered life of the Torah; instead, the daily task of turning the existing

Hellenistic social and family and intellectual life towards Christ. Both were converted lifestyles; but neither was complete in itself. Each needed the other, for both were building blocks in the New Temple, both were functioning organs in the Body of which Christ was head. Only as they came together could the Temple be built, the Body function aright, the full stature of Christ be realized.

When Ephesians was written, there were only two significant cultures, and thus two converted lifestyles, within the Christian community; and the time soon came when the original Jewish model of the faith of Christ dropped out of sight. The century since the World Missionary Conference has brought the return of the Ephesian reality, but in vastly magnified form. There are no longer two, but countless cultures into which Christ has come as people across the world have by faith received him. The multitudinous converted lifestyles that result from this belong together: they are all necessary building blocks in the New Temple designed for God's worship. They are all functioning organs in the Body of which Christ is the head. Some of the great tests of Christianity in the new age of the Church will be ecumenical. Ecumenicity is no longer a matter of how different confessions and denominational traditions relate to one another. It is rather how our Lord's prayer that all his disciples may be one, can be realized in a Body composed of African and Indian and Chinese and Korean and Hispanic and Caribbean and European and North American Christians.

The members of Commission One looked out on a world in which the Great European Migration was at its peak and the hegemony that the migration had established appeared beyond serious challenge. They looked on a church whose base lay firmly in Europe and North America. They called on that church to muster its forces for the evangelization of the Non-Christian world beyond the West and, incidentally, for the nurture and oversight of the tender plant they called 'the Native Church' that was quietly growing within that world. Today, we look out on a world in which the order of affairs established by means of the Great European migration is in gradual dissolution, and the powers of Asia await the succession. The migration has not simply ended, but reversed, so that Asia, Africa and Latin America have a permanent presence in Europe and North America. And the religious dimension of the reversed migration brings the World Church with it to the West; and it brings there all the religions of the world. In 1910, Western Christians rarely had the opportunity to meet Christians from elsewhere, and encounter with other faiths typically implied overseas travel; now both can be features of daily life. And as we look out on the Church, we see that what in 1910 seemed a tender plant has grown into a tree that is now the central feature of the garden. Its growth and its fruits offer fresh resources and fresh reserves for a new chapter of that mission to the world that brought the World Missionary Conference into being, a mission that must now include the re-evangelization of the West. It offers also the possibility of theological renaissance and of incomparably richer corporate Christian life. It has been a remarkable century.

Endnotes

[1] A somewhat different version of this chapter appeared as 'The Great Commission 1910-2010' in W. Stephen Gunter and Elaine Robinson, eds., *Considering the Great Commission: Evangelism and Mission in the Wesleyan Spirit,* Nashville: Abingdon Press, 2005, pp. 7–22. The author, editors and publisher are grateful to Abingdon Press for permission to see material common to both versions.
[2] The idea is pursued further in Andrew F. Walls, 'Mission and Migration: the Diaspora in Christian History', *Journal of African Christian Thought* 5, no. 2 (2002): pp. 3–11.
[3] On the conference see W. Richey Hogg, *Ecumenical Foundations: a History of the International Missionary Council and its Nineteenth Century Background*, New York: Harper, 1952, ch. 3; Andrew F. Walls, *The Cross-Cultural Process in Christian History*, Maryknoll, NY: Orbis, ch. 3.
[4] World Missionary Conference, 1910, *Statistical Atlas of Christian Missions*, Edinburgh: World Missionary Conference, 1910.
[5] 5 See, for example, J. Stanley Friesen, *Missionary Responses to Tribal Religions at Edinburgh 1910*, New York: Peter Lang, 1996.
[6] 6 Charles Howard Hopkins, *John R Mott, 1865–1955: A Biography,* Grand Rapids: Eerdmans, 1979.
[7] World Missionary Conference, 1910, *Carrying the Gospel into all the Non-Christian World*, Report of Commission I, Edinburgh & London: Oliphant, Anderson & Ferrier; New York, Chicago and Toronto: Fleming H. Revell, 1910, p. 5.
[8] *Carrying the Gospel*, pp. 281–2.
[9] *Carrying the Gospel*, p. 342.
[10] *Carrying the Gospel*, pp. 360–1.
[11] The effects of this are noted in the Report of Commission One, where the point is made that since missions arrived by sea they tended to concentrate on coastal areas and move inland by ports and waterways. By contrast Islam had traveled by the great overland trading routes. *Carrying the Gospel*, pp. 284–5.
[12] *Carrying the Gospel*, p. 33.
[13] *Carrying the Gospel*, p. 364.
[14] *Carrying the Gospel*, p. 96.
[15] *Carrying the Gospel*, pp. 298–316.
[16] *Carrying the Gospel*, pp. 434–6. Warneck makes strategic, as well as theological, observations.
[17] A volume similar to the Report of Commission One was published for each of the other commissions; a ninth volume, entitled *History and Records*, contains an account of the Conference.
[18] W. H. Temple Gairdner, *'Edinburgh 1910': An Account and Interpretation of the World Missionary Conference*, Edinburgh & London: Oliphant, Anderson & Ferrier; New York, Chicago and Toronto: Fleming H. Revell, 1910.

Commission One after a Century of Violence: The Search for a Larger Christ

Kosuke Koyama

The Commissioners' understanding of the theme

The Commissioners believed in the evangelization of the whole world within their lifetime. With fervent dedication to the truthfulness of the gospel, and confident in the supply of material resources from the Western Christian world, they accepted this responsibility. Christians of the West understood themselves to be the chosen people of God – the heart that pumps the gospel's blood of life to all extremities.[1] The pagan world was there to be 'conquered' by the gospel if the missionaries followed 'the three great laws of God': the law of sowing and reaping, the law of intercession and the law of sacrifice.[2] The world consisted of two worlds: the Christian world *and* the non-Christian world. The theology that supported this missionary geography was twofold. First was the conviction that human salvation is possible *only* in the name of Jesus Christ. Other religions, great and small, were seen as obstacles and menaces to the missionary effort of spreading the Kingdom of Christ. Second was a faith in God who is 'the Great Missioner'.[3]

The evolution of missionary thinking in the twentieth century

Edinburgh was a remarkable expression of Western Protestant Christianity's dedication to world evangelization, and yet it contained within itself elements of its own break down. The reason for this was that Edinburgh 1910 was a missiological monologue within the Christian West. To be sure this monologue was sincere and accompanied by many prayers. Christian mission, however, requires more than sincere theological formulation and piety. In order to prosper mission must be subordinated to the building up of human community. The missionary geography of two worlds, Christian and non-Christian, was facile and eventually made Christian dedication, though fervent, unable to communicate, and its material resources, though rich, ineffective. Soon after Edinburgh 1910 the world was to experience decades of deadly violence. Indeed with 187 million people perishing by human hostilities the century would become the most violent in the history of human civilization. One must consider how this has affected understandings of Christian mission. [4]

In terms of church and world history the missionary ideal expressed in Edinburgh is significant. It was based on a classical Christian worldview, associated with St. Augustine, that there are two worlds, the one pious and the other impious. This image of two opposing worlds has increased violence by justifying theologically the destruction of the people named 'enemy'. At the beginning of the twenty-first century the one world is split into two antagonistic worlds: Islamic and Christian. All the conflicts in this world are Cain/Abel fratricide. This conflictive dualism threatens the entire human family, yet it has been generally accepted as holy war. Given the advanced technology of the twenty-first century, the concept of holy war has proven to be not only irrelevant, but also barbaric. All wars are unholy because murder is unholy. The concept of the Christian world is as unrealistic as that of the non-Christian world. The complexities and ambiguities of human existence do not allow such a self-serving distinction.

In truth the gospel moves freely into the unholy zone. This has created the ever changing and expanding relevancy of the gospel's message for the world. Transformation, *metamorphosis,* is fundamental to Biblical theology. This motif has inspired a transition from a church-centered missiology to a world-centered missiology based on a theology of the kingdom of God. To say that all humanity is condemned (*massa perditionis,* Augustine), and to base missionary obligation on this thesis, disregards the presence of the grace of God in the so-called 'non Christian world'. Meanwhile in the 'Christian world' there are millions of people who confess the name of Christ yet do not practice what he said.[5]

Consideration of some seminal texts demonstrates how missionary thinking has developed since Edinburgh. The focus of Edinburgh 1910 was 'to persuade human hearts everywhere that Jesus Christ is their Saviour'.[6] It followed from this that: 'The chief aim [of the Christian proclamation] must ever be to persuade human hearts everywhere that Jesus Christ is their Saviour, standing ready in an attitude of love, compassion, and power, to realize to them, upon condition of repentance and faith, all that the Gospel promises to do for a soul that receives it'.[7] When the International Missionary Conference met in Jerusalem in 1928, it proclaimed:

> Our message is Jesus Christ. He is the revelation of what God is and of what man through him may become. In him we come face to face with the ultimate reality of the universe; he makes known to us God our Father, perfect and infinite in love and in righteousness; for in him we find God incarnate, the final, yet ever unfolding revelation of the God in whom we live and move and have our being. … Christ is our motive and Christ is our end. We must give nothing less, and we can give nothing more.

Ten years later, in Tambaram the 1938 International Missionary Conference stated:

> The core of evangelism is the presentation of the Gospel – the Christian message that God loves mankind and has sent His Son into the world to save men through

> the life, death and resurrection of His Son and the indwelling of His Holy Spirit. The Gospel concerns the individual. ... The Gospel likewise and equally meets the social needs and problems. ... It is a whole Gospel – personal first and social always. A Christian social order is to be achieved by Christians. The new world comes through new men and new women. There can be no new world without new world builders.[8]

The world plunged into the Second World War between Tambaram 1938 and Amsterdam 1948, the year the World Council of Churches was inaugurated. During this period of unprecedented human despair and turmoil, missionary thinking went through a process of change. Some decades afterwards at the Asian Catholic Bishops' Conference, held in Manila in 1979, the following was recorded:

> The purpose of mission is to proclaim salvation to the whole man and to all men. It is neither simply to convert people to an organized religion nor win them to membership in an institutional Church. It is rather to convert people to authentic human values and to deepen and fulfill these values in Christ so that the people who are evangelized may come to form the community, which is His Church.[9]

This line of thought is expanded in their 1991 statement:

> The Reign of God is a universal reality, extending far beyond the boundaries of the Church. It is the reality of salvation in Jesus Christ, in which Christians and others share together. It is the fundamental 'mystery of unity' which unites us more deeply than differences in religious allegiance are able to keep us apart. Seen in this manner, a 'regnocentric' approach to mission theology does not in any way threaten the Christo-centric perspective of our faith. On the contrary, 'regno-centrism' calls for 'christo-centrism' and vice versa, for it is in Jesus Christ and through the Christ-event that God has established his Kingdom upon the earth and in human history.[10]

Thinking along these lines led J. Mattam to the conclusion that: 'Salvation is therefore not necessarily linked to a religion but to the human community, to building up communities of love, justice and freedom, which Christians call the Kingdom of God'.[11]

This brief review indicates an adjustment in missionary thinking since 1910. Nevertheless the conviction that 'our message is Jesus Christ' stands firm. In Jerusalem 1928, the name of Jesus Christ is associated with 'the ultimate reality of the universe'. Jesus Christ means freedom in all aspects of life. These words point to the Kingdom of God beyond the church. God, who is 'perfect and infinite in love', is free to be gracious beyond the boundary of the church. The gospel affirms the centrality of Jesus Christ in the image of Christ crucified. This paradoxical centrality is the fundamental structure of theology and missiology. This is the theological basis on which regno-centrism calls for christo-centrism and vice versa.[12] In this light the following observations and questions may be considered.

1. The missionary will 'persuade human hearts everywhere that Jesus Christ is their Saviour'. Yet, Jesus Christ remains a stumbling block to *all* cultures and religions, including the Christian world. What does this mean?

2. Is there a specifically Christian understanding of repentance and faith? How are Islamic or Buddhist or Hindu repentance and faith related to the proclamation of 'our message is Jesus Christ'?

3. People are invited to convert to 'authentic human values' because the Christ of the Kingdom of God blesses such values. Can people of other Faiths find authentic human values within their Faith and world-view? And when their faith deepens, do they also encounter Christ?[13]

4. Japanese Lutheran theologian Kazo Kitamori says that God embraces the world in its rebellion against God.[14] God who embraces the world defines the nature of the church because it is only in this embraced world that the church can exist.

5. In 1995 Bishop Osthathios of the Malankara Orthodox Syrian Church in India wrote of the richness and comprehensiveness of the mission of the Holy Trinity: 'It is the outreach of this love that prompted God to create all things visible and invisible and also prompted Him to send His only begotten Son for the salvation of the world and the Holy Spirit for the consummation of salvation which is deification or *theosis*'.[15] True to the Orthodox tradition, *kosmos* is becoming *ekklesia.* The gospel embraces 'all things visible and invisible' and history is, by the providence of the Holy Trinity, moving towards the blessing of our *theosis.* The gospel is indeed 'a big story' that points to the Kingdom of God.

Addressing pluralism and globalization

Violence in the twentieth century dashed hopes that the great religions of the world could prevent humanity from falling into the abyss of destruction. Particularly disappointing was the spectre of one Christian nation going to war against another. Christianity is now seen to be **on the same level** with other religions. Missiology must fully acknowledge this historical judgment.

This thesis needs to be clarified. The world called non-Christian by Edinburgh 1910 has, in the last 500 years, been exploited, colonized and victimized by the nations of the West, which Edinburgh called Christian. The world judges 'Christian' civilization today, not on the basis of sublime doctrines and saintly presence, but on its observed association with the evils of racism, colonialism and militarism. Its founder says, 'The tree is known by its fruit.'[16] The tree is known by its power to create a healthy human community, the Kingdom of God upon the earth. Christians cannot establish wholesome human community by themselves; the participation of everyone is needed.

Religious **pluralism** must be discussed in the context of the creation of wholesome human community, free from racism and militarism. Pluralism, religious, moral and political, is necessary for the creation of healthy human community. The question of the truth is at stake in any genuine discussion on religious pluralism but truth must relate to the human endeavor to establish wholesome human community. Christian *shalom* will be truly Christian when it participates in the universal human *shalom*. To engage in a competition for doctrinal superiority among religions is counter-productive. It would be better for all six billion of us to live in a wholesome community free from fanatical religion-ism than to let doctrinal differences destroy us.

The truth of the Christian doctrine of justification by faith, for instance, is not self-contained. It *becomes* truth as it contributes to the creation of human community. This *becoming* process is open to the participation of those who feel alienated from the Christian world. All of us, with our different experiences of the human spirit, are involved in this common human mission. Missiology has a greater horizon than we knew, because God is the God of 'expansive vision'.[17] Religious pluralism is to be seen in the context of this participation in the realization of the kingdom of God upon the earth.

At this point, our thoughts on pluralism and **globalization** intersect. They come together, for our interest is in global health, *shalom*. Globalization, as we experience it today, is intensely ambiguous. It has creative potential, but is largely destructive. It is a world system that benefits the rich and powerful who control the media. The idea that the world has become a 'global village' is also a self-serving ideology that has been useful for dominant nations and/or corporations. Globalization is experienced differently by the poor of the world from those who are rich. The global gap between the rich and the poor has become staggering.

Religious pluralism should be judged by its ability to reject a monopoly-globalization in favor of a sharing-globalization. Sharing is the mark of the *vere religione*. It must also be the mark of a viable missiology. The power of the gospel is shown as it engages others, not in our way but in the way of the radical self-denial of the crucified. Georges Khodr, the Orthodox theologian writes, 'Christ is hidden everywhere in the mystery of his lowliness.'[18]

Great religious traditions – Christianity, Islam, Buddhism, Hinduism, and Taoism – are not enemies of Jesus Christ. The missiology of the mystery of the lowliness of Christ must ponder how the distance between Jesus Christ and Christianity compares with the distance between Jesus Christ and Islam, or Jesus Christ and Buddhism. The gospel of Jesus Christ is problematic to all religions and all civilizations. Yet, the gospel has power to baptize them and mobilize them for the purpose of the gospel. This is possible because of the mystery of Christ's lowliness.

Crucified, Jesus Christ accepted *all* without exception. That moment was the unparalleled moment of cosmic openness. When the one who is 'before all things' and 'the head of the body, the church'[19] was publicly crucified, all boundaries *we draw* – cultural, religious, linguistic, ethnic, racial, economic, educational, ideological, political, and gender – are abolished. This thought is deeply puzzling and threatening. The crucified Christ upsets all our value systems. 'There is no longer Jew or Greek, there is no longer slave or free, there is no longer male and female; for all of you are one in Christ Jesus.'[20] This is the work of the mystery of his lowliness.

Culture, context and mission

This vision is the foundation for the contextualization of theology. For such contextualization religious pluralism is not a threat, but an opportunity for fruitful mutually benefiting dialogue. Christ makes diversity a reconciled diversity. In the contextualization of the missionary message monopoly-globalization has no place. The truth of Christ moves from sharing to sharing. The gospel cannot be contextualized into a world system that leaves most of the world in dire poverty.

Human context is always cultural. To be human is to be cultural. Culture is always inter-cultural since cultures are always intersecting. The dynamism of the inter-cultural is always present in the situation of the inter-religious. Theological contextualization cannot be done apart from serious engagement with the complex reality of culture. There is not one *purely* theological word in isolation from culture. Culture prepares words; theology baptizes them and makes use of them. W. A. Visser't Hooft observed that Paul and John took the risk of using such Greek words as *logos, soter, mysteria,* and *metamorphosis* which carry heavy pre-Christian associations.[21]

The theological mind has been engaged in this act of baptism since the day of Pentecost. Mission/evangelism necessarily uses culture as a channel of communication. As Robin Boyd observes: 'Hinduism has been digging channels. Christ is the water to flow through these channels.'[22] The Second Vatican Council stated: 'The Catholic Church rejects nothing of what is true and holy in these religions.'[23] It is difficult to know 'what is true and holy in these religions' without thinking of culture as a vehicle of values. It is important, however, to know that culture is not concerned with moral examination. A gun culture accepts a profusion of firearms. A racist culture does not criticize racial prejudice. The chair culture of the Christian West allows people to worship with shoes on as would no other world religion. Is there a discontinuity between the practices of Christian culture and the dictates of the gospel?

It is striking that the gospel displays its power whatever the historical context. In 1945 both Shinto Japan and Christian Germany completed their own self-destruction through the misuse of transcendence, which the Biblical tradition speaks of as idolatry. In idolatry, Paul Tillich observes, 'something essentially partial is boosted into universality'.[24] Why does this 'boosting' always produce destruction? Why is the possibility of disaster indigenous to all cultures? Christian culture, as well as caste culture must be subjected to critical examination. All cultures stand under the judgment of God. Even as we criticize a certain culture, we may be living and breathing within that very culture. This is why the missionary act of baptizing words becomes a serious exercise.

The gospel cannot be completely contextualized within any theological tradition – black, feminist, Asian, *Dalit* or any other theology. The apostolic admonition for all of today's contextualization of theology is: 'we have this treasure in jars of clay'.[25] The cultures of the 'Christian world' are not necessarily closer to the gospel than the cultures of the 'non-Christian world'. 'Call the labourers and give them their pay, beginning with the last and then going to the first.'[26] Is missionary thinking prepared to express this 'scandalous' freedom of the gospel in the twenty-first-century world?[27]

Since life itself contains the interpretation of life, all religions are hermeneutically related. To think of religions as independent boxed-in units that can be identified by name is conventional and questionable. No religion can be isolated and contained in separation from others. All religions are in the state of mutual transformation. Simply put, they are webbed. Whatever one finds in one religion, may be found in its variation in others.

The human spirit cannot be boxed in. Missionaries are not called to persuade people to discard *this* box and take up *that,* like car-dealers asking people to exchange their old cars for a newer model. Careful examination must be given to the comment of the Commission One Report that: 'by far the greater part of the Mohammedan world is practically unoccupied. ... The unreceptive and even defiant attitude of Islam towards Christianity, and its unwillingness to acknowledge the supreme Lordship of Christ, will yield to the gospel if Christians do their duty.'[28] What does it mean to say, 'The Mohammedan world is practically unoccupied'? How can a territory be 'occupied' by Christianity? This sounds like the way Europeans spoke of the American continent in the sixteenth century. What are the reasons behind the 'defiant attitude of Islam towards Christianity'? What treasures do Christianity and Islam share? What does the doctrinal conflict between the religions mean to spiritual lives dedicated to Christ or to Mohammed? What kind of 'obstacle' does Islam pose vis a vis Christianity? These questions will free our missiology from boxed-in religion.

There can be no Muslim without Islam, no Christian without Christianity. Islam does not engage in dialogue with Christianity. Muslims and Christians can dialogue. Muslims are 'creatures' of cultural and theological complexity as are Christians and Buddhists. Though the expression 'people of other faiths' is useful, it is not a clear concept since people are a larger and a far more complex reality than the religions of their particular cultures. Buddhists create many Buddhisms. Christians have made many Christianities. There are all kinds of Buddhists just as there are all kinds of Christians. Not one of the great religions has one uniform faith, doctrine and confession. The biblical interpretation of life is discovered at the intersection of real life and the biblical witness. The same is true of Buddhism or Islam. If the *outsider* is lacking – if the *stranger* is not there – the possibility of meaning disappears. Yahweh speaks with force because Baal is there. Hermeneutics takes place in the borderland.

Christian fundamentalism reveals the hidden irritation of Western Christian civilization with the presence of the incomprehensible God. The finality of Christ is affirmed at the risk of being placed in a theological box. On the contrary, Christian insistence on the exclusivity of salvation in Jesus Christ[29] is a confession of faith in the incredible openness demonstrated in Jesus Christ. The astounding reach of his openness cannot be defined in terms of exclusiveness. The truth confronts us but ultimately the truth embraces us.

Harold W. Turner, however, raises a question. He writes: 'Indeed if the Christians of the first centuries had been "benevolent inclusivists" there would have been no Christian history at all, as the present-day pluralists are forced to recognize.'[30] Was exclusivity at one point necessary to the Christian message? True, Buddhism disappeared from India by its over-accommodation. Yet, no truth so perceived by humans can exist in history without some measure of accommodation. Raimundo Panikkar writes: 'It [Christianity] is the ancient paganism or to be more precise, the complex Hebrew-Hellenic-Greco-Latin-Celtic-Gothic-Modern religion converted to Christ more or less successfully.'[31] There is no unchanging identity. Christianity in China is different from Christianity in Sweden. The Christianity embraced by the rich is different from the Christianity in which the poor place their trust. Buddhism has, in fact, not disappeared at all. It has achieved the status of a world religion.

A missiology of the here and now

The time and space orientation of human salvation has shifted from 'over there' to the 'here and now'. A suggestion that this is a result of secular influence is superficial. Here and now is at the heart of responsible grace. The here and now is the zone of human responsibility. Salvation must be experienced, if at all, within this life, not *after* our personal end or the end of this planet or of the universe. This means that the location of transcendence is in this history. In fact, because history is ambiguous, all the more transcendence must be placed inside history, as the Christian teaching on the Incarnation and the Two Natures of Christ suggest.[32] The meaningful *beyond* is the beyond that is this side of the beyond. 'Where sin increased, grace abounded all the more.'[33] The salvation in the Buddhist *nirvana* is anticipated in the centrality of 'elimination of greed' here and now.

Biblical faith is time oriented. 'Time is the heart of existence', says Rabbi Abraham Heschel.[34] Biblical religion places time above space. Time is sacred. It is invisible, as God is invisible. It is beyond our control. It has the quality of transcendence, the *beyond.* It is proper to call God the eternal God. Christian liturgy does not invoke God as the spacious God. Indeed, a space-oriented theology is a dangerous concept. Space connects with Baal, time with Yahweh. The idolatry of *Lebensraum* has been used again and again by totalitarian regimes throughout history. Yet, is not the eternal God also the spacious God, though God is more eternal than eternity itself and more spacious than space?

The eternal God has become a distant God. Space is immediate to our everyday experience. Time-oriented Christian civilization expressed its vitality, not in the acquisition of time, but by the acquisition of space, even displacing 'native' populations! Now, after 500 years, liberation theologians, *Dalit* theologians, and black theologians are demanding dignified space for the people they represent. A theology of space, even more than a theology of time, makes the issues of justice and injustice in society visibly clear. The time-oriented eschatology has made humanity insensitive to the welfare of the *present* time. It inspired the program of 'building bigger barns'.[35] It has supported the *status quo.*

Eschatology is the doctrine of last things. The word 'last' is not about time but about the Kingdom of God. It is *kairos,* 'critical now'. Eschatology is not about a dispensationalist's elaborate schedule for the end of the world. It is about practising love of God and neighbour, now, in this moment of history. It is to 'do justice, love mercy and walk humbly with God' today because in this is the meaning of the beginning and end of history.[36] It is to respond *now* to a boy's question, 'Daddy, why do white people treat colored people so mean?'[37] 'Today salvation has come to this house', declares Jesus.[38] As Mattam observes: 'For Jesus salvation did not seem to be a matter of saving one's soul for a life after death nor even a matter of religion, nor religious practices, but a matter of proper relationship.'[39]

Whether the image of history is circular, straight, triangular, or zigzag is not important. To live in the *kairos* way of Micah is important. Colonial space must be replaced by the space of 'a single garment of destiny'.[40] All *beyond* stories must be brought into 'this side' because the location in which salvation is experienced is in this one Noah's Ark, the planet earth. This presents the new map of salvation inspired by faith in the freedom of the movement of divine grace among all creations. One may think of the ecumenical One Ship traversing the sea, the logo of the World Council of Churches. But in this image, as all are in one ship, believers and unbelievers, the spectacle of the masses drowning outside is erased by grace. Grace refuses to use the fear of damnation to draw people to salvation.[41]

Today we are more conscious than ever that mother earth is our Noah's ark. The destruction of the biosphere augurs global suicide. Humanity is terrorizing mother earth. The thought of an ecological crisis is new to our time. It was not there in 1910. The words 'ecological' and 'ecumenical' are derived from the Greek word *oikos* meaning 'house'. Ecological and ecumenical movements signify Good-House-Keeping. Ecological refers to the maintenance of the biosphere. Ecumenical refers broadly to the cultured spaces in which human languages are spoken, houses are built, things are named, education is conducted, ideas are exchanged, religions are conceived and practiced, political powers are exercised, time is measured and symbols are born and die. God's benediction embraces all beings. All beings exist in webbed-ness, interdependence, communication and reconciliation. This is the basic structure of the sacramental: 'If one member suffers, all suffer together with it; if one member is honored, all rejoice together with it.'[42] Here theology and ecology coincide. Tillich's 'Ground of Being' can be understood to mean that God is the relatedness of all that is. We read in a remarkable Orthodox theological book *Being as Communion*; 'Love as God's mode of existence "hypostasizes" God, *constitutes* His being. Therefore, as a result of love, the ontology of God is not subject to the necessity of substance. Love is identified with ontological freedom.'[43] If missiology is fully aware of the 'relatedness' of all beings it will have relevance for humanity. The eschatological and the ecological are one. The vertical and the horizontal, time and eternity, *this* side and *other* side are one. This is a missiology of Mother Earth as Noah's Ark.

Missionary thinking must be engaged in public dialogue. 'Seek the welfare of the city where I have sent you into exile, and pray to the Lord on its behalf, for in its welfare you will find your welfare.'[44] There is no individualistic *shalom.* In order to 'pray on its [the city's] behalf' one must have a good knowledge of the city. This exercise is crucial to missiology. 'City-study' (country study, world study, cosmos study) and mission study must come together. Missiology must become inter-religious, and inter-cultural. It must exist in dialogue with the various areas of human knowledge: physics, biology, anthropology, psychology, sociology. It must belong to the family of good knowledge. Christians, saying, 'Our message is Jesus Christ' and Buddhists, saying, 'Our message is the universal moral law, *dharma,* that the Buddha taught', must be brought into a dialogue. Werner Heisenberg says, 'In the beginning was energy.'[45] The Gospel of John says, 'In the beginning was the word.'[46] The *energy* thought and *word* thought must engage in dialogue, not in competition. If the world experiences *shalom* we all shall experience *shalom.* This is the future missiology of the 'Larger Christ' the image suggested by John R. Mott.

Endnotes

[1] World Missionary Conference, 1910, *Carrying the Gospel to all the Non-Christian World,* Report of Commission I, Edinburgh & London: Oliphant, Anderson & Ferrier; New York, Chicago and Toronto: Fleming H. Revell, 1910, p. 47.
[2] *Carrying the Gospel*, pp. 43–4.
[3] John R. Mott expressed the commitment of all eight Commissions when he wrote; 'the world's evangelization is a divine enterprise, … the Spirit of God is the great Missioner' *Addresses and Papers of John R. Mott,* Vol. V. The International Missionary Council, New York: Association Press, 1947 pp. 25–6.
[4] Eric Hobsbawn, *The Age of Extremes,* London: Michael Joseph, 1994, p. 12.

[5] 'To become aware of the secularity of God is to relativize the religious institutions as special and exclusive mediations of the Sacred', Michael Amaladoss, 'Mission in a Post-Modern World, A Call to be Counter-Cultural', *Mission Studies* Vol. VIII–1&2 (1996), pp. 68–79 [75].
[6] *Carrying the Gospel*, p. 312.
[7] *Carrying the Gospel*, p. 312.
[8] *Evangelism: 'The Madras Series' 1938*. Chapter IV, 'What is Evangelism? A Symposium of Views Collected by J.R.Mott' p.53f. Quotations from Edinburgh 1910, Jerusalem 1928, and Tambaram 1938.
[9] Gaudencio Rosales and C.G.Arevalo, eds., *For All the Peoples of Asia: Federation of Asian Bishops' Conferences, Documents from 197–1991*, Quezon City, Philippines: Claretian & New York: Orbis Books, 1992, p. 144.
[10] Ibid., p. 342.
[11] J. Mattam SJ, 'Evangelism in a Dialogical Context from a Third World Perspective', *Mission Studies,* Vol. IX–2 (1992), pp.148–55 {151}.
[12] Mott writes: 'He has been working through the non-Christian religions, not alone in using such truth as they may possess for the betterment of men, but also in making these religions a schoolmaster to lead the peoples to recognize in due time their need of Christ'. *Addresses and Papers of John R. Mott,* Vol V, p. 26.
[13] *Ibid.,* p. 342.
[14] Kazo Kitamori, *Theology of the Pain of God,* Richmond, Virginia: John Knox Press, 1965.
[15] Geevarghese Mar Osthathios, 'Mission and the Uniqueness of Jesus Christ', *Mission Studies,* Vol. XII–1 (1995), pp. 79–94 [87].
[16] Luke 6:44.
[17] Donald Senior and Carroll Stuhlmueller, *The Biblical Foundations for Mission,* London: SCM, 1983, p. 340.
[18] Quoted in Michael Kinnamon and Brian E. Cope eds., *The Ecumenical Movement: An Anthology of Key Texts and Voices,* Geneva: WCC Publications & Grand Rapids: Eerdmans, 1997, p. 403.
[19] Colossians 1:15–20.
[20] Galatians 3:28.
[21] W.A. Visser't Hooft, 'Accommodation – True or False', John R. Mott Lecture, Hong Kong, 1966.
[22] Robin H. S. Boyd, *An Introduction to Indian Christian Theology,* Delhi, ITL, 1969, p.107.
[23] Declaration on the Relation of the Church to Non-Christian Religions, *Nostra Aetate,* #2, *The Documents of Vatican II,* London: Geoffrey Chapman, 1966.
[24] Paul Tillich, *Systematic Theology,* Vol. I, London: Nisbet, 1953, p. 16.
[25] 2 Corinthians 4:7.
[26] Matthew 20:8.
[27] 1 Corinthians 1:23.
[28] *Carrying the Gospel*, pp. 36–7.
[29] Acts 4:12; John 14:6.
[30] Harold W. Turner, 'Historical Support for Pluralism? The 'Copernican Revolution' Revisited', *Mission Studies,* Vol. VIII-1 (1991), pp. 77–92 [8[illegible]].
[31] Raimundo Panikkar, 'Christians And So-Called 'Non-Christians', in Douglas J. Elwood ed., *What Asian Christians are Thinking,* Quezon City, New Day Publishers, 1976, p. 361.

[32] 'We have to discover transcendence as the depth or roots of the cosmos and of the human', Amaladoss, 'Mission in a Postmodern World', p. 75.
[33] Romans 5:20.
[34] Abraham Joshua Heschel, *The Sabbath* ,New York: Farrer, Strauss and Giroux, 1951, p. 3.
[35] Luke 12:16–21.
[36] Micah 6:8.
[37] Martin Luther King Jr., 'Letter from Birmingham Jail', 1963, http://almaz.com/nobel/peace/MLK-jail.html accessed 21 March 2007.
[38] Luke 19:9.
[39] Mattam, 'Evangelism in a Dialogical Context', p.150.
[40] King, 'Letter from Birmingham Jail'.
[41] See John 1:16.
[42] 1 Corinthians 12:26.
[43] John D. Zizioulas, *Being as Communion*, London: Darton Longman and Todd, 1993, p. 46.
[44] Jeremiah 29:7
[45] Werner Heisenberg, *Physics and Philosophy*, London: Allen and Unwin, 1958, pp. 70–71.
[46] John 1.

COMMISSION TWO

THE CHURCH IN THE MISSION FIELD

COMMISSION TWO
'THE CHURCH IN THE MISSION FIELD'

The Commission in Summary

Commission Two was entrusted with what its chairman, Campbell Gibson, declared to be 'one of the greatest subjects'[1] that 'now occupies so prominent position in the discussion of mission questions and methods'.[2] No longer the distant hope of early Christian evangelists, 'the Church in the Mission Field ... is now a complex body which has in some countries already attained, and in others is fast attaining, a high degree of organisation and corporate life'.[3] It represents 'the enormous force that exists, now established in the very heart of the pagan world, in the young Christian Church which missions have founded, but which is itself now the great mission to the non-Christian world'.[4] As such, it is no longer to be considered as 'a by-product of mission work, but as itself by far the most efficient element in Christian propaganda'.[5]

The Commission chairman, John Campbell Gibson, had an intimate knowledge of the Church in China, having served in Southern China since 1874 under the auspices of the English Presbyterian Mission (although he was born and educated in Scotland). He co-chaired the 1907 Shanghai Centenary Missionary Conference, one of the main precursors of 'Edinburgh 1910'. The American co-convener of Commission Two, Walter Lambuth, specialized in medical missionary work in both China and Japan, and in the United States was a leading figure in Methodist and ecumenical missionary circles. With its 18 other members, the Commission gathered information from 218 missionary correspondents, the majority in India, China, Japan and Korea. Africa, the 'Mohammedan Lands' of Western Asia, and 'other fields – *viz*. Southeast Asia, the Pacific, the Caribbean and Mexico, were less widely represented.

The Commissioners were uncomfortable with the title of their subject. As the introductory remarks of the Report emphasized, 'the world is the mission field, and there is no Church that is not a Church in the mission field'.[6] Some are 'older', others 'younger', but all 'are seeking to cherish the new life (of the Gospel) and to perfect its fruits'.[7] For purposes of its inquiry, however, the Commission identified 'The Church in the Mission Field' by two features: 'it is surrounded by a non-Christian community whom it is its function to subdue for the Kingdom;' and 'it is in close relation to an older Christian community from which it at first received the truth, which stands to it in a parental relationship, and still offers it such help, leadership, and even control, as may seem appropriate to the present stage of its development'.[8]

Within this broad definition, the Commission recognized the enormous diversity of the mission field. The Report's Introduction tried to evoke this in an imaginative journey through 'the course of the Lord's Day',[9] beginning with sunrise over the Fijian Islands, travelling Westwards across the Pacific, Asia, Africa, the European and American Artic regions, Patagonia, and finally to Samao and the Friendly Islands. 'It is inspiring to reflect how the younger Christian communities make good the lack of service of the older, and the older join with the younger, so that throughout the Lord's Day, from the rising of the sun to the going down of it, incense and pure offering ascend unceasingly to God, land answering to land as each in turn takes up the chorus'.[10]

While affirming that 'in many of the greater mission fields the Christian people are now recognized as a definite community whose social life and ideals, as well as their personal faith and character, are already becoming a powerful element in the reshaping of national life',[11] the Report does not examine the missionary initiative and potential of 'the Church in the Mission Field'. It concentrates instead on ecclesial issues of constitution and membership, on the edification and education of its members, the training and employment of workers, the character and spiritual fruitfulness of Christian life, and the need for Christian literature and theology that will support the development of these 'younger churches' into full maturity. Should this be surprising, even disappointing, it was justified by the fact that the Commission was constituted to address questions pertaining to the relationship of the Western 'parent' churches to those in the mission field. Given the paucity of representatives of the latter in the working of the Commission – none on the Commission itself, only 16 among the correspondents, only 4 among the discussants – no other course was possible.

The findings of the Report, based on the 218 missionary responses to its questionnaire, are recorded in eight chapters comprising 275 pages. A further 60 pages of appendices, and 35 that record summaries of the responses of plenary delegates, round off the Report.

Chapter 1, entitled 'Constitution and Organisation of the Church', addresses 'the fact that questions of polity and organisation are impressing themselves upon the minds of Christian folk all over the world in the mission field'.[12]The critical issue was 'the relation in which the Church life in the mission field stands ... to the life and government of the parent Church'.[13]The challenge lay in balancing 'the autonomy and liberties of the Church in the Mission Field' and 'the maintenance of such mutual affection and respect between the young Church and the older Church in the West, as shall enable the latter to continue to give the former helpful and sympathetic guidance'.[14] Fearing that a hasty growth of autonomy would multiply Christian divisions, the Report encouraged 'closer unity (of churches in the mission field) within larger denominational lines'[15] than those represented by Western churches.

Chapter 2 addressed 'conditions of membership', these being understood broadly in terms of the deepening Christian faith and discipleship rather than by narrow criteria of membership – though 'disqualifications and hindrances' such as 'bigamy and polygamy'[16] are examined. Chapter 3 discussed 'church discipline', concentrating on pastoral questions that arise in relation to Christian life in non-Christian cultures: for example, how to observe the Lord's Day in societies where Sunday is an ordinary weekday; inter-marriage between Christians and non-Christians; is it legitimate for Chinese Christians to associate themselves with ancestor worship, or Indian Christians with caste? Chapter 4 was devoted to the 'edification of Christian community', meaning 'building up in faith and godliness all ages and classes of the Christian people' through worship, Christian education, family life, conferences and visitation.

Chapter 5 to 7 focussed on issues of 'training'. Recognizing that each member of the Church has a personal vocation for some kind of Christian service, Chapter 5 was specifically concerned with 'workers' for whom 'the Church assumes some definite responsibility, and for whom it is bound to provide some form both of preparation and of oversight'.[17] First among these were workers employed as 'evangelists, colporteurs, and catechists, or in other posts in connection with hospitals, colleges and schools'[18] for whom 'general training' in Christian knowledge was considered sufficient. The greater challenge lay with a second category, namely 'the preachers and clergy of the Church in the mission field',[19] for whom more thorough theological education was necessary. The Report emphasized the inadequacy of the existing provision for theological education, lamented the paucity of students qualified for theological education, and enlarged upon the need for theologically trained missionary teachers who could avoid imposing 'in an external and mechanical way, systems of truth, knowledge, and practice, which are the results of Western experience, but do not vitally appeal to the mind, or even the Christian consciousness of the local Church'.[20] Chapter 7 was entirely devoted to issues of Christian literature, with extensive discussion of Bible translation as a missionary priority that is differently challenged by cultures without previous scriptural traditions (as in Africa), and those with their own ancient scriptures (as in Asia).

Chapter 8 was added after the plenary discussion of the Report, and contains general comments on the seven chapters of the Report itself. Among these comments three stand out as contributions to the plenary discussion by Asian Christians: (1) the danger of 'overloading the young Church in the mission field by the over-multiplication of organisations of a western type';[21] (2) the need for 'a due appreciation of the non-Christian life, religion, and social surroundings, out of which the Christian people have been gathered, in order to form a just estimate of the standard of character and life to which as Christians they have attained';[22] (3) the importance of encouraging 'native Christians of ability to write freely on subjects with which they are familiar, and in which they are likely to express the truth in forms adapted to the thought of their own people'.[23]

Endnotes

[1] World Missionary Conference, 1910, *The Church in the Mission Field*, Report of Commission II, Edinburgh & London: Oliphant, Anderson & Ferrier; New York, Chicago, and Toronto: Fleming H. Revell, 1910, p.340.
[2] *The Church in the Mission Field*, p. 2.
[3] *The Church in the Mission Field*, p. 341.
[4] *The Church in the Mission Field*, p. 341.
[5] *The Church in the Mission Field*, p. 2.
[6] *The Church in the Mission Field*, p. 4.
[7] *The Church in the Mission Field*, p. 4.
[8] *The Church in the Mission Field*, p. 5.
[9] *The Church in the Mission Field*, p. 6.
[10] *The Church in the Mission Field*, p. 9.
[11] *The Church in the Mission Field*, p. 2.
[12] *The Church in the Mission Field*, pp. 340–1.
[13] *The Church in the Mission Field*, p. 267.
[14] *The Church in the Mission Field*, pp. 267–8.
[15] *The Church in the Mission Field*, p. 268.
[16] *The Church in the Mission Field*, pp. 64–74.
[17] *The Church in the Mission Field*, p. 172.
[18] *The Church in the Mission Field*, p. 171.
[19] *The Church in the Mission Field*, p. 171.
[20] *The Church in the Mission Field*, p. 190.
[21] *The Church in the Mission Field*, p. 270.
[22] *The Church in the Mission Field*, p. 272.
[23] *The Church in the Mission Field*, p. 274.

THE CHURCH IN THE MISSION FIELD: A NIGERIAN/AFRICAN RESPONSE

Teresa Okure, SHCJ

Introduction

The task of the 1910 Edinburgh Conference 'The Church in the Mission Field' was 'to consider missionary problems in relation to the non-Christian world'.[1] Many of the issues addressed are still current today, especially in the African context. Among them are the understanding of mission; the need for solid theological formation of converts; education and adequate remuneration of church personnel; the issue of leadership, especially in the relation between the mother/daughter, older/younger churches; the abiding concern to promote women's participation in the work of evangelization; the need for original thinking by the evangelized set against the conditioning effect of received hymns, textbooks and theologies; the question of inculturation or the interface between Christianity and the African cultural reality including the use of its symbols in worship; the problem of finance which controls and conditions the training of local theologians and church personnel; the need for and difficulty of publishing works produced locally and of establishing sustainable theological institutions (other than seminaries); the problem of language in theological discourse (African languages *vis-à-vis* the colonial languages); issues of racism and ethnicity in the Church, and, last but not least, the issue of ecumenism rooted in awareness of the scandal caused by divisions within and among the churches.

In voicing these concerns, the Commission is strikingly balanced, even when it differs significantly from the missionaries in the field. Its Report shows a marked effort to present objectively the situation on the ground, and with great deference and respect for those in the field. In some instances the Commissioners even appeared content to work with the imperfections on the ground so as to present as fully as possible what was actually operative in the mission field. It helps to recall that three main groups are present in the Report: the Commissioners, the missionaries in the field, and the converts. When the Report speaks of 'the Church in the Mission Field' its primary frame of reference is the missionaries. Throughout one senses a strong spirit of ecumenism, a search for ways of collaborating among the different denominations and missionary societies, while respecting the individuality of each. The Catholic Church is strikingly absent from the Report. This may be indicative of the uncooperative relationship that existed between them at the time, though today the picture has changed. Apart from the conciliar and post-conciliar documents of Vatican Council II, and the many, as yet fully unsuccessful, moves by both Catholic and Protestant Churches towards ecumenism, the encyclical of John Paul II, *Ut Unum Sint* and his own concerted efforts to reach out to all and sundry (including the healing of the Great Schism of 1554) readily come to mind.[2]

On the negative side, the Report manifests a markedly derogatory attitude towards peoples of 'non-Christian' cultures (labelling them comprehensively 'heathenism') especially those in Africa. This betrays a racial bias rooted in colonialism and a White superiority complex – one that is perhaps still very much alive today. Its ambiguous and at times contradictory positions on issues may be traceable to this underlying racial bias, very much a feature of the time.[3] Yet the concern to promote the use of native symbols in worship and languages as media in theologising implies recognition of some goodness in the people's cultures.

The task of this submission is not to give a summary of the over 380-page Report of Commission Two, but to review the Report in its own context, identify twentieth-century developments that took place in 'the Mission Field' after it, and perhaps as a result of it, and highlight some challenges which these developments offer the Church in mission at the dawn of the twenty-first century. Of special interest is the image of Africa conveyed by the Commissioners; their understanding of mission; the question of inculturation (African cultural identity and its unique contribution to what it means to be Christian and Church) and the effect of these issues on those the Report calls 'the Christian people' or the 'home Church'. This submission reviews these issues from an African viewpoint and against the backdrop of the New Testament praxis of mission, especially since the Report sought to do for the churches in the mission field what the New Testament letters did for the young churches of their time.

Understanding of Mission

Remarkably, in defining 'the Church in the Mission Field', the Report says: 'The whole world is mission field, and there is no Church that is not a Church in the mission field. Some Christians are younger and some are older, but that is all the difference.' It further wishes for a time when, 'the younger Church being no longer dependent for the maintenance of its activities on the older . . . may be regarded as passing out of the domain of "Missions", and its future course (may be considered as belonging to) the region of general Church history'. Yet the Report likens mission to 'conquest', 'propaganda', and reaching out to people needing to be 'brought under'; converts are those who have been 'taken', 'gathered' or 'rescued' from heathenism, darkness and superstition.

This view of mission, current at the time in Catholic and Protestant Churches, is rooted in the conception of the non-Christian world, especially Africa, as heathen, savage, barbaric, sunk in vice, and having little or nothing to offer by way of virtue. Echoes of this occur in the New Testament (cf. Eph. 2:1–3; Col. 1:21). Nonetheless, the Report also ambiguously counsels due appreciation of 'the non-Christian life, and social surroundings, out of which the Christian people have been gathered'. But that they had to be 'gathered out' of their environment into a constructed Christian environment ('Christian villages' or 'mission compounds') implies that their natural environment was considered as being injurious to their Christian faith.

This view of mission is hardly tenable today. Mission is not about conquest but God's reconciliation and proclamation of the good news of liberation to all nations. No nation is to be conquered by another, even for Christ. This conquering attitude, located in the colonial mentality, justifies the observation of African scholars that the early missionary enterprise served in many respects as the handmaid of colonialism. In return, the missionaries enjoyed the protection of their national colonial governments. This illegal marriage between Church and Empire, mission and colonialism, has vitiated the Church's missionary witness for centuries. With a more enlightened faith and knowledge, Christians have a common responsibility to revisit their understanding of mission and listen to the Spirit who leads the Church progressively into the complete truth (John 16:12–15). Like the early Christians, today's Christians need to confront their inherited anti-Gospel cultural and racial prejudices in the light of Jesus, 'God's Gospel' (Rom. 1:1, 16).

The Report also deals with the practical questions of church organization, membership, discipline, the training and employment of workers, the promotion of Christian life through character formation and spiritual fruitfulness. Christian literature is a means of strengthening the Christian community. This literature should do for the young churches what the literature of the New Testament did for the early Christian communities. A marked difference here is that in the New Testament, the young churches themselves are the subjects of address. But in keeping with its mandate, the Report focuses on the evangelizers' responsibility for the young churches: how to train and promote them to leadership responsibilities, help them to develop their independent or 'native' theological thought, compose prayers and hymns, produce and publish locally suitable literature, and sustain their own theological institutions. For the Report 'the Church in the Mission Field' is 'now a complex body which has in some countries already attained, and in others is fast attaining, a high degree of organisation and corporate life', an 'enormous force . . . established in the very heart of the pagan world'; it considers 'the young churches which missions have founded' have become 'the great mission to the non-Christian world'. Yet the Church thus described seems to have conceded to the evangelized little responsibility for their growth in the faith or for evangelising. The issue of church leadership (the relationship between the mother/daughter, older/younger churches mentioned earlier) belongs here. Today, in the Catholic context at least, the churches in the former 'mission lands' are still referred to as 'the young churches', though some of them are over a hundred years old, older than any one New Testament Gentile Church.

While the Report laments the stagnating effect of too much control of the young churches by the missionaries and their home churches, it seems unable to do anything about it, except make its recommendations to the Conference. The Commissioners had to defend the Church in the mission field before the Conference and persuade the Conference against the fear of many that granting independence too rapidly to the young churches might result in doctrinal laxity. This recalls the situation at the Council of Jerusalem (Acts 15). To evince the ill-founded nature of such fear, the Report points to the number of converts who were prepared to die for their faith, for example the Ugandan martyrs of 1886. Nonetheless, the older churches continued to monitor the developments in the younger churches, retaining the power to withhold from them, should they disapprove of their actions, the liberty that was their right. Today the controlling measure may be the withholding of funds by the older churches. The Commissioners seemed to have had more faith in the evangelized than the 'home Church' and perhaps also the missionaries themselves.

Viewing converts as objects rather than subjects is still a major problem that African and Third World churches, theologians and historians, and indeed all marginalized sectors in the Church concertedly want to change. Women in the Church are the worst off here. Many teething problems of the young churches mentioned in the Report continue today because of the failure to treat these churches as subjects of their own life, a failure compounded by the neglect of the substantial and creative contribution of women. Jesus thought his not-so-well educated disciples were ready to carry his hard won mission to the ends of the earth, though all, except the women, failed the test at the crucial moment of his passion, death and resurrection.

The Missionary Constitution of Vatican Council II, *Ad Gentes* (2, 22) declares: 'Wherever the Church is, there is mission.' John Paul II, in his *Redemptoris Missio*, further offers a review of mission that seeks to correct some fundamental errors in the past approach to mission by emphasising the Holy Spirit as the principal agent of mission.[4] Strikingly, the Holy Spirit is not very prominent in the 1910 Report. Perhaps if the churches had focused less on themselves and on winning converts and more on the Holy Spirit as the principal agent and irreplaceable managing directress of mission, many mistakes in mission, and quarrels among and within the churches, might have been avoided. Not surprisingly, it has taken the advent of Pentecostal movements of the late twentieth century for Christians to recognize anew the indispensable role of the Holy Spirit, not only in primary evangelization but also in the on-going formation and transformation of the Christian in every location.

The Report's lament of the negative view of mission that was widespread among the home churches implies that 'the Christian people' at home had little interest or faith in missionary work itself. The foreign mission seems to have been regarded by some as the sending of a forlorn hope into the midst of a great darkness from which very little could be expected in return; a fad by a few crazy individuals who needed distraction from the quarrels at home or a safari to the newly discovered worlds. The missionaries' work was conceived to be a continual struggle with heathenism, and the converts gained were thought of as little groups of unimportant people whose conversion was gratifying for the sake of the individuals gained, but who had no important share in the missionary enterprise as a whole. This lack of interest contrasts sharply with the Great Commission of the risen Lord to his followers, to 'go out to the whole world and make disciples of all the nations'. (Matthew 28:20) The Report does raise the question of how the western missions can facilitate the further development of the young churches to full maturity, balancing their right of autonomy with 'the maintenance of such mutual affection and respect between the young Church and the older Church in the West, as shall enable the latter to continue to give the former helpful and sympathetic guidance'. Here is yet another area of difference between the Commissioners and 'the Church at home'.

It is doubtful that the pejorative view of new converts by the home Church inherent in the Report was ever abandoned. Today, African Christians, especially those living in the West, struggle for the right to be included in the definition of what it means to be Church. Reports abound of some 'home Church' members who refuse to kneel on the same pew, especially with Blacks. Many Africans (missionaries and migrants) are making great impact in a reverse mission to the West. But they are yet to be viewed as part of the Church, let alone as missionaries in their new locations. The 'we/they' mentality and language continue, on both sides, as an indictment of their common Christian witness.

The Report tacitly notes that the evangelized played indispensable roles in spreading the Gospel and transmitting the faith. Yet it gives little discernible attention to them. As a rule, ordinary people did not count in the history of the missions (written or oral), both before and after 1910. The current Project for the Documentation of Oral History (PODOH), spearheaded by the Overseas Center for Mission Studies (OCMS, New Haven, Connecticut), aims at retrieving and documenting the memory of such countless peoples; so too the monumental work, Dictionary of Christian Biographies, coordinated by Daniel Patte of Vanderbilt University. The role of nameless persons in the work of evangelization cannot be overestimated. In the New Testament era, such people effectively moved the mission of Church from an exclusive focus on the Jews to the inclusion of Gentiles, thereby ushering in the Church's worldwide mission. Yet in their context, too, their bold initiatives were narratively subjected to the role of 'the home Church', Peter and the Jerusalem Church.[5]

All this notwithstanding, the emphasis today on the importance of reception would requires a clearer attention to the missionary role of the evangelized. As Paul VI notes in his celebrated encyclical *Evangelii Nuntiandi*, evangelization is incomplete until the evangelized themselves become and are recognized to be missionaries at home and abroad.[6]

Strikingly, the Report gives a laudable attention to the ministry and mission of women. Yet, as a rule, women count among those most forgotten in the history and work of mission. Mercy Amba Oduyoye shared during an inaugural meeting of the Anglophone EATWOT Women's Commission in Port Harcourt, Nigeria in 1986, that her mother played key roles in the mission of the Methodist Church in Ghana, especially in teaching the faith to women; yet the written history of that mission remembered her only as having been 'an excellent cook'. Forgetting the memory of women in mission did not begin in the twentieth century. Jesus specifically mandated that the deed, at least, of the woman who anointed him for burial should be told whenever the Gospel was preached 'in the whole world' in her remembrance (Mark 14:8–9). But as Elizabeth Fiorenza has recalled, the Church over the centuries paid little attention to this injunction of the Lord.[7] The three years' training given in Ghana to all church personnel, mentioned in the Report, would no doubt have included the ministry of 'Bible women' as inspiration to local women in the mission field. According to the Report, the ministerial formation of women was more effective than that of men because women were freer to undertake such training. This implies that local women were very much a labour force for the missionary enterprise. Were any such women present at the Conference of 1910?

Today appreciable, though imperfect, efforts are made to recognize the contribution of women in mission and in the life of the Church. It is regrettable that the Interest Group of 'Women in Mission' of IAMS (International Association for Mission Studies) has not effectively taken off. The role of women missionaries of the Roman Catholic Religious Congregations is yet to be written. In Calabar, Nigeria, Mary Slessor of the Presbyterian Church is a well-celebrated pioneer missionary figure. On the theological sphere, the second EATWOT plenary meeting in Accra, Ghana opted for the inclusion of women in the doing of theology. It took the further practical step of forbidding a Region to present more members for admission to the Association unless at least a third of its Regional members were women. At the last two General Assemblies in Quito (2000) and Johannesburg (2006), more women than men attended. John Pobee, when in charge of the Programme for Theological Education at the WCC, promoted women's participation in doing theology by giving scholarships for their theological training and encouraging them to publish.[8] A key patron of 'The Circle of Concerned African Women Theologians', he sees in their work 'a source of relevant theology'. The agenda of 'The Circle' is reactive as well as creative and constructive. The Circle welcomes adherents of various religions in its membership and attempts to live the ecumenical principles of inclusiveness, connectedness and of following a participatory life-style in our journeying together as Christ's disciples.

If the attention given to the ministry of women in the Report (and emphasized in the last decades) had been systematically followed by all the churches, especially in Africa from 1910 onwards, the face of the Church, of ecumenism and society as a whole, would have been different today. It is still lamentable that the churches as a whole have not yet come to grips with the energising character of women's life-centred theology, dynamism in mission and their relevance for ecumenism. Women by nature have a way of accommodating differences and managing resources however meagre. African mothers know how to make a small supply of food go around the entire family, even if it means their doing without. Working the miracle of the loaves is a daily and natural experience for most of them. The Catholic Church, at its first Special Assembly for Africa of the Synod of Bishops, adopted the concept of the 'Church-as-family' of God as the best model for being Church in Africa, one with which Africans can naturally identify.[9] This model, as Pobee would put it, 'is not only typical of African ways of family gathering, but also is more faithful to the Church as *koinonia*'. It is equally characteristic of the Church as *diakonia*. Jesus charged his disciples, as a last wish, to 'wash one another's feet' in imitation of him (John 13:12–17), and Peter in particular 'to feed his lambs' as a mark of his love for him (John 21:15–17). If mission is rooted in and founded on God's love for the world (John 3:16), and if women are proverbially endowed by God to be selfless lovers, then the Church cannot succeed in its mission to mediate God's love for the world without integrating those most naturally endowed by God to love as God loves. The inclusion of women is indispensable for a new and renewed understanding of being Church or being mission.

Image of Africa

The Report projects a consistently negative, narrow and often conflicting image of Africa. Correctly described as 'one of the widest and most varied of all the mission fields of the world', Africa is yet discussed as if it were just one country. This applies both in the body of the Report and in the list of correspondents. They come from Japan and Korea (15), China (64), India (70) and Africa (35).[10] This portrayal is entirely incommensurate with Africa's rich diversity that is essential for appreciating its exceptionally rich resources and complex problems. The portrayal is largely responsible for the abiding distortions of Africa in Western media and minds today.

By contrast, the Report gives favourable attention to Asian countries, praising their good initiatives and cultural practices. Africa and countries with black populations (New Guinea and the Fiji Islands) receive prominence only when the Report describes negative cultural practices, especially in the areas of marriage and what it comprehensively calls 'heathenism' and 'barbarism'. The

Fiji Islands are said to be 'typical of the darkest depths of heathenism', while New Guinea is home to 'a wild and savage race', that is to be counted 'amongst barbarous tribes', they stand in sharp contrast to Japan, a country with 'an ancient civilisation'. Africa globally belongs to the non-Christian civilizations that manifest 'the lowest depths of barbarism and social depravity'. As one reads this and similar derogatory submissions about Africa in the Report, one cannot but ask: What were these depths of this barbarism? Did Europe of the time, or of any other time, ever qualify as a Christian civilization in the Gospel sense of the word? Was Europe devoid of its own barbarism at the beginning of the twentieth century in decimating, plundering and despoiling Africa?

The damaging knowledge of Africa is also evident in the Report's generalising of cultural practices in the continent. This is particularly true of marriage, polygamy, and sexual morality, especially in the section on 'Bigamy and Polygamy'. Here the Report gives prominent attention to Africa. Specific examples cited include 'a chief having three hundred wives' (like the current king of Swaziland) and 'both in Africa and Polynesia the wives are often numbered by tens or scores'. Not surprisingly, the Report's correspondents in Africa 'view with unanimous intolerance conditions of life which are not only unchristian, but which are at variance with the instinctive feelings of natural morality. With them there can be no question of polygamy. It is the gross evils of heathen society which, like habitual murder or slavery [the slave trade was still being practised at the time by peoples from Christian countries], must at all costs be ended'. One way the churches in the mission field sought to end this unanimously was to refuse 'admission to the Church to any man who is actually living with more than one wife'. The Report further identifies 'the Christian law upon this subject' as possibly being 'the greatest obstacle to the acceptance of our faith'. It regrets that in this matter 'the Church is placed at a disadvantage in her warfare, owing to the fact that the Mohammedan with his easier views on the subject is more in accord with the *average man of Africa*' (emphasis added).

Generalization and misrepresentations regarding sexual matters in Africa have sunk deep into the psyche of most Westerners and dies hard, and is today linked with the rampancy of HIV/AIDS in Africa. The causative role in this of the Report and the missionaries on home visits is not negligible. In traditional African societies, polygamy was not evidence of the man's sexual immorality or lewdness. Archbishop P.K. Sarpong of Kumasi, Ghana, among others, has identified some of the values that African societies attached to polygamy.[11] It gave the polygamist status in the community. Economically it provided a rich workforce for the man's farms. Society did not view polygamy as 'sin' (in Old Testament terms, 'missing the mark', in African terms, 'something intrinsically bad in itself'). To marry only one wife was evidence of poor social standing in the community. Given its emphasis on and respect for the Bible, the Report might have recalled Abraham's concubines (cf. Genesis 25:6). David, 'a man after God's heart', and bound by the Sinai Covenant, inherited Saul's wives along with Bathsheba, wife of Uriah the Hittite (2 Samuel 12:7). Yet these acts are hardly ever viewed as evincing a corrupt and barbarous or heathen way of life 'at variance with the instinctive feelings of natural morality'. Abraham too practised wife sharing in Egypt to escape death; in return, he became a great Sheikh through Pharaoh's generosity (Genesis 12:10–13:2). African scholars today ask that African traditional cultural practices be judged with the same yardstick as those of the Old Testament, most of which had their origins in Africa. The earliest theological literature from sub-Saharan Africa grappled with these issues.[12] African women's contribution offers both an appreciation of culture and a sustained critique of patriarchy within the culture. It also conducts a critique of colonial translations and interpretations of the Bible rooted in patriarchy, 'The Circle' being their celebrated flag bearer.[13]

Other cultural practices misrepresented in the Report (such as 'ancestor worship' and 'animism'), cannot be addressed here for lack of space. The Report underscores the evangelist's difficulty in addressing these issues. In fairness to the Report, one notes its common sense sensitivity and true Christian spirit in addressing the issue of polygamy. For it, 'There is no question about the sin of polygamy. The only question is, whether the solution of putting away, where there has been no unfaithfulness, may not be adding sin to sin'. Put differently, whether the 'heinous sin' of polygamy does not consist in the very fact that 'it is impossible to undo its results, without fresh violations of Christian righteousness'. These violations consist in the awareness that the wives put away will be badly and unjustly affected, as also the children of polygamous marriages whose mothers are put away. It notes that when polygamy has been thus entered upon by both parties in the times of *ignorance*, and where there are children recognising the two parties as their parents, for the Church to insist on breaking up the relationship is to deprive the children of either the protection of their father or the care of their mother; while the women who are put away find themselves in the gravest moral danger – 'relegated' 'to the position of a prostitute'. The dilemma remains till today. A way forward might be to distinguish between traditional polygamist (more accurately polygynists) and those who become polygynist as Christians. In the former case, the ruling should affect both the husband and the wives. The husband and all the wives, not just select wives, should be constrained to a life of perpetual celibacy as a condition for baptism and charged with the joint responsibility of looking after their children.

In its foreboding that denominational divisions might give rise to further divisions, the Report was unfortunately correct. The astronomical mushrooming of churches in Africa is almost proverbial. In some parts of Nigeria, every other house may be a church. Jesus must have a very sad time on Sundays listening to the cacophony of Christian voices shouting each other down, all in praise of him, each claiming to be his true follower.[14] The Report recommends refusing to admit those who changed denomination. Today 'soul harvesting' missionaries target not the unevangelized, but members of the established churches, especially the Catholic Church. Politically, the multiplication of Churches might be part of the legacy of the partitioning of Africa at the Berlin Conference, a measure calculated to decimate, subjugate and exploit the continent. Whatever the case, Africa wins the prize when it comes to the proliferation of Christian churches and suffers consequently in its Christian witness.[15]

Inculturation

African cultural reality suffered a great casualty in the Report. This problem is located in the general colonial caricature of things African as barbaric, savage and lacking in culture.[16] Not surprisingly, the main theological method of African theologians south of the Sahara and north of the Limpopo has been inculturation. From their earliest entry into the theological discourse, African theological scholars have sought to make their distinctive contribution to Christian thought (something the Report strongly encourages) by revisiting their cultural heritage – at least, what is left of it – and identifying the values (gospel and biblical values, such as hospitality), that were and still are present in them.[17] Topics treated include ancestor veneration (not 'worship' as the Report says), naming rituals, marriage rites, widowhood practices, initiation rites, age-grade and socialization processes aimed at inculcating sound human and moral values. The comprehensive rejection of African social life as embodying 'the lowest type of barbarism' is belied by the fact that African cultures themselves had criteria for discerning between the good and the bad in their cultural practices.[18] Ibibio culture, for example, clearly distinguishes the worship of God (*Abasi*) from the worship of wicked spirits (*ndem*). African diviners were comparable to early Old Testament prophets who pre-dated the writing prophets. People who practise sorcery and witchcraft are in bad standing in the community. To then condemn all African practice as fetishism is to do great injustice to African people. Inculturation theology does not only seek to identify what is good and compatible with the Gospel in African cultures; it also recognizes that much of what the West transmitted as the Christian religion was a form of western culture that had become part and parcel of the missionaries' expressions of the Christian message. Failing to perceive the cultural backdrop in these practices, the older churches felt that Africans must first become Europeans before they could be accepted as authentic Christians, as the Jewish Christians demanded Gentile Christians to become Jews through circumcision.

The related problem of circulating works published locally dies hard. To discover works published in Africa, one has often to go to Europe or America. Theological associations, such as the Conference of African Theological Institutions (CATI) and departments of religious studies in universities, provide avenues for the study of theology within the African socio-cultural context in ways that were unimaginable in 1910. But the issue of textbooks continues to be a problem. Texts used are for the most part written by Western scholars; they result in students modeling their theological thinking on Western concepts and reacting to questions set by Western agenda. African scholars in turn often write for the Western audience because of the financial factor. Many African scholars, however, have branched out under the umbrella of EATWOT to ask and answer their own theological questions. The Catholic Institute of West Africa in Port Harcourt, Nigeria, founded in 1981, had the specific mission to do theology within the socio-cultural context of the West Africa. Inculturation is its most natural theological method for both staff and students. Inculturation here goes beyond the interface between African cultural realities to identifying the cultural backdrop in the received traditions, dogmas, hymns and so forth.

The Report was thus right that missionary teachers should reject 'systems of truth, knowledge, and practice, which are the results of Western experience, but do not vitally appeal to the mind or even the Christian consciousness of the local Church'. Rather they should encourage 'native Christians of ability to write freely on subjects with which they are familiar, and in which they are likely to express the truth in forms adapted to the thought of their own people'. Pope Gregory the Great had counseled the same to Augustine of Canterbury through Abbot Milletus, both missionaries to England, back in 596. If to be human is to be cultural, it is impossible for any people to undertake a human act without culture playing its natural role. Intrinsic to human reality as is being male and female,[19] culture forms the prism through which human beings view life. It embodies both values and systemic, structural sin. Cultural liberation undertaken by its owners in the light of the Gospel is the most fundamental liberation of all. Negatively, Western culture has produced capitalism and individualism with its latest fruit of globalization. Radically opposed to Jesus' Gospel, all have unfortunately found a destabilising home in Africa. The mission forward of Edinburgh 2010 might deliberately tackle this culture in the light of the Gospel.

The impact on Africa of the culture of colonialism is not only of the past. The current neo-colonialism is perhaps worse than colonialism itself. In colonialism, as in apartheid, one knew and could identify the exploiter/oppressor. One knew the foreign master; one knew that one's territory was occupied, so one knew what to struggle against. In neo-colonialism, not only is the enemy hidden but often poses as a friend. African leaders are still economically dependent on the West that continues to impoverish and deplete African resources for self-gain. The common criticism of NEPAD is that it was forged for Africa by those very allies whose primary interest is to exploit the continent.[20] The UK alone (according to media reports in 2003), sells £400 million pounds worth of arms to Africa yearly. Yet the UK is one of those countries that have pledged themselves to help Africa. The exploitation of Africa is economic, political and academic. Africans now teaching in Western universities, mainly as a result of poor conditions at home, quickly lose touch with the vital forces of African life – the problems of development, economy, poverty, tough working conditions experienced daily and providing energy for doing life-centred theology.

The Church in Africa faces many challenges other than inculturation. Underlying all of them is the corporate responsibility of ministering the superabundant blessings, spiritual and material, which God has given to Africa. Ironically these very blessings have proved to be the major cause of the despoiling of Africa.[21] Yet Africa is noted for its incredible resilience. This inbuilt gift from God enables it to survive against all odds sustained by the deep awareness that it, too, is part of God's creation, and that no forces can ever wrest it from God's hands and destroy it indefinitely.

Challenges for the Church on Mission in the Twenty-first Century

Despite the inevitable criticism in this review, the overall impression is that the Commission's Report on 'the Church in the Mission Field' was in many respects very current and deeply committed to mission and ecumenism. The collection of Essays by Lombard mentioned earlier (note 2) documents many ecumenical initiatives that Edinburgh 1910 has given birth to in Africa.[22] A call of mission in the twenty-first century resulting from Edinburgh 2010 might be to work towards the restoration of denied dignity and humanity to Africans. The liberation of the 'home Christians' from the bondage of ignorance and denial is integral to this restoration, not so much for Africans but for the 'home Christians' themselves. Western Christians need to consciously undertake their own self-liberating mission. If the Church in any part of the world (north or south) fails to ask self-critical, faith-based questions in its own context, if it occupies itself only with monitoring other peoples, and if it exercises a supervisory role over their questions and presumes a superior right to judge their answers, then that Church has lost the sense of its Christian gospel life and mission. The much discussed crisis facing Christianity in the West could be successfully addressed if the Church there asks itself life-questions in light of the Gospel.[23] For too long the West has concentrated its energy on guiding the life of the young churches, neglecting itself. Meanwhile the young churches, having come of age, claim their right to ask their own questions, seek their own answers, and even offer some of those answers to the West as part of our common Christian heritage as members of the one family of God (Ephesians 2: 19–22; 4:6).

Finally, a post-celebration activity of Edinburgh 2010 might be to undertake a humbler and more detailed review of the past 100 years beyond the praiseworthy activities of the centenary celebration. *Novo millennio ineunte*, John Paul II's reflection at the close of the Great Jubilee, might serve as guide in this.[24] To this end, a truly international Commission (of Westerners and Southerners) could be set up to revisit the questions that Edinburgh 2010 will raise (not only in this review but also in responses to other Commissions), aware that 'wherever the Church is, there is mission'. The purpose would be to discover, claim and celebrate what the Spirit is doing and saying in all the Churches in their different locations, as She progressively leads the universal Church into the complete, liberating and life-giving truth in Christ.

Endnotes

[1] World Missionary Conference, 1910, *The Church in the Mission Field*, Report of Commission II, Edinburgh & London: Oliphant, Anderson & Ferrier; New York, Chicago, and Toronto: Fleming H. Revell, 1910, title page.
[2] Austin Flannery, ed., *Vatican Council II*, vol. 2, *More Post Conciliar Documents*, New York: Costello, 1982, pp. 82–189. For John Paul II's *Ut Unum Sint*, see the edited collection of his major encyclicals by J. Michael Miller, *The Encyclicals of John Paul II*, Huntington, IN: Our Sunday Visitor, 1996, pp. 895–976.
[3] It helps to recall that the slave trade was very much in force in 1910, though there were already some initiatives to stamp it out. The decree on the abolition of slavery, tied to the UN Declaration on Universal Human Rights, dates from 1948, about 38 years after the Report and the Edinburgh Conference.
[4] Miller ed., *The Encyclicals of John Paul II*, pp. 494–570.
[5] In the narrative sequence, Peter's welcoming of Cornelius to the Christian fold (Acts 10) with its sequel before the brethren in Jerusalem (Acts 11:1–18) is reported first. Yet the ordinary Christians who fled Jerusalem because of the wide scale persecution that followed the martyrdom of Stephen (Acts 7), had already proclaimed the word to Gentiles (Acts 11:19–21); prominent among them were Africans from Cyrene (Acts 11:20). Philip's divinely directed encounter with the Ethiopian Eunuch (Acts 8:26–39) and his mission to Samaria (Acts 8:1–18) also belong here.
[6] Paul VI, *Evangelii Nuntiandi*, nos 22, 24; Flannery, *Vatican II*, vol. 2, pp. 711–61.
[7] Elizabeth Schüssler Fiorenza, *In Memory of Her. A Feminist Reconstruction of Christian Origins*, New York: Crossroad, 1983; especially the section on androcentric translations, interpretations, historical traditions, etc., pp. 43–67.
[8] John S. Pobee and B. von Wartenberg-Potter, eds., *New Eyes for Reading: Biblical and Theological Reflections by Women from the Third World*, Geneva: WCC, 1986; Pobee attended, sponsored and supported the inaugural meeting of the Circle of Concerned African Women Theologians and was instrumental in ensuring Nyambura J. Njoroge succeeded him as a staff of the PTE at the end of his term of office.
[9] John Paul II, *Post-Synodal Apostolic Exhortation of John Paul II, Ecclesia in Africa, on the Church in Africa and its Evangelising Mission Towards the Year 2000*, Vatican City: Editrice Vaticana, 1995, pp.64–5; The Second Special Assembly aimed at reviewing and moving forward the outcome of the First, is now in preparation with the publication of its *Lineamenta* (Nairobi: Paulines Publications Africa, 2006), which will include a focus on Reconciliation, Justice and Peace.
[10] *Church in the Mission Field*, pp ix–xx; other correspondents are from Mohammedan Lands (9) and Other Fields (14).
[11] P. K. Sarpong, *Ghana in Retrospect: Some Aspects of Ghanaian Culture*, 2nd edn, Accra–Tema: Ghana Publishing Cooperation; Ostfildern, Germany: Schwabenverlag, 1974.
[12] John Mbiti, *African Religions and Philosophy*; London: Heinemann, 1969; idem, *Concepts of God in Africa*, London: SPCK, 1970; Kwesi Dickson and Paul Ellingworth,

eds., *Biblical Revelation and African Beliefs*, Maryknoll, NY: Orbis, 1969; Kofi Appia Kubi and Sergio Torres, eds., *African Theology en Route*, Mayknoll, NY: Orbis, 1988; See further, Teresa Okure, 'The Bible in Africa: A select Literary Survey', in *Yearbook of Contextual Theologies, MWI* Missio Aachen; Frankfurt and London: IKO-Verlag für kontextuelle Theologen, 002), pp. 174– 209, esp. 179–86 ; To date the most comprehensive resource is Grant Lemarquand, 'A Bibliography of the Bible in Africa', in *The Bible in Africa: Transactions, Trajectories, and Trends*, eds. Gerald West & Musa W. Dube, Leiden: E. J. Brill, 2001, pp. 633–800.

[13] Notable publications of the Circle include Mercy A. Oduyoye and Musimbi R. A. Kanyoro, eds., *Talitha Qumi: The Proceedings of the Convocation of African Women Theologians*, Ibadan: Daystar, 1990, pp. 1–7; idem, *Introducing African Women's Theology,* Sheffield: Academic Press, 2001); Mercy A. Oduyoye and Musimbi R. A. Kanyoro, eds., *The Will to Arise: Women, Tradition and Church in Africa*, Maryknoll: Orbis, 1992; Musa W. Dube and Musimbi R. A. Kanyoro, eds., *Talitha Qum!: Theologies of African Women*, Pietermaritzburg: Cluster Publications, 2001; Musa W. Dube, ed., *Other Ways of Reading: African Women and the Bible*, Atlanta, GA: Society of Biblical Literature; Geneva: WCC, 2001; Musa W. Dube, *Post-Colonial Feminist Interpretations of the Bible*, St. Louis, MO: Chalice, 2000; Musimbi R. A. Kanyoro and Nyambura J. Nyoroge, eds., *Groaning in Faith: African Women in the Household of God*, Nairobi, Acton Publishers, 1996; Isabel Apawo Phiri and others, eds., *Her-Stories: Hidden Histories of Women of Faith in Africa*, Pietermaritzburg: Cluster 2002; see further the bibliography in Teresa Okure, 'Invitation to African Women's Hermeneutical Concerns', in Mary Getui, Tinyiko Maluleke and Justin Ukpong ed., *Interpreting the New Testament in Africa*, , Nairobi: Acton Publishers, 2001, pp. 42–67; Emmanuel Martey, 'African Women and Theology in Africa and the Third World', *Voices from the Third World,* Vol. 13, No. 2 (1990), pp. 54–88; Leny Lagerwerf, 'African Women Doing Theology: Survey', *Exchange*, Vol. 19, No. 1 (1990), pp. 1–69.

[14] My most recent study on this is 'Christian Identity and the Challenge of Authenticity: A View from Africa', *Christian Identity, Forum Mission* 3 (2007): pp. 171–99; see especially 180–95; also, in the same work, André Kabasele Mukenge, 'Les manifestations de l'identité chrétienne au Congo-Kinshasa: De l'affirmation aux derives', pp. 72–89.

[15] See, for instance, David B. Barrett, *Schism and Renewal in Africa: An Analysis of Six Thousand Contemporary Religious Movements*, London and Nairobi: Oxford University Press, 1968; Inus Daneel, *Quest for Belonging*, Gueru, Zimbabwe: Mambu, 1982; Paulus Makubu, *Who are the Independent Churches?*, Johannesburg: Skotville, 1988; E. Welbourne and B. M. Ogot, *A Place to Feel at Home*, London and Nairobi: Oxford University Press, 1962; John Pobee and Gabriel Ositelu II, *African Initiatives in Christianity: The Growth, Gifts and Diversities of African Churches. A Challenge to the Ecumenical Movement*, Geneva: WCC, 1998.

[16] I have conducted a requested number of studies on Africa on this issue for *Concilium*. See, Teresa Okure, 'Africa: A Refugee Camp Experience', in Dietmar Mieth and Lisa Sowle Cahill ed., *Migrants and Refugees*, *Concilium* 1993/4, London: SCM Press; Maryknoll, NY: Orbis, 1993, pp. 12–21; idem, 'Africa: Globalisation and the Loss of Cultural Identity', in Jon Sobrino and Felix Wilfred ed., *Globalisation and Its Victims*, *Concilium* 2001/5, London: SCM Press, 2001, pp. 67–74; idem, 'Martyred Africa: Seed for a New Humanity', in Teresa Okure, Jon Sobrino and Felix Wilfred ed., *Martyrdom Reconsidered*, *Concilium* 2003/1, London: SCM Press, 2003.

[17] Kwesi Dickson and Paul Ellingworth's *Biblical Revelation and African Beliefs*, New York: Orbis 1969, counts among the pioneer works.
[18] Laurenti Magesa's *African Religion: The Moral Traditions of Abundant Life*, Maryknoll, NY: Orbis, 1991, gives a good précis of these practices.
[19] Teresa Okure, 'I will Open my Mouth in Parables: Matt 13:35, A Case for a Gospel Based Biblical Hermeneutics', *New Testament Studies*, Vol. 46 (2000): pp. 444–63. See further Stewart C. Bate, *Human Life is Cultural: Introducing Anthropology*, Pietermaritzburg: Cluster Publications, 2002.
[20] New Partnership for Africa's Development, signed into force by 53 African countries as the manifesto or constitution of the African Union (AU), metamorphosed from the old Organisation of African Unity (AOU) in Lome, Togo, 11 July 2000.
[21] Teresa Okure, 'The Beatitudes in African Context: A Bible Study of Matt 3:3–22', Nairobi: Joint Africa Theological Conference, 14–18 August 2000; and more recently, 'Impoverished by Wealth: Mama Africa and Her Experience of Poverty', Annual Pope Paul VI Lecture, London: Catholic Agency for Overseas Development, 10 November 2006.
[22] James Amanze, 'Some Large Ecumenical Organisations on the African Continent', in Christo Lombard ed., *Essays and Exercises in Ecumenism*, Pietermaritzburg: Cluster Publications, 1999, pp. 137–50.
[23] Philip Jenkins, *The Next Christendom: The Coming of Global Christianity*, Oxford: Oxford University, 2002.
[24] John Paul II, *Novo Millennio Ineunte*, http://www.vatican.va/holy_father/john_paul_ii/apost_letters/documents/hf_jp-ii_apl_20010106_novo-millennio-ineunte_en.html accessed 30 August 2007.

FROM MISSION TO CHURCH AND BEYOND: THE METAMORPHOSIS OF POST-EDINBURGH CHRISTIANITY

Kyo Seong Ahn

Introduction

From the moment the World Missionary Conference of Edinburgh in 1910 placed the issue of the 'Church in the Mission Field' on the agenda of the Commissions, missionary discussion would never again be the same. Although earlier missionary and ecumenical meetings had considered the issue, it was, at most, one among many missionary problems. In Edinburgh, the case is quite different. Although we still find the same attitude reflected in the Conference's full title, 'World Missionary Conference, 1910, To Consider Missionary Problems in Relation to the Non-Christian World', it must be admitted that since the Conference the issue of the national church has been treated as a distinct category of missionary understanding. As a consequence three fundamental questions began to be examined: the relationship between the churches in the West and mission field, the relationship between missions and churches in the mission field, and the ascendancy of the church over missions in the history of mission. The Conference, as A.J. Boyd contends, could be regarded as 'the last word, the memorable inspiring last word of the Age of Missions, soon to be succeeded by the Age of the Missionary Church'.[1]

Although the Conference put its hope on the missionary role of emerging national churches it still basically understood mission as a movement from the West *to* the non-Western world. This unilateral understanding was prominent in previous times, and showed its staying power in the post-Edinburgh years. It is against this background that scholars worked to modify the perspective of mission from 'transmission' to 'appropriation' of faith.[2] However, it must be noted that missionary movement involves not only the interchange of ideas. A people-to-people encounter lies at the heart of this movement. It is for this reason that missiology should take human relationships, together with ideas and ministries, into consideration.

This chapter aims to respond to three questions that pertain to the church in the mission field: how this topic was understood in the Conference, how it developed in the post-Edinburgh years, and the relevance of the subject for the contemporary church and for mission.

Assessing Commission II

In attempting an assessment of Commission Two, both in its original context and in its relevance for today, four main categories can be identified: the church, the member, the leader and theology.

The Church: from one centre to many centres

The recognition of the church in the mission field as a distinct issue is perhaps one of the most remarkable theological features of the Conference: 'not as a by-product of mission work, but as itself by far the most efficient element in the Christian propaganda'.[3] Nevertheless, its significance was yet to be fully appreciated. Missiological problems lie at the heart of the relationship between the churches in the mission field and at home. To begin with, there is some ambiguity on church polity and unity. While the Conference encouraged cooperation and unity in the mission field, at the same time it unashamedly declared that the participants would be loyal 'to that form of polity to which we belong'.[4] This equivocal attitude was reflected in the policy of church planting. Although a new pattern of united church movement was on the rise, which was examined in Commission Eight, both denominationalism and a virtual laissez faire policy still prevailed. The problem is that the church polity at home cannot be reproduced in the mission field in its pure form. No matter how strongly a denominational position is advocated the process of indigenization is inevitable. The problem is also that the churches planted by interdenominational missions 'could be as partisan and denominational as any'.[5] Moreover, this tendency suggests 'faith can be transmitted separately from any ordering of the church'.[6] Therefore, cooperation and unity in mission is a problem at home as much as on the mission field.

Although Commission Two neither developed a new theory of church polity nor suggested a practical solution to the challenges posed by church planting, it is worth noting that the three largest countries in Asia were deeply involved in united church movements which achieved partial success. This strongly suggests that the issue of church union has a political dimension. It has often been argued that in the three countries, in particular China and Japan, unity was closely related to nationalism.[7] In Korea, however, the rise of Asian imperialism caused the Korean church to regard Christianity as a comrade to cooperate with rather than a target to destroy in the movement of nationalism. This means that the Korean church benefited from the political incentive in church growth rather than church union.

On the other hand, there still lingered a dichotomy between the churches in the mission field and those at home. While the Conference recognized the existence of both churches, it was assumed that the former was subordinated to the latter. In practice, national churches were placed at the bottom of the four-layered hierarchy of authority: the parent Church, the administrative Board or

Committee of the parent missionary Society, the local governing body of the mission, and the ecclesiastical authority of the local Church itself.[8] We also discern a pattern of thought about the relationship between the two churches, which strikingly resembles imperial periphery-metropolitan connection: frontier and home, child and parent, learning and control. It would be fair, however, to note that the report also avows that: 'It should be remembered, however, that our use of the phrase "mission field" is inexact. The whole world is the mission field, and there is no Church that is not a Church in the mission field.'[9]

Although this voice was suggestive of the future idea of 'mission in six continents', it was, nevertheless, rarely heard. It was at the 1928 conference in Jerusalem that the relationship between Western and non-Western churches began to be understood in a more advanced way: sisterhood rather than parent-child relations.[10] At any rate, this way of thinking invariably brings home to us the problem of missionary paternalism and euro-centrism. Understandably such malaise also affected the practice of mission.

As a whole, although it was repeatedly emphasized that national churches should grow, it was also assumed that missions should continue to work or even expand their ministry. This is quite opposite to the idea of 'euthanasia of missions'.Though the report maintains that 'The Church in the mission field has become the predominant partner', and states that 'the Mission has to adjust itself to the new position, has to take the place of handmaid where once it carried chief authority', both missions and national churches were slow to implement this idea.[11] It is eloquent of such missionary attitudes that the evangelistic work of national churches was dealt with in Commission One. This means that missions regarded the native church as 'the indispensable complementary ally of the foreign force' rather than aiming to do mission through the native church.[12] It is encouraging, however, that in the 1938 conference in Tambaram, the previous missionary issues in Edinburgh such as education, indigenous ministry, Christian literature, cooperation and unity, and even the place, function and training of the future missionary were included in the life of the church.[13] Despite this effort, in the post-Edinburgh years, there had always been the conflict between missions and national churches, and thus the word 'missions' had gradually become a very loaded word. It is against this background that historians began to write church history from the perspective of the transition 'from mission to church'. In the post-colonial era, mission came to be understood as the ministry of the whole church, and then as the ministry from everywhere to everywhere. Even the 'mission to the West' has repeatedly been addressed.

Although their representation was lamentably poor, the rise of the church in the mission field was also manifested by the participation of nationals taking part in the Conference. J. S. Friesen notes, 'The seventeen members [out of 1200] from the younger churches were accorded positions on the program quite out of proportion to their number: of the forty-seven public addresses given at noon and in the evenings, they presented six.'[14] He argues 'This advance was prophetic of the growing place which the younger churches were to have in the ecumenical movement in the years ahead.'[15] He also contends that 'without a strong counterbalance from people in Asia and Africa there was a very real danger that the Christian message might be radically corrupted and compromised into a kind of spiritual imperialism'.[16]

Before we leave this topic, it is worth noting that the then Western churches and missions did not sufficiently sympathize with nationals in their aspirations, in particular of politics. It is remarkable that during the Conference imperialism was taken for granted and barely challenged. This weakness can be confirmed by the fact that, as Brian Stanley asserts, even Commission Seven, which was supposed to deal with *realpolitik* between missions and governments, confined its interest to pragmatic matters, evading 'the issues of ethical principle raised by missionary association with Western imperialism'.[17] For instance when mission leaders argued for 'such justice and generosity towards the Koreans as presently will make them proud of the flag of the Rising Sun', they revealed the callousness of imperialism.[18] If the Western church could have realized the importance of nationalism and have helped emerging nations to realize their heartfelt aspirations, the presence of the Christian church in the world would have been quite different.

The member: the un-evangelized, the un-christianized and the un-churched

As regards Christian edification in the mission field, we can discern two presuppositions in the Commission: the concept of evangelization basically going with that of Christianization, and the tendency to identify a faithful believer with a loyal churchgoer.

It can be said that membership and edification were understood from the perspectives of indoctrination and morality. Standards were high and demands were harsh. Indeed, it was so even for home churches. For instance, due to missionary scruples it took a convert as many as two to six years to be baptized.[19] Some churches even required 'a further period of probation and instruction' before being admitted to the Communion.[20] Moreover, catechumens were required to detach themselves from certain customs in a short space of time; customs that they had taken for granted until their conversion and to which other members of the society still attached importance. A convert was thus considered as an examinee, to be approved and accepted to an institution by passing a religious examination, rather than a new member of organism to which he or she was to be integrated through appropriate socialization.

It was this socialization process which enabled the Korean church to grow rapidly in a society which was inhospitable to Christianity and poorly equipped with Christian resources. The case of the Korean church can best be explained as familial transformation rather than personal conversion or mass movement. This familial transformation began with personal conversion, mostly that of men. Once tolerated, this personal change influenced the family unit and then possibly the whole community. If this did not occur the convert tended to be ostracized and move to a more favourable place. In this way the Korean family played the role of a basic Christian community for faith and nurture. With the family being its basis, the Korean church was eager for extra-ecclesiastical tasks such as socio-political responsibility and modernization, on the one hand, and intra-ecclesiastical tasks such as self-support and self-propagation, on the other. Indeed even when the church was gradually denied the possibility of furthering its extra-ecclesiastical tasks as an organization it continued to serve the society through socio-cultural movement and education.

No matter how eagerly missionaries made efforts to achieve their purposes, it has become gradually clear that they could not have accomplished these without the contributions of national Christians. By 1910 the Korean church was already famous for its rapid growth as well as the missions' consistent policy of the three-self principle. There had already been a heated debate about the feasibility of the principle, particularly of the Korean case, in the 1900 New York conference. Indeed at this time the Korean Christians were very active in promoting the growth of their own churches.[21] From the beginning the Korean Christians were renowned for evangelistic efforts, and fledging indigenous Christian groups were developed by the multifarious efforts of both nationals and missionaries. Finally the 1907 revival movement not only accelerated the growth of the church, but also consolidated the place of emerging national leadership in the church. It was widely acknowledged that the revival movement, which was to touch heart as well as mind, could best be run by indigenous Christian leaders, among whom the Rev. Gil Seon-Ju (or Sun Choo Kil) was the single most important figure. A missionary's report vividly testifies that:

> The meetings held by the native preachers at the different centers have been very fruitful ... One of the noteworthy things about this great revival has been the leading part taken by the native church. In many places the greatest results seem to have been accomplished when the native workers have had entire charge.[22]

Equipping Christians for witness and service was at the core of the work. Missionaries in general emphasized the total mobilization of national Christians. It is quite striking that the concept of equipping every Christian was strange to home churches at the time. It was not until the second half of the twentieth century that this idea was widely appreciated in the home churches.

The church at present faces a totally different phenomenon in terms of membership. On the one hand, the rise of the Pentecostal movement sheds light on the communal aspects of the church to the extent that 'believing is belonging'. On the other hand, the post-Christian context, of Europe in particular, produces a non-commitment faith of 'believing without belonging'.[23] There is also a new private movement of spirituality in which 'people express their personal relationships to the sacred'.[24] All these patterns of belief challenge the traditional institutionalism of the church and the tendency to identify faith with church membership. This means that the contemporary church is to cope with a new challenge of the 'un-churched'.

The leader: a Man Friday for Robinson Crusoe?

Special attention was drawn to the training of professional workers of the church. As regards leadership training, the main concerns of the Commission were twofold: theological training and employment. The questions as to the inadequacy of Westernized training and the status and payment of national workers were examined.

The professional workers of mission churches had belonged to missions. With the rise of national churches, however, the question as to the affiliation of these workers was raised: whether they belong to church or missions. This question is closely related to the understanding of evangelization. Nonetheless, no matter who took the leadership in evangelization, it could not be implemented without national workers. The complexity of this issue can be illustrated by the idea of the 'appointment of natives of foreign countries as missionaries to their own people'.[25] This idea was in general rejected, as this would duplicate the leadership of national churches and result in a financial gap between national missionaries and other workers. This issue of a financial gap between national missionaries and other indigenous workers brings home to us a more fundamental problem of missionary identification.

In most cases Western missionaries knew the importance of identification with the people to whom they were sent, but they applied this principle through national or indigenous church leaders, not through themselves. Jonathan Bonk describes this attitude as 'vicarious' identification.[26] An example may be taken from an English novel entitled *Robinson Crusoe*. The image of Man Friday tells much of national or indigenous church leaders. He was saved, given a name, taught Christianity and civilization by Robinson and accepted as a useful worker. He remained a helper and never became a friend on equal terms. It is in this context that V. S. Azariah called for friendship as a legitimate relationship between national workers and missionaries.[27] Yun Chi Ho, a Korean participant, even called for partnership or mutual accountability when he asked, 'Must all work carried on by foreign money be under foreign control?'[28]

When discussing leadership it is also appropriate to mention the Christian gender revolution that deeply affected both national and home churches. The modern missionary movement cannot be properly understood without due attention to the role of women, who comprised the majority of missionaries. Once the Korean society, a traditional society, was opened to Christianity, women began to outnumber men in the Korean church. Not only did women church workers play an active part in evangelization and pastoral care, but also grassroots women Christians were enthusiastically involved in various church works. As early as 1898 Korean Presbyterian women established the first missionary organization to support evangelistic work in the un-evangelized areas of Korea.[29] In 1931, the year following its establishment, the Korean Methodist Church ordained fourteen American women missionaries. In doing so, the Korean Methodist Churches was 'the first among world wide Methodism to receive women into full membership of the Annual Conference as ministers of the Gospel'.[30] This practice clearly shows the ingenuity of the national church, reminding us of the idea of 'mission in reverse'.

Over the last century a number of methods have emerged to promote national Christian leadership: devolution of leadership, contextualized theological training, homegrown leadership, informal and non-formal education, and even internationalization of leadership training. However, it must be acknowledged that the changed context of the church, seen for example in the rise of world Christianity, *missio Dei*, interfaith dialogue, and unity of the church and unity of humanity, challenges contemporary Christians and leaders to face enormous tasks. It thus requires a fundamental transformation in leadership training. In this context the question arises as to how theology can meet this need.

Theology: from theology to theologies

One of areas in which the so-called missionary *magisterium* was most strongly felt is theology, although indigenous theology was encouraged in the Conference. The Korean church is a case in point. While indigenous leadership became conspicuous in church politics, missionaries dominated theology and Christian literature, including Bible translation. Missionaries, at least early ones, seemed to be confident both of their theological viewpoint and of their literary ability to produce Christian literature on behalf of nationals. As a result, indigenous theology was seriously impeded or ignored. Instead, an indigenous conservative theology that was faithful to both missionaries' conservatism and Biblicism took root in the church. The monopoly of Bible translation ministry by missionaries is illustrative of the situation. It was not until the year of 1932 that indigenous translators were officially appointed; almost half a century after this ministry had been initiated.

Recently the relevancy, or authenticity, of non-Western theology and hermeneutics has been re-evaluated. For instance the Biblicism of national Christians has come to be understood in different ways. On the one hand, it has begun to be regarded as a way of interpretation that is close to and thus presumably more faithful to the New Testament message. It is this relationship between indigenous sensibility and early Christianity that Kwame Bediako was at pains to bring into relief in his study on African Christianity.[31] It is true that Harold Turner had already located this aspect, and that it was again emphasized by Paul Hiebert when he criticized the West for suffering from what he termed 'the flaw of the excluded middle'.[32] On the other hand, Richard and Helen Exley criticize this Biblicism for a tendency to make national Christians more familiar with the Biblical world than their real world and thus to isolate them from their socio-political context.[33] However, the case is quite different in Korea. David Suh maintains that the Korean Christians read out a strong message of liberation from the Bible, in particular the story of the Egyptian captivity. He indeed recollects 'My father was a religious fundamentalist, and morally a Korean-style puritan. But he understood the Christian Gospel in political terms.' [34]More importantly, it can be argued that the Biblicism of the church in the mission field was a way of theology that was appropriate for the occasion. Such Biblicism, free from the heavy investment of Western methodology and culture, enabled national Christians to directly approach the message of the Scriptures and to secure space for their indigenous theology. In this context it is no wonder that the early Korean Church, which was renowned as 'Bible Christianity', rapidly developed and that Pentecostal Christianity has become the fastest growing branch of World Christianity.

The relevance of Western theology has also been challenged. Its monopolized claim to be a reference in theology is directly confronted by emerging indigenous theologies. Instead it is advised to take into consideration its own cultural and socio-political contexts as these demonstrate it is a contextual theology of the West. It is in this connection that the contextual theologies such as Liberation Theology challenge the traditional Western theology, which has been satisfied with 'orthodoxy', and propose 'orthopraxis' as a legitimate way of theology. Rather than seeing itself as a reference, Paul Hiebert suggests that it should prepare itself to be an authentic partner in theological dialogue. He contends that 'As a result of the modern missionary movement, Western churches are being forced to leave their well-established Christian paradigms and to build houses large enough to accommodate Christians from a thousand different languages, cultures, and peoples.'[35]

Unfortunately not a few Western scholars still turn a deaf ear to such counsel. Nevertheless it is not only Western theology that is on trial. In the age of World Christianity the concept of 'local theology' has been on the rise. Since the right to formulate theology also means the responsibility for theology, every theologian of every church is required to develop theology that is responsible, communicative, and contextually adequate. In this sense, it can be said that we are entering into an age of cooperation and unity of theology, in contrast to that of the missionary practice of expelling theology, as was witnessed in the Conference of 1910.

Prospect: in search of an authentic missiology: from orthodoxy to orthopraxis to orthopathy

It cannot be denied that the last century was tumultuous, particularly in terms of mission. It may be well to say that in a different and qualified sense it was also a 'Great Century'. The last one hundred years saw a number of changes and challenges in mission. These include the 'shift of gravity' from Christendom to World Christianity, the transfer of the leadership of missionary movement from missions to church, and the transformation of missiological understanding from 'missions' to 'mission'. This process was turbulent, so much so that in many cases it led not only to institutional disruption but also to relational disillusionment. However, the fact remains that the Great Commission is still effective and the task is yet to be accomplished.

To be faithful to the command of the Lord the Christian church has made various efforts and in doing so, it came to realize different ways of doing mission as well as theology. It is against this background that theologians proposed 'orthopraxis' as an alternative to replace 'orthodoxy'. However, in Edinburgh, national delegates had already suggested another alternative, which gained a mere transient popularity at the time, and has never properly been appreciated. Admittedly, there has always been a genuine desire to have an authentic relationship with other churches and the world and to proclaim the truth not merely from head, nor from hand, but from heart. Such desire needs to be developed into a new authentic way of doing mission and can perhaps be named 'orthopathy' (right feeling), or pathos-oriented missiology.[36] According to Aristotle, persuasion or an effective communication 'occurs from the interaction of the ethos of the speaker, the logos of the message, and the pathos of the audience'.[37]

Kenneth Ross suggests repentance as a legitimate way of looking back upon the Conference.[38] This reminds us of the humility of Henry T. Hodgkin, Secretary of the Friends' Foreign Missionary Association, who admitted in Edinburgh one hundred years ago that:

> The Church will certainly make mistakes – yes, and it will learn from them as did our forefathers, and as to-day we, the infallible Church of the West, may learn by our mistakes. Growing out of this spirit of fellowship and trust we need to have consultation with the native Church.[39]

As the non-Western churches have participated in world mission, they put themselves in the Western churches' shoes. This means that both Western and non-Western churches have begun to understand each other on equal footing and from the same perspectives. In this way the centenary of the Edinburgh Conference is perhaps to be the place not only of consultation, but also of 'mutual' repentance and reconciliation.

Endnotes

[1] A.J. Boyd, *Christian Encounter*, Edinburgh: Saint Andrew Press, 1961, pp. 7–8; Eric J. Sharpe, *Not to Destroy But to Fulfil: The Contribution of J.N. Farquhar to Protestant Missionary Thought in India before 1914*, Uppsala: Gleerup, 1965, p. 275.
[2] See Andrew F. Walls, *The Missionary Movement in Christian History: Studies in the Transmission of Faith*, Maryknoll, NY: Orbis, 1996; Andrew F. Walls, *The Cross-cultural Process in Christian History: Studies in the Transmission and Appropriation of Faith*, Maryknoll, NY: Orbis, 2002.
[3] World Missionary Conference, 1910. *The Church in the Mission Field*, Report of Commission II, Edinburgh & London: Oliphant, Anderson & Ferrier; New York, Chicago, and Toronto: Fleming H. Revell, 1910, p. 2.
[4] *The Church in the Mission Field*, p. 14.
[5] Bernard Thorogood, ed., *Gales of Change: Responding to a Shifting Missionary Context*, Geneva: WCC Publications, 1994, p. 243.
[6] Thorogood, ed., *Gales of Change*, p. 243.
[7] See Sumiko Yamamoto, *History of Protestantism in China: The Indigenization of Christianity*, Tokyo: The Institute of Eastern Culture, 2000; Carlo Caldarola, *Christianity: the Japanese Way*, Leiden: Brill, 1979.
[8] *The Church in the Mission Field*, p. 13.
[9] *The Church in the Mission Field*, p. 4.
[10] International Missionary Council, *Report of Jerusalem Meeting, vol. III, The Relation between the Younger and Older Churches*, London: Oxford University Press, 1928.
[11] *The Church in the Mission Field*, p. 36.
[12] World Missionary Conference, 1910, *Carrying the Gospel to All the Non-Christian World,* Report of Commission I, Edinburgh & London: Oliphant, Anderson & Ferrier; New York, Chicago, and Toronto: Fleming H. Revell, 1910, pp. 318–43.
[13] International Missionary Council, *Report of Tambaram Meeting, Vol. IV, The Life of the Church*, London: Oxford University Press, 1938
[14] J. Stanley Friesen, *Missionary Responses to Tribal Religions at Edinburgh, 1910*, New York: Peter Lang, 1996, p. 25; see also W. Richey Hogg, 'Edinburgh 1910 – Perspective 1980', *Occasional Bulletin of Missionary Research* 4, no. 4 (Oct./1980): p. 148.
[15] Friesen, *Missionary Responses to Tribal Religions*, p. 26.
[16] Friesen, *Missionary Responses to Tribal Religions*, p. 136.
[17] Brian Stanley, 'Church, State, and the Hierarchy of 'Civilization': The Making of the 'Missions and Governments' Report at the World Missionary Conference, Edinburgh 1910', in Andrew Porter, ed., *The Imperial Horizons of British Protestant Missions, 1880–1914*, Grand Rapids: Wm. B. Eerdmans Publishing Co., 2003, p. 58.
[18] W. H. T. Gairdner, *Edinburgh 1910: An Account and Interpretation of the World Missionary Conference*, Edinburgh: Oliphant, Anderson & Ferrier, 1910, p. 80.
[19] *The Church in the Mission Field*, pp. 43, 46.
[20] *The Church in the Mission Field*, pp. 78–9.
[21] Ecumenical Missionary Conference New York 1900, *Report of the Ecumenical Conference on Foreign Missions,* vol. 2, London: Religious Tract Society, 1900, pp. 301–12.
[22] *Annual Report of the Board of Foreign Missions of the Methodist Episcopal Church*, 1907, p. 423.

[23] See Grace Davie, *Religion in Britain Since 1945: Believing without Belonging*, Oxford: Blackwell, 1995; Grace Davie, *Europe – the Exceptional Case: Parameters of Faith in the Modern World*, London: Darton Longman & Todd, 2002.
[24] Robert Wuthnow, *After Heaven: Spirituality in America Since the 1950s*, Berkeley: University of California Press, 1998, p. vii.
[25] World Missionary Conference, 1910, *The Home Base of Missions*, Report of Commission VI, Edinburgh & London: Oliphant, Anderson & Ferrier; New York, Chicago, and Toronto: Fleming H. Revell, 1910, pp. 246–8.
[26] Jonathan J. Bonk, *The Theory and Practice of Missionary Identification 1860–1920*, Lewiston, NY: The Edwin Mellen Press, 1989, p. 38.
[27] V. S. Azariah, 'The Problem of Cooperation between Foreign and Native Workers', *The History and Records of the Conference*, Edinburgh & London: Oliphant, Anderson & Ferrier; New York, Chicago and Toronto: Fleming H. Revell, 1910, pp. 306–15.
[28] *The Church in the Mission Field*, p. 358.
[29] Yon Ok Lee, *Daehanyesugyojangrohoe Yeojeondohoe Baeknyeonsa [Centennial History of the National Organisation of the Korean Presbyterian Women]*, Seoul: The Editorial Committee of the NOKPW, 1998, pp. 51–2.
[30] 'The First Annual Conference of the Korean Methodist Church', *The Korea Mission Field* 27, no. 7 (July 1931), p. 156.
[31] See Kwame Bediako, *Christianity in Africa: The Renewal of a Non-Western Religion*, Edinburgh: Edinburgh University Press, 1995; Kwame Bediako, *Theology and Identity: The Impact of Culture upon Christian Thought in the Second Century and Modern Africa*, Oxford: Regnum Books, 1992.
[32] For H. W. Turner, see Bediako, *Christianity in Africa*, pp. 93–6, 107; Paul G. Hiebert, *Anthropological Reflection on Missiological Issues*, Grand Rapids: Baker Books, 1994, pp. 189–201.
[33] Richard and Helen Exley, *The Missionary Myth: An Agnostic View of Contemporary Missionaries*, Guildford: Lutterworth Press, 1973, pp. 67–9.
[34] David Kwang-sun Suh, *The Korean Minjung in Christ*, Singapore: Christian Conference of Asia, 1991, pp. 19, 17–24.
[35] Hiebert, *Anthropological Reflection on Missiological Issues*, p. 94.
[36] I coin this term to match orthodoxy and orthopraxis.
[37] Aristotle, in George G. Hunter III, *The Celtic Way of Evangelism: How Christianity Can Reach the West Again*, Nashville: Abingdon Press, 2000, p. 57.
[38] Kenneth R. Ross, 'The Centenary of Edinburgh 1910: Its Possibilities', *International Bulletin of Missionary Research* 30, no. 4 (Oct. 2006), p. 177.
[39] *The Church in the Mission Field*, p. 353.

Commission Three

Education in Relation to the Christianization of National Life

Commission Three 'Education in Relation to the Christianization of National Life'

The Commission in Summary

> The subject of education in missionary work is of special and far-reaching importance. No one, who knows the history of missions, can doubt that missionaries were pioneers of education wherever they went, and it is hardly possible to exaggerate the debt of gratitude which is due to them for their labours in education, nor can it be doubted how important a part education has played in the process of evangelisation. At the same time, education, as pursued under missionary auspices, has exhibited certain weaknesses in its methods, and is exposed to certain perils …[1]

These are words with which Bishop Gore of Birmingham, Chairman of Commission Three on *Education in Relation to the Christianisation of National Life*, introduced the Commission's Report – a hefty document that, in its subsequent publication as a book, runs to 383 pages, or 455 with appendices. Framed by an Introduction and Conclusion, it comprises nine chapters: the initial five are regional surveys, summarizing the responses of missionaries in India, China, Japan, Africa and 'Muhammedan lands in the Near East' to the Commission's questionnaire; the final three chapters deal with thematic issues centring upon on training – both industrial and educational – and literature.

Between the two parts of the Report, Chapter Seven, entitled 'The Relating of Christian Truth to Indigenous Thought and Feeling', comprised the heart of the enquiry. In Bishop Gore's words: 'A universal religion, a catholic religion, needs a common message … but a common message comprehended by very different and various peoples and individuals, each with very different gifts, so that each in receiving the one message, brings out some different or special aspect of the universal truth or character which lies in the common religion. So it is, and only so, that the glory and honour of all nations are brought within the light and circle of the Holy City; so it is alone that the real breadth and catholicity of life is brought out.'[2]

Bishop Gore was an eloquent editor, and his Commission's message is as compelling in its relevance today as it was in 1910. He especially recommended the sixth paragraph of the Conclusion of the Report as the lens through which the rest of the Report should be read, and it merits quotation:

> In the work of training the native Christian Churches, and in particular those who are to be the leaders of the Churches, the greatest possible care will have to be taken to avoid the risk of denationalising those who are being trained. In

> particular, we desire to lay the greatest emphasis on the importance of giving religious teaching, not only of the elementary kind, but as far as possible throughout, in the vernacular. We feel certain that those of our witnesses are right who believe that religion can only really be acclimatized in the heart of the natives of any country if it finds expression in their native language – the language of their homes.[3]

Set aside sensitivities of 'political correctness', and allow the anachronisms of speech: 'native', 'denationalising', 'vernacular'. The fact remains that the Bishop of Birmingham – a city conventionally denigrated as parochial – had a visionary perspective on the world and the Church: not as a European or Western monolith, but – like Birmingham today – a community of peoples and nations, among whom those who respond to the call of the Gospel bring to church and society the wealth of their many social and cultural traditions. 'So it is, and only so, that the glory and honour of all nations are brought within the light and circle of the Holy City; so it is alone that the real breadth and catholicity of life is brought out.'[4]

How, then, did the Commission understand the nature of Christian education as an expression of Christian mission? The Report gives a three-fold answer.

- Education may be conducted primarily with an *evangelistic* purpose; being viewed either as an attractive force to bring the youth under the influence of Christianity, or as itself as evangelising agency.
- Education may be primarily *edificatory*, in so far as the school has for its object the development of the Christian community through the enlightenment and training of its members.
- Education may be *leavening*, in so far as through it the life of the nation is gradually permeated with the principles of truth.[5]

Evangelism, edification, leavening – three dynamic characteristics of missionary education.

The first, evangelism, meant disseminating the Gospel. Consistent with the other Commissions of Edinburgh 1910, this was broadly understood in terms of 'fulfilment' – i.e. 'recognition of the many elements of truth and value in non-Christian systems of religion and ethics' upon which 'the education of the world demands for its highest and best development those elements of truth which are the peculiar contribution of Christianity to the world's thought and life'.[6]

The second, edification, denoted 'the need of educating Christians to fill positions of usefulness and influence in the community'.[7] Preachers and teachers, certainly – but to concentrate on them 'disproportionately' is to distort the nature of Christian community and leadership. 'Providing for the laity' is equally important: 'Only as the Christian community contains a goodly proportion of men and women, trained to support themselves and serve the public good, can it exert its influence on the life of the community at large.'[8] It was in this connection that 'industrial education' – i.e. 'manual training as a factor of general education'[9] – (what we today term 'vocational training') – figured as prominently in the Report as intellectual attainment. The latter was highly valued, but not as an end in itself: 'Intellectual attainments are important, but personality, character, leadership go deeper.' In the training of both character and mind the Report emphasized the vital role of women, both as educators and as meriting education. In both respects they were considered equal with men: 'In view of the fact that character is largely determined in early years and by the influence of the mother in the home, the education of women acquires a place of first importance.'[10]

The third goal of missionary education, leavening, entailed 'the philanthropic desire to promote the general welfare of the people'. The Report infers that the Kingdom of God surpasses the realm of the institutional Church, an insight that prefigures current ideas of 'regnocentric' or Kingdom-centred mission. Constructive relationship with government is therefore 'the manifest course of wisdom'.[11] The Report recognizes that 'It may even be necessary for a time to put the stress of effort upon things that have to do with economic or educational conditions ... always of course keeping in mind the ultimate aim of Christian missions, the full Christianisation of the life of the nation'.[12]

Yet the Report concedes nothing to 'vague philanthropic aims', and therefore concludes: 'We wish to lay it down that we believe that the primary purpose to be served by the educational work of missionaries is that of the training of the native Church to bear its own proper witness. And inasmuch as the only way in which the native Church can bear its own proper witness, and move forward toward the position of independence and self-government in which it ought to stand, is through native leaders, teachers and officers, we believe that the most important of all ends which missionary education ought to set itself to serve, is that of training those who are to be the spiritual leaders and teachers of their own nation.'[13]

Endnotes

[1] World Missionary Conference, 1910, *Education in Relation to the Christianisation of National Life*, Report of Commission III, Edinburgh & London: Oliphant, Anderson and Ferrier; New York, Chicago and Toronto: Fleming H. Revell, 1910, p. 6.
[2] *Education in Relation to the Christianisation of National Life*, p. 406.
[3] *Education in Relation to the Christianisation of National Life*, p. 373.
[4] *Education in Relation to the Christianisation of National Life*, p. 406.
[5] *Education in Relation to the Christianisation of National Life*, pp. 369–70.
[6] *Education in Relation to the Christianisation of National Life*, pp. 368–9.
[7] *Education in Relation to the Christianisation of National Life*, p. 374.
[8] *Education in Relation to the Christianisation of National Life*, p. 375.
[9] *Education in Relation to the Christianisation of National Life*, p. 267.
[10] *Education in Relation to the Christianisation of National Life*, p. 377.
[11] *Education in Relation to the Christianisation of National Life*, p. 372.

[12] *Education in Relation to the Christianisation of National Life*, p. 370.
[13] *Education in Relation to the Christianisation of National Life*, p. 371–2.

To Hang a Ladder in the Air: An African Assessment

Ogbu U. Kalu

Introduction: the African road to Edinburgh

The Igbo people of southeastern Nigeria say that a man who does not know where the rain met him cannot possibly know where he is going. Edinburgh in 1910 may best be understood by Africa's encounter with the rain of the gospel and how it responded. There was no African present at the Conference; white missionaries spoke for Africans but their voices were so discordant that the conferees soon realized the vastness of the neglected continent, the complexity of the problems, and the challenging nature of the missionary enterprise there. The Commissioners felt like people trying to hang a ladder in the air and concluded that: 'so varied are the conditions with which missionary workers are confronted in different parts of Africa that only a few conclusions apply to the whole region'.[1]

The reflection here revisits the deliberations of Commission 3 about Africa, the voiceless continent. It examines how the West talked about African education during the Edinburgh Conference. Africa was at the periphery of Mission and its conditions conjured an image that was exotic and at the lowest rung on the evolutionary scale of both religion and civilization. After listening to twenty-eight correspondents, including prestigious veteran missionaries, the Commissioners were dumbfounded and concluded that it appeared that the core elements of a meaningful education did not exist. This chapter examines the historical background, the distorting lens through which the Commission saw Africa and the ideology of missionary education presented at the Conference.

Christianity in Africa in 1900

The story of Christian presence in Africa at the beginning of the nineteenth century is a gloomy one. In the Horn of Africa decline had been steady with the incursion of Islam from the seventh century. Nubia remained Christian till the fifteenth century. Ethiopian Christianity was left in splendid isolation. Early contacts in the sixteenth century portrayed the image of a muscular church with pristine first century Christianity, monastic spirituality, creative music, fine architecture and fascinating art. However by the end of the eighteenth century Ethiopian Christianity was in a traumatized state. Henry Salt in *Voyages and Travels* (1809) records: 'The nation, with its religion, is fast verging on ruin; the Galla and Mussulman tribes around are daily becoming more powerful;

there is reason to fear that, in a short time, the very name of Christianity may be lost among them.'[2] The state structure had grown soft, its boundaries dwindled and internecine theological debates on the Sabbath and nature of Christ created virulent divisions between the court, the leading monastic houses and the *abuna*. Its ancient liturgy in Ge'ez became less intelligible to Amharic speakers; learning declined as the infrastructure rotted. Hundreds of churches were destroyed or abandoned amidst violent strife.

South of the Sahara, in West Africa, the crusading spirit of the *padroado* meant that even indigenous chaplains could not sustain Christian evangelism in the midst of the inhuman slave trade. In Southern Africa, the major religious force was Islam. The Arab factor in African history was highly significant. At this point Islam expanded into the interior through trade (especially the slave trade), the fundamentalism of the *Wahhabis*, a resurgence of old *sufi* orders, and the formation of new orders such as the *Tiyyaniyya* and jihads. In West Africa, nine jihads prior to 1853 led to political formations in the Futa Jallon, Futa Toro and Sokoto regions. New centers of Islamic presence emerged such as Harar (Ethiopia), Zanzibar (East) and Sokoto (West). In Uganda, an astonished missionary, A. M. Mackay wondered, 'Is Arab or European power henceforth in Central Africa to prevail?'[3]

In the Cape region of South Africa the slave population outnumbered the settlers. The Dutch *predikants* on both sides of the Great Fish River (Albany District, Ciskei and Transkei) provided no mission for the local population who were exploited for labour. They mounted a psychological war against the early Moravian Brethren who tried to uphold the dignity of the indigenous population. Adrian Hastings concluded: 'Overwhelmingly the impression that a careful observer would have gained of Africa of 1820 was that Islam was substantially a missionary religion, and an effective one, while Christianity was not. The white Protestant presence in Cape Town for a century and half had led to no significant advance beyond the ranks of the settlers.'[4] How did the nascent forces of regeneration emerge in the midst of such a bleak scene?

Certain broad themes may be identified that emerged to reshape the religious landscape and revive the fortunes of Christianity in nineteenth-century Africa: philanthropy, abolitionism and African American missionary impulse, re-energized Protestant and Roman Catholic missionary resurgence, and geopolitics; that is European nationalism and the colonial partitioning of Africa. Another crucial and neglected dimension is how Africans appropriated the gospel through a variety of prophetic and charismatic movements and nationalist responses such as 'Ethiopianism'. It could even be argued that Islamic insurgence served as a missionary challenge in the 'Sudan' region of Africa.

In the period between 1800 and 1850 the most powerful force was the relationship between philanthropy, abolitionism and mission. Between this period and 1900 missions engaged in rapid, competitive, vertical expansion into hinterlands, often following the boots of colonial forces. The slave trade had sapped the moral authority of the gospel and the commercial dimension absorbed the energy and commitment of agents. Abolitionism, therefore, became the engine that moved the new missionary enterprise of the nineteenth century. An educated African-American elite drew up plans for equipping the young with education and skills. As Sanneh puts it, they adopted an ironic liberal stance: 'separation of church and state (that) was to create a vibrant civil society of lay agency, individual enterprise, personal responsibility, and equality before the law. This arrangement challenged people to believe in progress and in the improvability of society, rather than to cling to the past and established structures, and provide an encouraging and useful model of what was required in Africa. It also appealed to former slaves who found in the American experiment support for their own campaign for freedom, for a new society conceived in antislavery and anti-structure.'[5] They set the cultural tone of industry and religion that nurtured thousands of re-captives in Sierra Leone between 1807 and 1864. These freed slaves became agents of missionary enterprise throughout the West coast. The Colonization Society recruited enough African Americans to found Liberia in 1822. These intrepid blacks garnered spiritual sustenance for their vision from evangelical spirituality and through appropriating the power of the gospel.

In Britain a moral resurgence won support for the abolitionist cause. The temper of evangelicals grew more uncompromising as they canvassed a number of projects. Fowell Buxton's *African Slave Trade and Its Remedy* argued that a solution lay in pressing the indigenous participants into the task of dismantling the trade at source and installing legitimate trade in raw materials needed for British industries. Christianity would serve as a civilizing agent among the indigenous population. Charles Dickens derided the 1841 expedition to the Niger based on Buxton's plan as a failure but in the end, the use of commerce and Christianity, the Bible and the plough, won the day. Traders engaged in legitimate trade and provided the logistical support for missionaries. Abolitionist projects drew the power of the government into closer contact with indigenous peoples and increased access for missionaries.

Another strong feature of the century was the Evangelical revival of the era and the attendant resurgence of the missionary enterprise among Protestants and Roman Catholics. Its emphases within Protestant circles were Biblicism, the message of the cross, an attack on lukewarm Christianity, the conversion experience, a strong eschatology and social activism. Institutional revival and reorganization also occurred in the Roman Catholic Church in the nineteenth century. Structurally, the old missionary system came alive again: the Propaganda Fidei section of the Vatican was revamped as a clearing-house for the missionary enterprise; the Jesuits were restored; new orders and apostolates such as the White Fathers, Mill Hill, Verona emerged; and many educational and medical apostolates began to be staffed by nuns.

The story of Christianity in Africa took a specific turn in the 1880s, reflecting currents in European geopolitics. The Berlin conferences of 1884–5 on the partitioning of Africa among competing nations dramatically changed the relationship between Europeans and the rest of the world. Jingoism filled the air, drowning out the protests of the enemies of the imperial idea. Space, expansionism and migration to the non-Western world were matters of importance. One of the provisions of the Berlin treaty included the need to demonstrate actual presence instead of mere claims of areas of influence. Chiefs were treated in a cavalier, imperial manner; middlemen were brushed aside; and maxim guns became important in the pacification projects. Trusteeship replaced the vision of using indigenous agents to evangelize. There was an enlargement of scale in mission: in the number of missionaries, participating nations, areas evangelized, the level of participation by females and the funds raised for the enterprise. The goal of mission was for 'the kingdom of the Anglo-Saxons … to bring light to the Gentiles by means of lamps manufactured in America'.[6] Gustav Warneck criticized human-centred activism, the emphasis on proclamation to the neglect of discipling the nations, the danger of confounding the spread of European culture with the spread of the gospel and the replacement of the role of the church by voluntarist organizations and dangerous rhetoric; watchwords and slogans that could be quite misleading. Right up to the Edinburgh Conference, European missiologists remained hostile to the new spirit in the nineteenth-century missionary enterprise.

Yet Africans were not passive proselytes. Indigenous religions remained resilient. In spite of the control system Africans wrote their own hidden scripts. Missionary contributions, however, in education, medicine and the translation of the Bible into indigenous languages catalyzed changes in African Christianity. When people read the Word in their languages, the power brought about tremendous changes. Each regional context presented its own challenges, as culture became the contested ground. The effects of translation became more apparent after the First World War when the character and provenance of education changed, and revivalism grew more intense. In 1910 the Commissioners knew only of a haphazard and rudimentary education system.

Until the second half of the century the missionary enterprise was unsuccessful in many parts of Africa. This may explain why African Christianity was not central to the missionary discourse at Edinburgh 1910. Maturity and galloping changes would occur later in the twentieth century. These changes, however, came about through the forces of regeneration that started during the nineteenth century. Unfortunately, these were unrecognized when whites talked about Africans in 1910.

Wade Harris typifies what was missing at Edinburgh. In the year that whites met to talk about Africa, a bearded man, decked in a long white *soutan*, walked from his native Grebo Island across the Liberian coast, through the Ivory Coast to the Gold Coast. He carried a long staff, a Bible and a bowl of holy water. He preached; he composed his own choruses and taught them to large crowds. He baptized, healed and performed miracles. He was ecumenical; he founded no churches but convinced many to burn their idols and go to local churches. The Methodist Church in the Gold Coast exploded numerically because people took the old man seriously. The Roman Catholics in the Francophone colonies also benefited. Others created problems for him by means of the colonial governments. On his return through the Ivory Coast he found that the shipmasters had not stopped the practice of using Kru men to offload their cargoes on Sundays. He had warned them and decided to punish their recalcitrance. He threw holy water at some of the ships and these caught fire. The French authorities put him under house arrest. His missionary journey undoubtedly achieved more within months than the labours of many expatriate missionaries through many years.[7]

Images and lenses

At the Edinburgh Conference the regional distribution of white correspondents from Africa – there were no black Africans present – created a lens sure to distort the image: twelve came from South Africa, seven from Nyasaland, five from the whole of West Africa, two from East Africa and one each from Madagascar and Mozambique. Within West Africa, three came from Nigeria and one each from Sierra Leone and Liberia. Within Nigeria, one came from the northern region (the intrepid medical doctor, Dr Miller, who confronted the exclusion of missionaries from the Moslem emirates), and two came from Calabar (one Presbyterian and one Primitive Methodist). The vast south western region of Nigeria, where the educated religious nationalists were very strong, was not represented.[8] With hindsight, it is possible to see that the sampling distorted the image of Africa and African Christianity at the Conference.

The Commission received replies from over 200 missionaries and distributed these, by regions, to separate sub-committees. 'The English members of the Commission met in London for a week (1-6 November 1909), discussed these reports, and determined the lines to be taken by the report as a whole.'[9] They submitted their work for input by the American members, who suggested changes. At a meeting between the British members and a representative of the American members in London on 22 April 1910, the report, conclusions and recommendations were harmonized in order to be presented with the assent of the entire Commission. There is every indication the Commission dealt with the data on the role of education in the missionary enterprise with competence and clarity. It was the lens (the selective and incomplete nature of the data) that distorted the image!

The fourteen questions administered were exhaustive and will be considered along with other aspects of missionary education. The Commission was sensitive to the hardships of pioneering missionary work, and endeavored to balance the achievements with new theories of education. As the Report put it, 'It has seemed to us that we should probably best assist those who are actually engaged in the educational work of missions by formulating such a series of conclusions or recommendations…not to make final pronouncements or to arrogate authority to ourselves in any sense, but rather to stimulate thought and to provide a basis for discussion.'[10] The significance of Edinburgh 1910 in missionary discourse is the astonishing level of self-criticism that made the movement resilient. The Conference espoused high ideals. Having acknowledged the achievements by missionaries, it moved quickly to observe that, 'education, as pursued under missionary auspices, has exhibited certain *weaknesses in its methods*, and is exposed to certain *perils*, which make it necessary to review its *principles and its processes*'.[11] This startling acknowledgment opens up the discussion on the gap between the ideal that the Commission perceived and the practice that the missionaries pursued. The Commissioners started a conversation on African education that combined with geopolitical realities to nudge missionary practices in new directions.

The ideology of education at Edinburgh 1910

The Commission espoused an ideal of education that resonated with Roman Catholic ideals and practices. In many parts of Africa the Roman Catholic educational enterprise outpaced the Protestant. In southern Nigeria, Bishop Shanahan prosecuted the education apostolate with such vigor that inspectors from Lyon in 1929 wondered whether the Holy Ghost Fathers had deserted evangelism! The absence of their input to the conversation in Edinburgh was regretted. Protestants at Edinburgh, however, had arrived at the same conclusions. As Mott put it, quoting a German proverb, 'What you would put into the life of a nation, put into its schools.'[12] Education was the preferred instrument for mediating the missionary message.

Imagining the educational process

The Commission outlined the types of education required: primary, higher, teacher training, ministerial formation, industrial, education of girls, and education for evangelising Muslims. It derived its rationale for missionary education by exploring lessons from the early church. The early church recognized the *pilgrim/universal* and *indigenous/local* principles in Christianity. It sought to be universal and catholic without becoming exotic or foreign. In the early church, Christianity became indigenous in each race and place from the first, because it was entrusted to native teachers and rulers almost at once. There was accommodation to such national religious customs as were thought to admit of a Christian interpretation and use. The result was the diffusion of a catholic religion exhibiting local variations of customs and presentation.[13] Education was crucial to Christianity for several reasons: a commonly shared elementary education saved the catholicity of Christianity from becoming exotic or representing a foreign influence. Christianity was a religion of ideas and institutions that could only be maintained through teaching. It inherited from Judaism a profound respect for teachers and special instructions in catechism that were designed as a process of training and initiation into the religion.

The Commission recognized that in some places there was no commonly shared public education that could serve as a framework, so each mission had to design its strategy. The Commissioners may have been blind to indigenous models of education; they ignored the voices of educated Africans crying out for the indigenization of the gospel. Nevertheless they conceded that the ideal method of propagating Christianity in the contemporary period is that: 'the Gospel should be received by each race through the ministry of evangelists from nations already Christian but that the church should pass as rapidly as possible under the control of native pastors and teachers, so that while all churches hold the same faith, use the same Scriptures, celebrate the same sacraments, and inhere in the same universal religion, each local church should from the first have the opportunity of developing a local character and colour.'[14] Converts, they argued should, with their children, continue to share the education and social life of their own races and nations; and bring the distinctive genius and its products within the circle of the Holy Spirit. They not only promoted the Venn policy, shared with Rufus Anderson, but also moved towards a compromise with the German *volkskirche* principle that Gustav Warneck and other German missiologists urged. It was an espousal of a brand of ecumenism in which all nations and cultures stood equidistant to the kingdom of God. One suspects, however, that the Commission proffered this idea with Japan and China largely in mind, hardly Africa.

The ecology of learning

The Commission explored the tendency of Western people to reproduce 'strongly defined and intensely western forms of Christianity'. This created a gulf between the mental world of missionaries and that of the indigenous people. Missionaries paid insufficient attention to presenting the gospel in the form best suited to the context and spirit of the people. This tendency to plant 'the religion of conquerors, or foreign devils, and unwelcome intruders' lacked wisdom; especially when conquest, perception of the other, insularity, lack of sympathy for and study of other religions, may have caused alienation.[15] Paulo Freire was later to dub this model 'cultural invasion': 'the actors draw thematic content of their action from their own values and ideology; their starting point is their own world, from which they enter the world of those they invade'.[16] The opposite is 'cultural synthesis': 'the actors who come from another world to the world of the people, do so not as invaders. They do not come to teach or to transmit or to give anything, but to learn, with the people, about the people's world.'

The Commissioners did not go this far but called for a process that trains students for social functions, through music, poetry and dance. Education should train the individual for conscious and intelligent participation in the great social movements and challenges of one's environment. As South African educationist, Bongani Mazibuko said, 'It is in stressing the affective and experiential, rather than the narrowing rational and academic, that students are affirmed and empowered.'[17] The Commission urged missions to train native Christian leaders as teachers and church officers to bear the responsibility for building the church, to produce indigenous literature and use the vernacular in elementary schools because 'a man's mother tongue is that which reaches his heart, and always offers the best approach to the deepest subjects'.[18] Simply put, foreign language makes Christianity a foreign production.

This chimed in with African feeling. In 1891, the firebrand, Wilmot Blyden, gave a lecture in Lagos entitled, *The Return of the Exiles* in which he exhorted 'Africans must evangelize Africa' or, as Mojola Agbebi would say, the sphinx must solve its own riddle![19] The Niger Delta pastorate had split from the Church Missionary Society in that year. A young Ghanaian Methodist lawyer, J. Casely-Hayford wrote his play, *Ethiopia Unbound* in the year that white people met to talk about Africans in Edinburgh. There was ferment in the young mission fields but the din did not interrupt the discussions.[20] As J.R Mott read the signs there was an openness to receive the gospel in Africa. The challenge from Islam in Equatorial Africa contested the enterprise. Education was a core instrument and the distribution of Christian literature was imperative. This included devotional materials, apologetics, literature for moral formation and general, scientific materials that would provide information and aid reading abilities.

There appear to have been three different perceptions of the goal of education among the conferees in Edinburgh 1910. The first was the *assimilationist* position that argued that education could be deployed to uplift the culture to the European level. Mott may represent a second position held by the 'cultural invaders' when he said: 'As already seen, the influence of western learning has been in the direction of undermining the faith of the student class in the non-Christian religions and of breaking up the social and ethical restraints of the old civilizations.'[21] The Commissioners' third position was *indigenizing* - the task being to explore how to Christianize national life through education. To achieve this, they recommended changes in the content and method of education, with emphases on agricultural and industrial training.

The Commissioners suggested a gender sensitive model of education to mobilize the women and girls. This wove the traditional community's goals to white needs for domestic servants, nurses and teachers. The curriculum consisted of domestic science, hygiene, cooking, laundry, sewing, cleaning, spinning, lace-making, basket weaving and dispensary assistance.[22] The education ideology in response to Islam was creative. They urged the establishment of special facilities in Moslem countries manned by evangelists trained on how to witness without injury to the sensibilities of Muslims.

Questions of education

Using a social science model the Commissioners sought to assess the product-content or result of Christian education. They attempted to evaluate whether it had caused Christian conviction, that is if it had permeated indigenous thought, feelings and outlook; whether it had percolated into the learner's community; and whether 'the course of education is being gradually brought into more vital relation to the real needs of the different categories of native pupils'.[23] The Commissioners wanted to know whether the process had inspired higher ideals, equipped the learner for leadership roles and enhanced physical development. Most of the questions focused on curricula, the use of indigenous and other Christian literature, the mode of communication (English or vernacular) and the social ecology of learning.

The answers from the fields

The discussion of the responses of protagonists in the mission fields is exemplified by J.R Mott's characteristic hyperbole: 'it is not necessary to call attention to the economic, social and educational development of the native races of South Africa, which development, along with the political evolution, has advanced steadily through the past two or three generations. Suffice it to say that in no period has the progress been more marked, judged by every test, than during the last two decades. This progress is observable in almost every part of what is known as the Sub-Continent, the parts of Africa lying south of the Zambesi.'[24] In reality, 1910 was a dark year for the black population of South Africa. The Afrikaaners denied the indigenous people political and socio-economic status. In 1912, the year Mott's book came out, they were compelled to appeal for Britain's intervention.

The correspondents showed that missionary education in 1910 was at the elementary level, with little effort at the higher or secondary school level and with few Teachers' Colleges. Industrial education was either non-existent or rudimentary and girls' education remained the lowest priority. Education was focused on enabling pupils to read the Bible and devotional literature. The emphasis was on moral re-orientation, which tended to subvert the traditional worldview and culture. The brass ceiling of missionary education was moral formation, skill acquisition, and production of native teachers. Education in the Cape Colony had taught the people to improve their hygiene, physical surroundings, to acquire higher ideals in life and form the capacity to dissent from tribal ties and family control. The unintended consequence was intensified individualistic ethos, assertion of independence often amounting to license, and opposition to Europeans. Dr Stormont admitted that missionary education did not provide an adequate coping mechanism in the face of socio-economic changes in the lives of the indigenous people. The native teacher, he wrote, is unchaste, conceited, and lover of ease and money.[25]

Interestingly, the other leaders of institutions in the southern African region echoed Stormont. Henderson of Lovedale repeated the goals of moral regeneration and character formation, yet also confessed the lack of engagement in higher education, unfocussed goals in generating Christian influence in the communities, and low priority for industrial education (because the youth found it unappealing). Even less attention was paid to girls' education because, he argued, they would rather stay at home. He blamed polygamy, early marriage and love of ease.

Rev. J. D. Taylor of Adams Mission Station, Natal, devoted immense effort in answering the questionnaire. He applauded the moral dimension in missionary education, access to the Bible, arousal of interest in higher education, and the spread of Christian influence. Nevertheless he rated the enterprise a failure because of poorly trained native teachers, who despoiled primary schools and lacked earnestness in giving religious education. Blame went to parents who used child labour and encouraged indolence and absenteeism, as well as to Government under-funding. The teaching-learning environment, observed Taylor, is vitiated by an over-emphasis on academic subjects, undue attention to examination results by Government inspectors, lack of textbooks suitable for local conditions, and the multiplication of low quality schools. Industrial education had low priority because the Government capitulated to white labour organizations that resented skill acquisition by blacks.

The dark picture in South Africa is completed by Rev L. Fuller of Johannesburg who approved of a religious rather than academic emphasis in primary education, and would not encourage higher education for natives because it will afflict them 'with a horror of hard work, either mental or physical', and make them 'rather immoral and very far from religious'.[26] In Nyasaland and Central Africa the chorus continued as if orchestrated. All agreed that higher education was practically non-existent and industrial education was confined to producing artisans to work for the mission stations.

As late as 1950 little had changed. The World Council of Christian Education, in New York, conducted an elaborate global survey of the practice of Christian Education, and produced a source book for the convention in Toronto. Virtually all respondents linked evangelism to Christian education and stressed moral formation and destruction of indigenous religions as their aims.

Internal diagnosis: problems and prospects

The missionaries pointed to problems and possible solutions. In regard to the social environment, they commented on political resurgence (Ethiopianism - which spread throughout the Zambezi, Cape Province, Natal and Nyasaland);

the effect of increased demand for labour in the mines and its attendant moral consequences; the growth of Islam; the spread of materialism and urbanization; and competition by governments, some of whom were hostile toward (e.g. the French in Madagascar) or suspicious of missionaries (e.g. the Portuguese in Mozambique). Africa suffered from conflicting policies by the British, French, Portuguese and Belgians. The missionaries did not always agree on how to improve the results of missionary education. J.K. McGregor, of the United Free Church, Calabar, blamed the lazy 'natives'. Others wanted a review of the teaching-learning environment. Dr. Weatherhead raised the question 'whether (missionaries) may not have laid too much stress on Bible teaching in the past to the exclusion of the practical side of education'.[27]

Beyond content, the use of vernacular as a means of instruction and the use of indigenous literature became contentious. The Commissioners had been scandalized by the fact that:

> … so little has as yet been done in this direction that there is not even a school history of South Africa dealing with the subject in any way suitable for natives or from the native point of view. The musical gift of many of the African native tribes is remarkable. As at Hampton and Tuskegee in the United States, vocal music may be made a great factor in this connection. Much good is done by the introduction of hymns in the vernacular as an alternative to such of the native songs as are low and indecent.[28]

David Stormont, an influential correspondent and Principal of the Blythswood Institution of the United Free Church of Scotland in South Africa, insisted on the use of English as a branch of study and means of instruction at all levels because it would help blacks in their relationship with whites, be necessary for commerce and civilized life, and would enable good government and public morality. Moreover an English education would be economical as students could acquire cheap literature from Europe. Dr. Stormont represented those who fought against vernacularization because: 'there is no native literature in Africa. Tradition is largely based on myths and vague ideas. Thus, there is practically no stock on which to graft Christian ideas.'[29]

The Nigerian representatives disputed this because enormous translation work had been a part of the missionary task in West Africa. Educationists recognized that grounding in the vernacular was essential for transmitting and preserving indigenous knowledge and for developing mental and communication skills. The irony was that many communities wanted to learn English. When the CMS insisted on using vernacular as a means of instruction village chiefs chose to patronize the Roman Catholics, who obliged by teaching in English. Pundits say this explains the pre-eminence of Roman Catholics in education and the civil service and professions. Many missionaries conceded that translating the Bible into indigenous languages was one thing, using the vernacular as a medium of instruction was another. The debate among the correspondents said more about the minds of missionaries and the temper of the era than the subject matter.

Conclusion: ecumenism as an antidote

The Commissioners were overwhelmed by the discordant voices emanating from the mission fields, impressed by the breadth of the continent and complexities of its problems, and filled with 'anxieties as to the present results of some of the educational work upon which men and women are unselfishly spending themselves in many regions of the African mission field'.[30] The Edinburgh Conference proffered few solutions. It did, however, seek to bring modern educational theories into missionary practice. In considering the immense challenges it suggested an ecumenical endeavor as antidote, urging missionaries to co-operate in building inspectorate divisions in the system, operating joint training of teachers so as to harmonize the instructional methods, intensifying the care of alumni, improving the education of the girl child, and especially emphasizing handwork, manual labour, sports, industrial skill acquisition and agricultural education.

The conference was significant in revealing the capacity for self-criticism within the Missionary enterprise. The Commissioners and the men-on–the–spot differed over the ideals, content and method of education. The Commissioners set out to revamp the entire educational apparatus of evangelism by indigenizing it. That was a tall order. Yet on closer inspection, the Commissioners did not go far enough in distinguishing *training* from *education.* Missionary pedagogy did little to impress upon the learner the importance of knowing self. It was directed more toward promoting social maintenance than liberating the divine within the human spirit. It fitted individuals into the colonial caste system. It did not encourage reflection and analysis so much as uniformity of ideas and monolithic universality of response. It privileged training over education. Training is skill based, whereas education is identity based. Training focuses on learning mechanics; education focuses on learning one's place in the world through an emphasis on one's history or high culture. Education nurtures the human being and expands the person's understanding of the self through the identification of a cultural-social location.

The historian must see these educational ideals in their historical context. What is the significance of reconstructing this era? It provides a cameo, an insight into the adventurous Western imagination at the turn of the century and the backdrop to what happened later. The revolution in education in the aftermath of the Conference then becomes significant; it was the African who initiated the modern face of Christianity.

Mary Slessor wrote soon after the Edinburgh Conference that the chiefs at Itu 'want their boys educated and they want someone to guide them safely through the new world in which they are being enclosed by the white man of whom they know so little and whom they fear'.[31] But this is not representative of the whole. Because of the inadequate lenses used in reading the people, and understanding their responses to the presence of the kingdom of God in their midst, the Edinburgh Conference did not see the real face of Christianity in Africa. By focusing on the settler communities of southern and central Africa, it missed the ferment in the Western theatre and the signals of transcendence all over the continent. It ignored the key players in the indigenizing movement, misrepresented Ethiopianism and paid scant attention to the rising tide of charismatic revivals. Finally, Western education became the biggest factor in the underdevelopment of Africa because of its power of eradication. Early missionary ideas survived until the decolonization period and explain the resultant hostility towards missionary control of education. The study of the past always has meaning for the present and future. It is always useful to know where the rain met us.

Endnotes

[1] World Missionary Conference, 1910, *Education in Relation to the Christianisation of National Life*, Report of Commission III, Edinburgh & London: Oliphant, Anderson and Ferrier; New York, Chicago and Toronto: Fleming H. Revell, 1910, p. 213.
[2] Henry Salt, in Adrian Hastings, *The Church in Africa, 1450–1950*, Oxford: Clarendon Press, 1994, p. 224.
[3] A. M. Mackay, in Brian Stanley, *The Bible and the Flag*, Leicester: Apollo Press, 1990, p. 128.
[4] Adrian Hastings, *The Church in Africa, 1450–1950*, Oxford: Clarendon Press, 1994, p. 193.
[5] Lamin Sanneh, *Abolitionists Abroad: American Blacks and the Making of Modern West Africa*, Cambridge, MA: Harvard University Press, 1999, p. 13.
[6] Reinhold Niebuhr, *The Kingdom of God in America*, Chicago & New York: Willet, Clark & Co., 1937, p. 179; see also John F. Piper, *Robert E. Speer: Prophet of the American Church*, Louisville, KY: Geneva Press, 2000.
[7] See Gordon M. Haliburton, *The Prophet Harris*, London: Oxford University Press, 1973.
[8] *Education in Relation to the Christianisation of National Life*, pp. vii–xx.
[9] *Education in Relation to the Christianisation of National Life*, p. 3.
[10] *Education in Relation to the Christianisation of National Life*, p. 4.
[11] *Education in Relation to the Christianisation of National Life*, p. 6.
[12] J.R. Mott, *The Decisive Hour of Christian Missions*, New York: Student Volunteer Movement for Foreign Missions, 1912, p. 114.
[13] See *Education in Relation to the Christianisation of National Life*, p. 240.
[14] *Education in Relation to the Christianisation of National Life*, p. 244.
[15] *Education in Relation to the Christianisation of National Life*, pp. 245, 257.
[16] Paulo Freire, *Pedagogy of the Oppressed*, New York: Continuum, 1970, p. 181.
[17] *Education in Relation to the Christianisation of National Life*, p. 247; cited in Roswith Gerloff, 'Introduction', Roswith Gerloff, ed., *Mission Is Crossing Frontiers: Essays in Honour of Bongani Mazibuko*, Pietermaritzburg: Cluster Publications, 2003, p. 14.
[18] *Education in Relation to the Christianisation of National Life*, p. 252.

[19] Ogbu U. Kalu, 'Ethiopianism in African Christianity', in Ogbu U. Kalu ed., *African Christianity: An African Story*, Pretoria: University of Pretoria Department of Church History, 2005, pp. 258–77.
[20] See E.A. Ayandele, *The Missionary Impact on Modern Nigeria, 1842–1914*, London: Longmans, 1966.
[21] Mott, *Decisive Hour,* p. 114.
[22] *Education in Relation to the Christianisation of National Life*, pp. 208–11.
[23] *Education in Relation to the Christianisation of National Life*, p. 168.
[24] Mott, *Decisive Hour*, p. 22.
[25] *Education in Relation to the Christianisation of National Life*, p. 175.
[26] *Education in Relation to the Christianisation of National Life*, p. 183.
[27] *Education in Relation to the Christianisation of National Life*, p. 197.
[28] *Education in Relation to the Christianisation of National Life*, p. 203.
[29] *Education in Relation to the Christianisation of National Life*, p. 203.
[30] *Education in Relation to the Christianisation of National Life*, p. 166.
[31] Mary Slessor, 'Letter from Miss Slessor', *The Missionary Record of the United Free Church of Scotland*, Vol. XI (1911), p. 169.

Missionary Education: An Ambiguous Legacy

M. P. Joseph

The World Missionary Conference of 1910 was significant in many ways. Apart from laying the foundation for an ecumenical understanding between churches and people, and promoting a rational approach to faith and its practices, it will be recalled for raising subaltern voices from the mission fields.[1] Those subaltern expressions made a deep impact, not only on theological discourse and mission practices, but also on the social and political formations of the people in the colonies. An enquiry into missionary practices is important for churches in their attempt to promote freedom and liberation among marginalized societies around the world.

This chapter is divided into three sections: a brief evaluation of the impact of missionary education; an attempt to discover if and why missionary education has failed; and challenges to mission in the present context.

1. The impact of missionary education

Among the various debates on the impact of missionary education, four may invite special iteration. These are the introduction of scientific rationality and the promotion of technology, the promotion of the concept of social equality, the possibility of a religious renaissance, and the seeds of a new ecclesiology.

Towards a new rationality

Though Western scientific rationality based on dialectical reasoning is a matter of contention among social scientists today, missionary education is remembered for its effort to introduce Western theory of knowledge to the people of the periphery. A rational approach to science fostered the growth of technology and the development of communication. Urbanization coupled with industrial production initiated new approaches in production and labour relations. These changes accelerated the growth of production and its related social formations. This enhanced the ability of societies to meet their needs in food production and health care as well as offering a variety of services that improved the quality of life.

An East Asia Council of Churches meeting in 1964 observed that productivity and industrialization are gifts from God and signs of God's providence; signs of the abundant life that Christ has promised.[2] Rational knowledge meant freedom. In an agrarian context where traditional knowledge promoted a fear of nature, the missionary attempt to offer scientific knowledge freed people from mysteries and dependence upon nature. This appropriation of knowledge as freedom, however, was at the cost of decoupling freedom from responsibility.

Promotion of the concept of social equality

The concept of individual freedom was an alien concept in a majority of colonized countries. Community relations, mediated through tribal and caste social formations, created social hierarchies based on the relative location of each member. Social harmony was dependent upon the adherence of the members of the community to the rules of hierarchy. The concept of individual freedom that missionary education introduced favoured social equality over social hierarchy.[3] Conceptually, the emphasis on social equality strengthened the ability of respective individuals in the community to engage in social contracts with others as equal partners.

In India, where the right to education was mediated by the caste system and its rigid rules, promotion of the universal right to education was a subversive act. Caste rules prohibited the lower caste people from acquiring knowledge, and for those who dared to attempt it, there was severe punishment. The rights of women were no different from the rights of the lower caste people. Education was primarily a religious subject and the strength of the ancient educational methods was its capacity to perceive all human knowledge within the ambit of a theological system. Religious control of knowledge prevented women and the lower caste people from receiving education. Missionary efforts to educate Dalits, women, tribal peoples and other marginalized communities demonstrated its potential to initiate a social revolution.

The development of a political and legal structure, corresponding to the changing relations of the colonized nations from agrarian into industrial social formations, was an immediate outcome of the idea of individual freedom. Individualism, introduced by Western education, provided a new understanding of the human person and ultimately led to a redefinition of social legislation. Individual freedom was an alien concept in traditional societies where rights and responsibilities were determined by the structural priorities of communities. The introduction of the concept of individual freedom and the relative development of a legal structure promoted a culture of democracy. Suggesting that democratic culture was unknown to tribal societies prior to the introduction of Western educational philosophy would be a grave mistake. Yet the right of equal participation based on an equal valuation of the contributions of individual members was accentuated by the concept of universal education.

Equally important is the emergence of nationalism. This too owes its spirit to the rationality offered by Western educational priorities.[4] The concept of freedom furthered the assertion of self-hood among natives and was eventually translated into nationalism. Moreover, the ideal of universal equality offered by English education also helped the emergence of nationalism.

Religious and cultural renaissance

Religious and cultural renaissance in the colonies was not something envisioned by the missionary movement. Yet these came about as an outcome of education. The concepts of individual freedom and democracy were not clearly articulated within traditional religious systems. Their introduction challenged these faith systems to redefine themselves. Religious concepts were subjected to critical enquiry informed by secular science and hermeneutical principles. The outcome was a radical reformation of the relationship between tradition and ethics. Gandhi, for example, asserted that 'no scriptural text could supersede his reason for life'.[5]

This was a time when social practices were legitimated by theology and scripture, and thus earned spiritual meaning. The best-known example is that of widow burning, which in India is commonly known as *Sati*. The word *Sati*, a feminine noun derived from the Sanskrit root *sat* or truth, denotes virtuous women who submitted themselves to be burned in the funeral pyre of their dead husband out of devotion and belief in attaining the spiritual realm of *Satimata* or goddess.[6]

Hindu reformers, led by Mohan Roy, realized that treating the practice as a criminal act punishable under law would not stop it. Missionaries, including Alexander Duff, urged the colonial administration to ban the practice. Roy responded that only a counter theological formulation would be effective. This was initiated with the aim of providing new meaning to the belief systems of the people. It led to a rapid reformation of traditional religions. *Sati* was only one of such practices. Thus religious traditions and cultures were affirmed. It is an oft-quoted statement from Gandhi that 'I do not want my house to be walled in on all sides and my windows to be stuffed. I want the cultures of all the lands to be blown about my house as freely as possible. But I refuse to be blown off my feet by any. I refuse to live in other people's houses as an interloper, a beggar or a slave'.[7]

The emergence of fundamentalism

Another effect of missionary education was the presentation of two mutually exclusive worlds: the Christian world and the non-Christian world.[8] While the Christian world represents the ultimate truth, missionary Christianity presumed that other religions conveyed vain, foolish and wicked conceptions. Alexander Duff's statement is a categorical expression of this attitude. 'These religions', he said, 'are spread out before us like a universe where all life dies and death lives.'[9] The Christian task therefore was to demolish this gigantic fabric of idolatry and superstition. Duff, John Wilson, William Miller and other educational missionaries made the objective of education to unseat the superstitious gods from the consciousness of the colonized people. Unseating the traditional religious systems from the mind of the natives was considered a faith imperative by missionaries, which they believed would prepare the ground for the acceptance of the gospel. The rejection of the other faith systems was considered a service of the gospel. The Tambaram Conference of the International Missionary Conference reiterated the need for creating a sense of confidence in one's own faith.[10] Mission discourse during that time held the view that the fundamental problem for the people was the lack of absolutes in their lives, and in the absence of absolutes, they surrendered to relativisms, which would sooner or later lead them to a fundamental and radical uncertainty of the meaning of life.[11] Therefore providing an absolute was a mandate for mission. Such an absolute, as neo-orthodoxy iterated, is present in the Christian Gospel alone, because it alone is the work of God.[12] Overconfidence in their faith as the only absolute truth prevented the educational missionaries from appreciating the importance of self-criticism and repentance. Aggressiveness replaced humility; humility was perceived as weakness. It is unfortunate that there was no serious expression of repentance or confession expressed in the Commission Reports regarding the massacre in Jallianwala Bagh, in which missionaries were accused of having direct involvement. It was common knowledge that the opium trade financed missionary educational activities. Yet the Commission Report maintained an indefensible silence on such crucial issues. Uncritical absolutism led to over-confidence and failure to appreciate the 'other'. This absence of self-criticism promoted the absolutizing of the Christian interpretation of the divine presence in history, locking it within the boundaries of a given human comprehension. It rejected as heresy any non-Christian encounter with the living reality of the Divine.

At most times the establishment of absolutes is coupled with political and social functions, including the creation of cultural hegemonies. Political history reminds us that the establishment of cultural hegemony precedes political and economic hegemonies. In his inaugural address at the 1928 Jerusalem conference of IMC, Julius Richter observed that the theological understanding of absolutes cohabited with a social construction of superiority, and therefore Christian missionaries were convinced of the superiority of their religion over all others.[13] Or, in other words, the theological construct of absolutes provided a legitimation for totalitarianism.

Totalitarian Christianity was sponsored by Western nations and nationalist elements in the colonized nations. The response of other traditions was a fundamentalist and equally totalitarian approach to religions. The report acknowledged this fact in its statement 'What concerns this conference is that the new political consciousness … is almost inevitably anti-British and pro-Indian or pro-Hindu, and in Ceylon pro-Buddhist. Twenty-five years ago Buddhism was offering only a passive resistance to missionary efforts. Today it is establishing schools, founding Young Men's Buddhist Associations, publishing tracts, holding open-air meetings, publishing newspapers…'.[14] Within twenty-five years, a passive faith system had been converted to a militant outfit. The Report further observed that the coupling of anti-British and anti-Christian feelings led to a determined defense of Hinduism and Buddhism.[15]

Towards a new ecclesiology

Providing a new social base for the churches in the colonies was the fourth contribution of missionary education. The Commission report indicated that the development of self-governing native churches was an objective of education. The priority given to equipping native leaders found justification in this aim.[16] The Christianization of national life and growth of native Churches was possible, the Commission report suggests, only through the development of native leadership. To achieve this goal educational missionaries made Christianity accessible to all people irrespective of their caste, class or gender. In India, for example, the ancient St. Thomas Church was an upper-caste establishment, following the same taboos and rituals as other upper-caste groups and thus ensuring their privileged place in the hierarchical social structure. Thus the concept of a Church as a communion of all, irrespective of differences in caste, class and gender, was absent in the ecclesiological understanding of the ancient Indian Church.

The emergence of schools in the villages to offer education to the Dalits had an enormous impact in the emergence of a new ecclesiology. Education enabled the Dalit community to break the occupational basis of caste. The lack of social mobility and the absence of freedom in occupation was one of the dominant features of caste structure. Rules regarding purity, and pollution constituted other impediments for lower caste people. Educational opportunities for Dalits addressed both these elements. Moreover, missionaries invited them to the table fellowship of the Church. The impact of this invitation to the feast of fellowship forced the Indian Church to rethink the concept of purity and pollution and appreciate the inclusiveness of the gospel message and thus to reconstruct the concept of Church.[17] Newer discourse in ethics and theology, along with an innovative approach to reading the Bible, was a direct outcome of these new understandings of the Church offered by the consciousness of equality of caste. Scripture, translated into the vernacular, provided a new and liberating meaning when it reached the poor and the marginalized.

An agency for liberation?

One of the proclaimed objectives of missionary education was to civilize the non-civilized people in the colonies. What is meant by civilization is the blossoming of people's potential to resolve human problems in peaceful and mature ways. The emerging political ethos, however, demonstrates that barbarianism is the political norm. Military solutions are sought for conflicts. The War *on* Terror has turned into a War *of* Terror. Violence is meted out not only against humans and communities, but also against nature.

2. Missionary education: a critical appraisal

Education as a means

A critical appraisal should start with the object of education. Ironically, the correspondence from missionaries to the members of the Commission suggests that the primary objective of missionary education was not to educate but to convert. As W.A. Stanton of the American Baptist Telegu Mission wrote: 'The real purpose of educational missionary work is not merely to educate … but win our pupils to Christ'.[18] Furthermore educational work provided a legitimation for imperialist rule. Introductory reports of the Commission report confessed that it considered education a means, either direct or indirect, to fulfill the 'great commission' in Matthew to make disciples of all nations and to baptize them.[19] This observation was in agreement with a majority of educational missionaries including Alexander Duff, William Miller, and John Wilson. They argued that the chief aim of education was the conversion of individual pupils. To satisfactorily achieve this goal, education was narrowed down to a simple logic; reveal the 'revealed truth'[20] and have the pupil accept it without question. An uncritical appropriation of 'given truth' was promoted at the expense of any search for truth.

One of the correspondents to the commission, an American Baptist, was explicit in explaining this goal. He argued that the real purpose is not to educate, but to present the truth. 'We are not commissioned to teach a philosophy to be discussed, but to present the truth that is to be accepted'.[21] Drafters of the Commission report observed that the ethos of this correspondent is reflected in the majority of letters that they received.[22]

Educational philosophy holds that imposing a given truth is contrary to the aims of education.[23] This does not mean, however, that there is no accepted knowledge in any given discipline or faith system. Rather, knowledge is to be found through critical enquiry; by raising defining questions and sometimes by rejecting approved hypotheses. While explaining the philosophical basis of *Gurukulam*, Rabindranath Tagore asserted that the rational enquiry of the critical mind is the basis for learning. That process transcends the boundaries of teacher and student; both together assume the role of seekers of truth.

Social functions of education as 'not to educate'

One may wonder why educational missionaries failed to appropriate the spirit of freedom of enquiry. It amounts to a denial of the people's rights to determine what is good for them. Educational activities have expanded the knowledge of good and evil, but the students were deprived of the right to determine what is good for themselves. Those who controlled the mechanism of learning, or those in power, decided what was normative. People were deprived of their ability to construct normatives in their lives. The political projects of modernity and globalization adopted the same logic. Those who have a stake in the prevailing economic and social life have determined the so-called good and have made this normative for others.

The attempt to narrow down education to a means of conversion assumes a political strategy for homogenizing the mind. Educational missionaries took pride in the report that during the great mutiny in India there were limited disturbances in the cities where Christian schools were established.[24] Educational missionaries justified these assumptions through professing faith as a unifying logic in the political sphere. They assumed that social coherence would be achieved by accepting one interpretation of the divine in history. The implication of this approach was the denial of rational inquiry as a methodology for education. Education was reduced to a political method for unifying social forces. Fundamentalist approaches to religion also share the same logic and transform religion into a political programme for social unity.

Gautama Buddha suggested another way. Buddha advised his disciple: 'Kalamas, it is proper that you have doubt, that you have perplexity, for a doubt has arisen in a matter which is doubtful. Do not be misled by reports, or traditions, or by the authority of religious texts.' For Buddha, plurality of interpretations denotes the strength of any given system, exemplifying its inherent creativity, and expressing the beauty of the created world. Attempts for radical homogenization only expressed the fear of missionaries and fundamentalists in addressing the challenges of plurality.

Sadly the persuasive imposition of an unquestionable truth, denying critical enquiry only produced domination. Critical questions, challenges to authority, and rejection of a given social order were considered immoral and therefore anathema. Loyalty to authority and given social order was presented as morally normative. Reason was co-opted for the maintenance of status quo. The danger of depriving education of its potential as a praxis for freedom and liberation was further diminished when missionaries developed the diffusion theory; a theory parallel to the trickle down theory of capitalist economics.

The diffusion theory: reproduction of domination

E. Stanley Jones, a long serving missionary in India, explained the logic of this theory.[25] He argued that winning the educated classes would lead to winning the lower classes. The logic that Jones and other missionaries proposed was simple: influence people who have influence in society. They found justification in concentrating educational activities among the rich and powerful sections of society. The emergence of Christian colleges to provide 'quality education' was an outcome of this logic. However as Jotibha Phule, the Marathi social reformer, lamented, this shift in educational priority helped to reinforce inequality and social domination.[26] Upper-caste students used education as a means to attain higher status in the social hierarchy. The diffusion theory also refused to accept the social agency of the poor for change. The missionary understanding of social agency was not different from neo-liberal economic perspectives, which place faith only in those who have capital. One of the reasons for using English as the medium of education was the political aim of unifying the emotions and ambitions of the colonized people. English education was introduced as a component of the prevailing political logic of imperialism. In his famous thesis Thomas Macaulay (1835) argued that English education would promote a cultural revolution that would make Indians loyal to the crown. Once the revolution was achieved, he wrote, 'The Indian people will cease to opt for and aim for independence. The native shall not rise against us and thus the energy will be fully and harmlessly employed in acquiring and defusing European knowledge and in naturalizing European institutions'.[27] The majority of educational missionaries were enthusiastic about the Macaulay doctrine and, for them, teaching the Bible and English language education were inseparable.[28] Language, however, is not just a medium of communication or a symbol of civility but an experience of reality. The language one speaks positions one in relation to the basic truth of life.[29] It also defines truth and thus directs social praxis. Language is the medium of one's own social reality. Therefore alienation from the social self was the inevitable result of imposing an alien language – English – by means of missionary education. Depriving people of their mother tongue resulted in their alienation from the truth of life, creating a structural inability to discover the fundamentals of their own reality.

An implication of this approach to education was evident in emerging nationalism. The English educated elite devalued the concept of nationalism to the level of a polemic against the colonial leadership.[30] There was no attempt at the construction of an alternate theory of governance by challenging the exploitative logic of colonialism. This was because of the alienation of the nationalist leaders from their social selves. Nationalism fell short of demanding total liberation for the Indian masses from the forces of domination. Polemical nationalism was satisfied with a narrow goal – replacing the personnel in the ruling structure. It is possible to argue that English education was one of the major reasons that the nationalist movement failed to address the aspirations of the Dalits, the poor and the marginalized.

Education as justification for colonial rule

The second objective of education was to provide justification for the colonial administration. One of the moral questions that missionaries sought to answer was 'what right did the Europeans have to occupy, dominate, and to manage the people of Asia, Africa, and the Americas?'[31] An occupying power needs an ideology to explain why it dominates the other. A multi-billion dollar hi-tech industry is in operation to construct lies to justify the occupation of Iraq and the murder of innocent women and children. The occupation of the other's land was a moral issue for the missionaries, and therefore they struggled to find legitimate answers to this disturbing question.

In seeking rational justification for education and occupation, missionaries presented two arguments, which later assumed the role of an official explanation by the churches and the colonial political leadership. Missionaries argued, first, that colonialism was providential, allowing people to encounter the saving grace of God. Imperial success was therefore integral to God's plan to bless the world. Secondly they argued that the practice of occupying other lands and educating their occupants was driven by a moral imperative to modernize primitive economies and to civilize barbarians.[32] This second explanation was widely shared and regarded as the major objective of colonial domination. To meet these objectives the educational missionaries employed Western science to uproot superstition from the native mind and to develop in them a scientific consciousness.

Alexander Duff recounts an incident. In a junior class he asked his students, 'What is rain?' A student immediately offered an answer, 'Rain comes from the trunk of the elephant god Indra.'[33] To defuse this faith reading of reality, educational missionaries found a materialistic interpretation of science indispensable. Science assumed the role of destroyer: to uproot given meanings, faith explanations, values, moral principles, worldviews, and practices. Science was not a reason to govern, but it became a means to govern.[34] Science was used because it destroyed the existing knowledge system. As a result, the knowledge system that people had preserved for centuries was destroyed. These traditional knowledge systems that had been preserved for generations were informed by ethics and morality and were underpinned by a faith explanation of the cosmological and social reality of life. Within this system science and knowledge, including agriculture, carpentry, mathematics, medical science, and erotic knowledge, were situated as an extension of theological knowledge. Negation of this system of knowledge created a vacuum for moral and ethical discourse in science. Educational missionaries expected that the void created by the destruction of the traditional knowledge could be filled by Christian morality and faith; what they called Christian civilization. However, this attempt failed. What emerged in its place was an unethical and materialistic approach to social and physical realities. Science was turned into an instrument of exploitation rather than an agent to liberate the poor and the marginalized from the forces of ignorance and exploitation.

Materialist science has become a major threat to nature and the environment because new techniques designed to alter or manipulate the natural world are its primary features. Such an approach to science devalued nature as a 'thing' and suggested that distance from nature is a measure of progress, or a mark of civilization.

Education for de-earthization

Education as a form of de-earthization promoted the alienation of people from the earth. The earth is an object of study and not a subjective agency with which to be identified. It is ironic that at the time churches in the Western hemisphere were critical of a materialistic interpretation of science and social reality. Echoes of those critical warnings were heard in subsequent mission conferences. In 1910, Reverend Sloan Coffin reminded the Edinburgh conference that modern civilization probably was the greatest hindrance to the Christian gospel.[35] Later, Rufus Jones reiterated the same concern at the Jerusalem meeting of the IMC.[36] Educational missionaries, however, failed to appreciate the depth of Coffin's observation.

3. Mission and education: contemporary challenges

Two compelling realities of our time are globalization and fundamentalism, and mission education had a significant role in the development of both. Unfortunately these realities continue to shape and direct mission priorities and practices.

Rejection of un-god

Globalization is not just a prescription for a mode of production; it is a way of organizing collective life. It has assumed the role of a religion with well-articulated theologies, dogmas, rituals, priesthood, missionaries, cathedrals, and of course with its own concept of the divine. It also has a concept of hell. The heathens and sinners who dare to question the revealed truth of the divine market are condemned to life in eternal hell.

The doctrine has three pillars: market as the social principle; growth and modernity as normative culture; and the dictatorship of money.

The neo-liberal ideology that governs the present stage of globalization has made the market the foundation for social and community formation. The market assumes the exclusive right for mediation between individuals, communities, and nations – meaning that the market has become the functioning ecclesia of the present time.[37] This new ecclesia also comes with a soteriology, and an empirical explanation of utopia. In the market, however, all realities are transformed into commodities. If not commodities, realities hold no value. Therefore, educational institutions have restructured themselves as marketplaces where the buying and selling of knowledge and skills takes place. Knowledge has to be reshaped on a regular basis to attract prospective buyers. As the competition in the educational market intensifies, so does the advertising of its products. Teachers are converted into vendors selling specialized commodities. It is this perversion of education that missionary education needs to combat today. Unfortunately, Church schools around the world are embedded in market principals and are in a vanguard position for selling skills and knowledge and establishing the market as the governing norm of life.

The market in recent years has changed into virtual markets where value is added through virtual realities. In such subordination the function of wealth and resources are detached from the need to sustain life. Wealth has freed itself from having to be committed to a purpose and is beyond all social determinations. The result is the radical change to the status of capital in society. While in the capitalist system commodities assume the role of social subjects, in the globalized world 'capital' has become an ontological category and the foundation for all being.

In the religious level, the logic of the market has debased the memory of the divine in order to enthrone Money, with a capital M, as the presiding deity of individuals and nations. And that is the challenge new mission movements must encounter. In order to confront capital in the form of un-god, mission initiatives should attempt to build new solidarities between religions and create space for various faith systems to congregate.

Problem of 'otherness'

The second challenge of our time is fundamentalism. The 'other' has turned into a problem and furthermore, the ability to celebrate the presence of the other is rejected as an archaic idea. Educational missionaries were no exception in endorsing this view. They did not consider the 'other' because they perceived themselves as the norm. There is no legitimate space for the other to exist as 'other'. Missionary movements created a conscious ignorance of the 'other'. In recent political moralities 'otherness' has become a complex metaphor. The other is painted in dreadful colours. The social symbolization of the 'other' is used as an excuse to invade and conquer the space of the 'other'. 'Otherness' therefore is addressed through the language of war and the death of the 'other' is celebrated as a victory of the civilized world. The Biblical imperative, however, views the death of the 'other' as the death of God. This is because the face of the 'other' is the location where God revealed himself/herself in history. To counter the prevailing attitude to otherness mission should become a search for justice and healing by reestablishing the presence of God in community.

Unfortunately, faith has converted itself into a political statement and in that process religions are transformed into politics: political Christianity, political Islam, political Judaism, political Hinduism, and so on. The Iraq war has illustrated this phenomenon. In recent years religions have allowed abuse in the name of their deity and allowed their scripture to destroy innocent lives – victims of Christian texts.

Reading the mission document suggests that an imperative for mission is to decide whether we are for the Jesus of the Gospels or the Christ of Constantine. The Christ of Constantine is the presiding deity of all monarchic and imperialist rulers. This question is pertinent because the majority of the world's people presently consider the so-called Christian nations to be the greatest threat to world peace. This is not an ideological or political statement informed by any prejudice; it is informed by the concern to re-appropriate the fundamentals of faith. Have we failed to present 'the Prince of Peace'? There may be specious arguments claiming that the sword is a promise of Jesus and therefore a military response to disorder is justifiable. But the sword that Jesus promises is a sword for creating justice, equality, and peace. The sword of the so-called Christian nations is the sword of the market, to ensure access to oil and to provide protection for commodities and transnational capital, to defend deified money or the un-god of the market.

Have we failed to identify the Jesus of the Gospels? The major burden of Alexander Duff was the explicit idolatry he found in other religions.[38] This concern should lead us to identify a more deep-rooted and more tenacious idolatry buried in the triumphalist and invading Christianity that was carried around as an answer for all problems. Theological methodologies suggest that in order to reestablish faith in the Creator God, and to become a witness to the source of life, identification and naming of death-dealing idolatries is imperative. The dominant idolatries of the present time include patriotism, the concept of national security and so-called civilized values. Daring to reject the Christ of imperialism is the challenge of faith. This will also lead to recognizing the spirit of the divine moving through the ghettos with the outcasts, the poor, the women, the deprived, and others who are being cast out of the centers of power. This identification is one of the major mandates for mission today.

Endnotes

[1] V. S. Azariah, 'The Problem of Co-operation between Foreign and Native Workers', in World Missionary Conference, 1910, *The History and Records of the Conference*, Edinburgh & London: Oliphant, Anderson & Ferrier; New York, Chicago and Toronto: Fleming H. Revell, 1910, pp. 306–15.

[2] *Christian Community Within Human Community,* Bangkok: East Asia Council of Churches, 1964.

[3] M. M. Thomas, *The Christian Response to the Asian Revolution,* London: SCM Press, 1966, p. 39.

[4] Thomas, *The Christian Response to the Asian Revolution*, pp. 57–65.

[5] Gandhi, in M. S. N. Menon, 'Time to Bridle Religious Impulses', *Tribune,* 7 January 2002.

[6] M. P. Joseph, 'Suttee: A Critique from an Ethical Perspective', *The Sathri Journal* 1 (1993), pp. 65–95.

[7] Gandhi, *Young India,* Vol. 1 (June 1921), p. 170.

[8] See the analysis of Kosuke Koyama, above pp. 41ff.

[9] Alexander Duff, 'Speech at Free Church of Scotland General Assembly, 1855', in T. V. Philip, *Edinburgh to Salvador: Twentieth Century Ecumenical Missiology,* Delhi: CSS & ISPCK, 1999, p. 170.

[10] Michael Kinnamon and Brian Cope, eds., *The Ecumenical Movement: An Anthology of Key Texts and Voices,* Geneva: WCC Publications, 1997, p. 332.

[11] Hendrik Kraemer, *The Christian Message in a Non-Christian World,* London: The Edinburgh House Press, 1938, pp. 6–7.

[12] Kraemer, *The Christian Message in a Non-Christian World*, p. 7.

[13] Julius Richter, in T. V. Philip, *Edinburgh to Salvador: Twentieth Century Ecumenical Missiology,* Delhi: CSS & ISPCK, 1999, p. 180.

[14] World Missionary Conference, 1910, *Education in Relation to the Christianisation of National Life*, Report of Commission III, Edinburgh & London: Oliphant, Anderson & Ferrier; New York, Chicago and Toronto: Fleming H. Revell, 1910, p. 31.

[15] *Education in Relation to the Christianisation of National Life*, p. 31.
[16] *Education in Relation to the Christianisation of National Life*, pp. 52–5.
[17] See Eira M. Dalton, *Fellow Workers With God*, Kottayam: CMS Press, 1966.
[18] *Education in Relation to the Christianisation of National Life*, p. 17.
[19] The report reads, 'Go ye therefore and make disciples of all the nations.... We of this commission are concerned with education considered only as a means, direct or indirect, towards this end.' *Education in Relation to the Christianisation of National Life*, p. 16.
[20] *Education in Relation to the Christianisation of National Life*, p. 17.
[21] W. A. Stanton, 'Letter from Rev. W.A. Stanton, of the American Baptist Telugu Mission to the Commission', in *Education in Relation to the Christianisation of National Life*, p. 17.
[22] *Education in Relation to the Christianisation*, p. 17, records, 'Quotation to the same effects might be multiplied from the papers before us.'
[23] John J. Mearsheimer, 'The Aim of Education', Address delivered at Chicago University on 23 October 1997, <www.ditext.com/mearsheimer/aimsofeducation.html>, accessed13 April 2004.
[24] At a meeting held in Edinburgh in 1859, a letter was read from the Marquis of Tweeddale, the former Governor of Madras. It reads, 'It should be remembered that much of the excitement about India had to do with the Mutiny ... Madras, the most Christianised part of India , had remained quiet during the Mutiny ...'. Marquis of Tweedale, in J. C. Ingleby, *Missionaries, Education and India: Issues in Protestant Missionary Education in the Long Nineteenth Century*, Delhi: ISPCK, 2000, pp. 158–9.
[25] J. C. Ingleby, *Missionaries, Education and India: Issues in Protestant Missionary Education in the Long Nineteenth Century*, Delhi: ISPCK, 2000, p. 247.
[26] Ingleby, *Missionaries, Education and India*, p. 276.
[27] Thomas Babington Macaulay, in Jacob S. Dharmaraj, *Colonialism and Christian Mission: Postcolonial Reflections*, Delhi: ISPCK, 1999, p. 69
[28] *Education in Relation to the Christianisation of National Life*, p. 61.
[29] See Aloysius Pieris, 'Towards an Asian Theology of Liberation', in Virginia Fabella, ed., *Asia's Struggle for Full Humanity*, New York: Orbis, 1980, p. 77.
[30] See Sumit Sarkar, *Modern India: 1885–1947*, Delhi: Macmillan, 2000.
[31] Enrique Dussel *Beyond Philosophy: Ethics, History, Marxism and Liberation Theology*, New York: Ronman & Littlefield Publishers, 2003, pp. 53–81.
[32] William Wilberforce said that the Indian natives were barbarous and low in the scale of European civilization. Hence they should be civilized and converted. William Wilberforce, *Hansard* 26, First Series (22 June 1813), p.164, William Wilberforce, in Jacob S. Dharmaraj, *Colonialism and Christian Mission: Postcolonial Reflections*, Delhi: ISPCK, 1999, p. 33.
[33] Alexander Duff, in Sanjay Seth, 'Which Good Book? Missionary Education and Conversion in Colonial India', *Semeia* 88 (2002), pp. 120, 113–28.
[34] Ashis Nandy, 'Introduction: Science as a Reason of State', in Ashis Nandy, ed., *Science, Hegemony and Violence*, New Delhi: OUP, 1990, pp. 1–23.
[35] During the address to the 1910 meeting H. S. Coffin said, 'Modern civilization is probably the greatest hindrance to-day to the proclamation of the Christian Gospel.' H. S. Coffin, in World Missionary Conference, 1910, *The History and Records of the Conference*, Edinburgh & London: Oliphant, Anderson & Ferrier; New York, Chicago and Toronto: Fleming H. Revell, 1910, p.166.
[36] Rufus M. Jones 'Secular Civilization and the Christian Task', *Report of the Jerusalem Meeting of the International Missionary Council 1928*, vol. 1, London: Oxford University Press, 1928, pp. 284–338.
[37] See M. Douglas Meeks, *God the Economist*, Minneapolis: Fortress Press, 1989.

[38] In a 1858 issue of the *Wesleyan Methodist Magazine* Duff gave the rationale. He wrote, 'The most serious controversy that ever rose between God and man is represented in the system of idolatry. In every idol we see God's rival.' Alexander Duff, in Jacob S. Dharmaraj, *Colonialism and Christian Mission: Postcolonial Reflections*, Delhi: ISPCK, 1999, p. 63.

Commission Four

The Missionary Message in relation to the Non-Christian Religions

Commission Four
'The Missionary Message in Relation to the Non-Christian Religions'

The Commission in Summary

Commission Four stated its aim as being 'to study the problems involved in the presentation of Christianity to the minds of the non-Christian peoples'.[1] It was chaired by two Presbyterians: Rev. Professor David Cairns of Aberdeen served as convener, and Rev. Dr Robert Speer of the Presbyterian Church in the USA as the vice-chair. Cairns was a leading Scottish theologian. He had lost faith while studying divinity in Edinburgh, retrieved it through a sojourn in Germany and the poetry of William Wordsworth, was ordained a minister of the United Presbyterian Church, and taught a liberal theology with a strong commitment to overseas mission. Speer, if less a theologian, was a distinguished missions administrator, both in the PC(USA) and later the International Missionary Council that continued the work of the Edinburgh 1910 Conference. Their 18-person Commission included a cluster of professors and mission secretaries from the UK (7), the US (4), Germany (4), Holland (1) and Ireland (1). With a single exception they were male, Caucasian to a person, Protestant/Evangelical by confession, and mostly ordained clergy.

In preparing their Report the Commissioners drew on the written submissions of 125 missionaries 'in the field'. Each of these responded to an eleven-point questionnaire that inquired into their assessments of the moral, intellectual, and social differences, and points of contact, between Christianity and other religions, as these had bearing on the missionary communication of the Gospel. The 280-page Report comprised a summary of the responses. It was divided into chapters that dealt with the 'Animistic Religions' of the Bantu peoples of Africa and the tribal peoples of India and the Pacific; the Chinese Religions – Confucianism, Buddhism and Taoism; the religions of Japan – Shinto, and more Confucianism and Buddhism; Islam; Hinduism; and a final excursus on the Baha'i faith. Embracing a wide range of missionary opinion, the report is a rich deposit of Protestant Christian thinking about other religions in the first decade of the twentieth century.

Introducing the Commission's report to the Conference plenary, Professor Cairns reflected on the theological challenge that this mass of missionary correspondence represented. He asked,

> Does the evidence not disclose that we are face to face today with a new and formidable situation which is too great for our traditional thoughts about God? … Something very vast, something very formidable, something very full of wonder and promise is there, if we have the eyes to see it …. But inevitably the question

> arises, Whether the Church has within itself the forces to meet this great emergency? Is it equal to the providential calling? … Are we ready for it? Do we not need the broadening and deepening of all our conceptions of the Living God, the deepening and liberating of all our thoughts of what He has done for us in Christ, of what by His Providence and His Spirit He is ready to do for us today?[2]

The force with which Cairns pressed these questions reflects the inquiring nature of his own theology, and of his leadership of the Commission, and led him to affirm: 'For us this can only mean a new discovery of God in Christ.'[3]

The Report was fully debated in the Conference plenary, and in published form includes verbatim transcripts of some of the speeches from the floor. A broad consensus emerged that Robert Speer summarized in his concluding remarks in four points.

Firstly, Speer emphasised that 'we are all agreed that Christianity is the final and absolute religion'[4] But his point was less dogmatic than dialectic. 'Just because we hold so firmly to the finality and the absoluteness of the Christian faith, we dare go further than any other religion dare go, in laying down our goods for comparison with any other goods in the world.'[5] Confidence in the Gospel's truth, he argued, should be mirrored in a missionary confidence to explore the faith of other religions, secure in the principle that 'it is not what truth a man holds, but what truth holds the man that matters'.[6]

This brought Speer to his second point: 'The question before us is not whether we believe that Christianity is the final and absolute religion, but how we are going to get the world to believe it.'[7] The missionary responsibility is not primarily that of proving, but communicating the Gospel's truth. Rebutting the criticism that the Commission considered only the highest ideals of other religions, at the expense of criticising their less estimable aspects, he emphasized that '… exactly as we would wish ourselves to be approached, we must go to the men [that we wish to win to Christ] with the message by which we trust that they may be won'.[8]

Speer's third point was a further elaboration of the first: while Christianity is the true faith, 'no one believes we have the whole Christian truth'.[9] To put it another way: 'How is it possible for us, in a small fragment of the long corporate experience of humanity, to claim that we have gathered all the truth of the inexhaustible religion into our own personal comprehension and experience?'[10] The challenge of communicating the Gospel to the highest ideals of other religions – to the 'minds' of their best representatives – brings the missionary to a deeper understanding of the truth of Christian faith itself: 'We discover … truths in Christianity which we had not discerned before, or truths in a glory, a magnitude, that we had not previously imagined'.[11] Speer discerned a providential role in other religions for the missionary communication of the Gospel: 'As we bring our faith over against them, we shall not bring back into our own faith what was not in our own faith before, but we shall discern what we had not discovered was there before.'[12] He thus concluded the Report as follows: 'Our appeal has been not that we should seek in the non-Christian religions for truths that are not in Christianity, but that we should seek in Christ the truth which we have not yet known.'[13] Speer's last point draws out the significance of the Report for the home churches: 'We need an immense deepening and quickening of Christian life at home.'[14] While he did not elaborate this point, he anticipated the findings of the Commissions on the Home Church and Missionary Preparation.

The key principle in the Report's theological approach to non-Christian religions was the theology of the Word/*Logos*. As some of the Church Fathers likened the divine *Logos* to a 'schoolmaster' (*paidagogos*: Galatians 3:24–25) leading pagans to Christ, so the Commissioners discerned positive values in non-Christian religions. In some sense these values were deemed to prepare their devotees for the Gospel. Confucianism, the Report suggests, may be seen as a divine preparation of the Chinese for Christianity, as the Decalogue furnished a divine preparation for the Jews.[15] Hinduism may be regarded as a means being used by the Divine Wisdom to lead people to see their need of the truth, while its truths anticipate and provide a step toward the realisation of the higher truth revealed by and in Christ.' The Commissioners were persuaded by J.N. Farquhar's argument that: 'Christ's own attitude to Judaism ought to be our attitude to other faiths, even if the gap be far greater and the historical connection absent.'[16] Although the term 'fulfilment theology' was nowhere used in the Report, Jesus' words in Matthew 5:17 are frequently cited: 'Do not think that I have come to abolish the Law and the Prophets; I have not come to abolish them but to fulfil them.' Analogically, the Report suggested that Christ has not come to destroy Hinduism but to transfigure it.' But the Christological focus remained clear throughout the Report: 'One massive conviction animates the whole evidence that Jesus Christ fulfils and supercedes all other religions, and that the day is approaching when to Him every knee shall bow and every tongue confess that He is Lord to the glory of God the Father.'[17]

One of the architects of fulfilment theology, the late-nineteenth-century English missionary in India, Thomas Slater, is quoted more extensively than any other missionary in the sections of the Report dealing with Hinduism. 'The Gospel of Christ,' he wrote, 'enlightens the conscience (of Hinduism) to its great need, and is a message of salvation' that 'reveals the hidden craving of the human heart to possess a humanised God, which can only be satisfied in Christ.'[18] In terms of missionary method, such human yearning provides a starting point to lead the people 'up' to Christ's revelation. Such an approach calls for missionaries characterized by intellectual keenness, spiritual power, and a sympathy that can recognize and appreciate the view point of the other.'

The Scottish missionary in India, John Nicol Farquhar, who – unlike Slater – was present in Edinburgh 1910, went on to popularize 'fulfilment theology' in his classic work that presented the Gospel as *The Crown of Hinduism* (1913).[19] It remained the dominant missionary theology of other religions for the next quarter century until it was challenged, and largely replaced, by the 'discontinuity theology' of Hendrik Kraemer's 'Biblical realism' at the 1938 World Missionary Conference at Tambaram, India.[20]

Endnotes

[1] World Missionary Conference, 1910, *The Missionary Message in Relation to Non-Christian Religions*, Report of Commission IV, Edinburgh & London: Oliphant, Anderson & Ferrier; New York, Chicago and Toronto: Fleming H. Revell, 1910,
[2] *The Missionary Message in Relation to Non-Christian Religions*, p. 294.
[3] *The Missionary Message in Relation to Non-Christian Religions*, p. 294.
[4] *The Missionary Message in Relation to Non-Christian Religions*, p. 324.
[5] *The Missionary Message in Relation to Non-Christian Religions*, p. 324.
[6] *The Missionary Message in Relation to Non-Christian Religions*, p. 324.
[7] *The Missionary Message in Relation to Non-Christian Religions*, p. 324.
[8] *The Missionary Message in Relation to Non-Christian Religions*, p. 325.
[9] *The Missionary Message in Relation to Non-Christian Religions*, p. 325.
[10] *The Missionary Message in Relation to Non-Christian Religions*, p. 325.
[11] *The Missionary Message in Relation to Non-Christian Religions*, p. 325.
[12] *The Missionary Message in Relation to Non-Christian Religions*, p. 325.
[13] *The Missionary Message in Relation to Non-Christian Religions*, p. 326.
[14] *The Missionary Message in Relation to Non-Christian Religions*, p. 326.
[15] See *The Missionary Message in Relation to Non-Christian Religions*, p. 56.
[16] *The Missionary Message in Relation to Non-Christian Religions*, p. 173.
[17] *The Missionary Message in Relation to Non-Christian Religions*, p. 268.
[18] Thomas Slater, cit., *The Missionary Message in Relation to Non-Christian Religions*, p. 163.
[19] J.N. Farquhar, *The Crown of Hinduism*, Oxford: Oxford University Press, 1913.
[20] See Hendrik Kraemer, *The Christian Message in a Non-Christian World*, London: Edinburgh House Press, 1938.

Adventures in Christian-Muslim Encounters Since 1910

Guli E. Francis-Dehqani

The Edinburgh 1910 World Missionary Conference has been hailed as the most significant missionary event of the twentieth century. Delegates, participants and observers were acutely aware they were involved in something momentous. It was a *working* conference, for exploring theological and practical aspects of missionary work.[1] A large number of views were shared, through questionnaires sent to selected missionaries prior to conference[2] and in discussion sessions at conference. Amongst the topics covered by the Commission papers, it was generally accepted that the most remarkable was that of Commission Four, 'The Missionary Message in Relation to the Non-Christian Religions'.[3] This marked the first attempt to collect data on world religions from so wide a field, and to analyse missionary attitudes towards these religions from a Christian, or rather evangelical, perspective.

The first part of this chapter describes and analyses the report. The second part of the chapter considers the legacy of Commission Four, and how attitudes have developed both with regard to orientalist assumptions about East-West relations and interfaith concerns. Attention will be focused throughout on matters relating to the relationship between Christianity and Islam.

Part I: A Description and Analysis of Commission Four

The Report of the Commission

The report of Commission Four, and the ensuing discussion, formed a bridge between the two halves of the conference. The first three papers dealt with the people and religions amongst whom the missionaries worked, whilst the last four were concerned with the missionary Societies that had oversight of the work. Between these sat Commission Four which, from its significant position, presented views arising from missionary experience and reflected on how these might impact on churches at home.

In response to the questionnaire, which included 11 questions, an unprecedented 200 answers were received from the field, many of considerable length and importance.[4] Themes included the perceived religious value of other faiths; moral, social and intellectual hindrances in the way of conversion to Christianity; conversely, any points of contact with Christianity; attitudes to be adopted by Christians towards other religions; and the influence of contact with other religions on the missionary's faith.[5] Results were examined and evaluated by a committee, chaired by Professor David Cairns. In addition to an introduction and conclusion, the report was divided into five sections based on religions amongst whom the responding missionaries worked. These were the Animistic religions, Chinese, and Japanese religions, Islam and Hinduism.

The conference was an enormous organizational success. But the reason why we still look back at the conference today is because it represents a significant body of information based on grass roots experience and thoughtful theological reflection – all at a critical time in the history of missions, the British Empire and Western civilization.

Missionaries were among the earliest Westerners to have sustained contact with people of other faiths. At a time when East and West were still little known to one another they had unprecedented levels of contact with indigenous populations. They formed friendships and developed relationships, sometimes lasting many years. Among the most reliable social commentators, they were influential in providing the West with a more authentic account of a hitherto unknown and exotic East. For these reasons alone the report of Commission Four may be regarded as groundbreaking and deserves to be taken seriously.

Others have gone further, arguing that at a time when inter-religious understanding had barely begun, Edinburgh represented the laying of foundations for a more open, sympathetic attitude – sowing the seeds for a positive theology of religions. Kenneth Cracknell, for example, in *Justice, Courtesy and Love* claims that despite mistakes and a lack of consensus, the dialogical approach to other religions, usually considered an invention of the 1970s, are not a modern phenomenon, but existed in embryonic form as early as 1910.[6] Negative approaches regarding other religions as distortions or imperfect responses to Christianity were present, but Cracknell says these were in a minority.[7]

The special case of Islam

Cracknell's case is based largely on an undermining of 'the Islamic factor'. His thesis is damaged by the virtual silence, for the first two hundred pages of his book, on attitudes towards Islam. The positive trend he discovered through examining the questionnaires was not so apparent in Muslim contexts. There are exceptions, notably the views of William Shedd, an American Presbyterian in Persia, and Anna Smith of the Church of England Zenana Missionary Society in Bangalore. Cracknell himself admits that Smith was unusual in acknowledging truths in Islam from which Christians could learn, even discerning the presence of the Holy Spirit in the Muslim Community and faith tradition.[8] And Anna Smith, whose responses were remarkably positive, like most of the few *women* respondents, remained unquoted in the report. Despite these exceptions, both in the questionnaires and final report, the most negative views are from missionaries working among Muslims.[9] They represent a minority opinion, yet their significance cannot be minimized. Of the respondents only a small proportion were from Muslim lands. Therefore it is hardly surprising their views are in a minority. Only twenty were in Muslim countries and a further fifty in regions where Islam existed, though their work was chiefly among other religions. Had more responses come from Islamic areas, the negative views might well have increased in proportion.

Just when one assumes that Cracknell has ignored the significance of Islam, he presents a section entitled 'The special case of Islam'.[10] In it he outlines why the positive trends in evolving missionary thought did not impact upon those in Muslim lands. Most crucially, Islam had not appeared before Christianity and, as a later revelation, knowingly rejected Christian truths, claiming a higher place for Mohammad than Jesus. It could not therefore be regarded as a nascent tradition with potential for fulfillment through Christian transformation.

The Church Missionary Society (CMS) in Persia was represented at Edinburgh by two senior missionaries, Walter Rice and William St. Clair Tisdall. Not only are their questionnaires typical of other missionaries in Muslim lands, but Cracknell considers them amongst the most emphatic in calling for Islam's displacement.[11] Tisdall was certainly known as a fierce critic and author on Islamic matters.[12] His uncompromising and dogmatic attitude underpinned a wholly negative understanding of the essence of Islam. He maintained that the missionary, whilst recognising 'the truths that he [*sic*] finds hidden and buried under masses of error', still 'endeavours to cleanse the jewel from the mire into which it has fallen'.[13] Yet despite Tisdall's impassioned questionnaire and acclaim as a writer, he was noticeably under-used by Commission Four, whose report included a surprisingly positive slant on Islam for which his insights were presumably unhelpful. Maybe it was the Commission's eagerness to be as generous as possible that resulted in the section on Islam being somewhat shorter than those allocated to each of the other religions.[14] This was despite the prevalent view that Islam represented 'Eastern theism [at] its mightiest', and was of 'greater intrinsic interest' because of its greater 'religious and philosophical importance'.[15]

In the report, sections dealing with points of contact between Christianity and other religions provided a platform for positive comment. In the case of Islam, however, similarities were seen as a deformation of earlier Christian ideals, thus becoming 'a hindrance to, rather than a preparation for, the acceptance of Christianity'.[16] Sharing a missionary identity and a history of antagonism and misunderstanding, according to the report, of all the religions 'Islam offers the most bitter opposition to, and provokes the most severe condemnation of, Christian missionaries.'[17] Islam, which had either supplanted or subjected Christianity, issued the most direct challenge to the missionaries. It provided the greatest source of anxiety for strategic evangelical aspirations, breeding a Christian defensiveness. In words from the report, 'The Christian missionary to Islam must not only commend, but also defend his Gospel.'[18]

Evangelicalism, orientalism and missionary confidence

The conference took place at the height of the British Empire. A pre First World War confidence still sustained British culture, influencing the whole of western civilization and permeating the mood of evangelical Christianity.[19] The phrase 'the evangelization of the world in this generation' originating in America, was widely used in missionary circles.[20] Americans were ardent in their zeal. Continental Europeans displayed more caution. According to David Bosch, the German theologian and missiologist Martin Kähler had reservations about aspects of the conference. In particular, Kähler felt that under the chairmanship of the American John Mott the conference was 'structured largely on guidelines provided by North American assumptions'.[21] At any rate, it was a spirit of optimism and confidence that prevailed at Edinburgh, representing the zenith of missionary enthusiasm and pragmatism.

The evangelicalism that sustained the spirit of Edinburgh was based on a tradition of social action rooted in an individualistic spirituality dependant on personal salvation. Conversion was regarded as the solution for social problems. This provided the theory of 'pure evangelism' that under girded all missionary activities. In reality the theory was tempered. Experience showed the need for a more practical application of Christianity through reliance on medical and educational work, as well as the building of relationships. Nevertheless, the theory of pure evangelism remained in place, informing missionary language and justifying missionary efforts.[22] Temple Gairdner, for example, in his account of the conference, wrote: 'the purely *theological* parts of Christianity are at once the most effective, the most easily grasped, and the most quickly fruitful'.[23] So whilst the nature of missionary work was shifting to incorporate a more complex understanding of mission, a new theological language was not yet in place to express the changing experience. Missionaries still relied on old familiar linguistic structures provided by a particular evangelical vocabulary that promoted Christian superiority and called for repentance and conversion as the path to social improvement.

Alongside this *religious* theme ran a central concept underlying the British Empire, that the transfer of values and ideas was always from West to East. Again, in practice, the reality was often more flexible. Missionaries and other westerners found the current could run two ways as their own outlook and experience shifted. But the reality did not dislodge the philosophy of western superiority that upheld the notion of Empire. According to Edward Said these opposites coexisted surprisingly easily as generally accepted views about Islam were held alongside more personal experiences of it.[24] Said argues for a distinction between the 'particular' on one hand – whereby westerners could relate warmly to individual Muslims – and the 'general' on the other – whereby condemnation of Islam continued, often through unqualified generalizations based on theological and social suppositions. So, whilst experience was slowly changing, earlier theories and language remained embedded.

Such confidence inevitably bred a patronising tone both in terms of religious superiority and the critique of social conditions. Missionaries easily found fault with their adopted societies and in many cases the suffering and problems they encountered justified negative commentary. However, where these societies were Islamic, Commission Four was particularly quick to draw a correlation between religion and social or moral problems. To be sure, the report does acknowledge that:

> We must in fairness distinguish between moral defects which are due to 'the natural corruption of the human heart' and those which can be directly traced to the doctrines or practices presented in the Koran and by tradition. As regards the first class of moral offences we must not hold Islam itself directly responsible for them, but we are, nevertheless, entitled to ask the question whether the religion offers ... such restraints on sin .. as will effectively counteract ... natural sinful tendencies.[25]

The report then goes on to talk of widespread 'divorce between morality and religion' in Islam, of 'total lack of appreciation of the nature of sin', and of the moral example of Mohammad as being 'no inspiration to holiness'.[26] This stance was further exacerbated by a lack of a self-critical spirit within evangelical Christianity. By stark contrast, the evils of western Christendom or Victorian Britain are blamed not on religion but only on 'nominal Christians'.[27]

The constraints of evangelical and imperial ideologies heightened by lack of Christian self-criticism heavily influenced the missionary agenda in 1910. Analysis of the Muslim situation in Commission Four was based on an understanding of the natural link between a false religion and its resulting social degradation. By extension, embracing Christianity was the solution and the means of breaking the destructive cycle. In an uncomplicated way the WMC accentuated the belief that conversion would establish necessary theological structures from which would flow alleviation of Islam's social problems. This was based on fundamentalist and orientalist tenets. Evangelicalism promoted the salvation of individuals as the basis of social improvement; orientalism gave credence to the notion that missionaries were requisite catalysts in bringing about the transformation. By proclaiming the gospel message they would guide people from darkness to light, thereby passing on to the East, in the words of John Mott, the 'marvelous orderings of Providence' from which the West had benefited during the nineteenth century.[28]

The contradictions of Edinburgh 1910

Undoubtedly, the overall mood of Edinburgh *was* refreshingly positive, certainly compared with previous missionary conferences. There was a desire to find new and better ways of contact with other religions. Many wrote warmly about personal encounters and friendships, revealing the desire for better relationships and greater understanding. Whilst employing a confidently expectant tone, the general working principle of the conference was of courtesy towards others, and recognition of the need to move forward carefully. There was a desire to see the best in others but always alongside the belief that Christianity is 'the absolute best of all'.[29] Indeed, according to the report, it was this very confidence that allowed generosity to be shown.[30] The motivation for better relations was essentially to help find ways of communicating the Christian message more effectively and appropriately.[31]

Appreciative expressions and acknowledgement that truths could be found in other faiths make it possible to argue that Edinburgh provided the early stages for a positive theology of religions. The Commission Four report, however, and the analysis of theologians such as Cracknell, failed to adequately grasp the conservative views proffered by missionaries working in Muslim environments. Whilst it is possible to regard Edinburgh as a watershed in the history of Christian mission, this cannot be interpreted as a true reflection of the situation in many Muslim regions.[32] Overall, despite 'quite 'progressive' debates in some of the Commissions, the conference generally reflected a traditional conservative approach to mission, linking the proclamation of the 'gospel to the heathens' with the spread of Western civilisation'.[33]

Part II: The legacy of Commission Four

Changing perspectives on mission

Since Edinburgh 1910 changing perspectives have led to the emergence of a more complex view of church and mission. Events in Europe, Communism, secularism and the resurgence of religions have dented the confidence of the missionary movement. Liberals and Conservatives have clashed within the church over social issues, liberation theology and dialogue. Conferences subsequent to Edinburgh 1910 have reflected the uncertainty and tension felt by the church over the nature of its own mission. In relation to other faiths, and issues of social responsibility in particular, there has been an *articulation* of the underlying tension between loyalty to Christianity and commitment to working towards a safer, more peaceful, world. The context has changed and with it missionary language and motivation has shifted emphasis. This tension now explicitly acknowledged is one that has been present since Edinburgh and probably even before.

The significance of the different world we live in

The world was a very different place in 1910: better transport and communication, new insights in psychology, and socio-political changes have led to different priorities. The way in which we understand our selves and our relationships is more complex and multilayered. At Edinburgh these issues were not understood, nor could missionaries have imagined the degree of influence future political divisions would have on relations between East and West, Islam and Christianity.[34]

For centuries the relationship between Muslims and Christians has been characterized by conflict: theological, ideological, political and military.[35] Constructive elements have been in a minority, often buried in the writing of history. The balance of power and self-confidence has shifted at various times between the two, but generally their relationship has been blighted by suspicion and rivalry.

The effect of two world wars and a fading Empire was significant in changing attitudes. More recently growing numbers of Muslim immigrants to the West, and Europe in particular, has had further impact on the relationship between Muslims and Christians. Closer contact between the communities has raised questions about cultural, religious and ethnic identity as each side has tried to identify its own position in relation to the other. In Britain events such as the Salmon Rushdie affair have brought matters into the public arena. Meanwhile, at a grass roots level, especially through the efforts of mainstream churches since the 1970s, Muslims and Christians have ventured out of their trenches and entered tentative discussions.

In the West there has been growing demand for a more public Muslim voice and presence. Concurrently, the Arab and Middle Eastern world has seen a revival of Islamic consciousness through events such as the Islamic Revolution in Iran, developments in Egypt and Algeria and the heightening of tensions in Palestine. The intensifying tension between East and West was captured and further amplified in 1993 by the publication of Huntington's *The Clash of Civilizations*.[36]

For the West, largely through the media and political rhetoric, Islam has come to be identified – through a series of armed organizations – as the new enemy. For the East, events in Palestine, the American led liberation of Kuwait and the invasion of Iraq represent the rise of a new imperialism. Far from religion becoming obsolete – as secularism had predicted – it has taken centre stage. Religion has become a potent factor in unfolding world affairs. On one hand, there is a desire to avoid the clash of civilizations envisioned by Huntington. Efforts continue on both sides and various levels in neighbourhoods, amongst academics and even in centres of power to foster good relations and greater understanding. On the other hand, in a post September 11 world, East and West, Muslim and Christian, are more suspicious of one another than ever and the rise of fundamentalism and the power of religious and political propaganda on both sides represents a worrying phenomenon.

Faced with this we ask: what is our Christian responsibility towards other faiths generally and Islam especially? Certainly we need good theology to underpin our interfaith encounters. But more than ever we are drawn towards a vision in which doctrinal rigidity is loosened in favour of building good relations based on understanding, sympathy, forgiveness and generosity. Even at Edinburgh there was recognition that living and working amongst people of other religions had led some to become less concerned with church rules and dogmatic codes. One delegate, representing China, wrote of becoming 'less a Churchman and more a Christian'; another expressed the shift not in terms of *changing* doctrines but of 'greater hesitancy in fixing the circumference'.[37] A colleague in India was even more ardent that 'the essence of the Christian Gospel is not dogma and theology, but a distinct and unique spirit'.[38] Whilst such views were not proffered by any in Muslim regions, even then there was a commitment to finding more appropriate ways of expressing difficult Christian doctrines such as the Trinity and Incarnation.[39]

The personal dimension in the struggle towards interfaith dialogue

The problem is that whilst it is relatively easy to recognize the need for a more open approach to interfaith efforts today, even to be genuinely committed, the reality can be more difficult. Sometimes we are called to be generous in the face of suspicion, even hostility. At other times our integrity feels compromised, and we struggle for the right balance between loyalty to our own faith and generosity to another's. These are not simply signs of human weakness but illustrate a struggle to be honest as well as liberal and understanding. There is conflict between intellectual commitment to a liberal methodology and what Kenneth Cragg calls 'this impulse to disallow the other'.[40]

In my own experience the practice of interfaith dialogue found expression through events experienced by the Anglican Church in Iran after the 1979 Revolution swept through the country.[41] This small indigenous church came into being through the work of CMS in the late nineteenth and early twentieth centuries. It has, throughout its history, experienced periods of hardship according to the vicissitudes of socio-political events. The last twenty to thirty years, however, has been a time of sustained suffering with the confiscation of institutions and properties, a drastic reduction of numbers, imprisonment and even the loss of life. The situation as it stands today is no less precarious. Many Christians live in a climate of fear and the future of the church hangs in the balance.

There is a tension in dialogue between the call to Christian generosity and forgiveness in the face of suffering, and the need for justice or at least an acknowledgement of the pain and wrongdoing from the dialoging partner. The scandal of Christian forgiveness lies precisely in the undemanding nature of its giving. We forgive just as we have been forgiven, not because it is deserved but because forgiveness is a gift received and to be shared. Yet this is one part of a paradox in which Christians are also called to take a stand against injustice.

In dialogue with Muslims there is an acute need for honesty as well as generosity, although often such feelings remain unspoken. There is, for example, a troubled history that blights Christian-Muslim relations for which both sides are to blame. Christianity certainly has much to be ashamed of and for which to apologize. Even today in parts of the world Christians cause harm or hurt in the name of religion. Can Muslims then recognize the injustices not only from their past but which are part of their present? The response is invariably one of defensive resistance or refusal to engage. None of this is to suggest that Islam is faulty or that individuals should take responsibility for the actions of others. It is simply to state that there needs to be recognition of the dark side lurking within the history of all faiths.

Kenneth Cragg, one of the greatest advocates of fostering good relations with Muslims, believes there is an identity crisis going on between an Islam that *can* be accused of causing devastation and another which disavows violence.[42] In the Persian context, one is represented by recent events, the other by a 'vast and storied' culture in all its poetic and architectural beauty.[43] Cragg writes, 'The Islam that is indicated in what befell the Church [in Iran] might have stayed its hand by counsels no less claiming its name. Certainly *an* "Islam" was guilty.'[44] Without some recognition of this divided reality by Muslims, the path of dialogue is much more difficult and painful. For dialogue to be effective it must in the end be based on *mutual* respect and understanding, *reciprocal* honesty and generosity.

At the same time, however, there is a Christian calling towards generous hospitality regardless of what one encounters. This underlies the need to continue struggling towards a magnanimous dialogic spirit. For if Christians cannot make forgiveness and generosity part of their own experience how can they expect it from leaders and those in power? How can they desire it on a world scale? Relations between West and East threaten to tear the fabric of our global community apart. Neither side is prepared to relent, and the endless round of violence continues in an abhorrent tit for tat, with the result that some can save face and flex their political or religious muscles whilst others are caught up in the aggression that daily takes more lives.

Dialogue and witness

It seems that our context requires us to struggle in order to find a common basis for our shared humanity thereby ending the cycle of violence. Where then does faith fit into the equation and where does our ultimate loyalty lie? Do we foster good relations at any cost, sitting light to the spiritual dimension that sustains and motivates us? Or do we see dialogue as including the sharing of theology and experience as well as the easier, nonetheless important, task of co-operation in social and political programmes.

Theology cannot be entirely separated from lived experience. Nevertheless, the question about the right balance between dialogue and witness is also an intellectual one regarding the status of other religions and the extent to which conversion should be part of our motivation, as it certainly was in 1910. There have been concerted efforts by academics to set such an intellectual context for dialogue. The most enduring regards people of other faiths within the terms of one of three paradigms: exclusivism, inclusivism and pluralism.[45]

The controlling logic of exclusivism is that outside Christianity there is no salvation and, however respectfully approached, other religions are always being compared with the one true universal faith. Accordingly, whilst dialogue might be undertaken partly to enhance relations, the ultimate aim is to prove Christian superiority and convince the other of the need for conversion. Inclusivism also identifies Christianity as the universal religion representing the highest point of belief. However, it makes certain allowances for other religions, arguing that whilst the salvific process can be found within them its full efficacy remains the function of Christianity. In Christianity others can find fulfillment. So in dialogue it is possible to recognize some truths in the other, but their expression remains inferior to the Christian vision. Finally, according to pluralism there are many different but equally valid ways of reaching the one universal reality; there are multiple paths to salvation and none is superior to the others. The purpose of dialogue is to foster better relations and to learn from one another. These were not recognized categories at the conference in 1910. Indeed, there were no examples of a pluralist approach. It is possible, however, to discern some inclusivist attitudes (though not towards Muslims) amidst an essentially exclusivist stance.

Recently these paradigms have been expanded and subcategorized for greater breadth and flexibility.[46] Yet increasingly they are unsatisfactory in dealing with the reality of interfaith dialogue. All three models make assumptions about Christianity and other faiths before the process of dialogue has even begun. Exclusivism is patronising in its self-confessed superiority. Pluralism relativizes truth, denying either side its own conclusions and 'jealousies'.[47] And inclusivism, which for a number of years provided a helpful middle ground, is equally dismissive by ultimately subsuming the other into a Christian framework.

The threefold model now seems too neat and tidy. Dialogue is not just a question of whose salvation, secured where, when and how. It is also about exploring our common humanity and learning about one another. In a pluralist world the foundation for such an approach must be based on relationships and not on dogmatic presuppositions. A framework is needed that may not have all the doctrinal intricacies ironed out and which is characterized by 'creative tension'.[48] Such a framework would be based on certain principles and would include unresolved internal conflicts.

The principles, based on a foundation of good relationships, might include determination to understand the best of Islam, awareness of common ground alongside honesty regarding our distinctiveness, sensitivity to the wider world perspective as well as the local context, and a desire to share our faith.[49] The unresolved internal conflict would recognize that dialogue is an uncomfortable space in which to reside, representing an 'abiding paradox' which vacillates between commitment to one's own religion and openness to another's, always moving between certainty and doubt, recognising the possibility of change as much for ourselves as our dialoging partner.[50]

Such an approach has three advantages.[51] First, it aims to avoid the sentimentality of excessive liberalism whereby truth is relativized and anything goes. Collapsing our differences may seem acceptable from the comfort of our own position. However elsewhere Christians suffer persecution. How can a faith be worth dying for in one place if it is hardly worth proclaiming in another? Secondly, it attempts to take both self and other seriously by acknowledging distinctiveness. Thirdly, it offers a sympathetically critical approach to interfaith dialogue. Self-criticism is certainly an essential feature of Christian dialogue. But it is equally possible, perhaps even necessary, vigorously yet courteously to criticize the other. It is too easy to move from a position whereby Islam is demonized to a typically post colonial, guilt induced, appreciation of all it stands for. Rodinson warns against what she calls a distorted orientalism that simply classifies Islam in a diametrical manner. Rather than rendering it diabolic it goes to the other extreme and through an 'ideological about-face ... practically sanctif[ies] Islam'. This European version of 'Muslim apologetics', through its refusal to be critical of Islam in any way, loses its analytical edge, becoming little more than indulgence.[52] There must be no discrimination, vilification or scorn, but there is no obligation to applaud all that is Muslim.

Conclusion

Both dialogue and witness, based on honesty, criticism and generosity, are needed for the life of a religious community to find full expression. This leads to a kind of 'reciprocal testimony' in which phases of sensitive witness alternate with respectful listening.[53] Living with this paradox remains a vision for Christians and one with which I believe our faith requires us to struggle, regardless of what we encounter. Unless, however, it is a shared vision for our partners we will not see the full potential of interfaith dialogue blossom in our world.

Endnotes

[1] W. H. T. Gairdner, *'Edinburgh 1910': An Account and Interpretation of the World Missionary Conference*, Edinburgh & London: Oliphant, Anderson & Ferrier; New York, Chicago and Toronto: Fleming H. Revell, 1910, pp. 12–14.
[2] History has not recorded the reasons why certain missionaries were selected to respond to the questionnaires, though individuals were certainly hand-picked by the organisers.
[3] See, for example, Gairdner, *Edinburgh 1910*, p. 134.
[4] Gairdner, *Edinburgh 1910*, pp. 134–5.
[5] For a full list of the questions see World Missionary Conference,1910, *The Missionary Message in Relation to Non-Christian Religions*, Report of Commission IV, Edinburgh & London: Oliphant, Anderson & Ferrier; New York, Chicago and Toronto: Fleming H. Revell, 1910, p. 2.

[6] See Kenneth Cracknell, *Justice, Courtesy and Love: Theologians and Missionaries Encountering World Religions, 1846–1914,* London: Epworth Press, 1995.
[7] Cracknell, *Justice, Courtesy and Love*, pp. 227–31.
[8] Cracknell, *Justice, Courtesy and Love*, p. 219.
[9] Cracknell, *Justice, Courtesy and Love*, p. 231.
[10] Cracknell, *Justice, Courtesy and Love*, pp. 231–6.
[11] Cracknell, *Justice, Courtesy and Love*, p. 236.
[12] His writings include: William St. Clair Tisdall, *The Sources of Islam: A Persian Treatise*, translated & abridged by William Muir, Edinburgh: T & T Clark 1901; William St. Clair Tisdall, *The Religion of the Crescent*, London: SPCK, 1910; William St. Clair Tisdall, *Christianity and Other Faiths*, London: SPCK, 1912.
[13] William St. Clair Tisdall, in Kenneth Cracknell, *Justice, Courtesy and Love: Theologians and Missionaries Encountering World Religions, 1846–1914,* London: Epworth Press, 1995, p. 236.
[14] In the introduction to the report the Animistic religions and the religions of Japan are allocated 2.5 pages each, whilst the Chinese religions are given 3 pages. 1 page is dedicated to Hinduism whilst Islam only receives the attention of one brief paragraph. In the actual chapters on the different religions Islam is dealt with more briefly than any of the others, with the exception of the Animistic religions. Indeed the chapter on Islam is 15 pages shorter than the chapter on Japanese religions and 24 pages shorter than the chapter on Hinduism.
[15] Gairdner, *Edinburgh 1910*, p. 147.
[16] *The Missionary Message*, p. 142.
[17] *The Missionary Message*, p. 122.
[18] *The Missionary Message*, p. 138.
[19] Despite its shrinking authority, evangelicalism – which had its roots in eighteenth century revivalism – was still a significant and influential element at the time of the WMC. By 1900 it had been largely hijacked by the upper middle-classes, even becoming an avenue for upward social mobility. In the process it lost a certain amount of its incisiveness and spontaneity. Thus, the second evangelical awakening of 1860, considered by many to have begun in the States before arriving in England, marked a new phase of organized evangelism far removed from the unprompted nature of early revivals. Notwithstanding major changes, evangelicalism's primary characteristics (conversionism, activism, biblicism, crucicentrism) remained intact, and its influence remained alive, providing a milieu in which the missionary societies continued flourishing. For an excellent account of the history of evangelicalism see, David Bebbington, *Evangelicalism in Modern Britain: A History from the 1730s to the 1980s,* London: Routledge, 1989.
[20] The American mission theorist and promoter Arthur T. Pierson is credited with formulating the phrase. In 1889 the Student Volunteer Movement adopted it. See Arthur T. Pierson, *The Modern Mission Century Viewed as a Cycle of Divine Working*, London: James Nisbet & Co, [1901], p. 78.
[21] David Bosch, *Transforming Mission: Paradigm Shifts in Theology of Mission*, Maryknoll, New York: Orbis, 1991, p. 336; see also pp. 337–8 for more information on Mott's influence over the spirit of Edinburgh.
[22] For more on my views about the growing strain between the theory of pure evangelism and the practical experience of missionaries see Guli Francis-Dehqani, *Religious Feminism in an Age of Empire: CMS Women Missionaries in Iran, 1869–1934,* Bristol: CCSRG, University of Bristol, 2000, especially pp. 143–8; This is also available as Guli Francis-Dehqani, 'Religious Feminism in an Age of Empire: CMS Women Missionaries in Iran, 1869–1934', Ph.D., University of Bristol, 1999.

[23] Gairdner, *Edinburgh 1910*, p. 140. This was in a section discussing Animistic religions.
[24] Edward Said, *Orientalism: Western Conceptions of the Orient*, London: Penguin, 1987; reprint 1995, pp. 95–103.
[25] *The Missionary Message*, p. 133.
[26] *The Missionary Message*, pp. 133–4.
[27] *The Missionary Message*, p. 134.
[28] John Mott, *The Evangelization of the World in this Generation*, London: SVM, 1900 p. 106.
[29] Gairdner, *Edinburgh 1910*, p 138.
[30] *The Missionary Message*, p. 268.
[31] See, in particular, *The Missionary Message*, pp. 269–70, 324–6.
[32] This seems especially true of areas within CMS jurisdiction. The prevalent anti-Islamic stance adopted by many CMS missionaries may have partly resulted from the 'influence of some powerful ("domineering" is a better word) personalities within the CMS (Robert Stirling in Jerusalem, William Miller in Nigeria and Tisdall in Iran, to name but three) who had fixed negative views on Islam..'. By contrast with several other missionary societies, CMS was one of the least forward looking, with 'the general attitude of the ... General Secretary Eugene Stock set[ting] the tone at this period'. Kenneth Cracknell, personal emails, 18 –19 November 1996.
[33] See <http://www.mission2005.org/Edinburgh.563.0.html>, accessed February 2005.
[34] There was the hint of recognition at Edinburgh about political changes to come, with the report referring to the possible rise of a neo-Islam leading to the awakening of national consciousness (see *The Missionary Message*, pp. 132, 150). Delegates were unlikely, however, to have envisaged the extent and significance of the events that lay ahead.
[35] For one example of a helpful and concise history of Christian-Muslim relations, of which in the following section I make considerable use, see Jorgen Nielsen, 'Is there an Escape from the History of Christian-Muslim Relations?' in David Thomas, ed., *A Faithful Presence: Essays for Kenneth Cragg*, London: Melisende, 2003, pp. 350–61.
[36] Samuel Huntington published an article in 1993 in *Foreign Affairs* that was later expanded into a 1997 book entitled, *The Clash of Civilizations and the Remaking of the World Order.* Reprinted in 1998, New York: Simon & Schuster.
[37] *The Missionary Message*, p. 70.
[38] *The Missionary Message*, p. 208.
[39] *The Missionary Message*, p. 153.
[40] Kenneth Cragg, 'Editor's Postscript' in Hassan Dehqani-Tafti, *The Unfolding Design of my World: A Pilgrim in Exile.* Norwich: Canterbury Press, 2000, p. 262.
[41] Hassan Dehqani-Tafti, *The Hard Awakening.* London: Triangle, SPCK, 1981.
[42] Cragg, 'Editor's Postscript', p. 259.
[43] Hassan Dehqani-Tafti & Guli Francis-Dehqani, 'By Their Fruits Shall You Know Them', in David Thomas, ed., *A Faithful Presence: Essays for Kenneth Cragg*, London: Melisende, 2003, pp. 42–55.
[44] Cragg, 'Editor's Postscript', p. 250.
[45] For more on these paradigms see, for example, Alan Race, *Christians and Religious Pluralism: Patterns in the Christian Theology of Religions*, London: SCM, 1983; and Gavin D'Costa, *Theology and Religious Pluralism*, Oxford: Blackwell, 1986.
[46] Douglas Pratt, 'Pluralism and Interreligious Engagement: The Contexts of Dialogue', in David Thomas, ed., *A Faithful Presence: Essays for Kenneth Cragg*, London: Melisende, 2003, pp. 404–18.

[47] 'Every religion has its jealousies', was a phrase famously used by John V. Taylor in his 1977 Lambeth Inter-faith Lecture. Graham Kings, 'Mission and the Meeting of Faiths: The Theologies of Max Warren and John V. Taylor' in Kevin Ward & Brian Stanley, eds., *The Church Mission Society and World Christianity, 1799–1999,* Michigan & Cambridge: Eerdmans, 2000, p. 308.
[48] Bosch, *Transforming Mission*, p. 483.
[49] These principles are based on Colin Chapman's analysis of Kenneth Cragg's ideas. Colin Chapman, 'An Agenda for Dialogue', in David Thomas, ed., *A Faithful Presence: Essays for Kenneth Cragg,* London: Melisende, 2003, p. 385.
[50] Bosch, *Transforming Mission*, p. 483.
[5]1 In this section I have drawn on material from Martin Forward, ' "Is Thine Heart Right, As My Heart is with Thy Heart?" A Christian Spiritual Theology for Dialogue with Muslims', in David Thomas, ed., *A Faithful Presence: Essays for Kenneth Cragg,* London: Melisende, 2003, pp. 380–2.
[52] Maxime Rodinson, *Europe and the Mystique of Islam,* Seatle & London: University of Washington Press, 1991, pp. 78, 106, 127.
[53] Ulrich Schoen, 'Dialogue', in Karl Műller et al., eds., *Dictionary of Mission: Theology, History, Perspectives*, Maryknoll, New York: Orbis, 1997, pp. 109–10.

A World of Religions and a Gospel of Transformation

Vinoth Ramachandra

Introduction

There is a vast gulf that separates us from Edinburgh 1910. Three significant differences between their world and ours emerge from a consideration of the Commission Four Report. First, the racial, linguistic, denominational and theological complexion of the Christian world has been transformed in the twentieth century. The Report writers and respondents were white Western males who dominated the ecclesiastical and missionary centres of power. No African spoke for African Christianity, nor were there any representatives from indigenous churches outside the European world. It is Western Christendom that informs their conversation and constitutes its background.

Secondly, they were denizens of global empire, with the European nations and their former colonies in the Americas having political and economic control over 80% of the world. Not only have nationalism and de-colonization in Asia and Africa been prominent features of the twentieth century, but Europeans are now cynical towards all global projects except the march of consumerism and a narrowly defined set of rights.

Thirdly, while they were concerned about the threat of Western secularism and materialism on traditional ways of life, they could not foresee that modernity would develop in diverse ways, and even lead to a resurgence, rather than a diminution in religious identities in politics and national life. So convinced were they of the 'finality and absoluteness of Christianity' (which they could not distinguish from the 'finality and absoluteness of Christ') that the thought that Christianity would recede in Europe, while taking on new configurations in Sub-Saharan Africa, Korea, or China, lay beyond their imaginations.

Reading through the Report of Commission Four, one is struck not only by the gulf that divides our world from theirs, but also by a resonance with concerns of our day. It was perhaps unfair of the missiologist David Bosch to label Edinburgh a 'how to' conference the climax of American-inspired pragmatism. While it may have begun that way, one is humbled by the recognition in the Report's conclusion that 'the success of the missionary enterprise depends in the last issue, not on numbers, nor on wealth nor on organization' but by the desire to cultivate a 'living faith' and a 'living theology'.[1] And this re-vitalized theology is needed for the church 'at home' as much as for the churches abroad: 'There is assuredly more in God and in truth, and in that Gospel which is the truth of God, than we have yet attained.'[2]

The Report approached religious faiths under five headings, organized in separate chapters: Animism, Chinese Religions, Japanese Religions, Islam, and Hinduism. Clearly it is the religions of India and China that caught the imagination of the missionary movement and attracted some of its most gifted personnel. The lack of attention to Buddhism in South-East Asia was acknowledged, the reason being that only four responses had been received. One can only note the irony that Buddhism has been more successful than any of the other Faiths in winning Western converts in the twentieth century, and its influence (through the philosophy of Arthur Schopenhauer, for instance, or Edwin Arnold's epic poem on the life of the Buddha) was being felt in European intellectual circles even before the end of the nineteenth century. Parallels are drawn in the Report between the work of contemporary churches and the missionary challenge that had faced the early church: for instance, Animism today and pagan polytheism in Greco-Roman society; modern Islam and ancient Judaism in its 'legalistic conception of the God-man relationship'; Hindu Vedanta and the sophisticated intellectual systems of the Hellenist world.[3]

The Report is permeated by a sense of impending global crisis, perhaps a hangover from the apocalyptic pre-millennialism that marked much of the American missionary enterprise. With some prescience, the in-roads of an atheistic scientific naturalism into China and Japan are noted as potential catastrophes facing these nations. Paragraphs like the following, read with historical hindsight, are rather poignant: 'All history shows that without religion no civilisation can live. No man can tell the evils and the sorrow to China, and not to China alone but to the whole human race, that must follow the decay of religion throughout this great Empire. It would be far better for China to keep the religion that she has than to discard it for materialism and atheism.'[4] It is also fascinating to note that for the writers of the Report, 'There is perhaps no spiritual position in the missionary world of today of such strategic moment as the Island Empire of Japan',[5] and that 'sooner or later the issues here, as in China, must be fought out between naturalism and Christianity'.[6]

It is customary to regard Edinburgh 1910 as the high point of missionary triumphalism, Western Christianity's reflection of the high noon of empire prior to the dark horrors of the First World War. The Report belies this perception. No doubt some of the military metaphors jar on the sensitive postmodern reader, as when the Report concludes with the oft-quoted words: 'The spectacle of the advance of the Christian Church along many lines of action to the conquest of the five great religions of the modern world is one of singular interest and grandeur.'[7] But what is rarely quoted are the words that immediately follow: 'But at least as remarkable as that spectacle of the outward advance of the Church is that which has also been revealed to us of the inward transformations that are in process in the mind of the missionary, the changes of perspective, the softening of wrong antagonisms, the centralising and deepening of faith in the Lord Jesus Christ, the growth of the spirit of love to the brethren and to the world.'[8]

The overwhelming impression conveyed by the respondents and the Report is that deep understanding, sympathy and respect must mark the Christian approach to the non-Christian religions and their adherents. While our present vocabulary of 'inter-faith dialogue' may be missing, there is no doubt that most of those involved in the Report had been practising it to a remarkable extent. And their missionary experience of other faiths and cultures furnished a powerful challenge to Western Christianity. Anticipating the work of African theologians in the twentieth century, the Report dared to ask whether the animist worldview was not more helpful in understanding the Bible than 'conventional Christianity' and whether the post-Enlightenment 'theological view of nature as a closed system, sporadically broken on rare historic occasions, [was] really philosophically sound or religiously sufficient?'[9]

Even Islam, the 'great antagonist' of the Gospel, was a model of 'living faith' and it was 'this living faith, intenser [*sic*], more intimate and more comprehensive than sight', that the body of Christ had to recover if it was to have a credible witness in the world.[10] The Report dares to ask: 'Have we in our modern theology and religion sufficiently recognized what Islam stands for - the unity and the sovereignty of God?'[11] Anticipating later scholarship of Christian-Muslim relations, it suggests that it is not 'historically just' to say that Muhammad rejected Christ, and laments that 'The study of the conditions under which Islam came into being afford matter for heart-searching to Christendom.'[12] That same Christendom is chastised for 'all the rapacity and violence of national policy' towards China.[13] Temple Gairdner notes how, on the very first evening, one of the speakers had 'most uncompromisingly pointed to the failure of western Christianity to solve her social question, as well as to Christianize the foreign and colonising policies of the western nations'.[14]

Commission Four manifests humility, despite the triumphalist language. Along with a recognition of all that is good in non-Christian religions, the respondents share the 'massive conviction' that 'Jesus Christ fulfils and supersedes all other religions'.[15] But it is this conviction that led to the recognition that 'they and we alike need a new discovery of God',[16] and, what Gairdner calls the 'working principle' that guided the Commission: 'since the Church of Christ itself is partially involved in mists of unbelief, failing aspiration, imperfect realisation, this quest of hers among the non-Christian religions, this discovery of their "broken lights" may be to her the discovery of facets of her own truth, forgotten or half-forgotten – perhaps even never perceived at all save by the most prophetic of her sons'.[17]

The 'fulfilment' model

The language of 'fulfilment' *vis a vis* the relationship between Christianity and other Faiths surfaces especially in the sections on Hinduism. The Report recognizes that most of the papers received show a 'combination of what to the superficial observer seem contradictory elements, their penetrating judgment of the evils of Hinduism and their generous and profound appreciation of that in it which is true and eternal'.[18] It drew a parallel between the theological effort in India and the work of the Alexandrine Fathers: 'Indeed, at every turn one is reminded of the first meeting of Christianity and Hellenism in this meeting between Christian thought and the strange blend of crude, popular polytheism with a deep and subtle esoteric philosophy which is found today in India.'[19] Two native Indian readers objected to the Report as being inattentive to the view of Indian converts. Their experience of Hinduism from the 'inside' was not as 'roseate' as that of the missionaries who often only had contact with the 'best' of Hinduism.[20] In this, they were pre-figuring Dalit consciousness which champions Jesus as a fellow Dalit, one who, in solidarity with his brethren, subverts the oppressive power of the caste-system and its underlying religious ideology.

Edinburgh 1910's greatest legacy to the Christian Church lay in its setting up of a continuation committee, in the form of the International Missionary Council, to further the dialogue among Christians on the nature of the missionary calling. The Commission issued an appeal for deeper study of other religious traditions 'because the most direct way into the human heart of both Animist and Hindu and Moslem will be the study of what he holds most precious'.[21] An international journal was founded under the editorship of J. H. Oldham himself, the Secretary of the conference, and it was in these pages that much of the ensuing debates were initiated.

The 'fulfilment' approach dominated missionary and native Christian thinking in India right up to the IMC conference in Jerusalem (1928). Keshub Chander Sen was probably the first within the Indian nineteenth-century context to have used the term 'fulfilment' to describe the relationship of Christ to other religions. Max Müller's evolutionary view of religious development seems to have been the main influence on Sen's understanding of fulfilment. It is interesting to note that some African theologians continue to apply the fulfilment motif to their own pre-Christian religious experience. For John Mbiti, 'The Gospel enabled [African] people to utter the name of Jesus Christ ... that final and completing element that crowns their traditional religiosity and brings its flickering light to full brilliance'.[22]

J. N. Farquhar and A. G. Hogg came to represent the two poles of the 'fulfilment' debate in the period immediately before Edinburgh and until Jerusalem.[23] Farquhar's *The Crown of Hinduism*, published in 1913, and Hogg's *Karma and Redemption*, published a few years before Edinburgh, quickly became essential reading for missionaries serving in India. Their differences lay less in different assessments of Hinduism, or the uniqueness of the Christian message, than in matters of emphasis and of missionary approach. For Hogg, instead of asking what elements in Hinduism presented 'points of contact' with Christianity and constitute a preparation for it, it was better to ask 'where one can most readily create in the Hindu consciousness points of contact with the Christian consciousness, and thereby prepare the way for an Indian type of Christianity'. The Christian's aim should be to 'intensify' a dissatisfaction with the 'individualist ideals' of Hinduism: '... inspire the Hindu mind with the sense that its ideal is too narrow, that its attainment leaves the world too full of misery and wrong, and you have prepared the way for the Kingdom of God'.[24]

These two missionary approaches – the one building on what is good and true in the religious faiths of humankind, the other subverting them by intensifying the dissatisfaction of their devotees and leading them to a Christological transformation – both presuppose a deep and sympathetic engagement with the lives and thought-worlds of others. The most stimulating missionary theologies have come, not from academic theologians writing about the 'world religions' in general, but from scholar-missionaries who have lived a large part of their lives within another, particular, religious culture – whether Hendrik Kraemer among rural Javanese Muslims, Kenneth Cragg in the world of Arabic Muslim intellectuals, Lesslie Newbigin as pastor to rural churches in south India, or Kosuke Koyama among Thai Buddhist villagers. Their writings reflect the complexities and ambiguities of all religious systems. Even Kraemer, whose massive 450 page book *The Christian Message in a Non-Christian World* written (in just seven weeks!) for the 1938 Tambaram conference of the IMC has often been derided by religious pluralists for its Barthian denunciation of religion as human self-justification and idolatry, criticizes Barth for his (ironically) 'undialectical thinking' and 'rationalistic' arguments about religion.

Kraemer's argument against a 'rationalistic' approach to discussing religions cuts in two directions, not only against Barth but also against his detractors. Orientalist romanticism has marked several text-based defenders of 'religion'. Peter Cotterell, a missionary in Ethiopia for many years, has complained that 'in the contemporary debates about the world's religions the religions are hopelessly idealized.... The horrors of Canaanite religions are still with us, the *shaman* still claims the power to manipulate his gods, witchcraft still flourishes, the credulous are exploited, human achievement is exalted, the rich are filled with yet more good things, and it is the poor who are sent empty away. The fact is that religions do not prepare their adherents for the revelation of Christ.'[25]

The sheer otherness of what is heard in the gospel story by people of other faiths cannot be downplayed. Whatever may be the relationship between the Gospel and non-Christian experience of God, it cannot be described in terms of continuity alone. Lesslie Newbigin never tired of reminding us that it was not the sages but 'babes and sucklings' (Matt. 11:25) who received the Christ, while the highest in the land crucified him: 'The message of Jesus, of the unique incarnate Lord crucified by the powers of law, morals, and piety and raised to the throne of cosmic authority, confronts the claim of every religion with a radical negation.'[26]

The transformation of religions towards Christ

Indian Christian theology in the post-independence period has had a third partner in its dialogue with the dominant Hindu religious schools: Marxism. M. M. Thomas called for a 'Christ-centred syncretism', meaning a transformation of all religions around Jesus' liberating action for the poor and oppressed, and urged the Church to speak of this both in secularist and metaphysical categories.[27] The Dalit theologians of India have largely rejected Thomas' approach as being too naive in its estimate of changes within Hindu religious society.

There are similarities here to Kenneth Cragg's theology of 'retrieval'. Cragg is concerned with a Christian mission to the household of Islam.[28] He recognizes, more profoundly than does Thomas, that 'the Christian gospel is conversionist through and through',[29] and that the 'ardent hospitality'[30] that flows out of the Christ-event seeks to retrieve and mend distorted refractions elsewhere. We are summoned by the divine hospitality to exercise a like hospitality to unfamiliar and alien ways of thought and life, including where religion itself is neglected or denied outright. Christ 'belongs to us only because he belongs to all. He is ours only by virtue of his universality'.[31] This calls for a 'cross-referencing' style of doing theology, paying close attention 'those thoughts and inklings of him in the comprehension of other religions'.[32]

Thus Cragg confesses an incarnational Christology in dialogue with Islam, not by the traditional way of confrontation with Muslim views of Jesus, but by fully indwelling the Islamic discourse on missionary prophethood and moving that discourse towards the recognition that: 'truth-bearing from God, *via* prophethood, to the human realm reveals a logic in which message and messenger become indistinguishable, word passes into life and life becomes the word. When it does so, given human passion and prophetic steadfastness, the word that becomes life is likely to be the life that becomes suffering.'[33]

The pneumatological approach

What *is* of interest is the way that Roman Catholic theologians in India and elsewhere have begun to move from a Logos Christology to a Spirit Christology in dealing with religious pluralism. The shadow of Karl Rahner and of the Conciliar and post-Conciliar Vatican II documents falls on these theologies, but they are developed in different directions. Rahner's point of departure was 1 Timothy 2:4, 'the universal and salvific purpose of God towards all men', which he took to be actually effective 'for all men in all ages and places'.[34] This must imply that every 'individual ought to and must have the possibility in his life of partaking in a genuine and saving relationship to God, and this at all times and in all situations of the history of the human race'.[35] For Rahner, the non-Christian religions are 'lawful religions' but only up to the 'time when the Christian religion becomes a historically real factor' for their adherents. A 'lawful religion' is 'an institutional religion whose "use" by man at a certain period can be regarded on the whole as a positive means of gaining the right relationship to God and thus for the attaining of salvation'. Religions become 'unlawful right from the moment when they [come] into real and historically powerful contact with Christianity'.[36] Therefore, 'Christianity does not simply confront the member of an extra-Christian religion as a mere non-Christian, but as someone who can and must already be regarded in this or that respect as an anonymous Christian.'[37]

Rahner has been criticized for the paternalism implied by the term 'anonymous Christian'. In fairness to Rahner, since his thinking is Christocentric, he has to interpret the salvific value of other religions in Christological terms. His weakness is the way the argument from the universal saving purpose of God to the salvific efficiency of non-Christian religion assumes that God's saving action is experienced in the sphere of 'religion'. It is also unclear as to what constitutes the 'newness' in the 'good news' that the Church is called to proclaim.

Samuel Rayan has developed the post-Conciliar Vatican openness to salvation in other religions in a more radical pneumatological and political liberationist direction. Rayan makes the bold move, reminiscent of Hegel, of interpreting history as the movement of the Spirit across religious boundaries, bringing liberation and unity. Christ belongs to this 'history of the Spirit', which Rayan identifies with the Hindu concept of *shakti*, the universal divine energy, of which Jesus Christ is one instantiation. As Rayan sees it, 'The real question is whether the religions can now muster their resources to act together with the oppressed to struggle for the liberation of all and for a new-creative pro-existence.'[38] The Spirit works to conform human relationships to a socialist model of society. For Rayan and others, the concept of Spirit provides a way in which they can break out of what they see as the straitjacket of salvation-historical thinking, recognize truth and goodness in non-Christian peoples, and accord all histories equal significance. The irony of this approach is that it ends up being an ideological 'theology from above'; despite the intention to respect diversity, it tends to turn the particular into an example of a general principle. If the Christian message is reduced to the statement that in Jesus certain wonderful qualities such as love and justice were present in an exemplary manner, then we could dispense with the example once we had learned the lesson.

Unitary / monological pluralism

The editors of the much-publicized 1987 symposium, *The Myth of Christian Uniqueness*, expressed their confidence that 'a pluralist model represents a 'paradigm shift' in the efforts of Christian theologians to understand the world of other religions and Christianity's place in that world'. [39] John Hick maintains we must learn to think of the 'great world faiths' as equally valid responses to the Ultimate Mystery (or 'The Real' in Hick's later writings). Similarly, Paul Knitter proposed a model of 'unitary pluralism', asserting that: 'the world religions, in all their amazing differences, are more complementary than contradictory'. Knitter set a new 'goal and inspiration for missionary work' so that a process of 'mutual growth' may take place among people of all Faiths and none, the success of which would be measured in terms of 'a Christian becoming a better Christian and a Buddhist a better Buddhist'.[40]

It is in this *normative and programmatic* sense that the word pluralism has come to function in contemporary Christian discussions. This calls for the re-interpretation of all truth-claims. We can only speak, in a mythological way, of our culturally and historically conditioned perceptions of the Real/Transcendent, which are the religious traditions of humankind. Hick has invented a new 'pluralist religion'; tailored to suit the preferences of Western liberal intellectuals! He speaks of the 'great world faiths' or the 'post-axial religions', but ignores primal religions and the newer religious movements. Similarly, Hans Küng is quite sure that 'one cannot place magic or belief in witches, alchemy, or the like, on the same level with belief in the existence of God..'.[41] But why ever not? Because such phenomena do not fit comfortably within the liberal intellectual tradition to which most religious pluralists belong.

'Trinitarian' religious pluralisms

Raimundo Panikkar has vigorously championed an *oecumene* of world faiths. He has sought to marry the personalism of the Semitic faiths with the *advaita*, non-dualist experience of Asian faiths in such a way that diversity is not dissolved but anchored in a transcendent Mystery. He affirms the irreducible plurality of religious traditions, and then argues for their inter-penetration and mutuality on a different plane.

For Panikkar, as indeed for many recent pluralist theologians, the Christian belief in God as Trinity provides a way of accounting for the divergent spiritualities that we encounter in the world of religions. Belief in an ineffable ultimate ground, acknowledgment of a dialogical relationship with the ultimate, and a sense of the depth of our own being – these can all be found in the major religious traditions. Since the Christian doctrine of the Trinity has the *form* of a transcendent, personal and immanent principle, such a doctrine could be extended to serve as an explanation for how the various spiritualities may be grounded in the silence of the Ultimate.

This approach, however, runs the risk of confusing *form* with *content* and *goal*. Even if there are 'triadic' patterns or 'trinitarian' structures running through different religio-philosophical systems, it does not follow that the ultimate experience of *nirvana* or *satori* is equivalent to an experience of God, let alone salvation as understood in the Christian tradition. Experience is never unmediated, but always shaped by an overarching worldview. Thus neither concepts nor 'spiritual experiences' can be compared without paying attention to the narrative worlds in which they are embedded. The worship of God as Trinity did not arise from a speculative philosophy about God's relation with the world, but from the heart of the gospel narrative itself.

In the Christian tradition, Jesus is the unifying point of reference for all the creative acts of God. The *eschaton* towards which our life-stories are moving has a concrete pattern because of the life-story of Jesus. Human possibilities are defined with reference to Jesus who, as the Logos made flesh, not only becomes the normative form of human flourishing and response to God, but also brings the present disordered reality into a new intelligibility and unity. Christ is the redeeming presence in the unpredictable diversity of human histories; the divine action as Spirit is grounded in the divine action in Jesus, the incarnate Logos.

This is where Rahner, Rayan, Panikkar and others who follow them are vulnerable in their 'Spirit' terminology. There is a necessary and reciprocal relation between Jesus and Spirit. Jesus is both the gift of the Spirit and the giver of the Spirit. While the Spirit has been active in all of creation, the narrative identification of the triune God presents the Spirit as the Spirit of the crucified and exalted Christ, and not simply as the Spirit of the Logos. The giving of the Spirit is an eschatological event, a deposit and foretaste of the new creation. Surely this is the significance of Pentecost and of sayings like John 8:39 ('for as yet the Spirit had not been given, because Jesus was not yet glorified'). It is the coming of Jesus that makes the gift of the Spirit universally accessible to all; and the work of the Spirit is to bear witness to the Logos made flesh, to convict the world of guilt, sin, righteousness and judgment, and to lead people to truth by 'taking what is mine and making it known to you' (John 15:26, 16:7ff).

Responsible and responsive gospel witness

In conclusion, some brief questions may be raised with a view to deepening the integrity of our Christian missionary vocation.

(1) Is not any 'theology of religions' inevitably reductionist? Firstly, any generic notion of 'world religions' which embraces such diverse worldviews as orthodox Christianity, Jainism or Confucianism, but ignores Evolutionism or Marxism, is bound to be inadequate. Secondly, we should resist the temptation to seek conceptual neatness and theoretical closure. Not only does this distort the complexities of religious traditions, which are intertwined with cultural and

political factors, there are good theological reasons for retaining ambiguity. Thirdly, since the Spirit's activity is universal, why restrict it to world religions? God may give saving faith to men and women while they live in the context of a non-Christian religion, and even be at work in the transformations of religious traditions to reflect his purposes for the world but this is not the same as claiming that the religions themselves are vehicles of divine salvation and have been formed by God with that intent. If people encounter God in gracious friendship, may it be *despite* their religious practices and loyalties rather than *through* them?

As Chris Wright and John Goldingay have written:

> The gospel is good news, not a good *idea* ... However much theological and spiritual insight other religions may have, then, by definition they cannot encompass the gospel, because they do not tell the gospel story. So, while one can honour them as starting points for people, one cannot in love view them as finishing points. There is no salvation in them, not because they are somehow inferior as religions to the religion of Christianity, but because they are not witnesses to the deeds of the God who saves.[42]

(2) Does not gospel integrity demand that we hold together a high Christology and an open soteriology? The intent of God's action in Jesus Christ is universal; but surely it is important to distinguish this universality of *intent* from a kind of universality that many religious pluralists seem to endorse, which is actually the *relinquishment* of its content. 'To affirm the unique decisiveness of God's action in Jesus Christ is not arrogance; it is the enduring bulwark against the arrogance of every culture to be itself the criterion by which others are judged.'[43]

The biblical witness to Jesus Christ as the world's indispensable Saviour requires that certain questions remain open in eschatological hope. Until that day when all hostile powers are subject to Christ and we share in the resurrection of the dead (1 Cor. 15:24–28), we see 'in a mirror, dimly' (1 Cor. 13:12). I am *simul justus et peccator*, in Luther's immortal words. I have been grasped by the truth as it is in Christ Jesus, yet am ever growing into the fullness of that truth. In this pilgrimage, even as I share the story of Jesus with others, I find myself drawn deeper into the story and given fresh insights into it.

This is why the *other* is essential to our own pilgrimage. We do not know what we really believe, let alone how far our lives conform with what we profess to believe, until we engage in dialogue with others, especially those who are profoundly different from us. Evangelism, if authentic, changes the bearers as well as the recipients of the gospel.

(3) Does it not follow that gospel integrity demands a dialogical approach to mission? Dialogue proceeds from the belief that, in the missionary encounter with other peoples and their cultures, we are not moving into a void, but that we

go expecting to meet the God who has preceded us and has been preparing people within the context of their own cultures and communities.

Christians need to engage seriously with the *contemporary* art forms that embody the beliefs and values of our non-Christian neighbours. Sadly, the great bulk of writings on inter-religious dialogue that come from academic theologians, whether in the West or Asia, tend to be discussions of ancient Indian, Arabic or Chinese texts. There is comparatively little engagement with the novels, films, paintings and street dramas that represent the way that modern Muslims, Buddhists and others have re-interpreted their religious heritage in the light of both external critique and internal pressure. If we are relating the gospel to real people and their living traditions, then such critical attention is surely necessary.

Listening will lead, sometimes, to new appreciation. At other times it will result in disagreement and debate. The differences we discover through dialogue may be less important than we thought or the similarities we assumed may turn out to be superficial. In seeking to persuade others, but not in a manipulative or coercive manner, that the vision of the world that opens up through the gospel story is more true and more desirable than any alternative, we take seriously the 'otherness' of the other.

In conclusion, a 'postmodern' but orthodox Christian faith holds that it is in the incarnate life, death and resurrection of Jesus Christ that the divine character is decisively and supremely disclosed and the divine saving purpose effected; but not in a way that gives us finite and sinful human beings a unifying *theoretical* scheme that embraces the whole history and diversity of human experience. Rather, it is given in such a way that it becomes the *universal point of reference* for distinguishing between true and false visions of human flourishing. Otherwise, how do we distinguish the divine Spirit from the demonic? But reading the signs of how God is at work in the secular and religious activities of humanity is always hazardous and must be done with appropriate humility. It is the Spirit who makes a genuine 'hermeneutical spiral' possible, helping us to be critical of the church's language and practice and not identifying the absoluteness of Christ with the pilgrim church and Christianity.

'The biblical story', as Richard Bauckham reminds us, 'is not only critical of other stories but also hospitable to other stories. On its way to the kingdom of God it does not abolish all other stories, but brings them all into relationship to itself and its way to the kingdom. It becomes the story of all stories, taking with it into the kingdom all that can be positively related to the God of Israel and Jesus. The presence of so many little stories within the biblical metanarrative, so many fragments and glimpses of other stories, within Scripture itself, is surely a sign and an earnest of that. The universal that is the kingdom of God is no dreary uniformity or oppressive denial of difference, but the milieu in which every particular reaches its true destiny in relation to the God who is the God of all because he is the God of Jesus'.[44]

The closing words of the Commission Four Report are still as fresh and stirring as when uttered almost a century ago: 'But at least as remarkable as that spectacle of the outward advance of the Church is that which has also been revealed to us of the inward transformations that are in process in the mind of the missionary, the changes of perspective, the softening of wrong antagonisms, the centralising and deepening of faith in the Lord Jesus Christ, the growth of the spirit of love to the brethren and to the world. Once again the Church is facing its duty, and therefore once more the ancient guiding fires begin to burn and shine'.[45]

Endnotes

[1] World Missionary Conference, 1910, *The Missionary Message in Relation to Non-Christian Religions*, Report of Commission IV, Edinburgh & London: Oliphant, Anderson & Ferrier; New York, Chicago and Toronto: Fleming H. Revell, 1910, pp. 217–18.
[2] *The Missionary Message*, p. 235.
[3] *The Missionary Message*, pp. 216–17.
[4] *The Missionary Message*, p. 226.
[5] *The Missionary Message*, p. 231.
[6] *The Missionary Message*, p. 232.
[7] *The Missionary Message*, p. 273.
[8] *The Missionary Message*, pp. 273–4.
[9] *The Missionary Message*, p. 220.
[10] W.H.T. Gairdner, *'Edinburgh 1910': An Account and Interpretation of the World Missionary Conference*, Edinburgh & London: Oliphant, Anderson & Ferrier; New York, Chicago and Toronto: Fleming H. Revell, 1910, pp. 128–9.
[11] *The Missionary Message*, p. 241.
[12] *The Missionary Message*, p. 243.
[13] *The Missionary Message*, p. 228.
[14] Gairdner, *Edinburgh 1910*, p. 146.
[15] *The Missionary Message*, p. 268.
[16] *The Missionary Message*, p. 234.
[17] Gairdner, *Edinburgh 1910*, p. 138.
[18] *The Missionary Message*, p. 246.
[19] *The Missionary Message*, p. 245.
[20] *The Missionary Message*, pp. 276–8.
[21] Gairdner, *Edinburgh 1910*, p. 150.
[22] John Mbiti, quoted in Kwame Bediako, *Christianity in Africa: The Renewal of a Non-Western Religion,* Edinburgh: Edinburgh University Press, 1995, p. 217.
[23] For Farquhar, see Eric J. Sharpe, *Not to Destroy but to Fulfil: The Contribution of J.N. Farquhar to Protestant Missionary Thought in India before 1914*, Uppsala: Swedish Institute of Missionary Research, 1965.
[24] A. G. Hogg, in *The Missionary Message*, p. 185.
[25] Peter Cotterell, *Mission and Meaninglessness: The Good News in a World of Suffering and Disorder*, London: SPCK, 1990, p. 51.
[26] Lesslie Newbigin, *The Open Secret: Sketches for a Missionary Theology,* London: SPCK, 1978, p. 200.

[27] See M. M. Thomas, 'The Absoluteness of Jesus Christ and Christ-Centred Syncretism', *Ecumenical Review* Vol. 37 (October 1985), pp. 387–97.
[28] Christopher Lamb, *The Call to Retrieval: Kenneth Cragg's Christian Vocation to Islam*, London: Grey Seal, 1997, ch. 5.
[29] Kenneth Cragg, *The Christ and the Faiths*, London: SPCK, 1986, p. 17.
[30] Cragg, *The Christ and the Faiths*, p 17.
[31] Kenneth Cragg, *The Call of the Minaret* 1956, 2nd edn, London: SPCK, 1985, p. 168.
[32] Cragg, *The Christ and the Faiths*, p 5.
[33] Cragg, *The Christ and the Faiths*, p. 322.
[34] Karl Rahner, *Theological Investigations*, vol. 5, *Later Writings*, trans. Karl-H. Kruger, London: Darton, Longman and Todd, 1966, p. 121.
[35] Rahner, *Theological Investigations*, vol. 5, *Later Writings*, p. 128.
[36] Rahner, *Theological Investigations*, vol. 5, *Later Writings*, pp. 121–2, 125, 130.
[37] Rahner, *Theological Investigations*, vol. 5, *Later Writings*, p.131.
[38] Samuel Rayan, 'Religions, Salvation, Mission', in Paul Mojzes and Leonard Swidler, eds., *Christian Mission and Inter-Religious Dialogue*, Lewiston, USA and Lampeter, UK: Edwin Mellor Press, 1990, pp.138, 139.
[39] John Hick and Paul Knitter, eds., *The Myth of Christian Uniqueness* , London: SCM, 1987, p. vii.
[40] Paul Knitter, *No Other Name?: A Critical Survey of Christian Attitudes Towards the World Religions*, Maryknoll, New York: Orbis, 1985, pp. 220–22.
[41] Hans Küng, 'Christianity and World Religions: Dialogue with Islam', in Leonard Swidler, ed., *Toward a Universal Theology of Religion*, Maryknoll, New York: Orbis, 1987, p. 236.
[42] John E. Goldingay and Christopher J. H. Wright, '"Yahweh our God Yahweh One": The Old Testament and Religious Pluralism', in *One God, One Lord in a World of Religious Pluralism*, A. D. Clark and B. W. Winter, eds., Cambridge: Tyndale House, 1991, pp. 44, 45.
[43] Lesslie Newbigin, *The Gospel in a Pluralist Society*, Grand Rapids: Eerdmans, 1989, p. 166.
[44] Richard Bauckham, *Bible and Mission: Christian Witness in a Postmodern World*, Grand Rapids: Baker Academic, 2003, p. 110.
[45] *The Missionary Message*, pp. 273–4.

COMMISSION FIVE

THE PREPARATION OF MISSIONARIES

Commission Five
'The Preparation of Missionaries'

The Commission in Summary

Commission Five of the World Missionary Conference had the task of reporting on 'The Preparation of Missionaries'. Under the Chairmanship of Professor Douglas Mackenzie – born of Scottish missionary parents in South Africa, Edinburgh educated, Professor of Systematic Theology in Chicago, and from 1904 the President of Hartford Seminary Foundation – the Commission gathered evidence from the United States, Britain, Germany and Scandinavia, and from a wide cross-section of missionaries. The Commissioners were mainly theological educators from European and North American universities/colleges and theological colleges/seminaries. Thirteen were from Britain, seven were from the United States, and Sweden, Germany and Canada each had one representative: 24 men and 4 women.

The Report, running to 219 pages, with a further 115 pages of appendices, is divided into five Parts: (1) a review of world conditions affecting Christian mission; (2) a review of the current theory and practice of missionary training; (3) an elaboration of principles for missionary training, and their application to varies categories of missionary; (4) a consideration of what 'special missionary preparation' requires, and how it could be provided; and (5) a review of principles and practices of committees responsible for the selection and preparation of candidates.

The heart of the Report lies in Parts 2 to 4. In light of the rapidly changing world situation that was seen to challenge churches to produce a higher standard of missionary – the need being for men and women who combine genuine vocation with the highest possible professional and theological training – Part 2 offers a frank assessment of contemporary concepts and methods of missionary preparation. Reflecting views expressed by missionaries themselves, the Report recognizes 'a marked disparity between their ideals and their actual, or working, standard'.[1] This criticism is applied both to the standards of personal preparation – physical, social, intellectual, spiritual – and to the professional training of ordained, educational, medical and industrial missionaries, and lay evangelists. 'It is clear', this part of the Report concludes, 'that the Mission Boards of America, the continent of Europe, and Great Britain, are, as a whole, aiming at a high standard of all-round missionary qualification ... But in view of the admitted inability of the Societies to satisfy their own requirements, and because of the widespread opinion among missionaries that because of the modern situation abroad higher qualifications are needed, it is urgent that the richer resources of the Church should be more largely drawn upon'.[2]

This set the ground for the Commission's main task, 'to determine as precisely as possible what steps the Boards can take against such relative failure by a better system of preparatory training'.[3] Part 3 of the Report sets out the Commissioners' understanding of the principles that should underlie effective missionary preparation in relation to their definition of the three fundamental tasks of mission: to present the Christian message through 'direct evangelisation';[4] to manifest the power of Christian living in the 'personality and life of the evangelist';[5] and to organize 'a living and effective church in a Christian nation'.[6]

Missionary training, for all types of missionaries, should integrate spiritual, moral and intellectual elements. Since the spiritual element is 'purely a gift from God',[7] it has to be nurtured throughout a missionary's life, in which training both before and during missionary service is essential. Moral training should cultivate four qualities: 'docility'[8] in the sense of always being open and willing to learn; 'gentleness' or 'the spirit of courtesy'[9] that enables missionaries to understand the customs of the people among whom they are called to live; and 'sympathy' that empowers missionaries to love the people they serve. These combine to produce a fourth quality that all missionaries should seek to attain: namely, 'leadership' in respect of 'the special duties and responsibilities of a missionary's position'.[10]

In addition to such personal qualities, Part 3 of the Report addresses the importance of intellectual training. 'The missionary must have the best education which his own country and the Church can give him, whatever is to be his department of labour.'[11] For most missionaries this entails professional training for ordination, in medicine or education, or in nursing or a range of industrial skills, and it was recognized that such training can only be acquired in universities or colleges that are independent of the missionary societies themselves. But in nurturing potential missionary candidates in their professional studies, the Societies should encourage them to avoid the 'parochialism of specialisation',[12] and cultivate a wide culture that will inspire them 'to face the perils and the fascinations of independent thought', rooting themselves in the Bible – 'the missionaries' Book'[13] – while engaging the natural and social sciences and philosophy.

Anticipating that most missionaries would continue to be ordained clergy, and that their professional training would continue to take place alongside those preparing for home ministry, the Report gave extensive consideration to ways in which theological education could be improved by opening itself to missionary perspectives. Here the Commissioners spoke with the authority of theological educators themselves. Theological education, they opine, is best undertaken at the post-graduate level, on the basis of a good general education in the arts or sciences. Theological colleges/seminaries should pay more attention to missionary topics as an integral part of all theological training. Mission should not be considered an optional or elective subject, but should infuse the study of the Bible, the Church Fathers, historical and systematic theology, and practical theology. The Chair in Evangelistic Theology held by Professor Alexander Duff in New College, Edinburgh, was cited as an example, and it was regretted that it had lapsed.

The Report also gave extensive consideration to 'the supreme importance of the women's share'[14] in missionary work. While betraying the Commission's patriarchal complexion in the tone and content of its discussion of the preparation of women missionaries, it also produced one of its most insightful recommendations: that women missionaries should not be trained only for 'women's work for women', but for the realization of 'the vision of the place of women in the building up of the whole fabric of national life'.[15] The example cited was the Women's Missionary College in Edinburgh, the Principal, Annie Small, being one of the four women Commissioners. An Appendix to the Report describes the philosophy of the College.

Part 4 of the Report deals with 'special missionary training',[16] meaning the specific areas of training that could not be provided by universities or theological colleges. The ideal was a Central College, or Colleges, where missionary societies could co-operate in providing a curriculum including the sciences, history and methods of mission, comparative religion, social sciences, pedagogy, and linguistics. Yale and Hartford were already moving in this direction, as were German and Scandinavian colleges. To address the situation in Britain where there was less system, but no fewer resources, the Report recommended the creation of a Board of Missionary Studies, 'the general purpose of which will be to supply guidance and to render assistance to Missionary Societies in the preparation of missionaries for their work'.[17]

Endnotes

[1] World Missionary Conference, 1910, *The Preparation of Missionaries*, Report of Commission V, Edinburgh & London: Oliphant, Anderson & Ferrier; New York, Chicago, and Toronto: Fleming H. Revell, 1910, p. 15.
[2] *The Preparation of Missionaries*, p. 25.
[3] *The Preparation of Missionaries*, p. 97.
[4] *The Preparation of Missionaries*, p. 97.
[5] *The Preparation of Missionaries*, p. 97
[6] *The Preparation of Missionaries*, p. 98.
[7] *The Preparation of Missionaries*, p. 100.
[8] *The Preparation of Missionaries*, p. 101.
[9] *The Preparation of Missionaries*, pp. 102–3.
[10] *The Preparation of Missionaries*, pp. 104–5.
[11] *The Preparation of Missionaries*, p. 107.
[12] *The Preparation of Missionaries*, p. 108.
[13] *The Preparation of Missionaries*, p. 110.
[14] *The Preparation of Missionaries*, p. 147.
[15] *The Preparation of Missionaries*, p. 153.
[16] *The Preparation of Missionaries*, p. 155.
[17] *The Preparation of Missionaries*, p. 189.

Changing Images in the Formation for Mission: Commission Five in Light of Current Challenges A World Perspective

Anne-Marie Kool

In his account of the 1910 World Missionary Conference in Edinburgh, W.H. Temple Gairdner introduced the agenda for the last two days as follows: 'If THIS be the task before the Church: … the evangelisation of all the world, the Christianising of the nations … then *what manner of men must they be who are sent to set their hands to it, and what manner of Church must [it] be which sends them!'*[2] The focus was now on the missionaries, on the 'men … who are sent' to fulfill the task of 'the evangelisation of all the world'.[3] It was felt that this task largely depended on them. That is why the 1200 participants met to discuss the Report of Commission Five dealing with the preparation of these missionaries.[4] On the next day the focus was on the 'Church which sends them', the 'home base' in the 'Christian world'.

Since 1910 groundbreaking changes have taken place in the demographics of Christianity. It has become increasingly obvious that the 'home base' of Edinburgh 1910, Europe and North America, can hardly be called 'Christian' anymore. Christopher J. H. Wright reminds us that on an average Sunday more people are in church in Communist China than in all of Western Europe.[5] The churches in the West find themselves now in a completely new role – as missionaries being sent to their own Western contexts – considered by many as one of the toughest mission fields of today.

This chapter will focus on the changing images of the formation for mission since Edinburgh 1910 from a Western perspective. Wilbert R. Shenk has demonstrated that missiology and missionary training programmes in Western culture 'continue to be defined by the "foreign missions" paradigm of the past two centuries'.[6] This forces us to consider whether there has in fact been any change in mission formation since 1910. Though pragmatic approaches based on a functional ecclesiology have dominated the field for the last century, some authors have frequently asked more fundamental, theological questions regarding the nature of the missionary agent on whom this formation is focused. J. E. Lesslie Newbigin observes two responses of Western Christendom to this changed situation, showing a tendency to turn away from the reality of the Gospel and the contemporary world. There is the temptation 'to recapture missionary fervour by appeals to the models of the past', as well as the temptation 'to become victim of a sense of guilt'.[7] Referring to the situation in North America, Dana L. Robert suggests we have to go back 'to the basics', since we can 'no longer assume an educated consensus about mission in our churches'. She observes that 'a formation for mission in a post-modern, pluralistic world is seriously lacking'.[8] This chapter begins, first, with a brief examination of the Commission Report. Second, we will look at how the image of the preparation of missionaries changed and developed during the twentieth century. And third, we will turn to the question of missionary formation for today's world, especially in the Western context.

The Preparation of Missionaries: Assessing the Commission Five Report

The image of a missionary in this report is one who is trained for a lifetime career on the mission field, bringing Christian civilization hand in hand with the Gospel message. The impression is that the task of evangelizing the world largely depends on Western missionaries, and on the quality of these people. The missionary is *the* agent of mission. The chairman, Douglas Mackenzie, stated that, 'The whole matter on the human side of it hinges on the quality of the missionary... The quality of the missionary will triumph over the absence of money. The quality of the missionary therefore becomes a supreme question for this Conference'.[9] And what defined proper 'quality' was clearly outlined.

First, there was the quality of scholarship. The Report depicts the missionary not only as someone thoroughly rooted in the Bible, but also as someone who is academically competent in his or her professional field, be that medicine, education, or theology. The missionary should have the highest possible professional qualifications in the relevant field. He must be able to think independently and maintain a broad, academic outlook on life and culture. The general intellectual preparation of a missionary should give him a 'habit of ... weighing what is wanted, and for what purpose ... [It should also develop in him] a readiness to recognise the complexity of questions, and humility and patience to study them'.[10] Whether this ideal was ever achieved remains an open question.

Second, there was the quality of leadership. The Report acknowledges the 'unanimous call from every mission field' for 'men with a special capacity for leadership'.[11] The West was to send 'the ablest and best youth of Christendom', 'great leaders', not 'your average man'. The question is how does one identify and train such leaders. 'Real leaders are few ... those who think themselves to be such prematurely, perhaps before they have left home, usually fail, while the real leaders of the future are today content to be obedient and humble toilers at the daily task which is imposed on them by their own leaders'.[12]

Third, there was the quality of spirituality. A central stress in missionary preparation was the importance of their vocation, and of their spirituality. The necessity of spiritual formation was predominantly present in the principles laid out for raising the level of missionary training. The conference itself also had a strong focus on spirituality. In the plenary sessions 'the heart of the morning' was given to 'the cream of the day', the prayer hour, times of 'united silence, in the close presence of God'.[13] In regard to training, this spiritual element, the Report states, has to do with 'ways in which God rather than self becomes the actual centre of life', and should be considered as 'purely the gift of God'. Training could at best only 'remove some obstacles in the way of their development'. Nurturing a deeply rooted spiritual life, one that is independent from external aids, can be helped by general instruction, but more by 'intimate personal advice' provided by 'experienced Christian friends'.[14]

Finally, there was the moral quality. 'The secret of effective work' rested in an attitude of 'docility', of humility. This openness and willingness to learn was of crucial importance.[15] A special chapter in the Report examines the need for continuous education to assist the missionaries to avoid the danger of a certain mental fatigue brought about by climate, food or poor health, which affects both their spiritual and their intellectual life.

Underlying all that is said about the calling and character of the missionary is the matter of obedience to Christ's command, the Great Commission of Matthew 28:19–20, to take the Gospel to the world. The emphasis is on the task to be completed, rather than on the Gospel as something God *has* done once for all and for which we may all rejoice. This description of Christian mission approximates what Newbigin characterizes as a human 'programme of action' and moral reformation, which is marked by an 'atmosphere of strain and anxiety'.[16] Accordingly, the task of the evangelization of the world is depicted almost in the form of a huge business plan: a thorough, systematic and critical analysis of the current situation in the mission field. For this plan to be realized, better-qualified missionaries were needed. This basic assumption was followed by a set of principles for effective missionary preparation, and recommendations on how to implement them immediately. Finally, proposals were offered to fill certain gaps in this process: a Central Training Institute was proposed and a 'last word' was addressed to the church 'at the home base', calling it to provide the necessary resources.[17]

The Report conceived Europe, as well as North America, as 'fully evangelized'. The urgent issue was to point the home church to her responsibility to 'produce the missionaries and resources needed to tackle the unprecedented opportunities now being offered to evangelize the non-Christian world – before it is too late'.[18] However, between the lines – especially in the account and interpretation of Temple Gairdner – one senses that the survey had revealed that the home church was not as stable as the delegates conceived it to be.

Christendom Losing Missionary Zeal

One of the first discoveries was, as Gairdner recalls, the 'existence of a *non-contributing Church*',[19] that 'Christendom is not yet missionary'. Elsewhere he points to the standard of Christian life in the church, the 'lowness' of which is related to the 'mass of intellectual unsettlement' among students in the West.[20] With regard to the difficulties in recruiting missionaries, there was not simply a lack of interest in the missionary vocation. The 'ultimate explanation', put very 'bluntly', was that 'men are not coming forward into the membership of the Christian Church at all'.[21] It was even stated that 'something must happen to the church at home if it is going even to look at the work which has been put on it by this conference'.[22] Despite these bleak signs, the Report pointed the conference to God, the 'one solution of the problem of the home base of missions'.[23] People were urged to pray for a revival of a missionary spirit in the sending churches. Nonetheless, the first signs were already present for what Andrew F. Walls referred to as 'perhaps the largest and fastest recession in Christian history'.[24]

In identifying the weakness of the 'home base', the Report focused on the importance of making the home church more missionary minded. The idea dawned that 'the missionary enterprise ... must cease to be considered a matter for the specialists'.[25] This was no less than a restoration of the church to 'her proper function', or 'the re-creation of the church'. It is something 'which only God Himself can work, yet a work in which man can join by the almost forgotten secret of prayer'. This was the *Moravian Ideal*: the church itself as a mission society. At issue was 'how to make the passion for taking the Gospel to all the world permeate every rank and class and definable section of Christendom'.[26] We see here the contours of a new image of missionary agent, the church itself, later termed a 'missional church'.[27]

Finally, these issues, while of theological bearing, were essentially pragmatic. The concept of a missionary church was an individualistic one. It was to become an instrument for the goal of 'gathering converts', one by one, and in this way of Christianizing the non-Christian world. The focus was on *how to* secure, as soon as possible, the needed resources for completing the task. The Report was characterized by what James A. Scherer described as 'missionary traditionalism'. The *modus operandi* of missions remained unexamined. The theological, practical, vocational and intellectual tasks appear to be 'perfectly self-evident'. No fresh study was required.[28] Difficult questions were not asked, and the only things perceived as lacking were human and financial resources. Scherer, indicative of something of the shift, calls for a renewed biblical reflection on the goals and practices of mission. 'Our missionary practice must reflect that the Triune God fulfils His mission in the world through the church.'[29] He emphasized that the 'church needs to bring its missionary practice into conformity with a Biblical, theocentric and apostolic understanding of missionary vocation'.[30]

The Twentieth Century: Changing Images in the Formation for Mission?

Billy Graham, in his opening speech at the Lausanne Congress on World Evangelization in 1974, characterized Edinburgh 1910 as 'the most historic conference on evangelism and missions of this century'.[31] He identified two streams coming out of Edinburgh: an evangelical one and an ecumenical one. This split was due to several interrelated shifts in approach. Although some attempts were undertaken to reconcile the two streams, several dichotomies continued to dominate the discussions on mission theology and practice throughout the twentieth century. Aspects of this include: shifts from an individualistic to a communal approach, from evangelism to social action, from parachurch/mission society to church as the agent of mission, from man 'in this *and* the next world' to man 'in this world' alone, and from reconciliation with God to social reconciliation.[32] Graham sees the main reason for these shifts in an unclear relation between church and mission. In Edinburgh, church leaders were not there to represent their *churches;* they were there as 'evangelists or missionaries'. However, in later world missionary gatherings the participants were, increasingly, 'eminent leaders … in their capacity as *churchmen'*.[33] Graham considered these church leaders to be the main cause of a lack of evangelistic zeal that led to the disappearance of mission from the agenda. This strengthened the increasingly individualistic character of mission in evangelical circles, and impacted changes in the formation for mission. Profound theological discussions were taking place on the *what* and *why* of mission(s) in the ecumenical stream, while the evangelical stream was dominated by pragmatism and a complete lack of theological reflection. Fruitful interaction between the two concerning the church and mission relationship was missing. There was no mutual correction. This resulted in a continuation of a pragmatic approach to mission with no fundamental theological questions raised, and a stagnation of a missionary fervour, with some excellent documents on mission theory shelved in Geneva. What are the reasons for this stalemate? One wonders why Protestants write relatively little about a theology of mission.

The 1952 Willingen conference of the International Missionary Council revealed two different views on missionary ecclesiology that would be prominent in the ensuing years. For one, represented by Newbigin and Scherer, the church was perceived as continuing the mission of Jesus in the world. The other, 'emphasizing the work of the Spirit in culture', is represented by Hoekendijk. These two views remain in tension even until today.[34] Willingen was significantly influenced by the shock of China closing to Western missions and the 'alarmingly high' number of missionary withdrawals in the 1950s.[35] The conference made it clear that traditional approaches had to be re-evaluated and placed an emphasis on God calling the church to express her mission 'through an increasing flow of Christian laymen and women who go across the world in business, industry and government and who do so with a deep conviction that God calls them to witness for Him in all of life'.[36] Each member is called 'to share in the total mission of the church by his witness in his daily life and work'.[37] According to Newbigin, 'the primary witness to the sovereignty of Christ ... must be given and can only be given in the ordinary secular work of laymen and women';[38] they are the 'signs of His lordship in every area of life',[39] the 'subversive agents',[40] and 'the church's front-line troops in her engagement with the world'.[41] Early in his career Newbigin had come to the conclusion that 'the success or failure of the church depends supremely upon the witness to Christ of the ordinary lay member'.[42] For Newbigin, recovering the laity as the primary agents of mission had huge implications for missionary formation. His wide experience as a missionary in India had taught him the importance of 'exhorting pastors to give high priority to training people in their congregations for their callings', and to developing structures whereby 'the laity can be equipped for their witness in society'.[43] The patterns of ministerial leadership were the primary structure needing reform.[44]

Willingen's dealing with the missionary calling of the church did not rule out a foreign missionary obligation to be fulfilled by people in life-long service to the church, although this conclusion was prompted only by practical considerations.[45] The stronger focus on the missionary nature of the church implied for the foreign missionary that 'decisions in all matters of common concern should be made in mutual consultation, and in the spirit of partnership and obedience'.[46] Scherer points out that here we see a transition from the nineteenth-century missionary's role as 'a gospel herald standing on the frontier of paganism' to an 'ecumenical servant'. The interchange of servants of the church between countries belongs to the ecumenical nature of the church herself, not whether churches are older or younger.[47] 'The missionary now fulfils his personal calling by merging his vocation and identity with that of the receiving church'. He is not sent anymore as an 'agent or authority of the sending church', but as 'a servant loaned by one branch of the church of Christ to another'.[48] The terminology for 'foreign mission' shifted to 'inter-church aid', the foreign missionary became a 'fraternal worker'.[49]

Newbigin concludes that mission was being absorbed into inter-church aid and ecumenism. This was caused by a distorted ecclesiology.

> We have corrupted the word 'church' (and distorted the life of the churches) by constantly using it in a non-missionary sense. If it was always clear, both in our speech and in our ecclesiastical life that the Church *is* mission ... then inter-church aid would always be aid-for-mission and nothing else.[50]

He recalls that, whereas traditional Christian tendencies rejected the world, the mission and renewal of the church in the 1960s now 'depends on acceptance and affirmation of the secular world'. The vision of the missionary nature of the church, represented by Newbigin and dominant in the 1950s, was now considered 'pious talk and Geneva ideology'.[51]

Although it would appear that the age of the foreign missionary was over with the indigenous church now taking responsibility, Newbigin points to the cross-cultural missionary as an 'enduring necessity in the life of the universal Church', because in and through that person an ecumenical correction takes place. Through the 'reflexive action' of the missionary 'the gospel comes back to us in the idiom of other cultures with power to question our understanding of it'.[52]

In 1959, the International Missionary Consultation was asked to undertake a study of missionary training on a worldwide basis. Here, the foremost question asked was why it is at all necessary to train missionaries: 'Is not the missionary task self-evident to men of Christian conviction? Does not the church understand what mission is?'[53] The working definition of a missionary was accepted as 'the servant of the church who leaves his own country or culture to proclaim the Gospel in partnership with the church where it is already at work, or with the purpose of planting the church where it has not yet been planted'.[54] For the first time the emphasis was that 'every church is potentially both a sending and a receiving church', recognizing the need for missionaries also from the 'younger churches'.[55]

Whereas Edinburgh thought in pragmatic terms, now theological issues are given attention in missionary formation. Scherer states that 'theological clarity is no luxury to the Christian mission; it belongs to the indispensable equipment of the missionary'. Practical matters must also be given attention, implying 'a rigorous application of theology to missionary practice, so that the means and instruments employed are consistent with the Gospel'.[56] Missionary methodology should be grounded in theology, because 'missionary activity that is not consistent with the mind and purpose of God has no claim upon His blessing'.[57] Since in the ecumenical era the missionary's service has inter-church, inter-confessional and international implications, missionary training should deal with all three of these senses of ecumenical.[58] It should occur in an ecumenical community setting in which the missionary candidates should be helped to 'maintain and strengthen their evangelistic zeal and to deepen their sense of commitment to Christ as Lord'.[59] A special emphasis should be given to 'building genuine and vital relationships with persons' and working with groups. A significantly new note at the Toronto Consultation was an emphasis on the involvement of the receiving church in all phases of missionary orientation and training,[60] and in pastoral care – or, 'member care', as it is called today for expatriate missionaries.

Much attention has been and is given to the formation of individuals for missions, be it 'the laity', 'foreign missionaries' or 'fraternal workers'. But the missionary formation of churches seems to have been given less attention. Dana L. Robert reminds us that the Mission Education Movement in America taught ordinary churchgoers about the mission of the church, calling them to support missions. This was the way in which many denominations 'came to look beyond themselves to a grand vision of the Kingdom in which all of

Christ's people have a place at the table'. The 'simultaneously optimistic and self-critical' materials of the Mission Education Movement brought that 'grand vision down into the living rooms of small-town Christians across the country'. This located 'American experience in its place, as only one part of a worldwide Christian community'.[61] In the last three decades of the twentieth century the movement 'lost steam' because the number of missionaries from evangelical mission agencies and churches outgrew those of mainline churches, and thus mission in terms of missionary formation reflects the individualistic, pragmatic days of Edinburgh 1910.

Theological institutions were supposed to play a role in the missionary formation of the churches in the West, equipping them to take up their responsibility for mission in their own local and global contexts. David J. Bosch points out that one factor in the present crisis for missiology in the West is that the modern missionary enterprise was born and bred outside the church.

> The church did not regard [herself] as called to mission. The Reformation definitions of the church were concerned with what happened inside the church… a place where something was being done (passive voice), and not a people who did something …. Consequently when the missionary flame was eventually kindled, it burned on the fringes of the institutional church, frequently meeting with passionate resistance from the official church.[62]

Mission was an 'appendix' to the church, and missiology could be no more than that in the theological curriculum. Practical theology focused on the internal up building of the church in the West, missiology with the church in the 'Third World'. Other theologians often 'did not know how to cope with a department of foreign affairs in their institutions'.[63] That is the case in many institutions in Europe. A clear focus on missiology in their own context has emerged in only a very few institutions, although that number is increasing.

The most significant shift in mission formation since Edinburgh 1910 was the move from an individualistic, pragmatic focus on the missionary as the hinge on which the whole missionary movement depended, to a focus on God being a missionary God, who sends His church into the world. However, Willingen's focus on the missionary church remains deficient insofar as the relationship between the individual and the communal agent in missions remains ambiguous. Here, the individual missionary remains a functionary of the institutional church, dependent on the church, and confined by its institutional structures.

In the meantime a functional ecclesiology had taken over, which eliminated missions from the agenda of the mainline churches for decades to come. In 1958 Newbigin continued his Trinitarian-Christocentric perspective on the church in mission, and introduced a related, new image for Christian mission: that of One Body, One Gospel, One World.[64] Paradoxically, this was not initially taken up by the ecumenical movement, but by the evangelical wing of worldwide Christianity in its groundbreaking congress in Lausanne 1974.

Reaction: World Evangelization Back on the Agenda

Billy Graham formulated the goal for Lausanne as focusing on one sector of the church's responsibility, that of evangelism, because this aspect had 'not been adequately represented at some of the other world Church gatherings'.[65] Evangelical Christianity kept the 'unfinished task' of world mission on the agenda in the last decades of the twentieth century, taking up one of the main concerns of the Willingen conference to reinvigorate the missionary movement. It is striking how Newbigin's unity image for Christian mission is taken up in a modified way by the Lausanne movement – 'the whole Church ... the whole Gospel ... the whole world'. The structure of his statement is taken up, but its heart is relinquished – whole vs. one – possibly explaining the fact that Newbigin was not present in Lausanne. There was little attention at the Lausanne Congress 1974 to the 'formation for mission', or the training of missionaries, though some contributions dealt with closely related topics like the 'Church as God's Agent in Evangelism'.[66] Notably Jonathan Tien-en Chau raised the question of whether Evangelicals should cooperate with less mission-minded churches for the sake of biblical unity or to choose an independent route for pragmatic reasons so that mission strategy may be accomplished. Chau asked, 'Should we permit a pragmatic approach to cross-cultural strategy?' He concludes that 'the biblical doctrine of the unity of the body and the diversity of its members does not warrant such a pragmatic policy'. The evangelical world needs 'to re-examine its para-church structures in the light of the nature of the unity among local churches'.[67]

A major development in the formation for mission is related to the Lausanne movement. With the growth of the emerging missionary movement from the Two-Thirds World in the 1980s and 1990s, the Mission Commission of the World Evangelical Fellowship presented a study in 1991 called *Internationalising Missionary Training*: a 'world-wide perspective on the equipping of cross-cultural servant leaders'. It offers a 'spectrum of *models* from different countries, contexts and institutions' which are involved in the training of missionaries at a global level. The common thrust of the training is 'formation of character', and the 'development of cross-cultural ministry competencies' emerging from 'solid Christian educational philosophy'.[68] 'Nothing else like it exists.' Its global perspective offers 'the singular opportunity to do something new and fresh in this arena of equipping cross-cultural servants, while at the same time learning from both the successes and mistakes of the Western missionary movement'.[69] A sense of opportunity and optimism, like Edinburgh, is present here. But there is also a kind of amnesia. Were not Commission Five, and later the Toronto Consultation (1964), examples of internationalizing missionary training and involving the 'receiving churches' in the training process?

Stephen T. Hoke, in examining the paradigm shifts in 'Missions Training', states that 'the roles played by missionaries from North America must change'. He calls for 'servant-teaching' and 'a ministry of humility',[70] offering a good illustration of the current state of affairs in the formation for mission among evangelicals, and showing that in fact not much has changed since Edinburgh 1910. There seems to be a hidden resistance to speaking about Western culture as a mission field. One wonders, with this vestige of a 'West to the rest' attitude, whether 'real and active cross-fertilization' is truly taking place, so that we may become 'truly global in our missionary work'.[71] There is a real danger that the West will continue to 'dominate and impose strategy and structuring' of the partnerships between the West and the Two-Thirds World;[72] all the more so since most of the resources for missions are still provided by the West. Hoke presents us with a training model for missions characterized by a pragmatic ecclesiology. This is deficient in that it only focuses on the training of the individual missionary and not of the church. The basic assumption of the nineteenth-century image of a missionary and of the Western church as 'home base' is still present. Western culture is not explicitly considered a 'mission field'. The methodology of the formation for mission is uncritically taken from secular business models, which have their starting point in a radically different anthropology, and introduce non-biblical values into the mission movement. Shenk reminds us that 'we should become more self-aware of the assumptions that have controlled mission studies and missionary action up to the present'.[73] Interestingly enough, Hoke concludes his article similarly, with the observation that 'we have been depending too much on social sciences, management by objectives, and marketing techniques ... Where is Jesus in all this?'[74] He proposes a 'biblically responsible and reflective' answer from Christian educators, a response of 'doxological teaching', that is, 'recognizing or discovering that "God is here! God is in this place!" and then designing learning experiences which open the learner's eyes to see how big and glorious God is'.[75]

Surveying the 'images' of missionary formation in the twentieth century captures Newbigin's observation well, that two temptations have threatened the mission movement. On the evangelical side of the stream we notice the temptation 'to recapture missionary fervour by appeals to the models of the past'. A striking resemblance of continuity with Edinburgh 1910 can be observed in the image dominant among evangelicals: the individual missionary as the agent in missions. However, a shift has taken place from the career missionary to more short-term and tentmaker missionaries. Often partnership with local churches has been missing. It seems that in comparison to Edinburgh the academic focus has weakened. The pragmatic mission enterprise has continued. A weak functional ecclesiology gave way to the expansion of parachurch organizations. This led the missionary movement worldwide to splinter, causing duplication of effort, competition, division and conflicts within the body of Christ. *How* was at the forefront, and the *what*, and *why* questions were hardly raised. Theological questions into the nature of the missionary agents – the question of who should be included in the formation process – were not asked. A reductionist approach, lacking the biblical image, continued. No critical reflection took place on the methodology used in the formation. One wonders whether the drivenness for results and outcomes due to the use of secular business models in mission, and the continuation of an individualistic focus, does not lead to a situation in which missionaries are stretched to capacity, giving rise to increased 'missionary attrition'.[76] This image is as much a child of its time as the Edinburgh one. Few missionary training programmes have been set up for mission to Western culture, as the West seems not to be taken seriously as a 'mission field'. In the meantime, an emerging missionary movement is spreading up out of Central and Eastern Europe, often eastward into Central Asia and Siberia.

On the ecumenical side, Newbigin observes another temptation, 'to become victim of a sense of guilt',[77] has dominated. This second image of a missionary is a more corporate one, emphasizing since Willingen that the whole church was the agent in missions, with the responsibility of all her members to be witnesses. However, the ambiguity of Willingen resulted in a confused situation in which mission was dropped altogether. There was a failure to give these corporate and individual missionary agents a clear theological foundation, as well as uncertainty regarding how the two should relate to each other and to the world to which they were called. There was also ambiguity regarding how the *missio Dei* and the *missiones ecclesiae* were to relate. At most, churches were dominated by social agendas. Mission was out. Ecumenical unity without reference to mission was in. After the individualistic emphasis of Edinburgh 1910, the image of mission formation expanded to a more corporate, communal model. However, this change has not been of much impact, as the focus was no longer on mission.

Contemporary missiology also missed the opportunity to lead the formation of the church and its pastors for mission, helping them to understand the shift from Christendom to new missionary ecclesiology. Missiology continued to be the department for external affairs in Western theological curricula, focusing on the non-Western world, and hardly dealing with the Western world and its own missionary challenges! Few theological institutions aimed at teaching their pastors to be trainers of the members of their congregations to live a witnessing life and be missionaries, as Newbigin and others emphasized.

Resistance to Shift from Christendom to Missionary Ecclesiology

What is striking is a kind of resistance in Europe to thinking through issues related to the missionary nature of the church, although recently evangelism and mission are back on the agenda of mainline churches there.[78] There is no evidence of new missional structures in the church, which is indispensable for the Western churches to face the challenges of now being part of the non-Christian world. The emergence of non-Western Churches all over Europe has led to a situation where, on an average Sunday in cities like Amsterdam and Copenhagen, more 'non-Western' Christians worship than ethnic Dutch or Danes. Yet it seems that mainline European churches hardly take notice of these changes.

Wilbert R. Shenk states that the church in the West has long been marginalized, 'because it is confused about mission to its own culture'. The 'self-consciousness' inculcated by Christendom was non-missionary. Therefore the church in Western culture is characterized by a 'lassitude'. 'What is required is a fundamental reorientation of the church in modern culture to its mission to its culture.' In other words, 'missional ecclesiology must be at the top of our agenda'. Through the modern mission movement the church rediscovered her responsibility in the 'regions beyond', but 'nothing less than a reformation on that scale will deliver the church in the West from its captivity to its mission-less identity relative to its own culture'. A 'continuing conversion of the Church' to its missionary nature is needed![79] The missionary formation for Western culture must reckon with the 'ancient cathedral spires (which) continue to cast long shadows, ... but it must be based on a renewed understanding of the apostolic character of the church...'.[80]

One wonders why Newbigin's theological reflections did not have more impact on the Lausanne movement. Was he considered too much of a 'liberal ecumenical'? Why did his theological and practical reflection on the church's formation for mission not have more impact on the ecumenical movement? Was he considered too much of a 'missionary' in the traditional sense of the word? Probably the greatest asset in the formation for mission of the Edinburgh 1910 conference was that it was *one* conference, mission in unity, representing what were later referred to as the evangelical and ecumenical movements. But the greatest deficiency of Edinburgh was the dominance of the Western perspective on mission. Until now, 'solutions' for recovering a proper image of the formation for mission have been provided by 'the West'. As Joel A. Carpenter suggests, Western scholars would do well to listen to those voices of the body of Christ belonging to non-Western Christianity 'by allowing (them) to share in our projects here and shape our agendas'.[81] They are now in the majority. Their perspective in the training of missiologists and missionaries for Western culture could advance Shenk's observation that the formation for mission ought to be based 'on a biblical understanding rather than historical precedents and theological distortions'.[82]

The Twenty-First Century: 'Back to the Basics'! Changing Images in the Formation for Mission

African scholars remind us that the New Testament provides resources needed 'for offering a solidly grounded critique of the practice of mission'.[83] Newbigin, with his forty years of missionary experience in India, says that foreign missions, in the sense we know them, are a relatively recent occurrence and have been shaped by the movement of the cultural and political expansion of the West. He emphasizes that as we realize that our missionary methods have been 'too much conformed to the world of the 19th century, it is no adequate response to try now to be conformed to the world of the 20th century',[84] or, one could add, to that of the twenty-first century. We need to look afresh 'to our chart and compass and to ask how we now use the new winds and the new tides to carry out our sailing orders'.[85] That is what Newbigin considers a third possibility, apart from the two temptations mentioned earlier. It is another way forward, though it may not be 'broad and easy'. It is the 'costly, but exciting task ... of fundamental theological thinking, of Bible study, and of discerning the signs of the times'.[86] Dana L. Robert suggests 'we should go back to the basics', since 'one can no longer assume an educated consensus about mission in our churches'.[87] As we do so, Newbigin urges that, first and foremost, we recover the proper biblical and theological foundations for mission:

> The Christian mission began not as something to be done for the world, but as something God *has* done for all – the conquest of death. The risen Lord with us – that is the starting point. Jesus reigns; He is the *Alpha* and *Omega*; all authority in heaven and earth is His. He builds up and casts down, He roots up and He plants. He is not struggling against a world too strong for Him. He is not appealing to us to help Him to overcome the world. He *has* overcome the world, and all things – the things that so baffle us and frighten us – are in His hands to deal with as He will. How foolish we are when we allow ourselves to be tempted to seek some other source of authority and assurance for our mission… As if who Christ is and what He has done were not good enough reasons to go singing to the ends of the earth.[88]

Christian mission does not begin with a programme of action, but with the Risen Lord. 'It does not have about it that atmosphere of strain and anxiety, which always characterizes a human programme. It begins with a shout of joy … He is risen from the dead!'[89] Christian world mission starts with the resurrection of Jesus Christ, 'that explosion of hope (which) carried the believers to all the points of the compass'.[90]

The Twofold Antioch Mode of Missionary Existence

Shenk reminds us how Luke describes in Acts the unfolding of the church's missionary existence. Following His ascension Jesus entrusts the disconsolate and disoriented disciples with their defining purpose (Acts 1:8), which serves as the basis for the constitution of the church at Pentecost. In two passages Luke provides a twofold normative model for how this missionary existence of the church is to work out in the world,[91] and to the ends of the earth.

There is, first, the *organic mode*, with the disciple community scattered under the impact of persecution. They went as far as Antioch, one of the largest urban centres of that time, maintaining their witness indiscriminately to both Jews and Gentiles. This mode, Shenk emphasizes, has been the main vehicle of the expansion of the church historically. Secondly, there is the *complementary mode*: certain individuals set apart for itinerant ministry.[92] The innovative action of the Holy Spirit set apart certain individuals for an itinerant ministry, enabling faith to spread to key places in the Roman Empire. Shenk argues, 'This creates the precedent for the sending mode and, by extension, cross-cultural mission, which played a critical role in the expansion of the church precisely because it guards against parochialism… which is the slow death of the faith'.[93] Newbigin reminds us that the Holy Spirit Himself is the agent of mission who empowers the disciples (Acts 1:8) to continue the work of Christ Himself.[94] The 'Antioch Mission' does not advance after the manner of a 'humanly organized campaign',[95] or as a 'corporation to which Christ has entrusted it, but as the living body quickened and directed by the Spirit. The Spirit remains free and sovereign. He leads the way, goes ahead of the Church, surprises the Church with new things, leading her through her mission into fullness of the truth..'.[96]

The two-fold Antioch mode of mission leaves us with a surprising method for the formation for mission. There is a corporate dimension, focused on the disciple community in Antioch as they *organically* fulfill their mission, and a two-fold individual dimension, constituted by the members of this community and those sent out on a *complementary* mission. Both are closely related, as those who are sent on an individual mission have been actively involved in the formation of the former, and they continue to do so as they share their missionary experiences. One could even argue that special formation for mission is not even on the agenda; it is part of the everyday formation to be a disciple of Jesus Christ, empowered by the Holy Spirit who sends them to witness in Antioch and the ends of the earth. It was part of the nature of this community. On this basis Newbigin argues that: 'Church and mission belong indissolubly together'.[97] When the two are separated, he argues the result is that 'the Church becomes an introverted body, concerned with its own welfare, rather than with the Kingdom of God, and even if successful missionary work is carried on by others – the Church will be no fit home for those who are gathered in'.[98] In addition, he notes that, 'where new converts … are taught from the very beginning that being a Christian means being involved in a continuing mission to the world, they take their place quite naturally from the beginning in the van of the Church's evangelistic work'.[99] In arguing for a missionary ecclesiology – that mission belongs to the essence of the church – he sounds almost blasphemous to a Christendom ecclesiology still widespread in Western culture. 'If churchmanship does not mean fellowship with the Lord Jesus Christ through the Spirit, it means nothing; and you cannot have fellowship with Him without being committed to partnership in His mission to the world'.[100]

The question for theological institutions in the West is how to turn their inward looking theological curriculum into one which deals with the realities of their own Western context as a mission field, drawing on experiences gained in the worldwide mission movement. How can theological education provide for pastors to be missionaries to their own contexts, training their churches for the *organic mode*, to become missional and their members to be missionaries in the market place? A related issue concerns the role of academic missiology in the training of 'complementary mode' missionaries.[101]

The scope of this chapter does not allow for more than an outline of the implications for missionary formation. In Western culture, this task has as its starting point the reality of a widespread Christendom ecclesiology. Shenk reminds us that we are preoccupied with power, which is heightened in modern culture by a confidence of being in control of our environment, our life, and even our destiny.[102] In Christendom, the church has lived for 1500 years in a position of power. Her calling is now to let go of power, accepting a minority position, and to recover the redemptive power of the Gospel message as defined by the cross. Nothing less than a *metanoia* of the church is needed, a re-formation.

This reorientation needs to take place first of all where the formation of missional leadership for the church takes place, in theological education, which is often geared to achieving individual academic 'success'. Alternatively, it should focus on the training of pastors, helping them to lead their church community and its members to live 'worthily of the Gospel', to expose the idols of modern culture, to correct dichotomies, to reflect critically on the culture, and to be examples of love and grace of Jesus Christ in their families and in the market place. This radical reorientation should be based on a redrafted, global map of Christianity, with the West as a major focus of attention as a 'mission field'. Indeed, this might well be the 'most demanding mission frontier … the church has yet to face'.[103] At the same time, it is important to build in adequate corrective elements to help theological students from the West discover their own provincialism and the richness of the colourful worldwide body of Christ. This can only be provided by the non-Western church. With current global mobility, the introduction of off-site courses, faculty and student exchanges, extended exposure trips and field assignments in cross-cultural settings and in the non-Western world are much more realistic than a century ago. Students should be exposed to vital models of missional churches on other continents, with the persistent question in mind of how these experiences can be related to their own Western context.

Such cooperation in programs by sharing resources of different kinds could bring out one aspect that was very important in Edinburgh that of unity for the sake of a stronger witness. John 17 still reminds us of the importance of that element. The Western church should be willing to conduct programs on the basis of a 'sharing of resources among equals, not equals in strength but in status'.[104]

Valuable, untapped resources for the formation of missional leadership are people who have served as missionaries in other contexts, but have returned to their home countries. They are often considered a threat to the *status quo* of the home church, instead of a resource in the formation for mission. Such cross-fertilization of the church with the experiences of those who have been sent to engage in cross-cultural mission is more vital than ever today.

A curriculum for missiology in this context should focus on four different spearheads. One would deal with the biblical/theological foundation of mission and with the history of the missionary movement from a global perspective. A second would deal with ecclesiological issues, focusing on issues related to old Christendom, post Christendom and missionary ecclesiology. Thirdly, one ought to deal with contextual issues like gospel and culture, sociology of religion, and the relationship of Christianity to other religions. And finally, one ought to deal with issues of missionary spirituality, leadership, conflict resolution, adult education and, discipleship training.

Apart from formation for mission aimed at the local church and its leadership a curriculum for missiology should focus on reminding the local congregation that it is part of a worldwide community. In addition to the *organic mode* of the Antioch model, it must have the formation for mission of the *complementary mode* – which reminds the congregation of 'the ends of the earth', of being part of a worldwide community, and guards the church against parochialism. These two modes clarify to the church that there is an 'unfinished task' in world mission to fulfill in partnership with local churches on 'the mission field', wherever that mission field is.

Spiritual formation for mission to Western culture demands special attention. David J. Bosch calls this a 'spirituality of the road'.[105] Newbigin reminds us of John 20, where the risen Jesus greets His disciples: 'Peace be with you'. Peace refers to 'the fullness of God's blessing in His people, peace with God, peace with man, shalom'.[106] Newbigin challenges us: if that is what we have, why are we so often infected by anxiety and restless busyness?[107] He asks whether we show that the peace of God is at the heart of our activities. Often missionaries have been seen more as elements of Western cultural invasion than as emissaries of the peace of God. Many people today long for that peace, and 'if we are to be God's messengers today, we need to be able to speak to that longing for peace'.[108]

W.H.T. Gairdner used two images to introduce the last two days of Edinburgh 1910. One was of missionaries, on whom the task of evangelizing the 'non-Christian world' largely depended. The other was of a sending church in the 'Christian world' which had long ago become 'an encapsulated community... unable to evangelise the society around them'.[109] Since 1910 attempts have been made to clean and clarify these two images, and the relationship between them. Only by going back to the place where these images originate do we find under the ages of dust that there is the single image, in which both the Christian community and the individual participate in God's mission. Christopher Wright reminds us that 'all mission or missions that we initiate, or into which we invest our vocation, gifts, and energies, flows from the prior mission of God. *God* is on mission, and we, in that wonderful phrase of Paul, are "co-workers with God"'.[110]

The question is whether the Christian churches in the West are willing to surrender their resistance and fear of change, accepting to be formed for mission to impact their own culture as well as serving the rest of the world. In this, non-Western churches have much to teach us.

Endnotes

[1] This chapter is an abbreviated version of a paper presented in Edinburgh in October 2006.

[2] W. H. Temple Gairdner and John Raleigh Mott, *Echoes from Edinburgh, 1910: an Account and Interpretation of the World Missionary Conference*, New York, Chicago [etc.]: Fleming H. Revell, 1910, p. 215.

[3] Gairdner and John Raleigh Mott, *Echoes from Edinburgh, 1910*, p. 215.

[4] World Missionary Conference, 1910, *The Training of Teachers: with Supplement*, Report of Commission V, Edinburgh & London: Oliphant, Anderson & Ferrier; New York, Chicago and Toronto: Fleming H. Revell, 1910.

[5] Christopher J. H. Wright, 'An Upside-Down World', *Christianity Today* 51, no. 1 (2007), p. 42.

[6] Wilbert R. Shenk, 'Training Missiologists for Western Culture', in *Changing Frontiers of Mission, American Society of Missiology Series,* no. 28, Maryknoll, N.Y.: Orbis Books, 1999, pp. 129–38.

[7] J. E. Lesslie Newbigin, 'The Future of Missions and Missionaries', *Review and Expositor* 74, no. 2 (1977), p. 211.

[8] Dana L. Robert, 'The Mission Education Movement and the Rise of World Christianity, 1902–2002', Program Committee on Education for Mission, November 2002, <http://www.ncccusa.org/missioneducation/about_us/about_history.htm>, 3 May 2007.

[9] *The Training of Teachers*, p. 300.

[10] *The Training of Teachers*, p. 108.

[11] *The Training of Teachers*, p. 105.

[12] *The Training of Teachers*, p. 106.

[13] Gairdner and Mott, *Echoes from Edinburgh, 1910*, p. 67.

[14] *The Training of Teachers*, pp. 100–101.

[15] *The Training of Teachers*, p. 104.

[16] J. E. Lesslie Newbigin, 'Bringing Our Missionary Methods under the Word of God', *Occasional Bulletin from the Missionary Research Library* XIII, no. 11 (1962), p. 2.
[17] *The Training of Teachers*, p. 300.
[18] See above, Andrew F. Walls, 'The Church's Transforming Century', p. 27ff.
[19] Gairdner and Mott, *Echoes from Edinburgh, 1910*, p. 240.
[20] Gairdner and Mott, *Echoes from Edinburgh, 1910*, p. 247.
[21] Gairdner and Mott, *Echoes from Edinburgh, 1910*, p. 262.
[22] Gairdner and Mott, *Echoes from Edinburgh, 1910*, p. 262.
[23] Gairdner and Mott, *Echoes from Edinburgh, 1910*, p. 263.
[24] Walls, 'The Church's Transforming Century', pp. 27ff.
[25] Gairdner and Mott, *Echoes from Edinburgh, 1910*, p. 241.
[26] Gairdner and Mott, *Echoes from Edinburgh, 1910*, p. 242; cf. pp. 249–50.
[27] Darrell L. Guder, ed., *Missional Church: A Vision for the Sending of the Church in North America*, The Gospel and Our Culture Series, Grand Rapids, MI: William B. Eerdmans Publishing Company, 1998.
[28] James A. Scherer, 'The Preparation of Missionaries in an Ecumenical Era', *Occasional Bulletin from the Missionary Research Library* XV, no. 2 (1964), p. 4.
[29] Scherer, 'The Preparation of Missionaries', p. 4.
[30] Scherer, 'The Preparation of Missionaries', p. 4.
[31] James Dixon Douglas, *Let the Earth Hear His Voice: Official Reference Volume, Papers and Responses*, Minneapolis: World Wide Publications, 1975, pp. 26–7.
[32] Douglas, *Let the Earth Hear His Voice*, p. 26.
[33] Douglas, *Let the Earth Hear His Voice*, p. 26.
[34] Michael W. Goheen, *'As the Father Has Sent Me, I Am Sending You': J. E. Lesslie Newbigin's Missionary Ecclesiology*, Zoetermeer Netherlands: Boekencentrum, 2000, p. 5.
[35] International Missionary Council, *Minutes of the Enlarged Meeting and the Committee of the International Missionary Council, Willingen, Germany, July 5th to 21st, 1952*, London and New York: International Missionary Council, 1952, pp. 69–74.
[36] International Missionary Council, *The Missionary Obligation of the Church: Willingen, Germany, July 5–17, 1952*, London: Edinburgh House Press, 1952, pp. 19–25; Scherer, 'The Preparation of Missionaries', p. 5.
[37] International Missionary Council, *Minutes of the Enlarged Meeting*, p. 69; see also p. 152 {Günther, 1970 #7168} where Günther states, that 'laypeople are the bridgeheads of the church in the world'.
[38] J. E. Lesslie Newbigin, in Goheen, *As the Father Has Sent Me*, p. 44.
[39] J. E. Lesslie Newbigin, *Unfinished Agenda: An Updated Autobiography*, St. Andrew Press, Edinburgh, 1993, p. 203.
[40] Goheen, *As the Father Has Sent Me*, p. 361.
[41] Goheen, *As the Father Has Sent Me*, p. 308.
[42] Newbigin, in Goheen, *As the Father Has Sent Me*, p. 18.
[43] Newbigin, in Goheen, *As the Father Has Sent Me*, p. 95.
[44] Newbigin, in Goheen, *As the Father Has Sent Me*, p. 97
[45] Scherer, 'The Preparation of Missionaries', p. 5.
[46] Scherer, 'The Preparation of Missionaries', p. 6.
[47] Scherer, 'The Preparation of Missionaries', p. 6.
[48] International Missionary Council, *Minutes of the Enlarged Meeting*, p.7.
[49] Wolfgang Günther, *Von Edinburgh Nach Mexico City : Die Ekklesiologischen Bemühungen Der Weltmissionskonferenzen (1910-1963)*, Stuttgart: Evang. Missionsverlag: 1970, p. 150.
[50] Goheen, *As the Father has Sent Me*, p. 320.

[51] Newbigin, *Unfinished Agenda*, pp. 164–5.
[52] Goheen, *As the Father has Sent Me*, p. 365.
[53] International Missionary Council, *Minutes of the Enlarged Meeting*, p. 2.
[54] Scherer, 'The Preparation of Missionaries', pp. 5–6.
[55] Scherer, 'The Preparation of Missionaries', pp. 5–6.
[56] Scherer, 'The Preparation of Missionaries', p. 3.
[57] Scherer, 'The Preparation of Missionaries', p. 5.
[58] Scherer, 'The Preparation of Missionaries', p. 7.
[59] Scherer, 'The Preparation of Missionaries', p. 8.
[60] Scherer, 'The Preparation of Missionaries', p. 11. The changed role of the young church is also observed in the fact that they painted a composite picture of the desiderata in a missionary, emphasising such qualities as servant-hood, lifelong identification, embodiment of Christian vocation and spiritual depth and maturity; Scherer, 'The Preparation of Missionaries', pp. 13–15.
[61] Robert, 'The Mission Education Movement'.
[62] David J. Bosch, 'Theological Education in Missionary Perspective', *Missiology: An International Review* 10, no. 1 (1982), p. xix.
[63] Bosch, 'Theological Education in Missionary Perspective', p. xxi.
[64] J. E. Lesslie Newbigin, *One Body, One Gospel, One World: The Christian Mission Today*, London and New York: International Missionary Council, 1958.
[65] Douglas, *Let the Earth Hear His Voice*, p. 27.
[66] Douglas, *Let the Earth Hear His Voice*, pp. 327–51.
[67] Jonathan Tien-en Chau, 'The Nature of the Unity of the Local and Universal Church in Evangelism and Church Growth', in Douglas, *Let the Earth Hear His Voice*, pp. 1109, 1110, 1113.
[68] William David Taylor, ed., *Internationalizing Missionary Training: A Global Perspective*, Exeter: Paternoster Press; Grand Rapids: Baker Book House, 1991, p. ix.
[69] Taylor, *Internationalizing Missionary Training*, p. ix
[70] Stephen T. Hoke, 'Paradigm Shifts and Trends in Missions Training – a Call to Servant-Teaching, a Ministry of Humility', *Evangelical Review of Theology* 23 (1999), pp. 329–46; see also Stephen T. Hoke and Jim Roché, 'The Missionary Training Assessment: A Best Practices Case Study in Missionary Training', *Common Ground Journal* 4, no. 2 (2007). Accessed: 3 May 2007.
[71] Hoke, 'Paradigm Shifts', pp. 330, 331.
[72] Hoke, 'Paradigm Shifts', p. 331.
[73] Shenk, 'Training Missiologists', p. 132.
[74] L. Grant McClung, in Stephen T. Hoke, 'Paradigm Shifts and Trends in Missions Training – a Call to Servant-Teaching, a Ministry of Humility', *Evangelical Review of Theology* 23 (1999), p. 346.
[75] McClung, in Stephen T. Hoke, 'Paradigm Shifts and Trends in Missions Training – a Call to Servant-Teaching, a Ministry of Humility', *Evangelical Review of Theology* 23 (1999), p. 346.
[76] William Taylor, ed., *Too Valuable to Lose: Exploring the Causes and Cures of Missionary Attrition*, Pasadena: William Carey, 1997; Kelly O'Donnell, *Doing Member Care Well*, Pasadena: William Carey Library, 2002.
[77] Newbigin, 'The Future of Missions and Missionaries', p. 211.
[78] See, for example, Michael Bünker and Martin Friedrich, eds., *Evangelising: Protestant Perspectives for the Churches in Europe*, Wien: Community of Protestant Churches in Europe, 2007, <http://lkg.jalb.de/lkg/documents/lkg_doc_en_2089.pdf> 2 May 2007. However, the little attention given to the discussion of this document at the

Budapest 2006 General Assembly does not seem to imply that it is considered a major agenda item.
[79] See Darrell L. Guder, *The Continuing Conversion of the Church*, ed. Craig van Gelder, The Gospel and Our Culture Series, Grand Rapids, MI: William B. Eerdmans Publishing Co., 2000.
[80] Shenk, 'Training Missiologists', p. 130.
[81] Joel A. Carpenter, 'The Christian Scholar in an Age of Global Christianity', *Minds in the Making* 1, no. 2 (2004); http://www.calvin.edu/minds/vol01/issue02/global-christianity.php accessed 26 Febuary 2007.
[82] Shenk, 'Training Missiologists', p. 132.
[83] See above, Teresa Okure, 'The Church in the Mission Field: A Nigerian/African Response', pp. 59ff.
[84] Newbigin, 'Bringing Our Missionary Methods', p. 2.
[85] Newbigin, 'Bringing Our Missionary Methods', p. 2.
[86] Newbigin, *One Body*, pp. 11, 12.
[87] Robert, 'The Mission Education Movement'.
[88] Newbigin, 'Bringing Our Missionary Methods', p. 2.
[89] Newbigin, 'Bringing Our Missionary Methods', p. 2.
[90] Newbigin, 'Future of Missions', p. 209.
[91] Shenk, 'Training Missiologists', pp. 132, 133.
[92] Shenk, 'Training Missiologists', pp. 132, 133.
[93] Shenk, 'Training Missiologists', pp. 132, 133.
[94] Newbigin, *One Body*, p. 18.
[95] Newbigin, *One Body*, p. 19.
[96] Newbigin, 'Future of Missions', p. 215.
[97] Newbigin, *One Body*, p. 46.
[98] Newbigin, *One Body*, p. 46.
[99] Newbigin, *One Body*, p. 46.
[100] Newbigin, *One Body*, p. 46.
[101] J. J. (Dons) Kritzinger, 'Training for Mission', *Missionalia* 30, no. 1 (2002), p. 127.
[102] Shenk, 'Training Missiologists', pp. 136, 137.
[103] Shenk, 'Training Missiologists', p. 138.
[104] Newbigin, *One Body*, p. 38.
[105] David J. Bosch, *A Spirituality of the Road*, Pretoria: IMER, 1994; See also Timothy C. Geoffrion, *The Spirit-Led Leader: Nine Leadership Practices and Soul Principles*, Herndon, Va.: Alban Institute, 2005.
[106] Newbigin, 'Bringing Our Missionary Methods', p. 3.
[107] Newbigin, 'Bringing Our Missionary Methods', p. 3.
[108] Newbigin, 'Bringing Our Missionary Methods', p. 3.
[109] Newbigin, 'The Future of Missions', p. 209.
[110] Christopher J. H. Wright, 'An Upside-Down World', *Christianity Today* 51, no. 1 (2007): <http://www.christianitytoday.com/bcl/areas/missions/articles/070502.html>, 3 May, 2007.

Commission Six

The Home Base of Missions

Commission Six
'The Home Base of Missions'

The Commission in Summary

Introducing the remit of Commission Six, the Report states its concern as being 'the whole subject of the means by which the Church at home may adequately discharge its responsibility for the evangelisation of the world'.[1] The titles of its eighteen chapters indicate that the subject was understood as 'scientific', not merely practical: 'mission intelligence' and 'the science of missionary societies' are the terms that define the opening and concluding chapters of the Report, setting out the conceptual framework in which issues of missionary recruitment, funding, home leadership, and administration are discussed. 'The science of the home base', and 'the science of the operation of Missionary Societies' were to be understood as essential to the science of missions as a whole – a science yet in its infancy, to which the Report aspired to make a formative contribution.

A US American, James Levi Barton, chaired Commission Six. After distinguished missionary service in Turkey, where he manifested a combination of administrative and scholarly talents, he was appointed Foreign Secretary of the American Board of Commissioners for Foreign Missions. His experience and thinking imbues the Report. Its espousal, at this early point in the twentieth century, of today's 'management science' makes it a very American report in its provenance, principles and prognoses.

'In every point in our investigation', Barton told the plenary conference, 'the Commission has been confronted by the one stupendous fact, that there is not a Missionary Society in any of the countries named that is properly supported today for the conduct of its work.'[2] At a time when the home Church enjoys abundant material resources, the paucity of its giving to missions deadens the life of the Church that sends them forth. With this remedied, 'the Christian Church … possessed, mastered, and dominated by the faith which it professes, could easily evangelise the world'.[3]

The root problem being thus diagnosed as spiritual, 'the science of the home base' begins with prayer: 'the necessity of intercession, and of securing a widespread and intelligent scheme of intercession based on knowledge'.[4] While encouraging churches to commit to the practice of intercessory prayer for mission, and recommending several methods, the Report emphasized that 'multiplication' is not in itself sufficient: 'proficiency in the practice of prayer', and above all prayer that avoids nominalism, is required.[5] '*Learning* (original italics) to pray' in this way, 'from first to last with the Holy Spirit of God', opens human instruments to the Divine Spirit, and teaches the Church what makes for 'the coming of the Kingdom'. In this manner 'a revival of missionary interest must wait upon a spiritual revival'.[6] 'Missionary intelligence', as the Report uses the term, is neither primarily concerned with, nor confined to scholarly interest. 'Systematic study' has its place, but anchored in 'the power of prayer' it is quickened with spiritual enthusiasm that inspires effective application. ' "Knowledge" is what is needed – knowledge of the obligation to evangelise all men, knowledge of the open doors, the imperative call, the rewarding service.'

In light of its opening chapter on 'The Spiritual Resources of the Church', the following seven chapters each deal with 'the Promotion of Missionary Intelligence' in particular areas of activity: church services and agencies; religious and secular newspapers and periodicals; special literature; mission study classes; educational institutions; visits to mission fields; conferences and exhibitions. Four promotional targets emerge. Firstly, the pastors, among whom missionary enthusiasm, once fostered, ensure that their 'people ... gain much the same spirit and become a missionary force'.[7] Secondly, the youth, who are to be trained through Sunday schools, secondary and college education, with the aim of shaping them to become future recruits for missionary service. Thirdly, 'laymen' (*sic*), especially the young educated elite, were given extensive attention. At the time the lay were considered an 'unoccupied field' for missionary recruitment. The Report praised the successful methods of the Laymen's Missionary Movement, which had been founded a few years earlier (1906) in the United States (the General Secretary, John White, being brother-in-law to the Conference Chairman, John Mott). Fourthly, the Report also recognized the special role of women in missionary promotion: 'in not a few congregations the only missionary interest discernible is that engendered and kept alive by devout women, while most communions are indebted to women for large measure of their missionary activity'.[8] In a chapter devoted to the role of women's missionary organizations, the Report acknowledged that the day has passed when the nineteenth-century watchword 'Women's Work for Women' could still be applied. 'Women have been real leaders, both in wide plans of organisation and in details of execution' across a wide range of missionary activity.[9] The separation of women's work from the general missionary task was an artificial division. The future called for women to be included, alongside men, in the leadership of mission societies, and for existing women's missionary societies to be associated with the missionary councils and societies of the Church.

The chapter of the Report dealing with women's missionary societies was one of seven devoted to issues of missionary administration. These touched repeatedly on the problem of missionary funding; a subject that received detailed analysis in two chapters. Should missionary societies decline suitable candidates for lack of funds? Should initiatives in the mission field be constrained by budgetary stringency at home, or should the home churches be allocating greater proportions of their budgets to mission? Recognising the value of 'faith missions' that trust the Spirit of God to provide the material support necessary for work that the Spirit approves, the Report was at pains to avoid a polarization between these and centrally-funded missions; 'in both cases the entire work is one of faith', the difference being only on whom a deficit fell. The Report recommended 'a medium ground' that expected financial sobriety on the part of missionaries, and an increase of financial provision by home churches 'that they more nearly reach the standard required'. Drawing again from recent American experience, the Report commended the success of the 'Apportionment Plan', whereby a denomination made annual budgetary provision for mission, and apportioned the funding responsibility to its regional synods or their equivalent, which in term subdivided the apportionment among local churches. This gave local congregations a 'share' in mission, often connecting them directly with missionaries overseas.[10]

The Report ended as it began, with the spiritual value of mission.[11] As intercessory prayer for mission is the hallmark of a spiritually intelligent church, material support for missions brings spiritual vitality to home churches. Quoting the Scottish theologian and missions' advocate, Thomas Chalmers, the Report stood on the principle that 'charity works not by a process of exhaustion, but by one of fermentation'.[12] Churches that give generously are spiritually renewed and extend their generosity further. The fundamental value of mission for the home Church can be measured in terms of education, international sympathy (for example, in the struggle against racism and negative facets of imperialism) the promotion of Christian unity, a 'new spirit of beneficence'[13] in which mission takes the place of war, a quickening of evangelical zeal, and a strengthening and deepening of the faith of the Church itself. 'It is as we see the Gospel demonstrating its power of universal appeal that we receive confirmation and fresh evidence of its essential truth.'[14]

The Report appended 'The Findings of the Medical Conference' that medical delegates and medical missionaries convened on the fringe of the main Conference.[15] Complementing the many references to medical missions in the eight Commission Reports, this conference re-affirmed that medical missions should be recognized as integral and essential parts of the missionary work of the Christian Church, and asked Commission Six to recommend 'that there should be a definite Medical Department in connection with all foreign missionary societies'.[16]

A second appendix, nearly two-thirds the size of the Report itself, comprised a *Bibliography: Missionary Publications* classified under nine sections covering the main fields of missionary science as defined in the Report: 'the study of the extension into the world, among non-Christian peoples, of the principles of Christianity and the results that follow'.[17]

Endnotes

[1] World Missionary Conference, 1910, *The Home Base of Missions*, Report of Commission VI, Edinburgh & London: Oliphant, Anderson & Ferrier; New York, Chicago and Toronto: Fleming H. Revell, 1910, p. 6.
[2] *The Home Base of Missions*, p. 294.
[3] *The Home Base of Missions*, p. 6.
[4] *The Home Base of Missions*, p. 10.
[5] *The Home Base of Missions*, p. 11.
[6] See *The Home Base of Missions*, pp. 15–16.
[7] *The Home Base of Missions*, p. 17.
[8] *The Home Base of Missions*, p. 201.
[9] *The Home Base of Missions*, p. 201.
[10] See *The Home Base of Missions*, pp. 147–9.
[11] *The Home Base of Missions*, pp. 270–1.
[12] *The Home Base of Missions*, p. 259.
[13] *The Home Base of Missions*, p. 262.
[14] *The Home Base of Missions*, p. 267.
[15] *The Home Base of Missions*, pp. 286–90.
[16] *The Home Base of Missions*, p. 286.
[17] See *The Home Base of Missions*, pp. 333–558.

Mission from Everywhere to Everyone: The Home Base in a New Century

Samuel Escobar

The Report of Commission Six argued that without a strong 'home base', missionary work on the field would lack its necessary foundation. Striking a strongly spiritual and evangelical tone, the Report argues that intelligent prayerful commitment and practical support from the church at large is the great need of the missionary movement. This chapter will address three of the core features of the Report. Firstly, it will focus on the Evangelical ethos of Edinburgh 1910 and the theological and practical questions that it poses for 2010. Secondly, it will consider what the Report calls 'intelligence for mission' and the way it has developed in our time. Thirdly, it will deal with the way the base for mission has changed during the twentieth century to place us in a totally different setting.

The evangelical ethos and the aftermath of Edinburgh 1910

If Edinburgh represents a key point in the Protestant missionary movement it is a matter of historical record that such movement had what Latourette described as the evangelical-pietistic-puritan spirit which marked world Protestantism.[1] The Report reveals that participants place themselves in continuity with the Evangelical Awakenings of the nineteenth century and with the Evangelical conventions such as Northfield in the USA and Keswick in the UK.[2] John R. Mott himself owed his experience of conversion to that Evangelical movement, and especially to the Student Volunteer Movement, which by 1910 had mobilized almost 4,000 students to become missionaries. It was out of this spontaneous ferment, coming up from the grassroots of the church, that the well-organized institutional movement represented at Edinburgh emerged. The agenda and language of the Report reflect a continuity of what we could call an Evangelical spirit. If we look for a continuity from Edinburgh 1910, as we move into 2010, where do we see signs of it?

One way of grasping the situation is to follow the development of missionary activity from Europe and North America during the twentieth century. There is always the risk of simplification, but we may trace the development of two cycles of Protestant mission. We can place the first cycle in the time between the Edinburgh World Missionary Conference of 1910 and the end of World War II. During this period there is a development of missiological reflection that takes place in connection with the missionary activity of the mainline Protestant denominations that were playing the key role both in the practice of mission and in the theologizing about it. Edinburgh had a missionary vision and a sense of urgency for the evangelization of the world 'in this generation'. Out of the continuation movement arose the International Missionary Council. The meetings of this organization became the platforms for missiological reflection. In 1948, three years after the war ended, the search for unity and cooperation in mission had evolved into the formation of the World Council of Churches. However, in spite of the missionary vision that in 1910 had started it all, the period following the formation of the WCC was a period of continuing decline in the missionary activity of what we could call mainline Protestantism.

In contrast with that decline, a second cycle of Protestant missionary activity developed especially after 1945 through the growth of conservative Protestant agencies mainly in North America, but also in Europe. There was an explosive growth of faith missions and para-church agencies.[3] These new mission organizations were very critical of developments in the ecumenical movement. Some of them were strongly influenced by the liberal-fundamentalist debates of the 1920s and 1930s in the United States, and came from new denominations that were the result of separatist movements in mainline churches or from denominations that had been reluctant to enter into the ecumenical movement. The formation of the WCC polarized attitudes among such organizations and mission agencies. Especially in the USA, Protestantism became divided.

If it is true that Edinburgh 1910 reflected the mindset of the imperial expansion of Europe, the second cycle reflected the mindset of the Cold War. This was especially the case for the missionary work that sprang from conservative Protestantism. For instance, in the case of American missionary work in Latin America, both Roman Catholic as well as conservative Protestant missionaries embarked with a desire to save these societies from Communism. In the process of missiological reflection that followed both cycles there was eventually a revision of the mindset and a search for more biblical patterns of mission.

The history of American Protestantism after World War II, and its corresponding missionary activity, is still in the process of being researched. Two American scholars have recently argued that it is necessary to review the way in which the history of the classic divide has been understood. For my part I have sought to demonstrate how the divide between liberal/mainline and fundamentalist/evangelical had been crossed and blurred by some mission agencies, *for the sake of mission.*[4] In my view, it was a deep evangelistic and missionary concern which prompted evangelist Billy Graham to move away from the extreme separatist stance of fundamentalist Christianity and contribute to the development of an Evangelical stance; which became operative in the birth of a movement that could claim continuity with Edinburgh 1910.

Missiologists from the ecumenical movement did not always welcome the new actors in the missionary panorama. Dana Robert has captured well the kind of polemical encounter of the two moments, or cycles, to which I have referred. She reminds us that the great historian of mission R. Pierce Beaver, in his book *From Missions to Mission*, placed the future of mission in the new missiological ideas and methods that were being fostered within the ecumenical movement, and he referred to the missionary activism of conservative Protestants or Evangelicals as 'sectarian and partisan ... disrupting the unity of mission'. Robert goes on to observe that 'The ecumenical movement that Beaver touted as the source of new forms of mission had within ten years so modified the definition of mission that confusion over its meaning was widespread in mainline churches.'[5] On the other hand she says, 'The "sectarian"evangelicals that Beaver had excoriated in 1964 reached such a level of institutional maturity and ecclesiastical dominance that critical historical analysis became possible and necessary.'[6]

A number of developments in the mid twentieth century contributed to the emergence of a clear sense of Evangelical identity which stood in the tradition of Edinburgh but had misgivings about the direction being taken by the World Council of Churches as the institutional heir of the 1910 Conference. *First*, the renewal of mass evangelism that reached public notice with Billy Graham in Los Angeles, 1949. Some classic elements of revivalistic Protestantism combined with the use of mass media shook the dormant religious routine of people, especially in the big cities, first in North America and then in Europe. Graham's perception of the world and of Christianity developed significantly as he traveled and preached in other continents. *Second*, there was a renewal of serious Evangelical scholarship in Biblical studies and theological reflection, following a renewal of evangelical university life in Europe and especially Great Britain. *Third*, strong Evangelical churches and movements had emerged around the world, connected to the post- World War II stream of missionary fervor and activity from North America and Europe. Independent 'faith missions' played an important role in this emergence.

These three movements exemplify the type of Evangelical churches, missionary organizations and denominational renewal groups that find a way of expressing their concern for Christian unity and cooperation in loose alliances such as World Evangelical Fellowship (now WEA) or the Lausanne movement. Their variety also explains the tensions that develop within those alliances or umbrella movements which sometimes are unable to contain them. The volunteerism which is the genius of Evangelical life and mission is a key factor in understanding these developments. The 'faith mission' type of missionary activity contributes to the rise of vigorous Evangelical churches in the majority world, which are independent and have no connection with the historic Protestant denominations. Ecclesiology is undefined in these independent churches. Their participation in Evangelical alliances brings them into contact with Evangelicals inside the mainline churches. The encounter is mutually enriching but it also accounts for a long and difficult process of theological dialogue and definition. There is a dialectical interaction between the vitality that comes from these movements at the grassroots and the direction and stimulation that the alliances themselves provide. In order to understand the Evangelical position, both the promise and the precariousness of this dynamic have to be appreciated and its historical significance has to be evaluated theologically.

The Lausanne Congress of 1974 provided the forum that was required for an exercise in critical self-reflection on the part of the second cycle of Protestant missionary engagement. The pragmatic concerns of Evangelicals from North America, and the theological and missiological acumen of European Evangelicals, were matched by the restless sense of mission of Evangelicals in the young churches of the majority world or among the oppressed minorities. The agenda of the ongoing reflection had to make room for the burning questions of those who were witnessing to their faith in Jesus Christ within situations where the ferment of nationalism, social upheaval and ideological conflict were testing the theological depth of both Evangelical and non-Evangelical missionaries and churches. Lausanne 1974 was not a missiological and theological monologue of European or North American Evangelicals, but a brotherly global dialogue of a community that had grown beyond expectations all over the world: a dialogue in search of ways of obedience to the missionary imperatives of Jesus, our Savior and Lord.

The *Lausanne Covenant* expresses this unique missiological moment. Precisely at the point in time in which Evangelical Christianity became joyfully aware of its global dimension, it also developed a painful awareness of its serious shortcomings. Liberated by its missionary thrust from the bonds of sterile fundamentalism, Evangelicalism was able again to rediscover the holistic dimensions of the Christian mission that are clearly presented in the Bible. The Lausanne Covenant restates convictions that are characteristic of Evangelicalism. It starts with a Trinitarian confession, a statement on the authority of the Bible and an expression of Christological conviction.[7] At the same time the Covenant expresses repentance for what was wrong or missing in the way in which Evangelicals had been performing their missionary task.

We may summarize in four points the direction taken by the Lausanne Congress.

(1) The Congress made a commitment to a concept of *holistic* mission that retains the Evangelical emphasis on the proclamation of the Gospel of Jesus Christ while also describing the kind of missionary presence it requires, a presence that calls to discipleship and incorporates converts into the Church.[8] Inherent in this is self-criticism over the type of dualistic spiritualization that had come to be prevalent in the practice of Evangelical missionaries. Mission relates to every area of human need. For the majority of Evangelicals, however, holistic mission has evangelism as a key and primary component: 'In the church's mission of sacrificial service evangelism is primary.'[9]

(2) The Congress called for *cooperation* in the mission task – between church and para-church, mainline and evangelical, Pentecostal and Reformed – based solely on the missionary passion shared in the Lausanne event, and the basic theological consensus reached in the Covenant itself. The sheer magnitude of the task of world evangelization, and the scandal of sterile division and competition among missionary agencies, demanded a new attitude. A sense of urgency for reaching those still unreached makes room for the type of concern that had been underlying the call for a 'moratorium'.[10]

(3) The Congress was aware that in the post-imperial era the missionary and the theological tasks have a *global* dimension. Christians and missionaries from the European and North American regions, once strongholds of Evangelical faith, had to acknowledge the spiritual decline in those regions and the rise of new thriving churches in Africa, Asia and Latin America. Thus, neither imperialism nor provincialism could be tolerated.

(4) The Congress made a commitment to seriously consider the *context* of mission. Issues such as culture, education of leaders, spiritual conflict and persecution were addressed.[11] The need was recognized for an evaluation of the social, ideological and spiritual struggles that surround and condition the missionary enterprise, in order to design a relevant type of discipleship for our own times.

These insights have enabled the Lausanne Committee for World Evangelization to promote an active theological-missiological discussion within the second cycle of missionary engagement. However in the ongoing discussions evangelical leaders from the more pragmatic sector (related to the Church Growth movement) have been reluctant to deal with theological issues. It is worth remembering that as the second cycle of mission activity, especially in the United States, had a polemical stance and did not benefit from the experience and reflection of the first. New generations of missionaries without an adequate historical awareness or biblical training were condemned to repeat the mistakes of the past. It became necessary for theologians to embark anew in the search for a critical missiological reflection. This is what historian William H. Hutchison called 'familiar debates in an unfamiliar world'.[12] At the same time a remark by Joel Carpenter that points to the evangelical isolation from previous missionary practice and experience is sobering. Carpenter observes, 'when a post-fundamentalist, "neo-evangelical" theological movement appeared in the 1950's and 1960's, it virtually had to reinvent evangelical missions theology'.[13]

Lausanne 1974 was a missiological reflection on the Evangelical missionary activity of the second cycle we have mentioned, just as Edinburgh 1910 was to a certain degree a reflection on the missionary practice of the nineteenth century that preceded it. It is a well known fact that Edinburgh 1910 avoided theological definition. James A. Scherer, an ecumenical missiologist, says, 'In overall character, Edinburgh 1910 was not a conference on the "theology of mission" as we now understand it. It was a conference to design the *strategy* for a final campaign by the concerted forces of the kingdom of God as they assayed what was needed to complete the "unfinished task".'[14] Anglican Evangelical John Stott offers a historical explanation. He notes the contrast between the confident and optimistic mood in which the conference ended and the developments that followed. He thinks that two influences undermined the expectations engendered at Edinburgh. The first were socio-political events such as the two world wars. Stott argues, 'These devastating conflicts sapped the moral as well as the financial strength of the west, and signaled to the rest of the world the collapse of western culture and of its foundation, Christianity.'[15] The second influence was theological. Here I quote Stott extensively:

> Theologically, the fatal flaw at Edinburgh was not so much doctrinal disagreement as apparent doctrinal indifference, since doctrine was not in the agenda. Vital themes like the content of the gospel, the theology of evangelism and the nature of the church were not discussed. The reason is that Randall Davidson, Archbishop of Canterbury, as a condition of Anglican participation in Edinburgh secured a promise from John R. Mott that doctrinal debate would be excluded. In consequence the theological challenges of the day were not faced. And during the decades which followed, the poison of theological liberalism seeped into the bloodstream of western universities and seminaries, and largely immobilized the churches' mission.[16]

With its orientation to the practical task of world evangelization, the Lausanne movement today runs the risk of failing to develop an adequate theology of mission. If it does not learn from history it may be condemned to repeat the mistakes of history. Two factors ought to be taken into account as we seek to offer critical missiological reflection to the practice of mission today. First, by the mid-1970s there was what has been called a 'convergence' in the reflection about mission. The Lausanne Covenant of 1974 became, as Scherer says, 'a rallying cry for intensified evangelical mission efforts and a challenge to non-evangelicals'. He goes on to say that in the same year the Roman Synod of Bishops stated that 'the task of evangelizing all people constitutes the essential mission of the church' and that the bishops asked the Pope to reflect on the mission of the Church. The following year Pope Paul VI promulgated the Apostolic Exhortation *Evangelii Nuntiandi* about the evangelization of the modern world. In the same year the WCC held its Fifth Assembly in Nairobi. Themes of mission and evangelism were the object of renewed attention. Scherer says that 'Assembly statements about "confessing Christ" had a strongly Christocentric, Trinitarian, and churchly ring, echoing Eastern Orthodox and Roman Catholic influence but also responding to evangelical criticisms.'[17] The second factor is that in the field of Missiology a practice of dialogue between representatives of the Protestant, Roman Catholic, Evangelical and Pentecostal traditions had been established. This is evident in the work of such bodies as the International Association for Mission Studies and the American Society of Missiology.[18] Such collaborative missiological efforts are generating a capacity to underpin the missionary enterprise with a much more critical theology than has heretofore been apparent.

Intelligence for mission

Seven chapters of the Report have to do with what is called 'The Promotion of Missionary Intelligence'. We do not currently use the phrase, probably because of its militaristic connotations. At the outset it is evident that, for the Commission, such promotion is necessary for what we would today call the 'mobilization' of the church for mission (another term taken from military or political imagery). The idea is that the promotion reaches the rank and file, or the grassroots, of churches. At present, information and analysis is available to interested Christians as never before. We may think for instance of David Barrett's three volume *World Christian Encyclopedia*; a scholarly reference work that can be placed side by side with Patrick Johnstone's *Operation World*, a more popular book of missionary promotion that offers, in the best William Carey tradition, a vast amount of information as an incentive to prayer.[19] Barrett's figures are now used as a source of information about Christianity by Christians of all traditions, and also by secular agencies. Barrett, and also Johnstone, have created data centres that are independent of church control, and have established themselves as quotable authorities in the field of Missiometrics – the new discipline they have developed.

Data processing has been used to provide a map of the missionary challenges that are still ahead of us. However, missiological discernment is necessary. For example, missiologists of the school that I call 'managerial missiology' have developed the concept of 'unreached peoples'. This helps us to see the missionary need more precisely. The missiologists use linguistic and cultural indices to determine need, going beyond what could be the misleading categories of the nation-state. This allows them to take account of such peoples as the Kurds, a people with no nation of their own. However, there is need for the concept of 'reaching' and 'reached' to be cleansed of the imperialistic overtones of conquest and subjection that may be conveyed. Because of the use of technology and electronic media, 'unreached' tends to sound like a militaristic 'target' to be conquered, for the sake of the conquerors. Indeed even 'reaching' them can apparently be reduced to having them in the screen of our computers. The term has to be humanized by ascribing to it a biblical meaning of compassion, intercession, and willingness to serve. It is the love of Christ for those other sheep that are not yet in the fold, the zeal of Paul to preach where Christ has not yet been preached, which must shape our concept of the 'unreached'.

There is another aspect of intelligence for missions that, to my surprise, I have found in the Report: 'The greatly improved facilities for travel have led in recent years to a great extension of the practice among Americans and

Europeans of making tours to non-Christian countries.... It is desirable that missionaries and Mission societies should encourage such personal contact between tourists and missionaries and missionary work to the utmost extent in their power.'[20] The Commission would be delighted and surprised to find the turn that this idea has taken in the contemporary situation. At a recent consultation on 'Short Term Missions' (STM) in Lima, Robert Priest quoted figures that show that close to a million and a half Americans went overseas on an STM trip during 2005.[21] All indicators seem to point to the fact that the phenomenon will continue to grow. The consultation was an effort to evaluate the trend from a missiological perspective. Peruvians who had been hosts to short term teams, persons who regularly lead them, and scholars who are trying to measure the impact of the phenomenon, are using the tools of the social sciences. What emerges is a mixed picture. If the 1910 Commission recommended such a method as a way to promote 'intelligence for mission', the trend we are observing today could well undermine the long-term missionary enterprise. In the final analysis it could become just a form of glorified tourism.

Mission from everywhere to everyone

The late twentieth century witnessed a continuous and steady growth of intentional missionary activity from the non-Western countries to other parts of the world. The records we have are approximate and need to be qualified, but they show significant growth. Those who attend missionary conferences, missionary celebrations, or missiological gatherings know that the presence of representatives of young and flourishing mission organizations from the non-Western world have become more evident also in North America and Europe. Increasing numbers of nationals sent by non-Western agencies are involved in pioneering missionary situations among Muslim, Buddhist or Animistic peoples. Indeed non-Westerners are becoming involved in the new evangelization of Europe and North America and in the programmes of traditional Western mission agencies.

This trend was already evident during the Lausanne Congress of 1974 when evangelicals expressed a firm consensus about the urgent need to acknowledge that global Christian mission had become the responsibility of a global church and not only the privilege of the Western missionary enterprise.[22] The *Lausanne Covenant* expressed it clearly, 'We rejoice that a new missionary era has dawned. The dominant role of western missions is fast disappearing. God is raising up from the younger churches a great new resource for world evangelization, and it is thus demonstrating that the responsibility to evangelize belongs to the whole body of Christ.'[23] The Covenant went on to ask all churches to participate in global mission and to practice a continuous re-evaluation of their role. For Lausanne the new forms of partnership had theological and testimonial significance: 'Thus a growing partnership of churches will develop and the universal character of Christ's church will be more clearly exhibited.'[24] The Covenant also unfolds some of the consequences of taking seriously the new missionary era that has dawned: 'Missionaries should flow ever more freely from and to all six continents in a spirit of humble service. The goal should be by all available means and at the earliest possible time, that every person will have the opportunity to hear, understand and receive the good news.'[25] This has proved to be a prophetic insight.

In 1989, Larry Pate gathered data about the dynamic involvement of Third World churches in global Christian mission. He referred briefly to the gloomy picture that Western missions faced because of restrictions by countries that were closing their borders to missionaries and the activity of resurgent religions. Pate counterbalanced this with a glowing report about 'the burgeoning growth of missions by Christians in the Two Thirds World'. He stated that 'a large part of the future of mission belongs to the missionaries from Latin America, Africa, Asia and Oceania'.[26] He also offered a series of statistical studies showing the steady growth of that missionary movement, some valuable case studies, and a directory of Third World agencies that were sending missionaries to other parts of the world. He even predicted that soon non-Western missionaries would be more numerous than Western missionaries. More recently Michael Jaffarian, one of the world experts in missiometrics, has corrected Pate's enthusiasm by reminding us that in his comparative tables he included in the figures about the non-Western missionaries those that worked in mission inside their own nations, but that his figures for Western missionaries included only those that worked abroad.[27]

In any case, the figures of growth are impressive. Non-Western missionaries have gone from 6,634 in the year 1990 to 20,570 in the year 2000, which means a growth rate of 210%. Western missionaries numbered 62,927 in the year 1990 and by the year 2000 they had grown to 70,323, which means a growth of only 12%. In the year 2000 non-Western missionaries numbered 3,126 from Africa, 13,607 from Asia, and 3,837 from Latin America.[28] According to the Korea Research Institute for Missions, in the year 2002 there were 10,745 Korean missionaries sent by 136 mission organizations.[29] COMIBAM, the largest coordinating agency of Latin American missions shows that the number of Latin American missionaries in the year 2001 was 6,455. These figures do not take into account the number of migrants from the majority world that carry on missionary work in the countries where they move as migrants or refugees.

From a sociological perspective, Paul Freston says that: 'The British diaspora and Anglo-Saxon missions responsible for much worldwide expansion of Protestantism since the eighteenth century have now been overtaken by other diasporas (African, Caribbean, Latin American, Chinese and Korean) and by other missions.'[30] This growth is not just an imitation of the Western churches or a response to the mobilizing techniques that Western agencies may have developed. The spiritual vitality of persons, churches and denominations has nourished the vision and the willingness to obey and made possible great advances in mission. Revival has been the cradle for missionary vocations. Howard Snyder has offered a very convincing analysis that demonstrates revival has resulted in an environment in which new structures for mission have been imagined.[31] The sheer numerical weight of a church does not naturally produce missionary vocations. Catholics in Latin America are concerned by the fact that though half the Catholics of the world live in Latin America only 2% of the Catholic missionary force comes from that region.[32]

The Holy Spirit seems to be at work especially in the periphery of the world, giving Christian people a vision and mobilizing them for local and global mission in spite of poverty, lack of experience and absence of training. On almost every continent migration movements have brought to cities, and industrial or commercial centres, legions of mission minded lay people from Third World churches. The spiritual warmth and the sacrificial commitment of those whose parents or grandparents had been recent converts from other faiths, or from a dead nominal form of Christianity, is rejuvenating old established forms of Christendom. If this is the way the Spirit is moving, what needs to be done in order to walk in step with his reviving and transforming activity? What kinds of global partnerships have to be imagined and developed for this new stage of mission history? Obedience to Christ's commission and the Spirit's missionary drive will keep Christian mission advancing in the twenty-first century, but it will also demand a humble and reflective missiological expertise to propose avenues of obedience to biblical imperatives about *the way and the style* in which such advance is to take place.

My observation of churches in Asia and Latin America, also among minorities in the USA and Spain, is that those with dynamic mission awareness are located in impoverished communities. Newly formed churches experience life together in Christian community as a continuous effort to prolong the possibility of survival. As missiologists we cannot fall into the trap of idealizing these churches, but neither can we afford to bypass them as we think of future global partnerships for mission. Their missionary dynamism is the expression of a thankful response to the experience of the power of the Holy Spirit and the love of Jesus Christ. The marginal, the lonely, the displaced and the refugee find in these churches a home for the homeless and they experience *koinonia*. The oppressed who are 'nobodies', because they do not have a name, money or education, find a community where they may unburden their hearts or express their joy in their own way, without censorship. Those desperate because neither psychology, nor the fear of police, can deliver them from alcohol or drugs experience the liberating power of the Holy Spirit in the name of Jesus. One can then understand the joyful response by which, out of their poverty, they become stewards of God's grace and their churches are born with a special ability to be self-sufficient.

What is distinctive about the stewardship of these churches of the poor? It is what we could call a stewardship for survival. Popular churches planted among the poor cannot depend on a tradition, on the help of the state, on the endowment of rich benefactors or on a body of professional ministers. They have to be fellowships where members join forces to make the community live, grow, propagate the faith and survive. The stewardship of the totality of life is experienced as total missionary mobilization. What seems to be more difficult to obtain in the case of developed and old established churches is lay mobilization, or total participation in the holistic welfare of the Christian community. Among the churches of the poor such mobilization is the normal lifestyle of the community. No other form of life and ministry is possible. After the reality of survival has been possible for a certain time it is then also possible to speak of patterns of stewardship that will project the community to the great tasks of centrifugal mission. But that experience of voluntary contribution for the survival and growth of the church creates a discipline, a pattern of timing and budgeting, that is a new and foundational experience.

As we are well into the twenty-first century, the Covenant's reference to shocking poverty, as well as the call to simple life-style, has become more relevant to our discussion about global partnership for mission. On the one hand, an accelerated globalization process has facilitated communication to the point that we could say that material and technological means are available for the creation and development of transnational and transcontinental partnership for the recruitment, training and sending of missionaries. On the other hand, that process is generating a world of economic and social disparities that militate against the possibility of effective and legitimate global partnerships. Within this ambivalent situation it is a timely missiological exercise to ask about what is implied in the development of new global partnerships.

What kind of expectations may these churches from the majority world bring to the table of discussion about future partnerships of interdependence for mission? First, these churches would not like to lose the missionary vigour expressed in the total mobilization that characterizes their missionary patterns. As they come to participate in global mission their drive and willingness to be obedient to the prompting of the Spirit is their best contribution. There may be naive pre-modern tones in their confidence that the Lord will provide, or that God will open a way even in the most difficult missionary situations. That naivety may take them to missionary situations that, from a Western perspective, are disastrous. However the disposition to obey and the willingness to go are a very important asset.

Secondly, because their involvement in global mission is new, these churches need assistance in training of missionaries for participation at that level. However, such training has to be contextual because otherwise it may stifle spiritual initiative and it may de-contextualize missionaries to the point of making them irrelevant in their own environment and insensitive to the needs of the new environments to which they work. One serious problem in the development of theological education has been the difficulty of achieving true independence in terms of curriculum design, pedagogical patterns and content organization. Theological education in the non-Western world has been excessively dependent on Western patterns, not only financially but also theologically and pedagogically. Missionary education should avoid this pitfall. The tendency in the West has been always to assume that Western training programs and patterns are immediately transferable and translatable. The assumption must be radically revised. I would dare to say that one should start cooperative ventures with the opposite assumption; working in a creative search for adaptation.

Thirdly, participation in global mission requires established and durable institutional structures. Some young churches in the south are characterized by institutional fragility and weakness, which make it difficult to provide a continuous pattern of support and care for the missionary effort. In the enthusiastic or charismatic phase of a movement institutional structures are secondary and there is even a revolt against them, because revival has broken the structures. Structures are indispensable. However, they have to be contextual. This contextuality is very important in relation to the frame of disparity that has been observed above. The reproduction of support structures that reflect the needs and demands of an affluent society requires drastic revision. With an adequate ecclesiological basis we may be able to see patterns of partnership in which Western and non-Western churches enter into a relationship characterized by the principles of reciprocity and mutuality that we see in the practice and teaching of the Apostle Paul.

The pattern of stewardship for survival that I have outlined is not the only pattern that has developed in mission from the south. A sociological study of the expansion of Pentecostalism shows that what starts with humble origins, even in places like Brazil or Africa, may develop into a sophisticated corporation in which it is difficult to separate what would be religious business from what is Christian mission. A case in point is the Universal Church of the Kingdom of God in Brazil, which was established in 1977 and has expanded to over fifty countries including Europe and the United States. Paul Freston describes it in the following terms:

> While seeing itself as an heir to the Evangelical tradition, the UCKG also has links with traditional Brazilian religiosity. In the phrase of one leader 'We do not follow a European or American Evangelical tradition; we start from the religious practice of the people.' As a result in the opinion of the president of the Brazilian Evangelical Association the UCKG is a new syncretic religion which mixes 'Evangelical teachings, precepts of the medieval Catholic Church and Afro-Amerindian elements.' But it is also (thanks to constant methodological innovation facilitated by centralized control) a bricolage of practices from diverse sources adapted to times of globalization.[33]

I dare to ask the simple question, should the UCKG be invited to Edinburgh 2010? With such a successful record of missionary expansion should this church enter our dialogue about mission? This brings us back to the fundamental issue that cooperation in mission requires some kind of theological consensus. In 2010 it will be impossible to avoid theological issues. In order to be consistent with the ethos and spirit of Edinburgh 1910 we should find a way to avoid the pitfalls into which it apparently fell.

Endnotes

[1] Kenneth Scott Latourette, 'Carnahan Lectures 1956', in *Descfio a los Protestantes*, Buenos Aires: La Aurora, 1957, p.78; Kenneth Scott Latourette, *A History of the Expansion of Christianity*, vol. 7, Grand Rapids: Zondervan, 1971, p. 448.
[2] World Missionary Conference, 1910, *The Home Base of Missions*, Report of Commission VI, Edinburgh & London: Oliphant, Anderson & Ferrier; New York, Chicago and Toronto: Fleming H. Revell, 1910, pp. 104–5
[3] A brief but valuable compendium is Joel A. Carpenter and Wilbert R. Shenk, eds., *Earthen Vessels: American Evangelicals and Foreign Missions, 1880–1980*, Grand Rapids: Eerdmans, 1990.
[4] 'The Two-Party System and the Missionary Enterprise', in Douglas Jacobsen and William Vance Trollinger Jr, eds., *Reforming the Center: American Protestantism, 1900 to the Present*, Grand Rapids: Eerdmans, 1998, pp. 341–60.
[5] Dana L. Robert, 'From Missions to Mission to Beyond Mission: the Historiography of American Protestant Foreign Missions since World War II' *International Bulletin of Missionary Research* 18, no.4 (1994), p. 146.
[6] Robert, 'From Missions to Mission to Beyond Mission ', p. 146.
[7] Lausanne Covenant Par. 1–3; John Stott, ed., *Making Christ Known: Historic Mission Documents from the Lausanne Movement 1974–1989*, Grand Rapids: Eerdmans, 1996, pp. 7–55.
[8] Lausanne Covenant, par. 4.
[9] Lausanne Covenant, par 6
[10] Lausanne Covenant, par. 7, 8, 9.
[11] Lausanne Covenant, par. 10–13
12 William H. Hutchison, *Errand to the World: American Protestant Thought and Foreign Mission,* Chicago: The University of Chicago Press, 1987, p. 176.
13 Carpenter and Shenk, *Earthen Vessels*, p.131.
[14] James A. Scherer, *Gospel, Church and Kingdom: Comparative Studies in World Mission Theology*, Minneapolis: Augsburg, 1987, p.15
[15] 'An Historical Introduction', in John Stott, ed., *Making Christ Known: Historic Mission Documents from the Lausanne Movement 1974-1989*, Grand Rapids: Eerdmans, 1996, p. xii.
[16] 'An Historical Introduction', in John Stott, ed., *Making Christ Known*, p. xii.
[17] Scherer, *Gospel, Church and Kingdom*, p. 40.
[18] See *Mission Studies*, which is the journal of the International Association for Mission Studies, and *Missiology: an International Review*, which is the journal of the American Society of Missiology.
[19] David Barrett, *World Christian Encyclopaedia* , Oxford: Oxford University Press, 2 vols., 2001; Patrick Johnstone and Jason Mandryk, *Operation World 21st Century Edition*, Carlisle: Paternoster, 2001.
[20] *The Home Base of Missions*, p. 102.
[21] Robert J. Priest, Terry Dischinger, Steve Rasmussen, and C. M. Brown, 'Researching the Short-Term Mission Movement', *Missiology: an International Review* 34, no. 4 (October 2006), pp. 431–50.

[22] See further Samuel Escobar, 'New Patterns for Interdependence in Mission', in Manuel Ortiz and Susan S. Baker, eds., *The Urban Face of Mission: Ministering the Gospel in a Diverse and Changing World*, Phillipsburg: Presbyterian and Reformed, 2002, pp. 97–114.
[23] Lausanne Covenant, par. 8.
[24] Lausanne Covenant, par. 8.
[25] Lausanne Covenant, par. 9.
[26] Larry Pate, *From Every People*, Monrovia: MARC, 1989, p. 5.
[27] Michael Jaffarian, 'Are There More Non-Western Missionaries than Western Missionaries?', *International Bulletin of Missionary Research* 28, no. 3 (July 2004), pp. 129–30.
[28] Jaffarian, 'Are There More Non-Western Missionaries than Western Missionaries?', pp. 129–30.
[29] Steve C. Moon, 'The Recent Korean Missionary Movement: A Record of Growth, and More Growth Needed', *International Bulletin of Missionary Research* 27, no. 1 (Jan 2003), pp. 11–17.
[30] Paul Freston, 'The Transnationalization of Brazilian Pentecostalism: The Universal Church of the Kingdom of God' in André Corten and Ruth Marshall-Fratani, eds., *Between Babel and Pentecost: Transnational Pentecostalism in Africa and Latin America*, Bloomington: Indiana University Press, 2001, p. 196.
[31] See Howard Snyder, *Signs of the Spirit*, Grand Rapids: Baker, 1999.
[32] *Memorias del COMLA*, minutes of the Fourth Latin America Missionary Congress, Lima 3–8 February 1991, Lima: Ediciones Paulinas, 1991, p. 267.
[33] Freston, 'The Transnationalization of Brazilian Pentecotalism', p. 199.

Commission Seven

Missions and Governments

Commission Seven
'Missions and Governments'

The Commission in Summary

'Missions and Governments' – the title of Commission Seven – denotes the relationship between missions and the governments under which they operated: indigenous national governments, European colonial governments, and 'native chieftainships'. Within the concern for church-state relations, the Commission was specifically interested in 'the contact of the expanding (i.e. among "non-Christian peoples") Church with Governments which, for the first time, have to take account of Christianity both as a destructive and constructive power, contending for a law and loyalty different from, and higher than, those recognised by any State'.[1]

The task was entrusted to a twenty-one man (not a woman among them) Commission, ten of whose members were British, six US-Americans, three Germans, one Norwegian and one Canadian. Lord Balfour of Burleigh – Scottish politician, cabinet minister, and Presbyterian elder – who presided over the Edinburgh 1910 Conference, served as Commission Chairman.

The Commission Report runs to 121 pages – considerably shorter than the other commission reports – but includes a longer (nearly 40 pages) summary of the plenary discussion, as well as 20 pages of appendices. This reflects the way the Commission dealt with the challenge facing it. How to elaborate and apply general principles from situations of mission-government relations that differed widely from one part of the world to another? In line with the general policy of the 1910 Conference, it opted for an empirical approach.

Part One, 'A Survey of Existing Conditions in Various Mission Fields', examines relationships between missions and governments in Japan, China, India, the Dutch East Indies, 'Mohammedan Lands', Mid Africa and Southern Africa, with additional contributions from missionaries in all these regions in the plenary discussion. Part 2 extrapolates 'Principles and Findings', and applies them to a range of problems that recur in mission-government relations across the regions. The colonial ethos of the Report reflects the nature of the times, and the fact that Part 1 was drafted entirely by the British commissioners. Part 2, by contrast, is the work of the entire Commission, and succeeds in articulating principles that criticise aspects of colonialism and, at least to an extent, transcend the colonial mentality.

The Report classifies the survey evidence on a graduating scale of where it perceived societies to stand in relation to 'civilisation', the latter being defined relative to the missionary task itself. Thus, Japan was deemed the most civilized of 'mission fields', since its government had established 'such internal order and toleration that problems of missionary policy, *in relation to government* (original italics), have ceased to exist in any acute form'.[2] At the lowest end of the scale was 'the absolutely independent savage chief'.[3] Between the two stood governments that were 'of higher civilisation and independent' (e.g. Persia, China and Turkey), 'of low civilisation, under Christian rule or influence' (e.g. the African Protectorates), and 'of higher civilisation, under Christian rule and influence' (e.g. India and Egypt.)[4]

Irrespective of where governments were perceived to stand on this scale of civilized administration, it was agreed that missionary policy should be based on the New Testament principle, 'give to Caesar the things that are Caesar's, and to God the things that are God's'.[5] Respect for civil authority, regardless of religious identity, was deemed essential, provided civil authority obeyed its God-given mandate of caring for the welfare of the people. This included, as the Report tirelessly reiterates, the rights of indigenous Christian communities, and of the missionaries themselves, at least on par with other 'domiciled aliens' residing in a state, as determined by treaty or international law. The Report emphasizes, however, that Christians have a higher loyalty to God. Christianity is 'a revolutionary moral force' that desires the 'spiritual and personal transformation' of every human society.[6] In order to protect this Christian obligation, the Report considers it essential that missions should scrupulously avoid 'the identification of the Christian faith either with the aggression of Foreign Powers or with the spirit of lawlessness'.[7]

The Report recommends a policy of missionary obedience to 'settled government', and cautions against missionary participation in 'political agitation'.[8] At the same time it speaks with approval of situations where missionaries become 'the champion of the people' among whom they live.[9] This may be in missionary support of local cultures and languages, or advocacy of social change, or criticism of civil governments that are responsible for gross oppression and injustice, or sympathy with the awakened social and political aspirations of the people. The Report accepts that tension may therefore occur between missions and governments.

To guide the missions in such situations, the Report recommends the following principles:[10] (1) missionaries are legally subjects of their own governments, unless they choose to naturalize, and are therefore bound by such treaties as exist between their national government and the government of the country in which they serve; (2) indigenous Christians are, in terms of civil status, subjects of their own governments; (3) the relationship between missionaries and indigenous Christians is therefore 'purely religious', and does not legally permit missionaries to 'interfere in the general administration of the country'; (4) every independent state has the right to make its own laws, and is not answerable to any other state except in terms of international law or special treaties; (5) the spiritual obligation under which missionaries work does not confer any civil or legal rights upon them; (6) in other than exceptional circumstances, such action as missionaries undertake to apply their spiritual and moral teaching in society at large must be within the framework of the national law; and if, in exceptional circumstances, they act outside the law, they also place themselves out with its protection; (7) missions should deal with governments in a conciliatory and reasonable manner; (8) where missions feel morally or spiritually obliged to make representation to governments, they should do so in the spirit of St Paul's teaching: 'Let each of you look not to your own interests, but to the interests of others.'[11]

Under these same principles the Report considers several 'general questions' arising from its survey of existing conditions: e.g. appeal to civil authority, and compensation of missions. Especially in situations where governments restrict missionary work, the Report recommends that (a) contact with civil authority should be entrusted to a senior missionary, preferably acting on behalf of a joint missionary council (the institution of the Dutch Missions Consul was sympathetically described in Part 1 of the Report);[12] and (b) on the Pauline distinction between what is expedient and what is lawful,[13] missions should be willing to forego their legal rights where such sacrifice may benefit the indigenous Christian community.[14] This is the principle on which the Report concludes: 'We would emphasise that Christian teaching inculcates respect for civil authorities ... and would affirm the reasonableness of granting to (indigenous) Christians all the protection, rights and privileges of loyal and law-abiding citizens'.[15]

Endnotes

1 World Missionary Conference, 1910, *Missions and Governments*, Report of Commission VII, Edinburgh & London: Oliphant, Anderson & Ferrier; New York, Chicago and Toronto: Fleming H. Revell, 1910, p. 2.
2 *Missions and Governments*, p. 89.
3 *Missions and Governments*, p. 88.
4 *Missions and Governments*, p. 88.
5 Matthew 22:21; Mark 12:7; Luke 20:25.
6 *Missions and Governments*, p. 93.
7 *Missions and Governments*, p. 93.
8 *Missions and Governments*, p. 95.
9 See *Missions and Governments*, pp. 115–16.
10 *Missions and Governments*, pp. 97–9.
11 Philippians 2:4.
12 *Missions and Governments*, p. 103.
13 1 Corinthians. 10:23.
14 *Missions and Governments*, p. 106.
15 *Missions and Governments*, p. 120.

CHRISTIAN MISSION AND POLITICAL POWER: COMMISSION SEVEN REVISITED

Tinyiko Sam Maluleke

1. Edinburgh 1910: Character and Assumptions

The full title of the theme for the Edinburgh 1910 Conference is worthy of our careful recollection: *World Missionary Conference to Consider Missionary Problems in Relation to the Non-Christian World.* At least five things are remarkable about the vision behind Edinburgh 1910.

The first is the firm idea of the world as one unit, hence the boldness of declaring a 'world' missionary Conference:

> … one world, waiting, surely, for who shall carry to it and place in its empty hands one Faith – the only thing that can ever truly and fundamentally unite it or deeply and truly satisfy it, bringing its one human race into one Catholic Church.[1]

Clearly therefore, not only was there a growing vision of the world as one, such a vision was also inspired by (and in turn, inspired) an understanding of a world without Christ being as a person with 'empty hands' and in need of 'one faith'. The vision of unity here is not merely the scientific (the Earth as one planet among others) or the merely technological (the Earth 'organically knit by the nerves of electric cable and telegraph wire'[2]). Rather it speaks of a unity of the world that, despite its apparent scientific and technological unity, will never be truly united until and unless it is united by coming to faith in Christ.

The second remarkable thing about the theme is its clear and specific focus, namely 'to consider missionary problems in relation to the non-Christian world'. Commentators may have sometimes spoken of Edinburgh as if it was a Conference about everything to do with missions. But as the title delineates, Edinburgh 2010 is a clearly focussed Conference with a distinct and limited brief: to consider missionary problems in relation to the non-Christian world. Another way of amplifying this is to speak about what the 1910 Conference was *not* primarily about. It was not a Conference about the challenge of missions to the 'Church at home'. Indeed, it appears that mission was understood mainly in terms of foreign missions so that the 'Church at home' was only conceived of as 'the home base of missions' and not a site of missions in its own right and its own context. More positively stated, the 1910 Conference focus was on the non-Christian rather than the Christian world. It seems to have been the overwhelming view then that there was nothing wrong with the Christian world; hence, attention ought to be focussed on the non-Christian world. Ironically, the non-Christian world was represented by mainly Western missionaries working in that world rather than the peoples of that world themselves. Not a single native African was in attendance at Edinburgh 1910 – the exception being the Reverend Alexander P. Camphor, an African-American missionary to Liberia.[3]

Third, from the preceding point, it is clear that although the notion of the world as a single unit was making inroads in missionary thinking, the dominant reading at Edinburgh 1910 was of a world divided into two: the Christian and the non-Christian world. It is clear that this was the main diagnostic manner in which the world was viewed. The major challenge for missions and missionaries, therefore, was one of how to expand the Christian sphere at the expense of the non-Christian sphere in the world. As well as the notion of Christian vs. non-Christian, the world was further interpreted in terms of high civilization and low civilization. Note how the Commission on missions and governments goes about classifying the 'mission lands':

> Without entering into detail, we may divide mission lands roughly into five groups: a) those of low civilisation, but independent; b) those of higher civilisation and independent; c) those of low civilisation, under Christian rule; d) those of higher civilisation, under Christian rule or influence, e) those of the highest international rank.[4]

Fourth, the 1910 Conference is touted as 'deliberative and consultative' rather than taking the form of a practical demonstration.[5] This is true insofar as when Edinburgh is compared to similar conferences before it. However, the slant of Conference topics and discussions did bear a very practical 'how to' rather than a 'why' tone. It is significant that the planners of Edinburgh 1910 coined the problem and deliberations of our Commission (as they did with other commissions), not in terms of the apparently more theoretical construction of Christian mission and political power, but rather more practically in terms of mission and governments – in fact in terms of specific missions/missionaries and specific governments. A huge chunk of the principal sections of the Report of the Commission on Missions and Governments pertain to the roles, attitude, and functions of the missionary rather than towards missions as such.

Fifth, for Edinburgh 1910 mission was understood in an immediate and pragmatic sense. In this pre-Barth and pre-Hoekendijk era, talk was of missions rather than of mission. Mission was understood mainly as 'foreign missions', as the missions of the missionaries rather than in terms of a theological understanding of missions *per se*, the mission of mission societies and mission as the work of evangelization in a so-called mission field. In those days, the current of mission did flow, not from everywhere to everywhere, but rather from the Christian world to the non-Christian world. These are the prevailing understandings of mission that informed Edinburgh 1910 and certainly the understanding that informed Commission Seven on 'Missions and Governments'. Theologically, this overt man-based and Church-based understanding of missions was nevertheless grounded in God. Gairdner reported that the Conference methodology and objectives were the following:

> Like Solomon it sought wisdom – *to know* … to know *what*? The work abroad, of course, with its thousand facets; the nature of the supreme crisis that faces the Church; the Church Catholic itself, to which the whole [mission] enterprise has been committed; and – God.[6]

We sense here a kind of latent missionary theology built around an understanding of mission, with the Church as the main driver of mission. In understanding and performing its duty in the world, it was optimistically believed that the Christian Church had 'possibilities as illimitable as God Himself …. The issue to which the consideration of the world task of Christianity drives us back is *whether the Church really possesses Christ's thought about God, and, if not, whether it can get it back'* (emphasis mine).[7] The overwhelming sense was one of mission as an immensely achievable duty of the Christian Church – albeit a duty to be accomplished in faith and faithfulness to God. The countenancing of failure in achieving the goal of evangelizing the world was regarded as a sign of both a lack of faith in God and a lack of faith in self. 'Can anything stand in the way of the accomplishment of the good will [of God] but the unbelief of the Church?'[8]

2. The 'Unusual' Subject of Mission and Governments

2.1. Its Theoretical Underpinnings

> In all the other commissions … the Conference kept, so to speak, within the sphere of the Christian Church; but in the Report now to be considered it was dealing with an external power, the power of the State all over the world. It was one more of the novel features of this Edinburgh Conference, that this unusual subject had received treatment…[9]

From the above, it becomes clear that the *first* notable matter underpinning the approach of Edinburgh 1910 was the subject of external power. At the time, this was considered unusual if not daring. It was a subject considered to be beyond the normal purview of Christian missions. This was driven by an understanding of society as organized into different and separate spheres. This understanding governed the way in which the Commission understood the relation of the sphere of the Christian Church and the sphere of the State. The daring and peculiar nature of the work of this Commission is attributable to the fact that the Conference was seen as overstepping its proper sphere and moving into another sphere. To this notion of separate spheres, we must keep, at the back of our minds, other tools used to interpret society, already alluded to, such as the schemes of high and low civilizations, Christian world and non-Christian world, Christian and non-Christian religions. These form the 'Edinburgh toolbox' of conceptual instruments with which the world was to be read and to be understood. In this regard, the sphere of Christian mission was seen to be different from, for example, the sphere of government.

Second, it chose to conduct its task in terms of an analytical-descriptive rather than an analytical-critical approach to the subject. It was, in the first instance, not concerned with theoretically or theologically debating, let alone defining, the ideal. And this was not for lack of awareness of the issues at stake. The Commission noted that its subject, '... may be theoretically regarded as a study of one aspect of the great problem of the relation between the Church and the State and the discrimination between the two spheres'.[10] The mouth-watering issues and complex theoretical and theological issues implied in the above quotation notwithstanding, the path chosen by the Commission was one of accurately establishing the *status quo*, its problems and promises and:

> ... not the ambitious one of defining the ideal relations of Church and State. It is the humble work of ascertaining, by a survey of existing facts, what attitude the various governments assume towards missions working within their borders, how they help and are helped by missions, how they hinder them and, perchance, are hindered by them, with a view to disentangle the principles upon which missions do work and should work in order to avoid needless offence, and to promote the common end, both of governments and of missions – the welfare of the nations.[11]

Third, although recognizing the different spheres occupied by the two, as discussed in the first principle discussed above, the Commission ultimately recognizes and recommends a 'co-operant', rather than a conflicting relationship, between missions and governments. The reason is that 'to restrain evil and promote good is the duty of government', and both missions and governments are interested and invested in 'the welfare of the nations'.[12]

Fourth, there were, even after the decision for the Commission to seek non-confrontational principles upon which to build mission and government relations, there were at least 'three wrongs' discussed at the Conference where confrontation between mission and government lurked. These 'three wrongs' were: i) opium traffic, ii) liquor traffic and iii) enforced labour. All three impinged on the income and profits which major Western countries were making in relation to other countries.[13]

2.2. Findings and Recommendations of the Commission

It is necessary to recall here the distinctions between governments highlighted above, namely countries of a) low civilization, but independent; b) higher civilization and independent; c) low civilization, under Christian rule; d) higher civilization under Christian rule or influence, and e) those of the highest international rank. How missionaries should behave in relation to government and how the relations between missions and governments are to be structured depends on the type of government in place, as sketched out in the foregoing scheme. For the rest, the findings essentially contain a set of elucidated guidelines for missionaries in terms of how to relate to various governments in such a way as to advance the missionary cause. These guidelines were themselves compiled from the input of missionaries in various mission fields controlled by various types of government.

Concerning loyalty to political governments, the report suggested that missionaries should generally be guided by the principle of 'rendering unto Caesar the things that are Caesar's and unto God the things that are God's' regardless of the form and face of Caesar in the various contexts of the world. This included a recommendation to pray for the ruling prince. In this regard, the Commission rejoiced in the knowledge that 'the Gospel is the Gospel for the national and not the product of Western thought nor a means of advancing Western interests'.[14]

Concerning the heightened sense of political aspiration in many parts of the world, combined with the missionary efforts to 'disentangle the essentials of Christian faith and life from the Western outgrowths and accompaniments…',[15] the Commission found that the work of missions could not but be affected, 'especially in the many lands where the missionary belongs to a dominant race'.[16] In this regard, the Commission highlighted three crucial principles: a) missionaries were to desist from 'political agitation' for 'this is outside their sphere', b) missionaries have a duty to 'teach and practice obedience to settled government', c) they also have duty to 'exercise their influence for the removal of gross oppression and injustice, particularly where the Government is in the hands of men of their own race … provided that in so doing they keep clear of association with any political movement'.[17]

Concerning the public services of missionaries, the Commission was most articulate and full of praise for the numerous ways in which the work of missionaries was of great service to governments, claiming that 'they have won an influence which has made the task of governments comparatively easy; and everywhere they continue to manifest and inculcate that loyalty to and co-operation with governments, without which the latter indeed may rule, but without which they cannot fit a people for the higher task of ruling themselves'.[18]

Concerning other more generalized principles governing missionary relations towards governments, the Commission pronounced thus:

- Missionaries remain subject to their own governments as domiciled foreigners, 'entitled to all the privileges and subject to all the disabilities of domiciled aliens'.[19]

- The convert remains subject of his government. 'His *[sic]* civil status is not changed, except insofar as the law of the country may impose civil disabilities upon the profession of Christianity.'[20]
- Relations between missionaries and converts are 'purely religious'.[21]
- All independent states have the right to control and regulate the civil and municipal lives of its subjects.
- All independent states have the civil right to admit or refuse missionaries.
- '...where settled government exists, it is the protector of all within its borders; and the missionary should act on the presumption that it will protect'.[22]

Concerning the main points of difficulty between missions and governments (in restrictions on movements and settlement of missionaries, their acquisition of property, persecution or discrimination against converts, compensation for injuries, cooperation in matters of public welfare) the Commission made the following general observations:

- 'The government has the legal right in its own order (civil) to lay such regulation as it thinks necessary upon the missionary's action.'[23] (Recognizing that the missionary may choose to disregard, but only at the pain of relinquishing, his civil rights).
- Missionaries are urged to appeal to civil powers sparingly and to exercise wisdom/restraint in claiming extra-territorial rights.
- Missionaries should always seek to strike a balance between 'Christian expediency' and their demand for legal rights.
- The work of the Commission was not without a certain prophetic edge. The Commissioners were prepared to stick their necks out on such contentious issues as the following:
- The Commission contended that 'a respectful remonstrance' should be made to the British government for the excessive deference to Islam and the excessive restrictions placed upon Christian missionaries in such countries as Egypt, the Sudan, and Northern Nigeria.[24]
- It was strongly suggested by the Commission that the Conference should 'make a decided pronouncement upon the Congo question', where massive atrocities were being committed by the Belgian rulers in the context of forced labour in pursuit of profits connected with the acquisition of rubber.[25] In this regard, the Commission also noted that 'a system of forced labour is always liable to the greatest abuses'.[26]
- Concerning the difficulties faced by Christian missionaries and their converts in so-called Mohammedan lands, the Commission asked the rhetorical question of whether 'the time (has) not come in the development of a world civilisation and of international

relationships when the enlightened nations of the world may make freedom of action in religious profession the birthright of every man?'[27]

- Notwithstanding all the 'hindrances put in the way of missions by the policy of governments … nothing is a greater hindrance than the feebleness of the sense of responsibility for the welfare of the more backward races which is felt by the more advanced … (so that) even men in high public positions do not hesitate to speak of all "coloured" races as if they were doomed to perpetual national servitude …'.[28]
- The Commission advocated that 'the traffic in opium should cease unless under the restrictions proper to a dangerous drug' whist also expressing the hope that the British government 'may be able to meet the financial difficulties created by the cessation of opium revenue without further burdening the people with tax'.[29]
- The Commission further urged the 'severe restriction, if not the absolute prohibition of the sale of intoxicating liquor to native races, among whom its use has hitherto been practically unknown, or on whom its use is manifestly producing deteriorating effects'.[30]

3. How Far Have We Come?

3.1. Church State Relations before Constantine

The question of Church and State is a topic steeped in the earliest memories of Christian history. The original context of 'Church-State' relations was one of, on the one hand, a vast, powerful and extensive State demanding both taxes and allegiance, and on the other, a small, weak, but determined formation of followers of Christ who believed and confessed him as Lord and Saviour. Here lies the inherent subversive nature of the Christian faith: the *admission* that upon being crucified Christ died, the *belief* that Christ rose from the dead and the fervent *hope* Christ will come again to usher in a new dispensation. This is the triad of beliefs in which is contained the seeds of Christianity's relations to civil authorities. It was in this context that the nascent Christian Church was born – developing its identity, defining its mission, developing its theology and perfecting its rituals and structures.

Jesus' engagement of Pilate as the procurator sought to establish whether Jesus was king or not is quite instructive. First, he seemed to brush the question aside by fearlessly implying that Pilate might not be able to think independently, retorting, 'Do you ask this on your own, or did others tell you about me?' (John 18:34 NRSV). Later, Jesus puts it to Pilate that, 'You say that I am a king. For this I was born, and for this I came into the world…' (John 18:37 NRSV), even though he had also said his kingdom was not of this world. When Pilate asserted his 'power' (from Caesar) either to crucify or free, Jesus disputes the source of Pilate's 'power' declaring, 'You would have no power over me unless it had been given you from above...' (John 19:11 NRSV). With these words, Jesus seems to dismiss both the 'power' of Pilate and the authority of Caesar deferring instead to the real power and real authority of God. Denuded of his 'power' both by Jesus and by the crowds who were determined to coerce him to do their will, Pilate, as a final resort, takes to a 'what-I-have-written-I have-written' stance – all in a pathetic and hollow attempt to salvage some semblance of 'power' and to mitigate the indignity of being stripped of power so completely and so publicly. This same insistence of Jesus on a higher form of allegiance, allegiance to God and not to 'man', was to be invoked by Jesus' disciples and followers many times in the course of the first few centuries of Christianity, even in the face of persecution and death.

3.2. Church State Relations after Constantine

The conversion of Constantine and the resultant mainstreaming of Christianity eased Church-State relations considerably. From then on, Christians had to reorder their relations with the State – now a benevolent and friendly State. To speak of Church and State is ultimately to speak about power – its understanding and its exercise as well as the social and economic arrangements between people. In this regard, the Deuteronomic and prophetic teachings of the Bible become relevant alongside the teachings and practice of Jesus and the early Church. The topic invokes a discussion of how the Church understands power and its structuring, purpose and exercise. For example, there are really no Church and State relations to discuss when both Church and State understand, structure, order and exercise power in essentially the same way. The advent of the Constantinian era did not erode the importance of Biblical teachings; if anything, such teachings become an important resource as the Church defines and redefines its own attitude to power both internally and externally. To return to the phraseology we used at the beginning of this essay, after Constantine, the Church can no longer afford to ignore the 'politics' of its message, or assume the innocence of its own 'political existence' any more than the Church can afford to ignore the mission of the Constantinian State. After Constantine, the State is no longer satisfied (if it ever was) with being given what belongs to it because it is now possible for the Church to be drawn into the sphere of the State. After Constantine, the Church is no longer innocent, but it is implicated in the State even as the State is implicated in the Church. This mutual implication is complex and subtle, overt and covert, voluntary and involuntary, normal and abnormal, obvious and not so obvious. After Constantine, there is formal and legalized mutual seduction between Church and State. In this regard, the Reformation notion of spheres is a helpful hermeneutical key, but the actual determination of what aspect of what issue belongs to which sphere is not easy to decipher.

4. Evaluating Commission Seven for our Times

4.1. The late David Bosch has been criticized by, among others, Greg Cuthbertson, in one of the early reviews of his book, for overstating the influence of the Enlightenment on mission.[31] While we agree with some of the criticism in Cuthbertson's review, we do not think that (at least for Protestant missions) it is possible to overstate the influence of modernity. The long shadow of the enlightenment was cast over the 1910 Edinburgh Conference, perhaps in more ways than many of the subsequent conferences. This does not mean that Protestant missions were a carbon copy of Enlightenment thinking. Rather, it means that the Enlightenment provided the major and the dominant framework upon which the theory and practice of missions was developed. Protestant thinking on mission – even thinking that was decidedly opposed to aspects of Enlightenment thinking – was often either mirrored or modelled on Enlightenment paradigms.

4.2. We have already noted how the growing scientific belief of the earth as one planet among others was used by the participants in the Edinburgh Conference to argue for: i) the uniqueness of earth as *that* one special place where God chose to send His Son with ii) the coherence and oneness of earth interpreted as a metaphor for a single world emptily and hungrily awaiting *one* salvation, *one* baptism; *one* Lord. Indeed, its scientific oneness was transfigured into a necessary and imminent oneness in Christ which would come with missionaries doubling their efforts and governments assisting accordingly. It is in this belief that the missionary cause sometimes appeared indistinguishable from the colonial project. What confronts us today is the notion of the world as a 'global village' – one of the most subversive expressions of our times –with instant links of communication and travel, cultures, peoples, sounds, tastes and smells from afar, available at the touch of a button. But how real is the global village to one and all? Is it a global village for goods, people or money? Is it a global village for all or is it just for some? Is the global village available and amenable to mission? What is the difference between 'globe' and 'earth'?

4.3. Edinburgh 1910 participants not only borrowed from enlightenment descriptions of the word and enlightenment ordering of the world's peoples, cultures and religions, they also adapted and, in some cases conservatively resisted, enlightenment interpretative frameworks in order to construct their theology of mission and *vice versa.* We now live at a time when the economic metaphor reigns supreme. Countries and peoples are defined by their placement on the economic scale – the time of the market, the emerging market, the established market and the self-regulating market. We speak today of the developed, developing and underdeveloped world. How has missiology appropriated and dealt with the grammar? Is Christian mission an aspect of developmentalist and market paradigm or is it a challenge to this agenda, or both? One of the remarkable things about the notions of the world as globe and the world as market is how both seem to eschew and eclipse human beings.

Neither the term 'globe' nor 'market' necessarily foreground people. It is one thing to criticize our forbears for having depended heavily on the language and socio-analytical tools of their times; it is quite another when we have to consider our own captivity to the metaphors of our own time. If we were to do away with the economic grammar of our times; if we were to revise or do away with the notions of globe, market or development, what would we put in their place? If we were to discard the vision of a development as propounded by the International Monetary Fund (IMF) and the World Bank, what alternative vision of society would we put in its place and from what source would we draw the building blocks of such a vision? In a world that was scientifically defined as a unit, our missionary forbears proceeded to argue that the world was not really 'one' until and unless it was evangelized. What, then, is the role of faith in Christ in the quest for economic development and control of the markets?

4.4. One of the big suggestions of David Bosch in his *Transforming Mission: Paradigm Shifts in Theology of Mission* (1991) – the most controversial in my opinion – is the suggestion that one of the big moves we have to make in terms of our understanding of mission is the shift from 'mission *is*' to 'mission *as*' – his suggestion that mission has to be carried out in many modes. Bosch then makes a list of 'mission as' suggestions: liberation, justice, contextualization … etc. The real question is whether Bosch sees the transition from 'mission is' to 'mission as' a complete and single movement so the one replaces the other, once and for all. My sense is that 'mission as' is not a replacement of 'mission is', but an expression of it. Each generation therefore has the challenge both to define (i.e., mission *is*) and to contextualize (mission *as*) mission. Since Edinburgh 1910, we have moved from missions to mission – the mission of God who so loved the world that he gave his only Son. Herein lies also our understanding of the power of Christian mission as opposed to the power of our missions. While God is powerful, the Church may need to come to terms with the power of its powerlessness. We may need to engage in mission at the tactical rather than the strategic level – tactics being, as Michel De Certeau has taught us, the art of the weak.[32] By and large, we want to suggest that we persist in subscribing to power models of mission, relying more on Matthew 28 than on John 3, even though the context we live in confounds our assumptions and methods.

4.5. It is clear that our forbears operated with the idea that, although there was much overlap, there was nevertheless a government sphere and a 'missions' sphere. The problem is that there was not always a clear-cut space of intersection and non-intersection. Indeed, whenever the boundaries between Church and State are too clearly defined and too easily recognized by both sides, it is a sign of danger. In South Africa, the problem of spheres was often invoked by Apartheid-era politicians who cautioned against the mixing of politics and religion – so that the sphere of politics was meant to be totally detached from that of religions. Armed with the tool of distinct spheres our

Edinburgh forbears proceeded to map out some principles in terms of which Church and State were to relate. The challenge we face in the globalizing world is that spheres are harder not merely to distinguish one from the other but also to identify – for a variety of reasons. The walls surrounding most spheres are constantly being undermined and dissolved. No sooner are they set up than they are brought down. Think of the sphere of government as opposed to the sphere of the so-called private or corporate sector; the sphere of the private as opposed to the sphere of the public, the sphere of the personal as opposed to the sphere of the political. Have we perhaps reached a stage where, owing to the fluidity and porous nature of the spheres, we should consider either rethinking the whole scheme radically or abandoning it altogether? Think of the extent to which the nation-State has either ceased to have meaning and influence or ceased to exist. In this regard, the notion of government becomes elusive. Governments are important but perhaps not such centres of power as they once were. It also reveals the futility of limiting our focus to one government (or to government alone) when there is a network of other players benefiting from, or influencing, the government in question.

4.6. It is remarkable that Edinburgh 1910 managed to identify and speak out against some clear wrongs in relation to the action of governments, for example the opium traffic, liquor traffic and enforced labour, plus atrocities in the Belgian Congo. All three impinged on the income and profits of the major powers of the day. One of the most remarkable things about African wars and instabilities is the way in which some of them are able to rage on without seriously affecting the sale of platinum, diamonds and oil taking place in the same context. Similarly, there are business arrangements between countries that affect and regulate sales of drugs, which arrangements do to address the crises faced by humanity today – the case of anti-retroviral AIDS drugs being a candid example. The trafficking in women and girl children, as well as the scourge of sex tourism, is another poignant example.

4.7. Power relations in the world. The influence of the World Trade Organization (WTO), G7 countries and the United States of America (note that we have excluded the United Nations) has long been recognized as one of the main drivers of power and powerlessness, wealth and poverty, in the world today. We cannot discuss the question of mission and political power without confronting this reality. Indeed the most pressing question for mission today is how we conceive of Christian mission in the light of globalization as driven by the World Trade Organization (WTO), G7 countries and a rampant United States of America – which also happens to be Christian.

4.8. Will the 2010 Missionary Conference look different from its 1910 predecessor? In 1910 Commission One's membership included, so far as my forbears are concerned, Arthur Grandjean and Henri-Alexander Junod, Swiss Missionaries in the north of South African and the South of Mozambique respectively. Will the Commissions be any more representative in 2010? This is the third decade in which we have listened to arguments indicating that there has been a shift in the centre of gravity of Christianity from the global-north to the global-south. But what does this mean and why is it taking so long to sink in? One of the reasons why it has taken so long is that the global-south remains, by and large, an economically and politically powerless hemisphere. The swelling numbers of Christians in the global-south do not translate into power. Indeed, as Jesse Mugambi of Kenya has rhetorically asked:

> … how [can we] explain the apparent contradiction, that contemporary Africa continues to be, perhaps the most religious continent in the world, and yet its peoples remain the most abused of all in history. How could it be that peoples who continue to call on God most reverently are the ones whom God seems to neglect most vehemently? Could it be that irreligion in the key to success, and that religion is the key to backwardness?[33]

The shift in gravity has not moved the World Council of Churches (WCC) from Geneva to Accra, Ghana. It will not move Wall Street, New York to Soweto, South Africa and it has not moved the World Alliance of Reformed Churches (WARC) office from Geneva, Switzerland to Seoul, South Korea. Perhaps we need a much more quantitative basis, a much more tactical basis, for creating a new vision for mission than numbers and gravities.

4.9. An aspect to which we have hinted above regarding the 1910 Edinburgh Conference is the extent to which it was comfortable with the practice of naming others in terms of Christian criteria and standards. The notion of the 'non-Christian world' may have seemed obvious and self-explanatory to them, but it has over the past ninety-five years become hugely problematic. It is, for one thing, a massive generalization. It also seeks to confer on 'the other' a description whose intention it is to evaluate and to prepare for eventual take-over. Admittedly, the notion of civilization was employed to balance out the notion of non-Christian, for example Japan and China were granted the status of being civilized, though non-Christian. Yet the overarching frame under which they and all the rest fell was that of 'non-Christian', just as the world was seen to be either 'Christian' or 'non-Christian'. Ninety-five years later, we have learnt that it is fair and preferable to call people what they call themselves rather than describe them in terms of who we are. The insistence on naming others in our terms has many implications. It speaks against genuine exchange, stunts our capacity to listen, and militates against genuine mission.

Endnotes

[1] W. H. Temple Gairdner, *'Edinburgh 1910': An Account and Interpretation of the World Missionary Conference*, Edinburgh & London: Oliphant, Anderson & Ferrier; New York, Chicago and Toronto: Fleming H. Revell, 1910. p. 6.
[2] Gairdner, *Edinburgh 1910*, p. 6.
[3] Stanley J. Friesen, *Missionary Responses to Tribal Religions at Edinburgh 1910*, Frankfurt: Peter Lang, 1996, pp. 27–8.

[4] World Missionary Conference, 1910, *Missions and Governments*, Report of Commission VII, Edinburgh & London: Oliphant, Anderson & Ferrier; New York, Chicago and Toronto: Fleming H. Revell, 1910, p 88.
5 Gairdner, *Edinburgh 1910*, p. 13.
[6] Gairdner, *Edinburgh 1910*, p. 14.
[7] Gairdner, *Edinburgh 1910*, p. 16, quoting the pre-conference communiqué.
[8] Gairdner, *Edinburgh 1910*, p. 16.
[9] Gairdner, *Edinburgh 1910*, p. 154.
[10] *Missions and Governments*, p. 2.
[11] *Missions and Governments*, p. 2.
[12] *Missions and Governments*, p. 2.
[13] *Missions and Governments*, pp. 116–17.
[14] *Missions and Governments*, p. 94.
[15] *Missions and Governments*, p. 94.
[16] *Missions and Governments*, p. 95.
[17] *Missions and Governments*, p. 95.
[18] *Missions and Governments*, pp. 96–7.
[19] *Missions and Governments*, p. 97.
[20] *Missions and Governments*, p. 97.
[21] *Missions and Governments*, p. 97.
[22] *Missions and Governments*, p. 112.
[23] *Missions and Governments*, p. 104.
[24] *Missions and Governments*, p. 113.
[25] *Missions and Governments*, p. 113.
[26] *Missions and Governments*, p. 117.
[27] *Missions and Governments*, p. 114.
[28] *Missions and Governments*, p. 115.
[29] *Missions and Governments*, p. 117.
[30] *Missions and Governments*, p. 117.
[31] Greg Cuthbertson, 'Protestant Paradigms of Mission. Review of *Transforming Mission: Paradigm Shifts in Theology of Mission*, by David J. Bosch', *Journal of Theology for Southern Africa* 81 (1992), pp. 78–85.
[32] Michel De Certeau, *The Practice of Everyday Life,* trans. Steven Rendall, Berkeley: University of California Press, 1984.
[33] Jesse N. K. Mugambi, *From Liberation to Reconstruction: African Christian Theology after the Cold War,* Nairobi: East African Educational Publishers, 1995, p. 33.

Commission Seven in Light of a Century of Experience in Cuba

Adolfo Ham

Commission Seven: a Latin American Reading

From a Latin American perspective, the Commission Seven Report is marked by Constantinian thinking. Most of the governments of the 'First World' protected, and some even helped, the churches in their missionary endeavours. The mentality of the *corpus christianum* was prevalent in that the churches comfortably regarded their different societies as genuine realizations of the Kingdom. Missions were still guided by the *Vasco da Gama* approach: a joint project of the governments and the churches, with missions seen as a civilizing drive. Non-western nations were seen as having yet to 'learn to appreciate the blessings of Christian civilization'.[1] The Report is marked by an almost eschatological sense of triumphalism, an uncritical acceptance of the missionary endeavour. The participants were unconscious of their underlying ideological presuppositions: a kind of capitalism somehow balanced by a moderate democratic socialism. However they affirmed that: 'Christianity is a revolutionary moral force, and should be conscious also of not permitting its character to be misunderstood, keeping in the forefront the spiritual and personal transformation which Christianity aims at.'[2] Europe was naively considered a Christian continent, especially the Protestant nations, while other races and countries were considered 'backward'. And yet they could affirm that 'the Gospel is for all nations, and not a product of Western thought nor means of advancing Western interests'![3]

The question of compensation illustrates the prevailing presuppositions. The Report suggested that in some circumstances, when some wrong was done to missionaries, they could claim for compensation.[4] Now it is just the opposite: many people allege that the missionary societies and churches should pay some form of compensation for the damage done to indigenous cultures and races. This claim for 'restitution' (or reparation) has been dear to the aborigines and the black population in North America. Thomas Aquinas dealt with it in his *Summa Theologica*, expressing that in an unjust war to appropriate booty is spoliation and restitution has to be made.[5] This principle was applied in a surprising way by Bartolomé de las Casas when he argued that the only way to evangelize the Indians was to free them, and to restore to them whatever was taken from them by force.[6] Las Casas refused to give absolution of their sins to the *encomenderos* and those who participated in wars, and therefore they could not participate in the Eucharist.

W.R. Hogg, in his well-known book *Ecumenical Foundations*, comments on 'Edinburgh's omissions', mentioning women's work, literature, medicine, and emphasizing that for many 'the most important omission was Latin America'. Since the Roman Catholic Church fulfilled the missionary task, Latin America was not considered Protestant mission territory. The self-imposed limitation for the conference subject was 'missions to non-Christians'. Hogg comments: 'The great difficulty proved to be the fact that Latin America was a 'border line' case and in the hectic pressure that was Edinburgh there was no time to work it out. The whole question was the 'gravest issue' with which J.H. Oldham as conference secretary had to cope.'[7] R. E. Speer, Secretary of the Board of Foreign Missions of the Presbyterian Church in the USA, led the opponents to this exclusion and organized informal meetings of interested delegates who planned a 'Conference on Missions in Latin America' in New York in 1913. In an attempt to address this issue, they created the 'Committee on Cooperation in Latin America' which convened the Panama Missions Congress in 1916 and was for many decades, until the creation of CLAI (the Latin American Council of Churches) in 1982, the main ecumenical agency for missions and collaboration in Latin America (the American way, of course!). Speer claimed that the exclusion of Latin America from Edinburgh 1910 led to its inclusion on the missionary map of the world! Perhaps it would not have been so if Latin America had been in the Edinburgh agenda. Nevertheless the legitimization of Protestant missions does not remove the problem of the relation between Roman Catholic Missions and Protestant missions and the fact that many Protestant churches do not regard the Roman Catholic Church as capable of engaging in authentic Christian mission.

The Conference participants were convinced that the programme of the missionaries was beyond any suspicion, so that they had the right to demand freedom of action. No doubt that they start from respecting the constituted authorities and governments. They are following the rule stated by our Master: 'Render unto Caesar the things that are Caesar's and to God the things that are God's.'[8] We can share their conviction that 'Alive as missionaries are to the fact that Christianity is a revolutionary moral force, they are equally alive to the danger of permitting its character to be misunderstood, and to the necessity of keeping in the forefront the spiritual and personal transformation that Christianity aims at.'[9]

Christian Faith and Political Power: the Latin American Experience

The history of missions in Latin America, as elsewhere, has its shadows and its lights. Roman Catholic missions featured the *requerimiento,* requiring the Indians to swear a double loyalty: to the Catholic Church and the Spanish Crown. On the bright side, we remember missionaries like Bishop Antonio de

Valdivieso in Nicaragua who was assassinated by an *encomendero*,[10] Antonio de Montesinos, Bartolomé de las Casas, Obispo Toribio de Mogrovejo, Pedro de Córdova and others. Bartolomé de las Casas was the first priest to be ordained in the Americas in 1510. He was an *encomendero* in Santo Domingo, but in 1511 he heard Father Montesinos preach a sermon against Indian exploitation and from that time on he became the most brave and consistent defender of the Indians before the Spanish Crown and a forerunner of the Theology of Liberation. In 1542 he was able to speak personally to the Emperor Charles V and succeeded in making the Consejo de Indias in Valladolid to approve the 'Leyes Nuevas de Indias', by which more freedom was granted to the Indians. For him the whole system of *encomiendas* was 'unjust, impious, scandalous, irrational and absurd'.[11] He was one of the main actors in the first theological and philosophical controversy over the Americas: the issue of whether or not the Indians were human beings. Francisco de Vitoria held that the Indians were 'animals'. Although Juan Ginés de Sepúlveda defended the Spanish conquest, which las Casas disparaged, both he and las Casas defended the full humanity of Indians, as did Pope Paul III.

The ideology of that time made a difference between 'lands of peace' and 'lands of war' (as today!) In lands of war it was justifiable to inflict all evils (the 'just war' theory). If the Indian territories were considered 'lands of war' then evangelization was violent, if 'lands of peace' it was done in great sympathy with the aborigines. Who made the decision? In terms of the law of the 'Patronato Real' (Royal Patronage), approved by Pope Alexander VI in his bulls *Inter Caetera* (3–4 May 1493) to the benefit of the Spanish crown, the Catholic Church was under the direct supervision of the Spanish Crown, as was the case with the Portuguese colonization. Mission meant, in our case, 'hispanization', as later on at the end of the nineteenth century with the arrival of US missionaries it meant 'americanization'! Of course, the religious beliefs of the Indians were considered idolatrous, superstitious and atheist and had to be eradicated. The Catholic missionary was in the best of cases seen by the Indians as 'a more human sorcerer'.

Rivera Pagán observes:

> *Novus mundus, nova ecclesia.* The utopian imagination of the late Renaissance, so dramatically expressed in Thomas Moro's *Utopia*, the fusion of the missionary spirit of the mendicant orders and the inexorable violence of the conquistadores, not only transferred Christianity to the Americas, but also created the conditions for the renewal of the church of the poor, the distinctive characteristic of the apostolic *ekklesia.* It was a complex combination of material and spiritual forces which tried to save the soul of the aborigines, but at the same time made possible the enslavement of his body and sometimes legitimated his annihilation. The avarice and greed of the conquistadores seemed to be a divine paradox through which God calls the indigenous population to redemption.[12]

No wonder that when Pope John Paul II visited Salta in Argentine in April 1987, 2,500 aborigines presented him the following statement:

> Welcome John Paul II to these lands which originally belonged to our ancestors and that we do not possess any more! On their behalf and those of us who survived massacres and genocide, we declare you our guest and brother … But we were free and the land belonged to us. We lived out of what the land gave us generously, and all ate abundantly. We praised our God in our language, with our gestures and dances, with home made musical instruments. Until one day, the European civilization arrived. It planted the sword, language, and the cross, and crucified our peoples. The Indian blood of those made martyrs yesterday because they defended their land, were the seeds of the silent martyrs of today who with slow pace carry our cross of five centuries. In this cross you brought to the Americas you changed the Christ of Judea for the Christ of the indigenous population … May it be that all this blood poured by the ethnocide and genocide, which our native nations have suffered, serve to become the new consciousness of humankind, for the new relations based on justice and fraternity among the peoples.[13]

One of the best experiments in missions in Latin America was the 'Jesuit reductions' or 'Missions' in the seventeenth century. Around a hundred of them were launched in Brazil, Argentina and mostly in Paraguay among the *guaranies*. These *reducciones* were outstanding attempts to put into practice a 'utopian' Christianity.[14] But over a century and a half of clashes unfortunately finished them. This outstanding experiment was suffocated by conflicts with the colonial powers, rivalries with other religious orders, and the opposition of all the persons who benefited by the oppression of the Indians. But the main cause may have been their failure to form an authentic church for the natives.

In Cuba, Protestant missions began in 1898, during the first intervention by the USA at the end of the Spanish/American/Cuban war. Earlier, during the Spanish domination (1498–1898), there had been no religious tolerance. In the Cuban case the first missionaries were 'Cuban missionary patriots' who had become Protestants during their exile in the USA, where they had fled as exiles and where they had gathered funds for the war of liberation. These patriots had an ecumenical spirit and fostered collaboration among the different Protestant churches. Unfortunately the patriots were soon replaced by American professional missionaries whose ideology was clearly in favour of the American way of life and ideals.

The professional missionaries in Cuba were under Home Mission Boards. Though these Boards denounced colonial intentions the US government and intellectuals at that time were speaking of their 'Manifest Destiny'. Most missionaries came from the South and/or had studied in conservative theological seminaries. Many of these saw themselves as the 'new chosen people of God' who would implant the Kingdom of God on earth. Such individuals could also advocate the 'Monroe Doctrine'. In 1823 President

James Monroe and the US Congress determined that the US could intervene in the Americas if necessary to 'keep order'.

The patriots and founding fathers saw the risks in the position of those Cubans who were in favour of 'annexing' Cuba to the USA. The most outstanding of these was José Martí (1853–1895), who can be described as the period's most important intellectual and the patriot who led the war of independence from Spain. In his writings Martí often denounced the ideology of those pastors in the US who were 'instruments of the government and in favour of the rich against the poor!'[15] Two examples will suffice.

E. E. Clements, Methodist Missionary and also Editor of *The Cuban Evangelist*, in 1907 wrote an editorial entitled 'Americanism and Cuba' in which he said:

> The most potent force in American influence in Cuba is to be found in the spirit called Americanism, which grows out of the prevailing sense of freedom, justice, truth and moral obligation. ... Today the bulwark of our civilization is our holy religion. ... Every American that comes to the island becomes a centre of influence and in a sense an interpreter of Americanism. ... The business man is also called of God whether he heed or not, to practice the gospel, to be a living example, known and read of all men. His obligation is just as sacred as that of the missionary, and his manner of life should be such as becometh the gospel of Christ.[16]

Bishop W. A. Candler wrote the same year in the same publication an article entitled 'The peculiar appeal made to us by our Cuba Mission' and commented:

> It is a matter of our interest as well of our duty to give the gospel to the Cuban people. The world knows by the history of the French Revolution what comes to pass when a nation throws off both monarchical government and Christianity at the same time. ... When the Cubans cast off Spanish rule they threw off in a great measure such Christianity, and their revolution therefore, went to the very foundations of their social, as well as their political system. If faithlessness now prevail among them, so will disorder and faithlessness prevail among them unless Protestantism shall rescue many of them from the abyss of doubt which opens before them. And disorder in Cuba is damage to America. Our country stands pledged to preserve order there. It is better and cheaper to do this by the power of an enlightened and enlightening faith than by force of arms and acts of statecraft.[17]

This very kind of ideology not only prevailed in Cuba for many decades but in all Latin America. The two premises were: (a) Protestantism is modern and progressive; Christianity means freedom, while Roman Catholicism (often called 'Romanism') represented retrograde and reactionary Medieval Christianity. (b) The USA had received the commission from God to be the vanguard of Protestantism and the saviour of the world. As late as 1951 a committee which was preparing a continental Ecumenical Council, the predecessor of the present CLAI (Latin American Council of Churches), translated and published as preparatory material a book by a French Protestant, Frederick Hoffet, entitled *Protestant Imperialism* (imperialism in a positive sense!) which argued that all the Roman Catholic countries were backward and ignorant and should turn Protestant, since these countries were the richest, most civilized and progressive![18]

Christianity and Politics in Latin America Today

In most of the Latin American countries, relations between church and state have been regulated by the *Concordats* (short for *Pactum Concordatum*, referring to the legal agreements between governments and the Holy See). The countries which have signed concordats with the Holy See are: Argentina, Bolivia, Brazil, Colombia, Dominican Republic, Ecuador, El Salvador, Haiti, Paraguay, Perú, and Venezuela. Nevertheless, in some countries, there has been a separation of church and state with freedom of worship and missions being granted to other Christian denominations and religions. Liberal governments have sought to change the status of the Roman Catholic Church as the state church and liberalize the obligations of the Concordats.

Perhaps the most radical situation in the early twentieth century was that of Mexico. Between July 1859 and December 1860 Benito Juárez promulgated the Reformation Laws: nationalization of the properties of the Roman Catholic Clergy, the law on freedom of worship and others. The Roman Catholic Church had been the State Church but from that time onwards the Church was separated from the State. The State was the owner of all the Church's property and the Church could not possess legal capacity. Clergymen were forbidden to participate in politics. In July 1992 several articles of the Constitution were revised, granting the churches the right to own property, to have legal capacity and to teach religion in the schools. In Nicaragua the liberal revolution of 1893 abolished the Concordat, but it is said that the present Head of State is seeking its re-instalment. In Bolivia the third article of the Constitution states: 'The state recognizes and supports the Roman Catholic and Apostolic Roman Church. It guarantees the public function of any other cult. The relations with the Roman Catholic Church will be regulated according to the concordat and other agreements between the Bolivian state and the Holy See.'[19]

Today, with the ever-greater participation of Protestant pastors and leaders in politics, a new situation is developing in Latin America. The change can be traced to the 1950s and countries like Brazil and Peru. It has been documented that Protestants participated in the Mexican revolution of the 1920s. In Guatemala two pastors from the Neo-Pentecostal churches came to power as Dictator Generals, E. Ríos Montt in 1982-83 and J. Serrano Elías in 1991-1993. Carlos Garcia, a Baptist Minister was Vice-President in Peru, and Jaime Oriz Hurtado, an Evangelical lawyer and theological educator, was member of the Constitutional Assembly in Colombia. Three pastors – a Baptist, a Presbyterian and an Anglican – are at present members of the Cuban Parliament. In other countries Protestants have organized political parties, parties with differing political orientations (Venezuela 1978, Brazil 1986, Peru 1990, Argentina 1991, etc.).

Influential mega-churches, and movements like the 'Universal Church of the Kingdom of God', originated in Brazil in 1977 and now extend to many countries, including North America. Such churches have promoted the theology of the 'prosperity gospel'. Although in these churches the emphasis is on personal conversion, they create networks of mutual help that contribute to moral change. This explosive growth (mainly in Brazil, Chile, Guatemala and Nicaragua) and the phenomenon of 'charismatization' and 'pentecostalization' of the churches in Latin America, even in some of the 'historical churches', is an outstanding missiological challenge. Samuel Escobar poses the important question: will this Popular Protestantism become the heir of the sixteenth-century European Reformation?[20] On the Roman Catholic side we should not forget the great contribution of the Theology of Liberation and the Base Ecclesiastical Communities. Inspiration is drawn from the lives of Father Camilo Torres (who was killed in action after serving as a Columbian guerrilla from 1956 to 1966) and Archbishop Oscar Arnulfo Romero in El Salvador (1917-1980) who took sides with the poor and was assassinated as he was leading mass on 24 March 1980.

Jose Miguez Bonino gives a good assessment of the overall situation:

> The difficulty of characterizing in absolute and unequivocal terms the different groups and churches in Latin America results from an important phenomenon that we must take into account. Some of the more acute tensions and conflicts on the Latin American religious scene have to do with theological interpretations, social commitments, and visions of the mission of Christianity which do not correspond to confessional or denominational divisions but across them. The result is that we have – and I think we will increasingly have – forms of association which will bring together Christians from different churches for common tasks and witness without, in many cases, breaking the ties with their own communities. But this, no doubt, will be potentially conflictive. Or it may introduce a ferment for change, even as it opens up the possibility of new unities.[21]

Church and State in the Cuban Revolution

The situation in Cuba is characterized by the triumph of the Cuban Revolution in 1959, which quickly developed into a Marxist-Leninist type of revolution. In terms of the relation of churches to the state, at least five different periods can be discerned.

1. Honeymoon 1959

The whole population was united against the dictator Fulgencio Batista who had come to power by a *coup d'etat* on March 1952. The struggle was led by

Fidel Castro, who unsuccessfully attacked an army garrison in Santiago de Cuba on 26 July 1953. In early December 1956 Castro landed in the south-eastern part of Cuba with a group of followers and in the mountains of the Sierra Maestra began the guerrilla struggle against Batista, which finally won over his army. Castro's second-in-command was Frank Pais, the son of a Baptist pastor. Pais was a very committed Christian. He organized civic resistance and was responsible for supplying the guerrillas in the mountains. There were other Christian leaders, both Catholic and Protestant, who promoted the insurrection, such as J.A. Echeverria, Esteban Hernandez, and Oscar Lucero. Batista quit office on 1 January 1959 and a new revolutionary government led by Fidel Castro was installed.

2. *Mistrust and confrontation 1960–1968*

In 1960 the revolution became more radicalized. All banks, foreign concerns and sugar mills were nationalized. In 1961 the USA broke diplomatic relations with the Cuban government, a situation that has continued to the present. The literacy campaign was launched and one of the key figures was a Presbyterian minister who was then serving as the Executive Secretary of the Cuban Council of Churches. During this same year masses of people started to flee to the USA as part of a propaganda plan to de-stabilize the revolution. In April 1961 the Bay of Pigs invasion, led by a group of anti-Castro mercenaries, was quickly defeated when at the last minute the US Government refused its support. One effect was the proclamation of the Socialist (Marxist) character of the Cuban revolution. All education began to be controlled by the government and all the private schools were nationalized. As a result the churches lost their schools (primary, secondary and university) thereby losing their most important instruments for evangelization. In August 1960 the Roman Catholic Bishops released a series of Pastoral Letters in which the Revolution was strongly condemned. On 17 September 1962, 132 Roman Catholic priests and one Auxiliary Bishop were deported. Of the 800 priests on the island before the Revolution only 200 remained.

3. *Peaceful Coexistence 1969–1978*

The Second Vatican Council (1962-1965), and the Second General Conference of the Latin American Roman Catholic Bishops (CELAM) held in Medellin, 1968, brought some renewal to the Cuban Church. An example was that in April 1969 the Bishops' Conference published a Pastoral Letter condemning the US embargo against Cuba.

4. *Rapprochement 1979–1989*

In 1983, together with US Presidential Candidate Jesse Jackson, President Castro attended an ecumenical gathering in memory of Martin Luther King Jr., The same year, and for the first time, President Castro met with a group of Protestant leaders. 1985 saw the publication of *Fidel y la Religion*, conversations between the President and the Brazilian Frei Betto.[22] The President's comments resulted in the beginning of a more positive attitude between the government and Party *vis-à-vis* the churches. In January 1985 a delegation of Roman Catholic Bishops representing the Conference of US Bishops visited Cuba.

5. Openness and Opportunity 1990–

There is not yet any legislation that regulates or grants legal status to churches in Cuba. Relations are conducted under a *modus vivendi* basis, which varies according to particular authorities and pragmatic considerations. Church properties in general are not nationalized. The exception is schools, which were nationalized in June of 1961, when all private schools were nationalized. This is more striking since most of the Protestant property is still owned by the USA mission boards. There is no persecution. But there is a tight regulation of religious activities. As a rule, after 1959 no new denominations or religious movements have been allowed to enter the country. Only those denominations which had legal status before that year can function. The existing churches are happy about this arrangement! It has prevented the new religious movements from entering the country. The church does not own public mass media and have not access to it, except on very special occasions, such as the visit of the Pope John Paul II in 1998 with his huge open air masses in the provincial capitals, and the large Protestant rallies that were held in the most heavily populated Cuban cities in 1999.

Although freedom of religion was allowed the first Constitution after the revolution (drafted in 1976) was Marxist-Leninist. In 1992 a new constitution changed the Marxist basis of the state into a non-sectarian state that would not support any particular ideology (what we call in Latin countries *estado laico* - a 'lay state'). The Roman Catholic Church, due to their lack of priests, has been able to bring in some foreign priests, mostly from Spain and other Latin American countries. On the Protestant side it is difficult for foreign missionaries to serve in Cuba. In 1990, due to the fall of the East European Socialist countries which subsidized Cuba and the disastrous effects of the US embargo against our government, the so-called 'Special Period' of economic crisis began. This prompted a massive attendance at the churches, particularly of the young people. The result was a revival. All the churches were filled with people, giving a new missionary opportunity and thrust to all the churches. The 'charismatic' churches, in particular, have been growing tremendously. However aberrations are compromising the credibility of the Gospel and posing difficult questions for the churches on what position to take. In 1991 the government authorized the functioning of 'house churches'. It is estimated that there are more than 5,000 of these, which give an outstanding missionary opportunity. A negative element to account for is the large amount of people who have migrated, particularly to the USA, because of the 'Adjustment Act' which allows automatic political asylum and residence to any Cuban arriving to any US territory. It also feeds the political tensions between the extremists at both ends. In January 2004 Bartolomeu, the Patriarch of Constantinople, visited Cuba to consecrate a new Greek Orthodox Cathedral in Havana. In many aspects his visit was similar to that of the Pope in 1998. He was received by the Cuban government as a Head of State.

The difficult relations between the governments of Cuba and the USA prompted the Cuban Protestant churches to become autonomous from their 'mother' churches in the USA. This process was accomplished with their blessings, and came about by natural development in the growth and self-identity of the Cuban churches. But this was aggravated by the embargo the US imposed on Cuba, which created a new problem of isolation and lack of funds and pressed the Cuban churches to seek relations with the WCC. In 1964 Bishop Lesslie Newbigin was the head of the Missions and Evangelization Section of the WCC. Newbigin took special interest in the situation and the 'Cuba Project' was launched. This resulted in many Protestant churches receiving emergency financial help, including those churches that were not attached to USA Mission Boards. This was the beginning of very fruitful relations, which extended to other sections of the WCC, to which Cubans, such as Israel Batista, Héctor Méndez and Ofelia Ortega, have given expertise throughout the years. The contribution of the WCC to the Cuban Ecumenical Movement has been enormous.

During the early years, after the triumph of the Cuba Revolution, the island represented a haven of revolutionary thinking and praxis. There was a very close relation between the Cuban Communist Party, the communist parties of Latin America, and some of the guerrilla foci in Latin America. This provided solidarity for Unidad Popular in Chile and Nicaragua. The Socialist government of the Unidad Popular in Chile was elected to power in 1970, until a *coup d'etat* in 1973 ousted and killed President Salvador Allende. The Sandinista Revolution in Nicaragua succeeding in overthrowing Dictator Somoza, who left the country in 1979, and governed until 1990 when they lost the general elections. More recent developments in Venezuela under President Hugo Chávez and in Bolivia with President Evo Morales point to a new coalition between Cuba and those regimes in opposition to the policies of the USA in the region.

Challenges Ahead

Churches in Cuba today are struggling with the challenge of redefining mission. From 17 to 23 February 2006 the Roman Catholic Church held an important Congress, mostly for lay people, in order to re-define Catholic missions in the present Cuban situation. The meeting was preceded by a period of preparation and surveys at the parish level in order to analyze better the situation and hear the voice of the laity. The text begins by offering a brief history of Christian evangelization in Cuba. Next there is an examination of the present Cuban situation, followed by a theological analysis which includes an assessment of the elements of mission, the relations between faith and society, faith and culture, the function of the laity and the ordained clergy and finally the elements for a *'pastoral de conjunto'* (an integrated mission programme). The priorities are: (1) a church which evangelizes, (2) a praying church, (3) an incarnated church, (4) a church in dialogue, (5) a church united in plurality, (6) a participating and co-responsible church, (7) a church which plans its missions programme and (8) a church that assumes poverty.

Among the 'lines of action' that are particularly important at this time in Cuba are: (1) renewing the mind of the church, (2) developing incarnation spirituality and (3) fostering the evangelization of the Cuban culture. When the hierarchy sponsored a parish survey seeking to identify missionary priorities, the general answer was that spirituality should be the main concern. The Bishops have said: 'we need a spirituality centred in the encounter with Jesus in order to illuminate life in all its dimensions, to make possible a committed style of life, producing hope and coherence … collaborating in the transformation of our reality and making possible a new hope.'[23] On the Protestant side, the Cuban Council of Churches has organized three international missiological gatherings in Matanzas 1984, Toronto 1988 and again in Matanzas 1999. The final document says: 'We need to develop a new mission paradigm, beginning at the national level, revising and re-actualizing our biblical and theological discourse, our ecclesiology, those structures which limit our missionary action, our models of theological education, our tradition and liturgical creations, our theoretical and practical models of the ministry. This new pattern should give the priority to liberating projects which can be multiplied.'[24] The document encourages supporting programs of South-to-South and South-to-North collaboration, as well as programs of equal dialogue between North and South. For a new type of dialogue between the North and South it is necessary to acknowledge the historical background of domination – conscious or unconscious – of missionary enterprise. All missionary activity should centre on the dynamic elements of economy, ecology and macro-ecumenics. Macro-ecumenism should further projects of justice, human rights advocacy and a common witness for the defence of life. Missionary ethics should be more respectful of the other, avoiding patriarchal legitimations. Missions cannot be separated from *Diakonia*

Concluding Remarks

1. Looking back to Edinburgh 1910 from our present point of view we have to admit that we are all children of our times. There is no point in reproaching those who participated in that agenda. Our responsibility today is to have the same loyalty and fervour, yet to be more conscious than they were of our ideological conditionings. Those who will read about our programmes a

hundred years from now, I am sure, will criticize us for being too subservient to present trends.

2. The Cuban experience teaches that it is healthier for missions and churches not to enjoy the support of governments. It is better to depend more on the strength and power of the Gospel than the favours of the State, which are often manipulative. If mission is the continuation of the project of Jesus Christ, and his project was the kingdom and not the church, the accent should fall on freedom, justice and integrity of all creation. The concept of the kingdom is holistic: it includes the material, the ecological, the cultural, and the spiritual. We do not do missions to make the church grow or be strengthened, but to consolidate the kingdom. The fundamental principles of mission are: (a) incarnation, (b) witnessing and (c) liberation. Thus the relation between missions and civil society is crucial, more important than the link with Governments and the state on which Commission Seven was focussed at Edinburgh in 1910.

3. We cannot do mission in Cuba behind the back of the people. This is especially true at present when there is a danger that people will become disillusioned with the revolution that was carried out in their name. But neither can we do mission that forgets history. It is a problem, for instance, that in 1998 we commemorated the centennial of the fall of the Spanish empire and the beginnings of the USA empire! In a similar manner in 1992 we celebrated the arrival of Christopher Columbus and Christianity in our lands, with its sequel of aggression and the beginnings of so-called 'modernity': Events that made Europe, with its domination over the 'periphery, the centre of the world. Too bad for the Church to have identified herself with these colonial and neo-colonial projects!

Endnotes

[1] World Missionary Conference, 1910, *Missions and Governments*, Report of Commission VII, Edinburgh & London: Oliphant, Anderson & Ferrier; New York, Chicago and Toronto: Fleming H. Revell, 1910, pp. 115–16.

[2] *Missions and Governments*, p. 93.

[3] *Missions and Governments*, p. 94.

[4] *Missions and Governments*, p. 108.

[5] Thomas Aquinas, *Summa Theologiae*, London: Eyre & Spottiswoode; New York: McGraw-Hill, 1975, Vol. 38: p. 83, 2a2ae, q. 66, art.8, ad 1.

[6] See Bartolomé de las Casas, *Obras Completas*, vol. 2, Madrid: Alianza Editorial, 1990.

[7] W. R. Hogg, *Ecumenical Foundations: A History of the International Missionary Council*, New York: Harper, 1952, pp. 131–2.

[8] Mark 12:17.

[9] *Missions and Governments*, p. 93.

[10] A person in charge [*encomienda*] of a group of Indians supposedly to educate them in the Christian faith.

[11] Charles V, Emperor, in Luis Rivera Pagán, *Entre el Oro y la Fe*, San Juan: University of Puerto Rico, 1995, p. 226.

[12] Luis Rivera Pagán, *Entre el Oro y la Fe*, San Juan: University of Puerto Rico, 1995, p. 28.
[13] Pope John Paul II, in Luis Rivera Pagán, *Entre el Oro y la Fe*, San Juan: University of Puerto Rico, 1995, pp. 30–31.
[14] The *reducciones* are accurately represented in the well-known film *The Mission*. Robert Bolt, *The Mission*, prod. David Puttnam, dir. Roland Joffe, 128 min., Warner Bros. Pictures, 1986.
[15] Rafael Cepeda, *José Martí: Perspectyivas Éticas de la Fe Cristiana*, S. José: DEI, 1991, p. 153.
[16] E. E. Clements, 'Americanism and Cuba', *The Cuban Evangelist* (1 May 1907).
[17] Bishop W.A. Candler, 'The peculiar appeal made to us by our Cuba Mission', *The Cuban Evangelist* (16 October 1907).
[18] Frederick Hoffet, *El Imperialismo Protestante*, Buenos Aires: La Aurora, 1951; Frederick Hoffet, *L'Impérialisme Protestant*, Paris: Flammarion, 1948.
[19] Vitelio Mejías, personal correspondence; Vitelio Mejías is the chairperson of Red Latinoamericana de Abogados Cristianos, Santo Domingo, Dominican Republic.
[20] Samuel Escobar, 'A Missiological Approach to Latin American Protestantism', *International Review of Mission* 87, no. 345 (April 1998), p.171.
[21] Jose Míguez Bonino 'The Condition and Prospects of Christianity in Latin America', in Guillermo Cook, ed., *New Face of the Church in Latin America: Between Tradition and Change*, Maryknoll: Orbis, 1994, p. 266.
[22] *Fidel y la Religión: Conversaciones con Frei Betto*, La Habana: Oficina de Publicaciones del Consejo de Estado, 1985.
[23] Cuban Bishops' Conference, *Plan Global de Pastoral: Construiremos Juntos el Mañana, 2006–2010*, México: Progreso S.A., 2006.
[24] Unpublished manuscript, held in the archives of the Evangelical Seminary, Matanzas, Cuba.

Commission Eight

Cooperation and the Promotion of Unity

Commission Eight
'Cooperation and the Promotion of Unity

The Commission in Summary

The mandate of Commission Eight represented one of the two central aims of the Edinburgh 1910 World Missionary Conference. 'Carrying the Gospel to all the Non-Christian World' (Commission One) necessitated 'Cooperation and the Promotion of Unity' if the goal of 'plant(ing) in every non-Christian nation one united Church of Christ'[1] was to be achieved. Commission Eight addressed this latter concern. It was the most ecumenically focussed of the Edinburgh 1910 Commissions – though the word 'ecumenical' does not appear in the Report – and it justified the Conference's subsequent reputation as the 'symbolic beginning of the modern ecumenism'.[2]

An experienced Scottish colonial administrator, Sir Andrew Fraser, formerly governor of Bengal, chaired the Commission. The Commission included four bishops, and church mission boards were as strongly represented as autonomous missionary societies. Although the Commission took evidence from less than one hundred correspondents – considerably fewer than other Commissions – they included a larger percentage of persons who could speak on behalf of the missionary boards and societies that they represented. While avoiding any semblance of speaking on behalf of churches, or of addressing them officially, the Report reflected the 'desire for closer fellowship, and for the healing of the broken unity of the Church of Christ' that was a concern for churches, church mission boards, and missionary societies, at home and overseas.[3]

The Report divided its subject into five main chapters: Comity, Conferences, Joint Action, Federation and Union, and Cooperation at the Home Base. The chapters were mainly descriptive in character. However they were introduced and concluded with two chapters that gave an insightful analysis of the hindrances and horizons of cooperation and unity. Twelve appendices comprise an invaluable archive of documents relating to the promotion of unity among churches, and cooperation between churches and missions in Asia – China, India, the Philippines, and Japan. These support the main argument of the Report: that Christians in these regions were 'the first to recognise the need for concerted action and closer fellowship',[4] and that their pioneering action called for 'hearty sympathy (on the part of western churches) with the movements toward unity in the mission field'.[5]

The flow of the Report began with a frank discussion of comity – i.e. the friendly and courteous recognition by one missionary society of the integrity and disciplines of another working in the same or proximate places. The American Board of Commissioners for Foreign Missions first enunciated the principle of comity in 1838. Its repetition by many subsequent missionary conferences evidenced the continuing need for 'delimitation' among missions to avoid proselytism, duplication, and waste of resources. Delimitation took both territorial and denominational forms. The migration of indigenous Christians, their freedom of choice, and their desire to evolve new forms of ecclesiastical identity made some forms of comity obsolete. While concluding that the principle of comity was still valid, the Report urged that comity agreements should be considered expedient rather than permanent, and that 'the preservation of comity … must lead to federation or some form of unity'.[6]

Subsequent to this the Report considered missionary conferences, and determined that they were 'indispensable preliminaries to all developments of cooperative action or ecclesiastical approximation'.[7] A range of missionary conferences were brought under review: local meetings; wider associations dealing with a particular areas of work or with more general missionary concerns; geographical or national groupings; informal conferences for discussion and meditation; and formal 'general conferences', which meant regional and international gatherings of missionaries and indigenous Christians. The Report distinguished between 'inter-missionary' and 'inter-mission' conferences: the former had informal constitutions and included missionaries as individuals, while the latter involved 'definite representation of the Missions … as corporate units'.[8] Inter-missionary gatherings demonstrated 'numerical strength for purposes of conference and fellowship', while inter-mission conferences achieved 'weight and authority for purposes of action'.[9] The Report concluded that each was valuable in 'the realisation of new fellowship and essential unity … that underlie and transcend all differences'.[10]

In the chapter on 'Joint Action', the Report reviewed the missionary activities that were either initiated or sustained by such conferences. First and foremost it instanced the interdenominational and international Bible Societies as 'the foremost among cooperative institutions',[11] whose work of Bible translation and distribution had, over many decades, tested and vindicated 'the value of cooperation'.[12] Education was also praised as a branch of missionary activity in which joint action is 'feasible and manifestly desirable'.[13] Special mention was made of the Dutch 'Missionary Consulate' in Java as an example of separate missions electing a single representative to mediate with the colonial government.

While efficiency was a self-evident value of joint action, the Report emphasized that missionary cooperation was motivated by a higher goal: namely, 'to plant in each non-Christian nation one undivided Church of Christ'.[14] In its chapter on 'Federation and Union' the Report amassed evidence from missionaries and indigenous Christians, especially in Asia, of 'movements in the direction of unity'.[15] In China the lead was being taken by Chinese Christian leaders for whom 'the sense of a common national life and a common Christianity is stronger than the appreciation of (denominational) differences which had their origin in controversies remote from the Church in mission lands'.[16] Respecting the theological integrity of many ecclesiastical differences, but eager to respond constructively to Asian Christian realities, the Report was careful in its phrasing: 'In the supreme work of laying foundations of national Church ... it is impossible that missionaries should refrain from giving the indigenous churches such help and counsel as they can that is part of their inheritance from the past'.[17] Organic unity among churches of common polity was relatively straightforward. Progress toward interdenominational unity was more difficult, though significant advances had been achieved in China, India and East Africa. The Report was equally appreciative of 'federations of Christian bodies which regard organic union as impracticable or undesirable',[18] yet still promote the ideal of unity in an 'experimental stage'.[19]

In its final chapter the Report turned its attention to the 'Home Base'. It asserted that 'movements toward unity in the mission field cannot proceed far without cooperation and support for those responsible for missionary administration at home'.[20] If this betrays a sense of *real politik*, it was also intended to challenge mission boards and societies in the West where progress toward unity was slower that in Asia. Promising progress was reported from North America and the Continent, but Britain lagged behind. The Report recommended greater unity across the 'home base' in the interests of promoting 'one united Church of Christ in every non-Christian nation', and 'the healing of divisions' in the West.[21]

The Report thus moved to its main recommendation: that 'some plan should be found of maintaining permanently the closer relations between missionary societies throughout the world into which they have been brought by the work of this (Edinburgh 1910) Conference'.[22] Conceding the Commission's limits, it confined itself to recommending a 'Continuing Committee' comprising elected delegates of the Conference, with agreed powers to consult and advise in taking forward the Conference concerns. It emphasized that the Continuing Committee should be authorized 'to confer with the Societies and Boards as to the best method of working towards the formation of a permanent International Missionary Committee'.[23]

The recommendation was unanimously approved by the Conference plenary on 21 June. The foundation on which the International Missionary Council would stand had been laid – though on account of the First World War its creation was delayed until 1921. Following the unanimous vote, the delegates joined together in singing 'Praise God from whom all blessings flow.'[24]

Endnotes

[1] World Missionary Conference, 1910, *Cooperation and the Promotion of Unity*, Report of Commission VIII, Edinburgh and London: Oliphant, Anderson & Ferrier; New York, Chicago and Toronto: Fleming H. Revell, 1910, p. 131.

[2] Michael Kinnamon and Brian Cope, eds., *The Ecumenical Movement: an Anthology of Key Texts and Voices*, Geneva: World Council of Churches Publications, 1997, p. 1.

[3] *Cooperation and the Promotion of Unity*, p. 131.
[4] *Cooperation and the Promotion of Unity*, p. 133.
[5] *Cooperation and the Promotion of Unity*, p. 144.
[6] *Cooperation and the Promotion of Unity*, p. 19.
[7] *Cooperation and the Promotion of Unity*, p. 28.
[8] *Cooperation and the Promotion of Unity*, p. 32.
[9] *Cooperation and the Promotion of Unity*, p. 32.
[10] *Cooperation and the Promotion of Unity*, pp. 50–1.
[11] *Cooperation and the Promotion of Unity*, p. 53.
[12] *Cooperation and the Promotion of Unity*, p. 56.
[13] *Cooperation and the Promotion of Unity*, p. 73.
[14] *Cooperation and the Promotion of Unity*, p. 83.
[15] *Cooperation and the Promotion of Unity*, p. 83.
[16] *Cooperation and the Promotion of Unity*, p. 84.
[17] *Cooperation and the Promotion of Unity*, p. 87.
[18] *Cooperation and the Promotion of Unity*, p.107.
[19] *Cooperation and the Promotion of Unity*, p. 117.
[20] *Cooperation and the Promotion of Unity*, p. 119.
[21] *Cooperation and the Promotion of Unity*, p. 131.
[22] *Cooperation and the Promotion of Unity*, p. 129.
[23] *Cooperation and the Promotion of Unity*, p. 144.
[24] World Missionary Conference, 1910, *The History and Records of the Conference*, Edinburgh & London: Oliphant, Anderson & Ferrier; New York, Chicago and Toronto: Fleming H. Revell, 1910, p. 98.

Cooperation and the Promotion of Unity: A World Council of Churches Perspective

Samuel Kobia

1. Partnership, Inter-Church Discipline and the Healing of Unjust Relations

Commission Eight's report and discussion emphasizes the importance of 'comity' – of discussions and regulations between mission societies of different nationalities and denominations to find agreements in the 'mission fields', so as to avoid duplication of missionary efforts.[1] The main aim was to deal with the inadequacy of the forces with regard to the task of bringing the gospel to the whole world. The Commission insisted on the importance of learning to know each other, of consultation, discussion and agreement as essential ways to avoid wasting time as well as human and financial resources. The report still deplores too much unconcerted policy, mutual ignorance, overlapping and competition among the actors in mission.

However, it is striking to discern how many efforts at mutual knowledge and greater co-operation already existed in the years preceding the Edinburgh conference. The participants could build on success-stories brought from several parts of the world, in particular from Asia, as to concrete ways to organize inter-missionary co-operation, with examples of by-laws of conferences, or rules and regulations of meetings.[2] The Edinburgh conference hailed these efforts and hoped they would be multiplied. It also expressed the wish to have the home base of missions and the related churches officially involved.

Reading the report nearly 100 years later, it strikes the observer that the questionnaire sent to missionaries as preparation for the work of the Commission is very interesting. There was careful attention put, for example, to the potential differences between the opinions of missionaries and those of 'natives'. We know that only very few Christians from the global South were present in Edinburgh. Their voice was not given the attention we would require today. Still, the care to try to find out potential differences is remarkable and a foretaste of the future culture of partnership. The Commissioners had even included questions about relationships to Roman Catholics in their enquiry and, had prior to Edinburgh, also contacted Archbishop Nicolai of the Russian Ecclesiastical Mission in Tokyo.[3]

Commissioners were aware of the advantages of full missionary freedom, but emphasized the hindrances created by evangelistic free-lancers who were unwilling to accept self-restriction through agreements. This, too, is an indicator of future trends.

Mission societies saw the urgent need to find territorial delimitations, and requested new arrangements for those intending to enter a country where other missions were already active. The desire was for discussions that would lead to an agreement prior to entry regarding engagements. In its core intention, this prefigures the principle of respect for the local church. The care with which conference participants went into details of the discussion of the best practices in co-operation and delimitation of tasks shows how much the later discussion on partnership and ecumenical discipline is rooted in Edinburgh's deliberations.

Highlights of the Debate since 1910

Two outcomes of Edinburgh made this conference the symbolic starting point of the ecumenical movement. It led directly to the creation, in 1912, of the *International Review of Missions*, and the formation, in 1921, of the International Missionary Council (IMC). As several scholars have underlined, this institutionalization of communication and co-ordination between mission actors made the difference between Edinburgh and the earlier world mission conferences of the late nineteenth and early twentieth centuries.[4]

Let us then highlight a few important milestones in the progress of co-operation between churches in different regions of the world. I consider the terminology of partnership, highlighted in the mission debate in the late forties (Whitby 1947), as a key turning point, insofar as it was linked with a change of language, moving away from the idea of 'mother' and 'daughter' churches, or 'sending' and 'receiving' countries. The International Missionary Council (IMC) progressed over many years towards a clearer recognition of the fundamental equality of all partners in world mission. Of course the partnership terminology was somewhat ambiguous, since it had been used within the policies of the British colonial empire[5] and could be interpreted as to allow for autonomy in the South while retaining power in the North. That ambiguity remains, in particular because in many circles the terminology is misused.

Throughout the 1950s both the mission and ecumenical movements wrestled with these issues. Mission bodies affiliated with the IMC tended to reduce missionary presence, and influence, in favour of increasing self-government by local churches. In the same period of the 1950s, however, diaconal institutions had been created to help refugees and countries damaged after the war. Once their immediate reconstruction work was completed, these organizations extended their operations in the direction of the global South. In the 1950s therefore, one could witness two dynamics. Whereas mission bodies linked to the IMC tended to reduce their direct activities in favour of leaving the control of mission to the local churches, the inter-church departments, at national and international levels,[6] increased their diaconal involvement in the same countries. We are still struggling with the consequences of these double dynamics.

The most radical attempt at putting the partnership ideal into practice happened in the early 1970s. As a consequence of the failure of the first decade of development, and the increasing injustice between North and South, partner churches in the South called for radical solutions, which surfaced internationally at the Bangkok conference in 1972/73. Representatives from Asia and Africa advocated the idea of a 'moratorium', consisting in calling back all missionaries to their countries of origin for a certain period of time, and stopping all transfer of financial resources from rich to poor churches during that same period of time. Personnel and finances were to be used to change the structures of injustice in the power centres, thus addressing some of the root causes of the injustice between North and South.[7] This time-bound 'ascetism' in mission would also create a space of freedom for churches in non-Western cultures, allowing them to develop theologies, church policies, ethics and spiritualities really rooted in their own cultural identity, without imposition from anywhere else.

The moratorium was rarely put into practice, but it had deep consequences. Where imposed, often by political authorities, the moratorium eventually proved fruitful for church development, like in China. But its proposals were so radical that even its most vocal advocates did not put it into practice in their own churches and organizations. In the North it allowed many people to involve themselves in advocacy movements for justice and peace. However, it also reinforced a growing anti-mission mood in mainline churches. The related negative publicity on traditional mission influenced a whole generation of church leaders. Indeed at present many remain highly critical of mission and evangelism.

An important alternative to the moratorium was also highlighted at the Bangkok conference. This was well illustrated by the structural change initiated by the Paris Mission.[8] A community of churches in mission, called Cevaa, agreed to share power in decision-making, independently of the resources put by each church into the common basket. In Cevaa, and later in other similar mission communities such as the Council for World Mission, the structural changes bear the mark of transformative justice between churches of North and South. We believe that this was an attempt at 'best practice', which realized some of the dreams of Edinburgh's Commission Eight. It has unfortunately not received the attention it deserves, in particular in North America, Northern Europe, among evangelical mission circles, and among those criticizing mission.

This model of sharing in mission was adopted by the Commission on World Mission and Evangelism, and the WCC as a whole, and led to programmes such as Ecumenical Sharing of Personnel and Ecumenical Sharing of Resources. The culmination of these efforts was the declaration adopted at El Escorial, in 1987, that provided the framework and formulation for a holistic ecumenical discipline of sharing power, resources and persons in the relations between churches in different parts of the world.[9] We would affirm that El Escorial and similar texts (which were coined in the language of their period) represent developments in the ecumenical movement that are a direct consequence of the aims and efforts of 1910. A missiological formulation of the model was given by the CWME in chapter 6 of its year 2000 statement entitled, 'Mission and Evangelism in Unity Today'.[10]

What are the challenges now on this question? Unfortunately, the political, economic and cultural developments of the late eighties and nineties jeopardized these remarkable efforts at self-restraint, respect of the partner and common discipline. The development of the charity market and the increased mediation of its activities; the explosion of numbers of development organizations; renewed individualism, in particular in postmodern cultural contexts, and the tendency of churches in the North to relinquish the effective control of, and decisions on development work, to relatively independent agencies led to trends quite opposite to the ideals of El Escorial. The increasing necessity of performance, that is to be efficient and rapid, as well as to excessively technocratic interpretations of planning, monitoring, evaluating and reporting, jeopardize the partnership-sharing model. Old practices of bilateral (not to say 'colonial') relations came to the front again, allowing for projects to be easily controlled by and responsive to the needs of donors. That the control strategies that affected mission in the past are being reinvented today is an easily observable phenomenon, and is a matter of concern.

In addition, the impressive growth of Pentecostal and neo-charismatic missions (both in and from North and South) show, if considered at world level, how limited are the co-ordinated mission efforts. Both the Lausanne movement and particularly the World Evangelical Alliance have made important attempts at better co-ordination and mutual discipline in mission, in ways quite parallel to some of the WCC's main concerns.[11] Greater networking is needed in this area. But meanwhile there are many Evangelical, Pentecostal and neo-Pentecostal churches and movements for whom discipline like the one dreamt of by Edinburgh is not – or not yet – an issue. In addition, work on building authentic contacts of co-operation in mission between long-established churches and more recent churches of other-cultural origins in North and South has only started. Finally, in the globalized competitive economy, and related neo-liberal ideology, denominationalism is increasing also among 'mainline' churches; each attempts to strengthen its own identity and 'uniqueness'. At the threshold of a new century, we feel we are again faced with similar concerns as our forefathers were in 1910.

We are all members of the same body of Christ – despite our ecclesiological differences. To what discipline does this call us? How can we define 'comity' in a way that is sustainable in the present economic and cultural conditions? The WCC is ready to work with its member churches, but also with the wider mission, and development networks, to find contemporary and credible answers to the concerns of Commission Eight.

2. Mission and Unity – Ecclesiology and Mission

At nearly every page of the report of Commission Eight, one can discern a strong advocacy for moving towards much greater unity than seemed possible and reasonable to expect at that time. A united church was considered to have more success in mission *and* also to be the essential aim of mission: 'for the achievement of the ultimate and highest end of all missionary work – the establishment in these non-Christian lands of Christ's one Church – real unity must be attained'.[12]

Commission Eight was able to formulate, with fascinating clarity, two very different ways of approaching the task and challenge of unity. To summarize in the language of the report:

For a *first group of Christians*, the essential lay in the transcending significance of faith in the Trinity, forgiveness of sins, life everlasting and Christian scriptures (as authority and guide). Christians were seen to be already united by faith and experiencing intimate fellowship. Matters on which they still differed – as serious as they were – appeared as secondary and subordinate. Christians were to be reconciled within the essential unity that exists. The model of cooperation which could be developed on this basis is that of a federation of churches in which every church would retain the full freedom of doctrine and polity, but recognize the ministry and ordinances of the others, and also allow members to freely transfer from one federated church to another. No complete uniformity would have to be reached. Divisions should not be imposed on churches born of mission work. They should be allowed to develop by themselves, adapting to their own context.

In opposition, a *second group* insisted that the full and rich tradition of Christianity had to be transmitted to newly planted churches. They agreed that there is essential unity, but considered the matters on which there is disagreement as also being essential to divine revelation and the means of grace. They saw the churches as having a responsibility to transmit both the essentials of faith, and the safeguards that secure them, to the future generations at home and abroad. They believed forms of church polity are not indifferent, but embody fundamental truths, essential for the future of Christianity. As a consequence, one cannot join a federation organized following the above-mentioned model, because there is no recognition of ministry. Unity would have to be sought by patient and prayerful thought until one reaches a form in which all that is true in principles and practices can be reconciled.[13]

The Commission did not want to choose between these two positions, but thought its duty was to bring these ideas to the delegates. In the report, the necessity to address ecclesiastical differences appeared more than once, in full awareness of their importance. However it was not the task of the conference to enter into debate on those matters. Nor was it recommended that missionary conferences, or other co-operative consultations, do so. But healing of divisions and of broken unity, as well as the visible demonstration of unity, definitely were among the major concerns of the participating missionaries and church leaders in Edinburgh.

Edinburgh also addressed factors other than theological issues that were jeopardising unity. The Commission took up an urgent request by correspondents who were arguing that 'national churches' should be encouraged. Obviously there had been disagreement within the Commission on this question. The report sees the danger that churches could be drawn to favour national antagonisms and, limited to a 'single nation', could offend the principle of unity. Finally, the Commission found a medium position: 'We desire only to lay emphasis on the importance of planting a united church, which would embody all that is deepest and truest in national life and which would make it possible for national gifts of mind and character to contribute in the largest possible way to the perfect and complete interpretation of the Lord Jesus Christ, the Son of Man.'[14]

Evaluation of Twentieth-Century Developments

It is fascinating how a conference that had decided not to address divisive theological questions did in fact emphasize the importance of ecclesiology and the visible unity of Christ's church. It looks as if Edinburgh prepared the agenda for the Faith and Order movement which was to start in Lausanne, Switzerland, some 15 years later (1927). The Edinburgh report proves that reflection on mission cannot, and must not, be separated from basic questions related to what the church is, how it is constituted, and its mandate and organizational form (including church discipline and pastoral care).

The relation between church and mission became particularly important at the IMC Tambaram mission conference in 1938, leading to what some have called a period of ecclesiocentrism in ecumenical mission thinking. One can consider that this lasted from the middle-thirties until the early sixties. This emphasis proved very fruitful, resulting, as it did, to the formation of the WCC and the merger of the IMC and the WCC. During that same period, the Church of South India offered, in 1947, both a model of unity and a form of integration of mission and church. This was, in particular, due to the influence of Lesslie Newbigin, who was a key figure in the debates on Christian unity. The legacy of that time has been preserved and developed by the United/Uniting churches. Many of these were born during the period. A number are located in the countries of the global south. In some ways these churches, and the movement of which they are a part, incarnate one of the dearest visions encompassed in the report of Commission Eight: having one united church of Christ that is both a consequence of and bearer of mission.

It soon became clear, however, that this kind of move towards unity could not be generalized, and that some of the ecclesiological questions that the report of Commission Eight highlighted called for other approaches. There was a need to take seriously the increasing number of Orthodox churches in the WCC, and after Vatican II it would also become necessary to consider new relationships with the Roman Catholic Church.

In 1961, the IMC merged with (and not 'into') the WCC, and this marks one of the most important consequences of the work started at Edinburgh, both as far as cooperation is concerned as well as in terms of the interdependence between mission and church. Integration happened both at world level, with the formation of the Division on World Mission and Evangelism in the WCC, but also at national levels in various countries. This has become one of the major points of debate between Christians of the evangelical mission family and Christians of the conciliar or ecumenical mission family. It seems that the questions that were raised during the late 50s and early 60s have not yet been dealt with sufficiently. We still need 'healing of memories', which I consider very important for any progress in co-operation around 2010 and following.

Let us try to briefly mention what is at stake:

First, it is essential to find structural forms of church life showing that the ultimate responsibility for mission lies with the church and not with particular groups of Christians, or para-church organizations. Matthew 28 is addressed to all disciples and not just to a few specialists. Those taking decisions in terms of mission must be church leaders or directly accountable to leaders and members of the church. Integration in that sense is an essential point of 'no return' in ecumenical missiology.

Second, one of the important fears raised by integration was, and is, that church authorities and politics would hinder missionary freedom and prevent missionaries from taking risks that would enable the gospel to cross new frontiers. This is a serious concern, as appears already in the Bible in the conflicts between James and Peter, or James and Paul. Keeping unity within an existing community can be in conflict with the move towards new forms of inculturation of the gospel among new groups of people, or new sectors of society. Yes, mission can endanger existing forms of church or unity, just as prophecy does. It is thus essential to safeguard both the final responsibility of churches as well as the freedom to engage in mission. Forms can vary, as one can see with the existence of missionary congregations in the Roman Catholic Church, the mission boards of evangelical free churches and their missions (many of whom do practise integration) or the history of CWME within the WCC. We must all struggle to find the right balance between freedom and responsibility.

The third problem could well have been the most important one. Seen retrospectively, the movement towards integration of mission and church, and the formation of the new WCC after 1961, became parallel to the intensive search for involvement in transformation of society in North and South. One must admit that in the sixties and early seventies, the mission of the church was somewhat neglected in the missiological discourse of the WCC. The emphasis was on discerning God's mission in the secular world and on the socio-political involvement of Christians for liberation and peace, rather than on the role of the church and the importance of evangelism. As we move towards 2010, we need to unwrap history and distinguish how much of that theological development was really linked to the idea that mission depends on the church and vice-versa, and how much of it was a response to specific political situations.

A clear turning point is found in the Ecumenical Affirmation on Mission and Evangelism of 1982, still the official WCC document on mission:

> The mission of the church ensues from the nature of the church as the body of Christ, sharing in the ministry of Christ as Mediator between God and his creation. This mission of mediation in Christ involves two integrally related movements – one from God to creation, and the other from creation to God. The church manifests God's love for the world in Christ – through word and deed, in identification with all humanity, in loving service and joyful proclamation; the church, in that same identification with all humanity, lifts up to God its pain and suffering, hope and aspiration, joy and thanksgiving in intercessory prayer and eucharistic worship. Any imbalance between these two directions of the mediatory movement adversely affects our ministry and mission in the world.[15]

Enriched by contributions from Catholics and Evangelicals, and taking more seriously its own Orthodox constituency, the WCC continued to move towards a renewed affirmation of the relation between church and mission. The CWME worked hard to keep a holistic understanding of *missio Dei*, to present the eschatological establishment of God's kingdom of justice and love as the overall horizon of mission. From 1982 on, but in particular since the 1990s, the CWME revisited the specific calling of the church to witness to Jesus Christ, and to form reconciling and healing communities, as part of *missio Dei* and not as opposed to it. The formulation of the theme of the world mission conference in Athens in 2005 related *missio Dei* and *missio ecclesiae* in a clearer way than before. The language and content of the CWME's work thus came very near to the study of the Faith and Order Commission on *The Nature and Mission of the Church*.[16]

We think these are good preparations for the contribution WCC will to make to the 2010 celebrations. The following year will also allow us to remember New Delhi 1961, as the key moment in which, at a worldwide level, the theological affirmation of the intimate link between missiology and ecclesiology took an interdenominational and institutional form. We have 50 years experience of theological wrestling with the relation between church and mission. We know we share this concern with the Roman Catholic and Orthodox churches, as well as with a number of missiologists and mission leaders from evangelical organizations and churches. We want to do whatever is possible to deepen the dialogue with all.

3. From the 'Evangelization of the World in This Generation' to 'This Generation's Mission in a Globalized World'

The famous watchword of the Student Volunteer Movement, which influenced so many Edinburgh delegates, was not a matter for debate in Commission Eight. Nonetheless, the Commission's focus on unity for mission challenges us to consider the way our understanding of mission has changed since 1910 and to determine how we would formulate the most urgent priorities in mission from an ecumenical point of view as we come nearer to 2010.

The world has profoundly changed since 1910 and despite all the missionary efforts of all the churches, including the impressive growth of Pentecostalism, there are today still as many or as few Christians in the world as at the time of Edinburgh, that is roughly a third of the world population.[17] Realistically speaking, it does not make sense today just to repeat the watchword of a century ago. The debates during the whole history of the IMC indicate the width of matters, concerns and struggles that were key to our missionary forefathers. Think of their involvement in the questions of racism, peace, education, health, economic injustice, and secularization, among others. When the WCC defends a holistic approach to mission, it is in the tradition of the missionary movement. Political activity does not represent a departure from its historic concerns. This should of course not be interpreted in the sense that there is nothing to criticise in the WCC! But discernment is requested as to what precisely is faithful, or unfaithful, to the gospel, or to the Edinburgh tradition.

In the middle of last century a significant shift took place with the move to understand mission first and foremost as God's own concern and involvement, expressed since Willingen 1952 by the famous concept of *missio Dei*. This was a turning point in the sense that the question of faithfulness was not just linked to the best way the church could fulfil a great Commission, but was associated with discernment regarding the trinitarian God's own presence and action in the world, inside and outside the faithful Christian community. The new watchword, which could have been 'God's mission for this generation', led to a liberation of mission from legalistic forms of interpretation of Jesus' mission command and allowed for an opening up to the Spirit's new and surprising involvement within all of humanity. In particular in the sixties, and around the Uppsala assembly of the WCC, a specific focus on the humanization of structures and the development of peoples empowered thousands of communities of the poor and downtrodden, the victims of colonialism, to rise up, to feel called, respected and liberated by God for a realistic hope of change towards an embodiment of the most intimate values of the gospel. This may have been linked with extreme interpretations of mission and with, at times, uncritical appreciations of political or social developments. Evangelical mission movements have reacted strongly against these tendencies, which they thought were unacceptable forms of 'social gospel'. Indeed, we moved into a huge confrontation, disastrous for the mission movement in general and alienating efforts at more unity. Therefore, as we turn our eyes to 2010 and beyond, we should find a way to confess mutual exaggerations and disrespect, and progress, *in this generation*, with the healing of memories, toward an authentic reconciliation.

The Lausanne covenant of 1974 appeared at the highest point of the conflict. Thanks to its recognition of the importance in mission of both evangelism (considered as priority) and socio-political involvement, it provided also a first step towards a renewed approach. At the WCC level, following the debates at the Nairobi assembly in 1975 and the publication of Pope Paul V's encyclical 'Evangelii nuntiandi', in the 1982 Ecumenical Affirmation we were able to find a new synthesized formulation of mission. This provided a key formulation on our way towards renewed faithfulness, and expresses and understanding of mission that still rings true for the WCC:

> There is no evangelism without solidarity; there is no Christian solidarity that does not involve sharing the knowledge of the kingdom which is God's promise to the poor of the earth. There is here a double credibility test: a proclamation that does not hold forth the promises of the justice of the kingdom to the poor of the earth is a caricature of the gospel; but Christian participation in the struggles for justice which does not point towards the promises of the kingdom also makes a caricature of a Christian understanding of justice.[18]

The world has profoundly changed in comparison with the context of the debates just mentioned – let us remember that the whole debate on mission in the twentieth century was caught up in the conflict between capitalism and socialism. Since then, we are in a period of a unilaterally polarized world with one superpower, and an economic and political structure sometimes referred to as the 'empire'. With the rise of new powers in East Asia, and the developments both in Europe and Latin America, that political context may change in the coming decades. Still, we are confronted with a globalization that has both economic and cultural consequences, many of which are most dangerous for humanity and creation. At the same time, the landscape of Christianity has profoundly changed, with strong acceleration of the growth of neocharismatic churches in the last 30 years. If Edinburgh was one of the most powerful mission centers in 1910, it will definitely be at the periphery of Christian majorities in 2010. The strongholds of Christian spirituality have moved towards the South and the East, even if formal power centers remain for a certain time in what is called the North. What then are the priorities of mission in this generation?

We may turn to an article of the WCC constitution which provides the guidelines for our understanding of mission and embodies the emphasis of Edinburgh on cooperation, unity and mission: 'The primary purpose of the fellowship of churches in the WCC is to call one another to visible unity in one faith and one eucharistic fellowship, expressed in worship and common life in Christ, *through witness and service to the world*, and to advance towards that unity *in order that the world may believe'*.[19]

Two forthcoming events can help us grasp what we think are priorities in Christian witness in the coming months and years:

The first meeting of the Global Christian Forum, scheduled for November 2007, is an attempt at creating, at the world level, a space of dialogue for representatives of the major Christian churches and movements of this generation. It will include invitations to many more churches and mission movements than was the case in 1910. The most recent world mission conference, in Athens, was like a foretaste of such a Forum meeting. It seems essential to offer such possibilities for encounter and dialogue in order to publicly acknowledge how the face of Christianity has changed in one century. Some of the most dynamic mission movements are to be found among Christian traditions not represented in any of the formal fora that exist as a consequence of the structures of last century. We must imagine new forms of meetings and dialogues, to give visibility and credit to the spiritual revolution brought by the Pentecostal and charismatic movements and churches. This is the pre-condition for starting a fruitful theological dialogue on priorities and disciplines in mission. In that sense, we need a new Edinburgh, and one can only hope that the celebration we foresee for 2010 will be a step in that direction! The history of the IMC and the CWME holds important lessons of successes and errors in mission, from which some of the newer movements with centers in the South could profit. At the same time, the older Christian traditions need the reinvigorating experience of, and theologising on, the Holy Spirit if they want to be renewed in their own missionary and evangelistic motivation.

We are preparing a convocation on just peace for 2011, which will be the concluding event of the *Decade to Overcome Violence*. In the present world context, with rising temptations at all levels to justify violence in conflicts, this is a priority. In particular because religions, Christianity included, are more and more misused to fuel conflicts and so increase their destructive effect by absolutising issues at stake. Fundamentalists of all religions, ours included, join ideological or nationalistic fundamentalists so as to appropriate power and might, and thus win their cause. It is urgent to react against such a trend. It is today's major form of the temptation to which our Lord was submitted at the very beginning of his ministry. We believe that the truth of the gospel is at stake, because Christ's death on the cross is the core of our message – a message confirmed on Easter: God chooses not to dominate the world 'from above', through a politically reigning Messiah, but to offer himself 'from below', in and through the person of the suffering servant. The convocation will highlight the best of the ideals defended within the IMC, where the struggle for peace was at the top of priorities.[20] We call on all to combat the logic and ideology of violence, the structures and traditions, the economic and political systems that favour and increase violence and destruction, both of humanity and God's creation.

It is of particular urgency that mission be understood and practised in a way which does not lead to an increase of hatred and violence. Some methods, thus, we believe, must be rejected, even though they are 'efficient' in the short term. Mission must be 'in Christ's way',[21] otherwise it must be challenged. In that sense, we hope that 2010 and 2011 will enable us to progress towards a better theory and practice of non aggressive, or non violent, forms of evangelism or proclamation, keeping the bold witness to Christ and God's kingdom in creative tension with respect for men, women and children of all convictions, all made in God's image. That is one of the reasons we are involved with Roman Catholic, evangelical and Pentecostal churches in searching for a code of conduct on conversion. In Athens, we managed to point towards the essential importance of the multiplication of healing and reconciling communities, whose radiating and welcoming influence would lead to such an ecumenically responsible evangelism.

WCC has not abandoned the concern for evangelism. But we think this has to be embedded as part of a holistic mission, and must be connected with the illumination and radiation brought by living missional communities. Ecumenically responsible evangelism has to be a proclamation which, while critical of human pride and sin, makes it clear that God wants peace and not war, life and not death, unity and not division, forgiveness and not vengeance.

Endnotes

[1] World Missionary Conference, 1910, *Cooperation and the Promotion of Unity*, Report of Commission VIII, Edinburgh & London: Oliphant, Anderson & Ferrier; New York, Chicago and Toronto: Fleming H. Revell, 1910.

[2] *Cooperation and the Promotion of Unity*, pp. 83–118, chapter on Federation and Union.

[3] *Cooperation and the Promotion of Unity*, pp. 2–4, introduction to the Report

[4] See, for example, Keith Clements, *Faith on the Frontiers – A Life of J.H. Oldham*, Edinburgh: T.&T. Clark; Geneva: WCC, 1999, pp. 95, 101 ff., 105 ff.

[5] Lothar Bauerochse, *Learning to Live Together: Interchurch Partnerships as Ecumenical Communities of Learning,* Geneva: WCC, 2001, pp. 88–93.

[6] At the Evanston assembly of the WCC, in 1954, its Division on Inter-church Aid and Service to Refugees received a mandate 'to develop its ministries outside of Europe'. That decision was two-fold: '1. To build on the foundations laid in Europe in the time of emergency a permanent structure of Inter-Church Aid; 2. To carry the concept and the ministries of Inter-Church Aid to lands beyond Europe'.; *Evanston to New Delhi 1954–1961: Report of the Central Committee to the Third Assembly of the World Council of Churches*, Geneva: WCC, 1961, p. 112–13.

[7] *Bangkok Assembly 1973: Minutes and Reports of the Assembly of the Commission on World Mission and Evangelism of the WCC, December 31, 1972 and January 9 – 12, 1973*, Geneva: WCC, pp. 24–5, 106–7.

[8] *Bangkok Assembly,* pp. 23, 105–6.

[9] 'Guidelines for Sharing. WCC world Consultation on Koinonia, El Escorial, 1987', in Michael Kinnamon and Brian E. Cope, eds., *The Ecumenical Movement. An Anthology of Key Texts and Voices*, Grand Rapids, MI: Eerdmans; Geneva: WCC, 1997, pp. 443–6.
[10] 'Mission and Evangelism in Unity Today', in *'You are the Light of the World': Statements on Mission by the World Council of Churches 1980–2005*, Geneva: WCC, 2005, pp. 84–9 (§§ 68–77).
[11] See, for example, the commitment on partnership contained in the 'Iguassu Declaration' (commitment 13), issued at a world consultation of the World Evangelical Fellowship (now: Alliance) in 2000; William D. Taylor, *Global Missiology for the 21st Century : The Iguassu Dialogue*, Grand Rapids, MI: Baker Academic, 2000; the Declaration is on pp. 521 ff., with comments by various theologians, the section referred to is on p. 535.
[12] *Cooperation and the Promotion of Unity*, p. 5.
[13] *Cooperation and the Promotion of Unity*, pp. 131–9.
[14] *Cooperation and the Promotion of Unity*, p. 9.
[15] 'Mission and Evangelism: An Ecumenical Affirmation', § 5, in *'You are the Light of the World': Statements on Mission by the World Council of Churches 1980–2005*, Geneva: WCC, 2005, p. 8
[16] *The Nature and Mission of the Church: A Stage on the Way to a Common Statement*, 'Faith and Order Paper No. 198', Geneva: WCC, 2005. The theme of the 2005 CWME Conference in Athens was: 'Come, Holy Spirit, Heal and Reconcile – Called in Christ to be Reconciling and Healing Communities'.
[17] See the annual 'Table on the Status of Global Mission, Presence and Activities, AD 1800 – 2025', prepared by David B. Barrett, Todd M . Johnson and Peter F. Crossing, *International Bulletin of Missionary Research* 31, no. 1 (January 2007), p. 32.
[18] *Mission and Evangelism: An Ecumenical Affirmation,* § 34; A fine analysis of the divergences and convergences between evangelical and ecumenical mission perspectives can be found in: Tormod Engelsviken, 'Convergence or Divergence? The Relationship between Recent Ecumenical and Evangelical Mission Documents', *Swedish Missiological Themes* 89, no. 2 (2001), pp. 197–220.
[19] Constitution of the WCC, article III, my italics.
[20] The Commission of the Churches on International Affairs was set up by the Joint Committee of the WCC and the IMC in its meetings in 1946 and 1947; See, *Minutes of the AD Interim Committee of the International Missionary Council, Geneva, Switzerland, February 16–19, 1946*, p. 42; See also, *Minutes of the Enlarged Meeting of the International Missionary Council and of the Committee of the Council, Whitby, Ontario, Canada, July –24, 1947*, pp. 45–50.
[21] The expression has been highlighted in the WCC since its use as the title of chapter 4 of the 'Ecumenical Affirmation on Mission and Evangelism', p. 19.

Cooperation and the Promotion of Unity: An Evangelical Perspective

Rose Dowsett

Introduction

Edinburgh 1910 was indeed an historic event, but it is easy to invest it with significance beyond the truth. As we re-consider mission and unity, and reflect on the Eighth Commission on Cooperation and the Promotion of Unity, it is important that we neither overstate nor understate the role Edinburgh 1910 played. While it is undoubtedly true that Edinburgh 1910 gave impetus to what came to be called the Ecumenical Movement, and facilitated the formation of the World Council of Churches almost forty years later, it is absolutely not true that Edinburgh 1910 marked the start of interdenominational unity in the cause and practice of world mission, nor does the Ecumenical Movement represent more than one strand in the story of twentieth-century world mission and church history. Indeed the WCC is neither the only nor the truest inheritor of 1910's legacy. In fact, had there not already been well-established and substantial evangelical interdenominational cooperation in world mission, it is doubtful whether Edinburgh 1910 could have happened in the form it did; and had not evangelicals continued to run with the baton of evangelization in the spirit of 1910 it is highly likely that many parts of the world where there is now a vibrant church would still be untouched by the gospel.

Evangelical mission in the nineteenth century

The Evangelical Movement was birthed in, and nourished by, a series of spiritual revivals. Each wave of revival led to a fresh wave of mission, either domestic or overseas. The context of world exploration on the one hand and the new technologies of the industrial revolution on the other, along with the political instabilities of North America and much of Europe – France, Germany, Italy – lent wings of urgency, as well as of exciting and expanding possibility, to evangelicals at the close of the eighteenth and the beginning of the nineteenth centuries. If James Cook could sail the world for commerce and for the sheer thrill of exploration, and capture the popular imagination in the process, then William Carey could go to Bengal,[1] and Henry Martyn[2] could go to India and Persia, and five American students sheltering under a haystack during a thunderstorm could pray and covenant to win people for Christ wherever he might choose to take them.[3]

It was a group of evangelical Anglicans who came to be known as the Clapham Sect,[4] led by William Wilberforce,[5] who not only turned their concern for the evangelization of Africa and India into the founding of the Church Missionary Society but also worked with gospel men and women from different denominations to bring about the abolition of the infamous slave trade in 1807 and the establishment of the British and Foreign Bible Society in 1804. At a time when divisions between Churchmen (i.e. Anglicans) and Nonconformists were often very deep, here were evangelicals engaged in a common cause where spiritual unity bridged structural chasms. This in turn paved the way for the establishing of the evangelical and interdenominational City Missions, an example of which is the London City Mission which began in 1835. Similarly, the YMCA (Young Men's Christian Association) was founded in 1844 as a distinctly evangelical and interdenominational ministry.

The revival of 1858–59 impacted both North America and Europe. Around one million new members joined American churches, and another million joined British churches. Some of these people had been spiritually dormant, but with some previous church connection. However records suggest that the overwhelming majority were completely unchurched prior to their conversion. From 1873 onwards, the mission campaigns of D.L. Moody led to many more coming to Christian faith, and this wave of evangelical mission also spread to Germany, Sweden and Russia. As a direct result of these two waves of revival – the 1858/9 period and then from 1873 onwards – a growing number of mission agencies were born.[6] These focused on many different geographical areas of the world, and a growing tide of men and women flowed into world mission. A high proportion of whom were evangelical. Many of them joined agencies which were interdenominational and soon international as well. Others were instrumental in starting mission agencies contained within their particular denominations, but which at that time were both theologically and in the practice of mission, hard to distinguish from evangelical societies.

Meanwhile, in 1846, just three years after the traumatic Disruption of the Church of Scotland, the Evangelical Alliance was formed.[7] The two events were not unrelated. Many of those who had left the Church of Scotland on conscientious grounds did so with very heavy hearts, and wished to demonstrate solidarity with those of other denominations with whom they felt a spiritual oneness that transcends structural divisions. At the same time, there were others in other parts of Britain and in America who also shared a longing to express their unity in the gospel even though their respective denominations might be firmly separate. At first there was a hope for establishing an international alliance. There was extensive agreement on a doctrinal basis and on principles of relationship; but there was also deep and painful disagreement over whether or not to admit American slave owners to membership. Reluctantly it was agreed that at that stage it was only possible to establish national alliances rather than a worldwide association. Because evangelicals were to be found across a variety of denominations, some of which were theologically quite varied, the evangelical alliances initially drew together only likeminded individuals, and denominations; congregations and agencies did not affiliate. Today there are both personal and corporate membership categories. But while this is a very different pattern of unity from that of the later WCC, it both then and subsequently built strong bonds of cooperation and friendship, with honesty about differences but also facilitating much common cause.

The case of the China Inland Mission

When James Hudson Taylor[8] founded the China Inland Mission in 1865, he was greatly influenced by his own spiritual background and also by the patterns that were developing in Britain at that time. From its foundation, the CIM was interdenominational. Members could come from any Protestant church, provided that they could agree to the statement of faith in good conscience. Hudson Taylor was clear that there could be no unity in mission unless there was agreement on fundamental doctrine, even though there might be considerable diversity of conviction on secondary matters. There was no distinction between ordained and unordained; both were equal in standing. What mattered was godly character, a clear sense of calling from God, a passion to see Chinese come to faith in Jesus Christ, and unity based on a shared commitment to the authority of Scripture. Missionaries were not employees but members of the mission, with mutual responsibility, accountability, and ownership in ministry and prayer, prayer for the financial and other resources with which to fulfil it. Women, both married and single, were equally missionaries with the men, and could engage in pioneer evangelism on their own if so gifted. There was a strong emphasis on pioneer evangelism: when CIM started, there were huge areas of inland China where there was no Christian witness of any kind at all, and never had been. Converts were to be gathered into congregations, taught, and trained in evangelism to reach and lead their own people. From the beginning there was also a strong emphasis on holistic care, through medicine, education, and other ministries of compassion. Since CIM members came from backgrounds with different church polity, church order must be treated as a secondary issue. A willingness to work with what had previously been established rather than insisting on replicating what was familiar from home was required.

These principles made it possible for CIM not only to be interdenominational but to soon become international as well. Evangelicals from different countries and different denominations had more features in common than they had distinctive points to divide them. Further, as many other agencies also arrived in China, both denominational and interdenominational, and from a range of countries, Hudson Taylor was a prime mover in establishing regular consultations and conferences between them all. Later he was to be a catalyst for the 1888 (London) and 1900 (New York) international mission conferences.

In 1875, the Keswick Convention began its annual meetings in the Lake District of northwest England, for the deepening of the spiritual life, and under the banner of 'All one in Christ Jesus'. For more than twenty years, whenever he was in England, Hudson Taylor was a regular visitor and speaker. By the mid 1880s consecration for foreign missionary service was a strong part of Keswick's ministry. In 1889, Hudson Taylor was invited by D.L. Moody to attend a similar conference on the Canada-America border, as a result of which North Americans began to join CIM in ever-increasing numbers. Among those present was Robert Wilder, who the previous year, together with John Mott, had founded the Student Volunteer Movement, which in its turn would be an important contributor to the vision for Edinburgh 1910. Shortly after this conference Hudson Taylor reported: '...one felt what a wealth of love and grace there is in the great Church – greater, perhaps, than one had ever conceived before – that, after all, all the wide world over, no matter whether in Africa, in India, in China, or in America, in Canada, in Scotland, or in England, all the Lord's children are children of one Father, all bound to one great central heart, and that they are indeed *one* in Christ Jesus. It is so glorious to realise that the Church is one. It is not uniformity that we want, but real manifested heart unity.'[9]

The fatal flaw of Edinburgh 1910

At the beginning of the nineteenth century, few Protestant denominational leaders were much interested in world mission, which is one important reason why so many mission initiatives began despite, rather than because, of denominational structures. By the end of the nineteenth century the picture had changed, and many denominational leaders were very interested in the Christianization of the world – a goal that fitted very comfortably with European imperialism – and most Protestant denominations had their own agencies. Further, where earlier in the century the majority of missionaries were working in pioneer situations, by the end of the century there were established churches in many new countries, many of them linked by a very strong umbilical cord to a mother denomination somewhere in the West.

There were cultural, political, and philosophical reasons for this change, as well as more specifically religious ones. For America, after the Civil War, growing wealth and confidence allied to its pioneer entrepreneurial spirit, made conquering the world for religion, as well as for commerce, a natural goal. For Europe, and most especially for Britain, the growing confidence in western civilization, in 'progress' along evolutionary lines, and the concomitant relentless development of high imperialism, similarly confirmed the assumption in church leaders that the entire world must be brought under the umbrella of Christendom, and indeed this could speedily be accomplished. This was not necessarily a matter of evangelization, as that had been widely understood fifty years before. It was much closer to the concepts that followed the Constantinian settlement of the fourth century, albeit with the crucial difference of the uneasy acceptance of Protestant denominational pluralism.

Allied to this were two developments in the Anglican Church. Because of the territorial expansion of the British Empire in particular, the Anglican Church in 1910 was regarded as a critical player. But in the second half of the nineteenth century, partly in reaction to Evangelicalism, the Anglican Church had changed in two significant ways. On the one hand, there was the High Church Anglo-Catholic wing, which was growing in dominance in the leadership of the Church, especially at the Episcopal level. On the other, there was the growing acceptance of the so-called Higher Criticism and theological liberalism. Both of these had critical relevance for world mission as it had largely been understood and practised in the nineteenth century. The liberals were anti-conversionist in general, and increasingly saw the role of mission as social improvement, education and westernization. Many elements of historic Christianity, including anything that smacked of supernaturalism, were now repudiated as primitive and outgrown. The Anglo-Catholics were happy to endorse mission among 'the heathen', but fiercely opposed to it in traditional parts of Christendom, such as Latin America or Europe; their highly sacramentalist view of baptism (also linked to a highly sacramentalist view of the episcopacy), whether Roman Catholic, Orthodox or Protestant, meant that in countries where a high rate of infant baptism still prevailed conversionist mission was deeply offensive and must at all costs be condemned. Proselytism is understandably a very sensitive subject, and raises profound questions as to our beliefs about what makes a person truly a Christian.

Where earlier conferences had largely been dominated by field missionaries, the leaders of mission agencies, and mission councils, there had been a gradual shift to include denominational leaders, and then for these leaders to take an increasingly influential role. For the organizers of 1910, the most coveted prize in this British Empire dominated world was the leadership of the Anglican Church. And at this time the senior leadership of the Anglican Church was largely Anglo-Catholic or at least High Church, and therefore opposed to mission in territory regarded as Christianized. This included Europe, America (except among native Indians), and –most controversially – Latin America, with further arguments about some parts of the Middle East with long Orthodox histories.

It is difficult to know how much evangelical mission leaders were aware in advance of 1910 of the fierce controversy that took place, the implacable conditions laid down by the Anglo-Catholic leaders of the Church of England, and the concessions that were then made. Behind the scenes J.H. Oldham, secretary to Edinburgh 1910, was desperate to have full Anglican endorsement. In America John Mott, organizationally inspirational but theologically not very astute, may not have fully grasped the long-term significance of what was decided. What is beyond doubt is that while Edinburgh 1910 has come to be regarded as a milestone in the development of unity in mission, it in fact led to a far more significant parting of ways in global mission. Further it reinforced the concept of Christendom in a way that has proved deeply damaging – see for example the huge losses from the churches of Europe since 1910. Moreover it reinforced the equally damaging and unbiblical belief that mission was what the west did to the rest of the world, rather than mission being at the core of the DNA of the church wherever it may be. This almost certainly delayed the development of the mission movement from the global south by decades, and also long hindered the churches from the global south from taking responsibility for the ongoing evangelization of their own people.

The recommendations of Commission Eight

In summing up the extensive research and consultation that went into the making of the Report on Co-operation and Unity, a number of points were firmly asserted: that evangelization was non-negotiable, and urgent; that attempts to develop only one united church in each mission field had so far proved unsuccessful, even among those who professed a wish to see their development; that some advocated at least a single federation of churches in any given area, with full mutual recognition, including intercommunion, while retaining domestically distinctives of order, practice and doctrine; that others could not accept that such a federation could work without violation of conscience, but they supported respectful consultation and prayer which might lead disparate bodies closer, and which would enhance recognition of spiritual unity even if structural unity was not possible; and that many of the problems of disunity on the mission field could not be resolved until and unless they were resolved in the home countries.[10]

Nonetheless the Commission recommended, there were certain steps that could be taken to strengthen mutual respect and understanding, and which might perhaps lead to greater visible unity in the future. First, everyone should observe comity agreements, whereby no denomination or agency would begin work in an area where another was already at work. If there were absolutely pressing reasons to break this undertaking the incoming mission must consult those already there, and work complementarily not in competition. Secondly, joint conferences had a key role to play in encouraging unity, as they would help people from different groups to know each other personally and let go of some of their prejudices and stereotypes. Thirdly, missions should look for every possible way in which to undertake joint action, for example in the capital-costly areas of educational institutions, theological training and producing Christian literature. Fourth, all should pray and look out for those individuals especially gifted as 'apostles of unity', and also look at achieving unity primarily as a spiritual and moral issue rather than an organizational one. Fifthly, the home bases of missionary societies must learn to work together. In passing, it is worth noting that many of the evangelical missions were already actively pursuing each of these five recommended actions, even though there was certainly scope for much further development.

Lastly, a Continuation Committee was established on the basis of the following three principles:

(a) It should, from the beginning, be precluded from handling matters that are concerned with the doctrinal or ecclesiastical differences of the various denominations.

(b) This being assured, it would be desirable that it should be as widely representative as possible.

(c) Yet it should be a purely consultative and advisory association, exercising no authority but such as would accrue to it through the intrinsic value of the services that it may be able to render.[11]

In due course the Continuation Committee became the International Missionary Council, which in turn was one of the three streams which in 1948 led to the formation of the World Council of Churches. The early vision of the WCC was certainly well beyond being a purely consultative and advisory association with no agenda of organic or ecclesiastical union.

The principles were problematic for evangelicals. On the one hand, they had plenty of experience of working interdenominationally in mission both in the West and in the mission fields of Africa, Asia and Latin America. On the other hand, especially in the light of the growing power of liberalism within the mainline denominations, many evangelicals were acutely aware of the inadequacy of unity or even very meaningful co-operation on pragmatic rather than doctrinal grounds. If there were no fundamental agreement on the nature of the gospel, the uniqueness of Christ and his atoning death, and on the authority of Scripture, there could not be any kind of unity that meant anything at all, even if there could be respect and courtesy. The desire for visible unity, as indeed the Lord himself had prayed, was strong, emotive and seductive. But if it were to be at the expense of clear agreement that people everywhere, including within Christendom, needed decisive conversion to Christ, then the price was too high.

Subsequent developments

All movements are birthed in a context, and it is arguable that after two disastrous, wildly destructive world wars, and in the face of the spread of Communism, Europeans in general, not just the churches, were desperate to find some transcendental unity, and to support the establishing of organizations that would give mutual strength to resist enemies (especially Marxism with its global ambitions) and promote peace. The United Nations was formally launched in October 1945 (it had informal antecedents) and in many respects the WCC's concerns mirrored it. It was this political chaos quite as much as more spiritual considerations that gave special impetus to the WCC to focus so much on unity. From an evangelical perspective, the WCC's preoccupation with unity, its focus on political and social issues, and the pressure during the 1950s, 1960s and 1970s for organic union between denominations, meant that evangelism was marginalized. Evangelical reaction focussed on the urgency of evangelism. For a while it lost some of its historic holism, on which it had an impeccable record, and retreated to a rather pietistic form of faith.

John Mott had been right to see the strategic importance of discipling students and mobilizing them for the cause of world mission. Following the First World War, the Student Volunteer Movement, whose energy had been so decisive in the decades previously, gradually fizzled out and the World Student Christian Federation that had grown out of it, supported by Mott's vision and enthusiasm, turned its back on its evangelical roots and embraced instead theological liberalism. In their (right) concern for post-war social reconstruction, and in the cultural mood of the day, they turned their backs on evangelization, as Mott had understood it. Indeed many mocked as obscurantist those who continued to take the Bible seriously.

Many evangelicals struggled in this new and hostile climate. Some retreated into highly separatist fundamentalism, while others were just confused. For several generations a high proportion of the most able evangelicals had gone overseas in mission. 'Back home' there was an acute lack of evangelical leaders in the churches. Few evangelical scholars were able to challenge the liberal theologians on their own turf. The Evangelical Movement was at its lowest ebb since the days of Wesley. The young men of the Cambridge Inter-Collegiate Christian Union responded to this context by insisting that because the SCM was not willing to put the atonement of Christ at the centre of its belief and actions they could not merge with the Student Christian Movement.[12] For them (and the resultant Christian Union movement) this was the very heart of gospel faithfulness. In other words, the grounds once again for evangelicals refusing structural unity were doctrinal. Without agreement in doctrine there could be no possibility of unity of purpose, practice and mission.

In successive decades, as the Evangelical Movement once again grew, these same issues of the centrality of the Cross of Christ, of the need therefore for personal conversion, and the place of Scripture as authority, were repeatedly decisive as to where there could be unity in mission. It was not that evangelicals were saying that nobody outside their own ranks could be a genuine Christian, nor were they saying that there were no circumstances in which they could join with others from other parts of the Christian family. Indeed many evangelicals have always chosen to be members of denominations that are not themselves exclusively evangelical. Since evangelicals do not believe the church to be co-terminous with the visible structure but rather with the community of all those born by the Spirit into the Body of Christ, ultimately known only to God, there is a God-sourced spiritual unity between believers that cannot be achieved by creating structures and organizations. This distinction between the visible and invisible church is of course not a new concept, but rather one adopted by Augustine and other Early Church Fathers as they observed the growing problems of disunity on the one hand and of nominalism and laxity on the other. Nonetheless, visible structures, be they of congregations or of mission agencies or of networks, are important as the physical expression of the spiritual communities – the invisible realities – into which we are called. And where those entities have a deeply shared commitment to fundamental gospel truths, alliances and federations naturally follow.

Twentieth-century advance

Evangelicals have played a very large part in the intentional spread of the Christian message during the past century, with a strong record of pioneering among previously unevangelized people groups. In many cases, where fifty years ago there were no known believers or only a tiny fledgling church, churches are now strongly established and engaged in mission. A high proportion of the churches of the global south, despite the historic dominance of Roman Catholicism in Latin America in particular, are evangelical, evangelical-charismatic, or Pentecostal. Further, to add to the complexity, many in the ancient churches of the global south are nonetheless evangelical in spirituality. In many cases, evangelicals are networked together through national and regional evangelical alliances, which in turn are affiliated to the World Evangelical Alliance (established in 1951). At present the WEA represents some 420 million members, linking denominations, congregations, individuals and agencies, in a common vision and task. The WEA fosters fellowship, understanding, and co-operation through conferences, commissions and task forces. Indeed, by means of these it facilitates joint action by a significant portion of the global church on issues as diverse as caring for refugees, working for justice for the disempowered, and co-ordinated mission to the unevangelized.[13]

Evangelical student movements and the Lausanne Movement

In 1947, representatives of ten national evangelical student movements formed the International Fellowship of Evangelical Students; today there are affiliated movements in 150 countries, discipling about a third of a million students.[14] Not only do these movements engage in local mission among the student population, but they have also produced many fine church and mission agency leaders, theologians, Bible translators, and Christian professionals who bear witness to Christ in their societies. Because their spiritual formation happens within an interdenominational setting, with a strong training element in relation to global mission, IFES people have proven well equipped to play a strategic role in developing deep bonds of friendship and co-operation between different parts of the world church.

This was a significant contributory factor in the convening of the 1974 Lausanne Congress, and of its outcomes. Billy Graham, with the support of the leading evangelical John Stott, initially called the Congress with the purpose of considering how evangelicals from around the world could work together for the evangelization of the world. The Congress was to birth the ongoing Lausanne Movement. John Stott had close association with IFES, and as a result many of the representatives, from the global south in particular, were from that background. It was their passionate input that probably changed evangelical mission from being a primarily a First World endeavour to one of a global teamwork of equals. The Lausanne Covenant remains to this day one of the most formative documents on the nature of mission to have been written in the whole of the century.[15] While affirming familiar evangelical foundational doctrine, it also recaptured the holistic nature of biblical evangelism. This had been a strong feature of eighteenth- and nineteenth-century Evangelicalism, but between Edinburgh 1910 and Lausanne 1974 it had been sometimes eclipsed. The Lausanne Movement has remained an important strand in fostering evangelical unity in mission to this day. There has also been some significant interface between evangelicals from Lausanne, the WEA and IFES, and personnel aligned with the WCC. They have worked together on mutually beneficial projects such as the Gospel and Culture initiative.

In turn, the co-operative movements of Lausanne, the IFES and the WEA have contributed greatly to the development of national and regional alliances of churches and agencies. The global south's missionary movements are overwhelmingly evangelical, charismatic and Pentecostal. This poses a special challenge to the ancient churches, whose life was shaped in the north, and in the long-ago past. From a southern perspective, the churches of the north are largely seen as lacking in spiritual life and fervour, in denial of the supernatural dimension of authentic Christian faith, captive to materialism and secular culture, and in dire need of re-evangelization. Will we be purely defensive, or will we have the humility to listen and learn? Paternalism may be more alive and well among us than we would like to admit.

Areas where evangelicals need to repent

It would be naïve and dishonest to imply that evangelicals have always been united. Sadly, the movement has been far from united. The very fact that structural unity is not our highest priority can of course make it easier rather than harder for new groups to begin, and some established ones to split.

In particular, I am ashamed of what happened after the USSR broke down in 1989. There is no way to defend the mad rush of countless denominations, agencies and local congregations to set up their own brand of work in the former Communist bloc. This was ugly and divisive. I accept that the Orthodox Church had persevered at great cost through the previous sixty years. At the very least it deserved greater respect. At the same time, as a matter of accuracy, while many of those groups were evangelical, many were not, and certainly by no means were all of them from the north. Furthermore, some of those who went to Russia and the other countries went at the pleading of national Christians who were not Orthodox, and who also had suffered.

It would also be naïve and dishonest to suggest that disunity is a western problem. In cultures influenced by Confucianism, loyalty to the top leader in a particular hierarchy is extremely important; and rival hierarchies, each with their own top leader, abound. In cultures where tribal or ethnic identity has been paramount, churches too frequently reflect tribal and ethnic lines rather than the new reconciled humanity in Christ. In one Asian country where I lived, some 40 imported distinct Baptist denominations had been joined by a further forty Baptist denominations that originated within the nation. Imagine how one could be Baptist in 80 different ways! Evidently, Asians, Africans and Latin Americans are quite as capable as Europeans or North Americans of being divisive. It is not accurate to say the plethora of denominations is all the fault of western missions. Nor is disunity simply a Protestant issue. There are some intriguing examples of groups that have broken away from the ancient churches.

The future

I do not believe we should deduce from the New Testament that the church is supposed to be one monolithic organization, with every local congregation or community of Christian people under one structural umbrella. The unity of the New Testament churches had more to do with unity in apostolic doctrine, shared purpose and the resulting one-ness of harmony than it had to do with any central human organization to which all must conform and submit. Despite the high hopes of some, even the Ecumenical Movement has not been the catalyst for more than a small handful of denominational unions, and I think the weight of church history is against many mergers in the future. In fact, new denominations are being created all the time, far faster than any mergers. Some mission agencies have merged – and others have been formed. Some of these have become wonderfully international, while others have remained mono-cultural. Globalization and migration bring Christian people from around the world to different places – and bring also amazing crowds of people from unevangelized backgrounds within reach of the gospel.

The ancient churches must come to terms with the collapse of Christendom, in Europe and beyond, and the impossibility of holding on to a pattern of territorial hegemony. Indeed, in the face of the massive migration that has been occurring, churches have been willing to establish congregations outside their own territory, initially to serve their own diaspora. However such churches commonly draw in local people too, people from very different backgrounds. In this way the ancient churches are themselves adding to the complex mosaic of Christian pluralism all over the world.

In my view, structural unity – which, it will be remembered, was explicitly rejected by the 1910 Conference – is less likely today than at any point in the past hundred years. This challenges us all, whatever our tradition, to ask what kind of unity we are really seeking. Evangelicals are better placed than most streams of the church to live with the realities of denominational pluralism, which is sure to be the pattern of the twenty-first century. We have, after all, a history of more than 200 years of evangelical co-operation across denominations in the cause of mission, and have been content to respect considerable diversity of conviction, practice, and culture in many areas of church and Christian life. But, wherever we stand, and whatever our convictions about the nature of unity, let us be sure that it is unity for mission, witness and world evangelixation – which was, of course, the context within which our Lord spoke in John 17. This, without a doubt, is the abiding message of Edinburgh 1910.

We live in privileged and wonderful days, where we see a global church, with men, women and children from countless people groups bearing witness to Jesus Christ in their communities. The church is very diverse – and maybe the Lord who delighted to create tens of thousands of different kinds of butterflies is less troubled by diversity than we are. Let us celebrate that and, while we wait for the return of the King, commit ourselves that the whole world, in each generation, might hear and see the gospel, and come to worship the one and only living God.

Endnotes

[1] Timothy George, *Faithful Witness: The Life and Mission of William Carey,* Leicester: Intervarsity Press, 1991.
[2] David Bentley-Taylor, *My Love Must Wait*, London: Intervarsity Press, 1975.
[3] Keith Hunt and Gladys Hunt, *For Christ and the University*, Downers Grove, Illinois: Intervarsity Press, 1991.
[4] John Patten, *These Remarkable Men*, London, Lutterworth Press, 1945.
[5] John Pollock, *Wilberforce*, London: Lion, 1977.
[6] E.g., China Inland Mission (1865), North Africa Mission (1881), Christian and Missionary Alliance (1887).
[7] Ian Randall and David Hilborn, *One Body in Christ: The History & Significance of the Evangelical Alliance*, Carlisle: Paternoster Publishing: 2001.
[8] A good one-volume biography is Roger Steer, *J. Hudson Taylor: A Man in Christ*, Singapore: OMF, 1990. For a more full treatment, see A. J. Broomhall's seven volume *Hudson Taylor and China's Open Century*, London: Hodder & Stoughton, 1981–90.
[9] J. Hudson Taylor, Anniversary Meetings at the Conference Hall, Mildmay Park. 30 May 1889, *China's Millions,* July 1889, p. 113.
[10] See World Missionary Conference, 1910, *Cooperation and the Promotion of Unity*, Report of Commission VIII, Edinburgh & London: Oliphant, Anderson & Ferrier; New York, Chicago and Toronto: Fleming H. Revell, 1910, pp. 131–48.

[11] World Missionary Conference, 1910, *The History and Records of the Conference*, Edinburgh & London: Oliphant, Anderson & Ferrier; New York, Chicago and Toronto: Fleming H. Revell, 1910, p. 96.
[12] For the story of the CICCU, including its relationship to SCM, see O. R. Barclay and R. Horn, *From Cambridge to the World*, Leicester: Intervarsity Press, 2002.
[13] For current information about WEA, see: World Evangelical Alliance, 2007, <www.worldevangelicalalliance.com>, 13 August 2007.
[14] For the IFES story, see Pete Lowman, *The Day of His Power*, Leicester: Intervarsity Press, 1983; and Lindsay Brown, *Shining Like Stars*, Nottingham: Intervarsity Press, 2006. For current information see International Fellowship of Evangelical Students, 2007, <www.ifesworld.org/home/> 13 August 2007.
[15] For the full text of the Covenant, see 'Lausanne Covenant', Lausanne Committee for World Evangelization, 1974, <http://www.lausanne.org/lausanne-1974/lausanne-covenant.html>, 13 August 2007.

Cooperation and the Promotion of Unity: An Orthodox Perspective

Viorel Ionita

1. Edinburgh and the Orthodox

The Orthodox Churches were not present at Edinburgh in 1910, first of all because of the fact that in the beginning of the twentieth century there were no Orthodox missionary councils at work. On the other hand almost all Orthodox Churches were confronted at that time with big problems, which prevented them from being actively involved in international gatherings. The report of Commission Eight mentioned a correspondence with Archbishop Nicolai of the Russian Ecclesiastical Mission in Tokyo. Archbishop Nicolai reported that: 'I am in friendly, more then that, brotherly relations with all the missionaries of other sections known to me, and so are our Christians with their Christians. So shall we be from our part always, because we know that the first duty of us Christians is to cultivate Christian love to all men, and particularly to our brothers in Christ. But, nevertheless, there is no real and full unity between us and other sections; more then that, we are far from such unity because we are divided in the Christian doctrine.'[1]

The Russian Archbishop expressed a position that is still valid for the Orthodox understanding of cooperation and unity in mission. Archbishop Nicolai pointed out the close relationship between the unity of the Church and unity in mission. Actually this Archbishop appears to have been quite progressive in his attitude towards cooperation with other missionary groups in the same context. Motivated by Christian love he considered that he should have a brotherly openness towards his fellow Christians, but felt constrained to underline that the unity that may exist between them is not a full unity, because full unity in mission would imply also full unity of the respective churches, which was not the case.

Coming back to the report of Commission Eight, we should point out some questions dealt with in this report challenge us even today. Speaking about 'Comity', the second chapter of this report refers to the very difficult issue of 'Delimitation of territory'. In this respect the report underlined that 'Few would refuse to accept as an abstract principle the view that it is undesirable to press in where others are working when neglected fields are calling for labourers.'[2] It also indicated 'The avoidance of overlapping and interference with the work of others is also demanded by the spirit of Christian charity, which should be preeminently manifested in the work of Christian missions.'[3] If this principle would have been respected everywhere many conflicts would have been avoided; such as the difficult debate around the concept of 'canonical territory', to which the Russian Orthodox Church has made reference during the last decades.

The report also referred to obstacles on the way to cooperation and unity in mission, 'which are grounded in differences of doctrine or ecclesiastical polity' and which 'are, perhaps, harder to overcome'.[4] It argued divisions between the churches weaken their 'testimony and confuse the total impression made by Christianity on the minds of the non-Christian people'.[5] Indeed the divisions between the churches have not been created by the situation in the mission field, but they do affect the mission field. Consequently one of the most significant contributions of the report from 1910 to the Ecumenical Movement as a whole was the reference to the close relationship between unity in mission and the unity of the Church. The issue of the unity of the Church had been a concern for the divided churches for a long period of time. But in 1910, more than ever before, the World Mission Conference pointed out the negative impact of this division for the mission of the churches at the world level.

The concern of Orthodox theologians over the close link between the doctrinal differences and the mission of the churches in the world of today was best addressed by Metropolitan Ignatios Hazim, the current Patriarch of Antioch, in his speech at the fourth General Assembly of the World Council of Churches, Uppsala 1968, on the theme *'Behold, I Make all Things New'*. In his presentation, which was probably one of the most prophetic addresses ever delivered at a WCC Assembly, the then Metropolitan Ignatios approached inter-church relations from an eschatological perspective, and asked whether the best way of solving the doctrinal dispute, which is still preventing full communion, would not be 'to turn together towards the Coming Lord?' He continued, 'There is no programmatic sentimentalism in this, but rather that same evidence of faith, which would enable us to re-centre everything in the heart of the Mystery. The dialogue between the churches has perhaps remained at the stage of the time before Isaiah 43:18, when one still considered "the things of old". But it is certain that the Lord is "doing a new thing"; now it springs forth, do you not perceive it?'[6]

The report from 1910 also makes references to some 'Joint Actions' in mission, which were very relevant for the Orthodox Churches during the twentieth century. We would like to underline two of these joint actions, namely the translation and publication of the Bible and the cooperation in philanthropy. On the first issue, the report emphasizes that 'there is no sphere of missionary work in which the value of cooperation has been tested and appreciated more than in the translation, publication, and distribution of the Word of God; and not least among the fruits of this work must be reckoned the friendships which have been formed between men separated ecclesiastically and diverse in nationality but called to work around the same translation board'.[7]

One of the most urgent missionary needs within the Romanian Orthodox Church during the time of oppression from the Communist regime (1945–89) was the publication of the Bible and liturgical books. With the support of the United Bible Societies the patriarch Justinian (1948–77) published two editions of the Bible, in 1968 and 1975, and several editions of the New Testament. The distribution of the Holy Scripture during that period of time proved to be one of the most fruitful missionary actions. This is only one out of many examples of cooperation between the Orthodox Churches and the Missionary or Bible Societies.

Finally another aspect underlined by the report of 1910, which has been relevant for the cooperation in mission from an Orthodox perspective, is, as the report formulated it, the 'work of philanthropy and Benefice'. The report stated that 'in time of famine, flood, earthquake, and fire, Christian men [*sic*] do not discuss whether they should co-operate, but simply do so as a matter of course. By the organisation of relief funds and the judicious disbursement of monies raised, countless thousands have been saved from suffering and death'.[8] The cooperation between churches of different confessional traditions, when facing catastrophic situations around the world, did bring the churches nearer and often helped them address the theological differences from a new perspective. The Orthodox theology underlined repeatedly during the last decades that diakonia, or service to fellow human beings, is an integral part of the mission of the church in the world of today and therefore cooperation in diakonia is cooperation in mission.

Although the Commission Eight Report did not have a direct impact on Orthodox mission, it opened up a complex process of reflection about mission in the world today, which would in due course include a specific Orthodox contribution. Already the Encyclical Letter of the Ecumenical Patriarchate from January 1920, which constitutes a Charta Magna for the Orthodox involvement in the Ecumenical Movement, strongly suggested a 'whole-hearted mutual assistance for the churches in their endeavours for religious advancement, charity and so on'.[9]

2.1 The Orthodox Understanding of Mission

His Beatitude Anastasios, Archbishop of Tirana and All Albania, one of the most representative Orthodox theologians in respect to the missionary renewal during the last century, considered that when talking about Orthodox mission the first thing to do is 'to state that by this word we mean witness to the living Trinitarian God, who calls all to salvation and binds human beings together in the church, who otherwise would not belong to it or who have lost their tie to it'.[10] In this respect 'for every local church, mission is "inward" or "internal", when it takes place within its geographical, linguistic and cultural bounds, and "outward" or "external" when it reaches beyond these bounds to other nations and lands'.[11]

The very purpose of the mission is to build up the 'communion with God and with one another through Christ in the Holy Spirit'.[12] According to this view mission is not just the exportation of new religious doctrine, but bearing witness to the love of God for the whole world, love which was revealed in Christ, communicated by the Holy Spirit and present in the hearts of those who are practising his commands. Therefore we should not forget that 'the famous text on mission – "go and make disciples from all nations ..." (Matthew 28:19) – has no complete meaning without the experience of what is said in the following verse, "I will be with you always even until the close of ages." In other words, those who preach Christ and make disciples of Christ must themselves experience the presence of Christ or of his Spirit in them.'[13]

Following Jesus Christ or living in Christ means being a member of the body of Christ, which means being a member of the Church. Strictly speaking, for the Orthodox the Church doesn't have her own mission, but she participates in God's mission. 'The very being of the Church is missionary, the Church is, indeed, a missionary event. Therefore, mission is not one of the "functions" of the Church, but the life of the Church that goes beyond itself to embrace the whole of humanity and the whole creation. The mission of the Church is not the expansion of the Church, but the establishment of the kingdom of God. Unity and mission must be understood in the perspective of the kingdom. They are for the kingdom and, as such, they are dynamically interrelated'.[14]

Mission is, for the Orthodox, exclusively a task of the Church. The Church is both the instrument and the purpose of mission. The real purpose of the mission is to bring people to Christ and to help them grow into the body of Christ, which is the Church. The preaching of the gospel alone without bringing new people into the body of Christ is not enough. The purpose of mission is not simply to bring new people into the Church, but also to continue to accompany them their whole life. The pastoral task of the Church is therefore an integral part of her mission. Finally the mission is the task of the whole Church, both of ordained and lay people, of men and women, of old and young believers.

The Orthodox understanding of mission could be summarized in the following four points: 1. *Kerygma*, or the proclamation of the Gospel; 2. *Leiturgia,* as public service for the praise of God; 3) *Martyria,* or the witness to the faith as a life style and 4) *Diakonia*, or the service to the neighbour, or the service to the whole world. The Orthodox theology is developing its mission, which is the mission of God in this world, following without break the tradition of the early church. The tradition, which in this context is the Holy Tradition and should not be mixed up with the church tradition or traditions, is not a dead letter, a collection of dogmas and practices of the past. This Tradition is for the Orthodox the history of salvation. It is the experience of the Holy Spirit in the history, who constantly illuminates men and women to become sons and daughters of God the Father, in Jesus Christ, through the grace of the Holy

Spirit. Through this Tradition the Orthodox Church of today stays in an unbroken continuation with the Apostles.

2.2 The Challenges of Mission for the Orthodox Churches in the Twentieth Century

During the whole of the twentieth century the Orthodox Churches were facing many difficulties in developing their missionary tasks. Living mainly in countries ruled either by non-Christian or by atheistic governments, the Orthodox Churches were confronted with basic existential questions. The mission of a church under such circumstances is, if at all, an internal mission. If we should take into consideration the situation of the Orthodox Churches in the former communist countries, then we cannot stop wondering how these churches survived and how a large majority of the respective peoples were continuously active members of their church. In spite of these circumstances the Orthodox mission went through a real and sometimes spectacular revival, mainly in the second half the twentieth century.

The immigration of Orthodox people during the twentieth century, largely to the West, challenged the Orthodox mission in a very specific way. The Orthodox believers from the Diaspora came in contact not only with new political, economical and cultural realities, but also with new religious views. The Orthodox mission in such a context could no longer be only an internal one, but it had to also take into consideration dialogue with other Christian traditions or even with other religions. In trying to defend and affirm their own confessional, or even their religious identity, in a foreign context, the Orthodox believers became in a certain sense missionaries. The missionary experience of the Orthodox in a Diaspora situation improved the missionary activity of the Orthodox Church at home.

One of the most important inputs for the renewal of the missionary ethos within the Orthodox Churches came not from outside but from inside; from a youth organization known as Syndesmos. The World Fellowship of Orthodox Youth, Syndesmos, was founded in 1953 to encourage contacts among Orthodox youth movements in Western Europe, Greece and the Middle East. Today Syndesmos has grown into a federation of 121 youth movements and theological schools in 43 different countries around the world.[15]

At the fourth General Assembly of Syndesmos in Thessaloniki (1958) an Orthodox movement for 'external mission' was established in Greece. Archbishop Anastasios of Tirana and All Albania, one of the main actors in this enterprise at that time, reported that with this initiative 'we had to face two difficulties: the amazement of Westerners, who thought the Orthodox Church was introspective and uninterested in mission; and a pathetic internal opposition from Orthodox, who considered such an interest as something imported. For this reason, during the first decade, not only was external mission stressed as an Orthodox theological and ecclesiological necessity, but a special attempt was made to study its history'.[16]

2.3 Orthodox Contributions to the Ecumenical Approach of Mission

When the International Missionary Council (IMC) became an affiliated body of the WCC, at the 3rd WCC General Assembly in New Delhi, India, the Orthodox Churches opposed this integration. They did so, first of all, for ecclesiological reasons. They did not consider the IMC to be a church. It therefore could not be a full member of a 'fellowship of churches'. Secondly, the Orthodox considered that they were the victims of proselytism exercised by churches or missionary agencies in membership with the IMC. However in 1961 a large group of Orthodox Churches became members of the WCC as well, and this fact opened up new perspectives for the cooperation of the Orthodox Churches with other churches, including work in mission and evangelism.

One of the most important actions, which improved the cooperation of the Commission for World Mission and Evangelism with the Orthodox Churches, was the creation, in 1970, of an executive position on Orthodox Mission Studies and Relations within the WCC. The first Orthodox theologian appointed to this position was the current Archbishop Anastasios of Tirana and All Albania, followed by Fr Dr Ion Bria, Mr. George Lemopoulos and Fr Dr Ioan Sauca. Through this desk several consultations have been organized, much material about the Orthodox understanding of mission has been published and a network of Orthodox theologians committed to mission has been established. In the course of these discussions a distinctive Orthodox perspective has been developed on a number of key topics.

2.3.a. Mission in Relation to Other Religions

For Orthodox theology the confrontation with other religions has been a painful one.[17] The starting point of an Orthodox theological approach for the relations to other religions, or for a possible Orthodox theology of religions, is a Christological approach. According to this approach the Logos (Word) of God inspired, already before his Incarnation, all the good ideas in the different Holy Scriptures, not only in the Old Testament, but also in the holy scriptures of the East, or even in the ancient Greek philosophy. Together with the Church Fathers from the Alexandrian tradition (like Clement of Alexandria or Origen) the Old Testament is not the unique Gospel-type scripture, 'it is rather the prototype of all other Holy Scriptures'.[18]

Metropolitan George Khodre of Mount Lebanon argues

> … God has also revealed Himself in these Scriptures. Our God is a hidden God. It does not befit us to define objectively the intensity of the Divine Presence in the Abrahamic Bible, for instance, but rather simply to seek in it the traces of Christ who is eternal Logos, and whose manifestation before the Incarnation and outside

> the historical heritage of the Incarnation are possible. These many modes of God's revelation can only be read in the light of the Gospel. They all point to the mercy and meekness of the Divine Logos manifesting itself not only within a sacred historical tradition but even in a certain manner outside this tradition where the veil is thicker.[19]

This veil will be taken away from the minds of people only by turning to Christ (2 Corinthians 3:16). In other words, the other religions should not be simply rejected as wrong, but considered in the perspective of their relation to the Logos of Christ. The Orthodox Christians came to this view not simply through an abstract theological, or even philosophical, reflection but rather through their long experience living next to or among people of other religions.

Along this view, the Middle East Council of Churches, which include not only Orthodox Christians but also Christians of other confessions, declared at its fourth General Assembly that if the Christian faith is authentically lived, then Christians have the responsibility to struggle for the rights not simply for a particular group, but also for the dignity of each and, above all, for the integrity of those who are victims of injustice. 'This responsibility of all people in every society, regardless of colour, race and creed, becomes a spiritual dimension, a fidelity to Christ, who calls us to assume on behalf of everybody all true human solidarity'.[20] In this way the Orthodox people learned to approach other religions not simply from an abstract theoretical point of view, but from their spirituality. This approach could be a specific Orthodox contribution to the theology of religions, or even to the very delicate issue of the Christian mission among other religions.

2.3.b. The Missionary Tasks of the Local Community

Mission is, first of all, the task of the whole church, and is best expressed through the local community. The issue of the missionary task of the local community was addressed at the consultation organized by the WCC with representatives from the Eastern Orthodox and Oriental Orthodox Churches (Neapolis, Greece from 16–24 April 1988). This consultation constituted a preparatory meeting for the World Conference for Mission and Evangelism that was then organized at San Antonio, USA, in 1989 under the theme '*Your Will be Done'*. According to the Neapolis statement, the mission of the local community is to make it possible for everyone to have the possibility 'to know Christ, to live in him and witness him by word and deed'.[21] In this respect the first missionary task of the local community refers to the 'internal' mission, which is the major pastoral task of every church. But when the Eucharistic assembly experiences the truth of the resurrected Lord, 'the necessity to share the joy of the resurrection with all people is a natural consequence'.[22] In this case the mission of the local community becomes an external mission, which 'includes even those who are baptized, yet ignorant of the calling and election they have received through baptism'.[23]

The same statement was formulated as a practical recommendation to the Orthodox Churches, namely that it is essential to develop contemporary means to help all the baptized believers 'return to the fellowship of the church. The church's mission also calls us to the task of peacemaking, reconciling and defending justice for everyone, especially in contexts where the people of God suffer from injustice, oppression and war. When the Eucharistic assembly does not engage in such outreach it fails to realise its missionary responsibility.'[24]

2.3.c. Liturgy after the Liturgy

The phrase 'liturgy after the liturgy' was formulated at the consultation organized by the WCC with Orthodox participants on '*Confessing Christ through the Liturgical Life of the Church Today*' (Etchmiadzin, Armenia, 1975). In that context Archbishop Anastasios of Tirana and All Albania, then a professor at the University of Athens, wrote that each of the faithful 'is called upon to continue a personal "liturgy" on the secret altar of his own heart, to realize a living proclamation of the good news "for the sake of the whole world". Without this continuation the liturgy remains incomplete.'[25]

The late Fr. Ion Bria, who was responsible for the most substantial contribution to the whole issue of Orthodox mission and the WCC, further developed the concept of 'liturgy after the liturgy', so that this expression has been more and more identified with his name. Bria underlined that 'in ensuing ecumenical discussions other dimensions of 'the liturgy after the liturgy' have been discovered. The church's liturgical and diaconal functions are connected, for liturgy reshapes the social life of Christians with a new emphasis on the sharing of bread, on the healing of brokenness, on reconciliation and on justice in the human community. The concept has also come to be associated with other facets of the life of the church, including education, evangelisation, concern for creation, spirituality and social ethics'.[26]

2.3.d. Mission and Unity

The issue of the mission and unity, or of mission in unity, was best addressed at the above-mentioned Neapolis consultation. In the final report of this consultation a special section was dedicated to the issue of 'Mission and Unity'. In this section the following aspects are addressed: 1) Ecclesiological perspectives; 2) Common witness; 3) Proselytism and 4) Ecumenical vision. From an ecclesiological perspective, the Church, as the presence of the kingdom of God in the world, is called to manifest the Trinitarian communion and love 'within its fold and towards the world. The church's mission is the expression of this unity and love.'[27] In other words the unity of the Church is based in the unity of the Holy Trinity, and from this unity results also the unity in mission, which is nothing else as the unity of the Church.

In relation to the issue of common witness, the consultation from Neapolis recommended some concrete actions for cooperation between all Orthodox Churches as well as for the cooperation of the Orthodox Churches with other churches. The common witness is a concrete expression of the unity in mission. In regards to the topic of proselytism, it was noted that from the Orthodox perspective proselytism is a most difficult obstacle on the way towards unity in mission. Finally the question of ecumenical vision was discussed. The Neapolis statement refers to the fact that one impetus for the modern vision 'was originally inspired by the committed search for a common witness to the good news of salvation. It still remains the primary objective of our ecumenical involvement – to offer common witness in love to the power of Christ, crucified and risen, so that those who are caught up in this world of division, conflict and death may believe and be transfigured'.[28]

2.3.e. The Issue of Proselytism

The representatives of the Orthodox Churches in the ecumenical movement have complained, from the beginning, about the fact that missionary groups from other churches are often stealing believers from Orthodox Churches. The statement of the consultation from Neapolis, mentioned above, addressed the issue of proselytism in connection with the question of unity in mission. In this respect the 'proselytism, along with the actual disunity among the churches, creates major obstacles for our common witness'.[29]

The statement recommended that 'all proselytism by any church should be condemned, and all antagonism and unhealthy competition in mission work should be avoided, as constituting a distorted form of mission'.[30] When these remarks were first made public they encountered heavy criticism for being in contradiction with religious freedom. Today such remarks are commonplace in the ecumenical circles. The Orthodox Churches were called, through the Neapolis statement, 'to continue efforts to persuade the churches and agencies involved in proselytism not to engage in dubious missionary activities detrimental to God's will for unity, and to seek the path of true Christian charity and unity'.[31]

2.3.f. The Eucharist and Mission

Through mission the Church makes people permanently aware of God's saving presence and action in the world, and invites them to partake in a new life of communion with the Trinity. Because this new life develops through, and in relation to, God and other people it decisively shapes their identity. Emmanuel Clapsis explains: 'This kind of new life is sacramentally actualised and communally experienced in the eucharist, which is the great mystery of our participation in the life of the Holy Trinity, the recapitulation of the entire history of salvation in Christ and the foretaste of the Kingdom of God. In it, the faithful, by the invocation of the Holy Spirit, become the body of Christ, in which all respect one another for their unique gifts that the Holy Spirit has bestowed upon them for the building-up of their unity, which is grounded in their baptism'.[32]

Clapsis further explains that the Church's mission in relation to the Eucharist is to reveal:

> … what we have already become in the risen Christ, and what we will fully experience in his kingdom. Thus, Christians, as it becomes evident in the Eucharist, draw the being of their identity not from the values of this world but from being of God and from that which we will be at the end of this age. Baptised Christians, therefore, in the Eucharist become a community of people who together unite prayer with action, praise with justice, adoration with transformation and contemplation with social involvement. As they disperse in history for the proclamation of the Christian gospel, their missionary task is affected not only by their words but also by what they do and how they relate to each other as different members of the same Eucharistic body of Christ in the context of the fragmented world.[33]

2.3.g. Gospel and Culture

The specific Orthodox contribution to the issue of Gospel and Culture, which was the theme of the World Conference for Mission and Evangelism at Salvador de Bahia (1996), was expressed at the Inter-Orthodox consultation on Gospel and Culture, organized in Addis-Ababa, Ethiopia, between the 19th and 27th of January 1996. The final statement adopted at this consultation underlined, among other things, that:

> … the eternal truth which is Christ, delivered to the Church in its fullness immediately became incarnate in many languages in Jerusalem on Pentecost. The Gospel is always inculturated, proclaimed, manifest in a particular time and place by a particular people which means in a cultural context. With its reception by a people, their pre-existing culture is fertilised by the Gospel and organically transformed into creative energies towards salvation. There will inevitably be elements, attitudes, values within any culture alien to the Gospel and incompatible with it, which will be purified, transformed or exorcised by the Holy Spirit as the Spirit witnesses to Christ in the continuing life of the local eucharistic community.[34]

At the European Forum on Gospel and Culture, an Orthodox theologian underlined that Orthodox theology neither identifies religion with culture, nor separates them completely, because the Orthodox Church 'has avoided both the sacralisation of culture and its secularisation'.[35] In relation to the very complex situations of today's world, the Addis Ababa document stated that:

> … in multi-cultural and multi-religious settings, different cultures and religions may compete with each other for predominance. This inevitably leads to violent conflict, exploitation and even persecution and death of the less powerful. In such situation of brokenness and violence, the Church by following the irenic life of Jesus Christ must actively work for the peaceful co-existence of all communities, enabling all to recognize the sanctity of life as a gift of God and the right of all to

> pursue the quest for human fulfilment not in opposition with the other but in meaningful conversation of enrichment that enhances the understanding of life as God's gift.[36]

2.3.h. Mission and the Whole Creation

The mission of the Church relates not only to human beings but also to the whole creation which 'itself also shall be delivered from the bondage of corruption into the liberty of the glory of the children of God' (Romans 8:21). Regarding the message of the Gospel as 'God's love and concern for the life of the whole world, the church cannot reduce its mission to the "salvation of souls". The cosmic Christology implies that the mission of Christians in the world includes also their responsibility for the whole life of society and even their attitude towards nature and creation. In this sense, the Christian mission includes the dimension of a global human responsibility for the life of the world'.[37]

It is well known that His All Holiness the Ecumenical Patriarch Bartholomew is very much committed to the protection of the environment, or to the integrity of the creation. For him 'all of our efforts to cultivate a sense of environmental responsibility and to promote genuine reconciliation among people comprise the immediate responsibility and initiative of the Ecumenical Patriarchate, which has served the truth of Christ for some seventeen centuries. Our Church regards the sensitisation of its faithful in relation to the natural environment and in regard to the development of inter-religious dialogue as a central and essential part of its ministry of solidarity and co-existence'.[38] The original privilege and calling as human beings lies, for the Ecumenical Patriarch, 'precisely in our ability to appreciate the world as God's gift to us. And our original sin with regard to the natural environment lies – not in any legalistic transgression, but – precisely in our refusal to accept the world as a sacrament of communion with God and neighbour'.[39]

3. A New Resonance

Instead of a conclusion we will simply quote His Beatitude Archbishop Christodoulos of Athens and of All Greece, who when addressing the last World Conference on Mission and Evangelism, held for the first time in an majority Orthodox context (Athens, Greece, 9–16 May 2005), rightly appreciated 'the holistic understanding of mission, being developed in recent years within WCC'. His Beatitude continued that his church 'considered this conference important and providential among other world mission conferences of this kind, because of its new shift in mission paradigm, which makes it resonate with the theology, spirituality and contextual realities of our Orthodox Churches. We Orthodox do not only benefit from the ecumenical encounter and dialogue but also bring challenges coming from our long history of mission experience and our mission theology with echoes from the time of the early Christian communities'.[40]

The World Missionary Conference from Edinburgh in 1910 opened up the process for a large ecumenical debate on the mission of the Church in the world of today. In preparing the centenarian anniversary of this conference we have to take into consideration the considerable ecumenical contribution towards a more comprehensive and more ecumenical approach of this issue during the last decades. In this perspective the Orthodox contribution will appear as a specific one, which enriched in a special way the holistic ecumenical approach of mission and evangelism towards a common witness of all churches to faith in Jesus Christ; that the world may believe.

Endnotes

[1] World Missionary Conference, 1910, *Cooperation and the Promotion of Unity*, Report of Commission VIII, Edinburgh & London: Oliphant, Anderson & Ferrier; New York, Chicago and Toronto: Fleming H. Revell, 1910, p. 4.
[2] *Cooperation and the Promotion of Unity*, p. 12.
[3] *Cooperation and the Promotion of Unity*, p. 13.
[4] *Cooperation and the Promotion of Unity*, p. 50.
[5] *Cooperation and the Promotion of Unity*, p. 9.
[6] Constantin G. Patelos, ed., *The Orthodox Church in the Ecumenical Movement: Documents and Statements 1902–1975*, Geneva: WCC Publications, 1978, p. 264.
[7] *Cooperation and the Promotion of Unity*, p. 56.
[8] *Cooperation and the Promotion of Unity*, p. 79.
[9] Patelos, *The Orthodox Church in the Ecumenical Movement*, p. 42.
[10] Anastasios of Androussa, 'Orthodox Mission: Past, Present, Future', in George Lemopoulos, ed., *Your Will be Done: Orthodoxy in Mission*, Geneva: WCC Publications, 1989, p. 63.
[11] Anastasios, 'Orthodox Mission', p. 64.
[12] Daniel Ciobotea, *Confessing the Truth in Love: Orthodox Prespectives on Life, Mission and Unity,* Iasi: Trinitas, 2001, p. 136.
[13] Ciobotea, *Confessing the Truth in Love*, p. 137.
[14] Aram Keshishian, *Orthodox Perspectives on Mission*, Oxford: Regnum, 1992, p.98.
[15] See 'Presentation', Syndesmos: The World Fellowship of Orthodox Youth, 2007, <www.syndesmos.org/content/en/presentation.php>, 20 August 2007.
[16] Anastasios, 'Orthodox Mission', p. 64.
[17] George Khodre, 'The Church as the Privileged Witness of God', in Ion Bria, ed., *Martyria/ Mission: The Witness of the Orthodox Church Today*, Geneva: WCC Publications, 1980, p. 32.
[18] Khodre, 'The Church as the Privileged Witness of God', p. 33.
[19] Khodre, 'The Church as the Privileged Witness of God', pp. 33–4.
[20] George Lemopoulos, ed., *Your Will be Done: Orthodoxy in Mission*, Geneva: WCC Publications, 1989, p. 97.
[21] Lemopoulos, *Your Will be Done*, p. 55.
[22] Lemopoulos, *Your Will be Done*, p. 55.
[23] Lemopoulos, *Your Will be Done*, p. 55.
[24] Lemopoulos, *Your Will be Done*, p. 55.

[25] Ion Bria, *Liturgy after the Liturgy: Mission and Witness from an Orthodox Perspective*, Geneva: WCC Publications, 1996, p. 20.
[26] Bria, *Liturgy after the Liturgy*, p. 21.
[27] Lemopoulos, *Your Will Be Done*, p. 47.
[28] Lemopoulos, *Your Will Be Done*, p. 51.
[29] Lemopoulos, *Your Will Be Done*, p. 51.
[30] Lemopoulos, *Your Will Be Done*, p. 51.
[31] Lemopoulos, *Your Will Be Done*, p. 51.
[32] Emmanuel Clapsis, 'The Eucharist as Missionary Event in a Suffering World', in George Lemopoulos, ed., *Your Will be Done: Orthodoxy in Mission*, Geneva: WCC Publications, 1989, p. 165.
[33] Clapsis, 'The Eucharist as Missionary Event', p. 168.
[34] Ioan Sauca, ed., *Orthodoxy and Cultures: Inter-Orthodox Consultation on Gospel and Cultures*, Geneva: WCC Publications, 1996, p. 183.
[35] Dumitru Popescu, 'Theology, Culture, Church: The Relation between Theology and Culture in Orthodoxy and in the Present Day Romanian Society', in Viorel Ionita and Dietrich Werner, eds., *European Forum on Gospel and Culture(s),* Hamburg: EMW Informationen, no. 113 (December 1996), p. 36.
[36] Sauca, *Orthodoxy and Cultures*, p. 186.
[37] Ciobotea, *Confessing the Truth in Love*, p. 142.
[38] His All Holiness the Ecumenical Patriarch Bartholomew, 'Address by His All Holiness the Ecumenical Patriarch Bartholomew: Oslo Sophie Prize Ceremony', The Sophie Foundation, 12 June 2002, <http://www.sofieprisen.no/Articles/48.html>, accessed 20 August 2007.
[39] 'Address by His All Holiness the Ecumenical Patriarch Bartholomew: Oslo Sophie Prize Ceremony'.
[40] Archbishop Christodoulos of Athens and of All Greece, 'Conference on World Mission and Evangelism: Welcoming Address', World Council of Churches, 10 May 2005 < www.oikoumene.org/uploads/media/ PLEN_10_doc_1_Archbishop_Christodolous.doc>, accessed 20 August 2007.

Cooperation and the Promotion of Unity: An Roman Catholic Perspective

John A. Radano

Part One: 100 years of thought and action in the Catholic Church

While it is true that the Catholic Church came full force into the ecumenical movement with the Second Vatican Council 1962–5, it is also true that concern for unity within the Catholic Church, on the part of Popes, theologians, monastic communities and others, is found long before the Council. Indeed even before Edinburgh 1910.[1] Catholic efforts for unity came, at first, parallel to, but separate from, those steps leading to Edinburgh 1910, the Life and Work and the Faith and Order movements, and the creation of the World Council of Churches. Only afterwards did they relate to these initiatives. We will trace the Catholic developments in three periods.

The first period, 1910–1948:
Edinburgh to the creation of the World Council of Churches

The document, during this period, reflecting the official Catholic attitude to the newborn ecumenical movement to which Edinburgh 1910 gave such impetus was Pius XI's encyclical *Mortalium Animos* (1928). It was issued after the World Conferences on Life and Work (1925) and Faith and Order (1927); it strongly repudiated the young ecumenical movement and forbade Catholic participation in it.[2] The Pope saw this movement as promoting *expressions* of the church which were alien to Catholic understanding. According to the encyclical, this ecumenical movement was led by 'pan-Christians' seeking to federate churches on the precarious bases of charity and doctrinal compromise. 'It is clear', emphasized Pius XI, 'that the Apostolic See can by no means take part in their assemblies, nor is it in any way lawful for Catholics to support such enterprises; … if they did so they would be giving countenance to a false Christianity, quite alien to the one Church of Christ.' The only way to Christian unity, he emphasizes, is that non-Catholics accept all Catholic dogmas and return to the Roman-Church.

The Popes during this same period nonetheless expressed hopes for Christian unity in different ways, often having more hope for unity with eastern Orthodoxy, though not exclusively. While their hopes for unity are sincere, they are often expressed with a particular interpretation of the division which occurred centuries ago, namely that those not in union with Rome had at some point separated from the Church, and if union were to come about, they had to return to the Catholic Church.

Leo XIII (1878–1903) tried to create a new climate of friendship and respect for the Orthodox.[3] In his encyclical *Praeclara Gratulationis Publicae* (1894) he expresses the hope that 'the day is not far distant when the Eastern Churches, so illustrious in their ancient faith and glorious past, will return to the fold they have abandoned. We hope it all the more, that the distance separating them from Us is not so great.'[4] Leo, in his Apostolic letter *Orientalium Dignitas* (1894), expressed the hope that Catholics of the Eastern rite could, in effect, be mediators between East and West, by living in such a way as to 'show themselves true heralds and peacemakers of holy unity between the Eastern Churches and the Roman Church'.[5] Leo promotes a goal of unity with diversity, not uniformity, when he says, in *Praeclara Gratulationis Publicae*, that there is no reason for Eastern Christians 'to fear … that We or any of our successors will ever diminish your rights, the privileges of your Patriarchs, or the established ritual of any one of your Churches'.[6]

Leo also made some important ecumenical gestures to Western separated Christians. He addressed letters to Christians of England, Scotland, Germany, and never referred to them or of them as heretics,[7] but rather as dissidents (separated). In his 1895 letter *Amantissima Voluntatis* ('to the English People'), Leo referred to non-Catholics in England as 'separated brothers' (*fratribus dissidentibus*). Placing unprecedented stress on the positive quality of their faith and practice, his letter notes 'the frequent and manifest works of divine grace' among them.[8] In an 1898 encyclical letter *Caritatis Studium* to the Catholic Bishops of Scotland he noted that the separated brethren owe much to the ancient Catholic Church, yet he also praised Protestants in Scotland because 'they have always shown reverence and love for the Inspired Writings' and 'in revering the Sacred Scriptures, they are in agreement with the Catholic Church. Why then should this not be the starting point for a return to unity?'[9] He affirmed also that they 'sincerely love the name of Christ, and strive to ascertain His doctrine and to imitate His most holy example'.[10]

On the other hand, Leo looked upon *Protestantism* as a destructive movement. He understood that the proper principle of Protestant religion was 'private judgment', and when this 'wedge of rationalism' was inserted into the divine religion of Christianity, it provoked a multitude of denominations, the decay of true religion, and the disappearance of faith in the divine Saviour.[11]

But in pointing to the similarities, Leo, according to George Tavard, was proposing 'the bases of a Catholic ecumenism. Initially it consists in seeking points of contact between Protestants and Catholics, such a Scripture and love for Christ. Starting out from here, it will bring to light the fullness of tradition, which is implied in Scripture itself, and the fullness of revelation, implied in the love of Christ.' Tavard argues that Leo was 'the first Pope to take up ecumenism. He must be given credit for laying the bases of modern Catholic ecumenism.'[12]

Pope Pius XI (1923–39) also expressed concern for unity. In regard to Eastern Christians, in some ways he goes further than Leo XIII. In his encyclical *Rerum Orientalium* (1928), published the same year as *Mortalium Animos*, an official document admits, perhaps for the first time, that obstacles to reconciliation are not all on the other side.[13] Mutual ignorance and prejudices are involved.[14] To remove prejudice and misconception between East and West, Pius, in *Rerum Orientalium* (no.12), promotes Eastern studies in Catholic universities. His predecessor Benedict XV had already founded the Oriental Institute in Rome (in 1917), which was intended, from the beginning, to welcome Orthodox students as well as Catholic. Pius believed that the benefits of reconciliation between East and West would go two ways. The Catholic Church itself would benefit as well as the separated Eastern churches.[15] Pius XII (1939–58) took the same position in the encyclical *Orientales Omnes* (1945), maintaining that Catholics too are in need of perfect unity.[16]

Besides the Popes, during this period ecumenical concern was also raised by many others. Examples include:

Fr. Fernand–Etienne Portal (1855–1926). In his contacts with the Anglican Lord Halifax (1839–1934) Portal believed that Anglicans' reconciliation with Rome could take place as a corporate body, and not by their renouncing the Church of England. He believed that an examination of doctrinal divergences between Rome and Canterbury would reveal more theological agreement than many supposed.[17]

Fr. Paul of Graymore (1863–1940), an Anglican who became a Roman Catholic in 1909. In 1908, while still an Anglican, he helped institute a Week of Prayer for Christian Unity. After becoming a Catholic he redoubled his efforts and promoted the Church Unity Octave.[18] Previously, Leo XIII had already introduced the idea of prayer for Christian union, seeking rapprochement of the separated brethren.[19]

The *Malines Conversations* (1921–6) led by Cardinal Mercier, Archbishop of Malines in Belgium. Portal and Halifax approached Mercier to host discussions between Anglican and Catholic scholars. By the second meeting in 1923, the participants had received the cautious approval of Pope Pius XI and the Archbishop of Canterbury Randall Davidson. They discussed disputed dogmas, including papal authority.[20] An important participant in the *Malines Conversations* was Dom Lambert Beauduin (1873–1960), head of a newly established monastery at Amay, Belgium (1925). This monastery was created in response to a request by Pope Pius XI (letter *Equidem Verba*, 1924) who asked the Benedictine Order to designate certain monasteries as centers for seeking union between separate Eastern Christians (especially Russians) with the Church of Rome.[21]

Other Catholic pioneers from this period include Yves Congar, Paul Couturier and Josepf Lortz. These pioneers planted ecumenical seeds that have continued to bear fruit. At the time, however, the wall of separation was still very high, and time was needed before the new thinking on ecumenism could be received in the Church. Indeed some of the theologians who promoted ecumenism ran into significant trouble with Church authorities. Nonetheless their efforts helped the Church to grow toward the commitment to ecumenism that developed in Vatican II.[22]

The second period, 1948–1962: The creation of the World Council of Churches to the Second Vatican Council: Cautious recognition of the modern ecumenical movement

The key document representative of the view of the Holy See regarding the ecumenical movement during this period was the 1949 Instruction of the Holy Office, *Ecclesia Catholica. On the Ecumenical Movement,* which states:

> In consequence of the common prayers of the faithful through the grace of the Holy Spirit, there has grown constantly in the mind of many persons separated from the Catholic Church the desire for a return to unity on the part of all who believe in the Lord Christ. To the children of the Church this is surely a cause of true and holy joy in the Lord ....[23]

The Instruction asked bishops not to only to 'watch over this entire activity' but 'also prudently promote and direct it'.[24]

Here we find a cautious recognition of the modern ecumenical movement as being inspired by the Holy Spirit. The Instruction reflected the growth of the ecumenical movement, referring to 'mixed assemblies and conferences of Catholics with non-Catholics' which in recent times had been held in many places to promote union in the faith. It wanted bishops to promote, but also to control, the phenomena. Two significant developments during this period call for attention.

First, as early as 1949 Catholic theologians had some, even if small, impact on the World Council of Churches. According to the first WCC General Secretary, Willem Visser 't Hooft, who previously had contacts with Catholic theologians, his meeting with Catholic theologians at the Istina Center in Paris, in 1949, helped him prepare a draft which in turn helped the Central Committee meeting in Toronto, in 1950, to clarify the self-understanding of the WCC. The resulting Toronto Statement was critical to ecumenical relations because it affirmed that a church does not have to abandon its ecclesiology as a condition for belonging to the WCC.

To facilitate discussion with the Istina group he presented the subject in the form of theses, the first six describing 'What the World Council is not', and another six attempting to explain 'the assumptions underlying the World Council of Churches'.[25] Visser 't Hooft speaks of some of the results of this meeting. First, that the discussion had proved useful, and that this had encouraged him to submit the theses to the Central Committee of the World Council for discussion, revision and adoption. Then, he says:

> I added to the theses some ideas which emerged from the Istina meeting, including I believe, the formulation: 'The World Council exists in order to deal in a provisional way with an abnormal situation'.
>
> The paragraph on the positive consequences to be drawn from the concept of *vestigia ecclesiae* (one of his theses) too was strengthened in the light of the remarks made on this subject by Father (Yves) Congar and Father (Jean) Danielou.
>
> I added two new theses, one on the solidarity of the member churches and their obligation to refrain from actions which were incompatible with fraternal relations, and another on mutual spiritual assistance for the sake of the renewal of the life of the churches.
>
> At the end of the document I pointed out that the distinction between the conditions which had to be fulfilled so that the churches might enter into relations of conversation and cooperation in the World Council and those which had to be fulfilled to achieve full unity was fundamental. The World Council was an emergency measure and had only a provisional task.[26]

These insights are reflected in the 1950 Toronto statement.

A second important development during this period concerns the Catholic Church itself. This was the founding of the Catholic Conference for Ecumenical Questions (CCEQ), in 1951, by Johannes Willebrands and Frans Thÿssen, two priests from the Netherlands.[27] During 1952–63, the CCEQ met in different cities of Europe when invited by the local bishop. Though it was a Catholic body, others appreciated its significance. The WCC General Secretary Visser 't Hooft, in his memoirs, comments that in 1952 the CCEQ 'attracted very little attention, but … was to have far-reaching consequences for the ecumenical movement'.[28]

Two aspects of its impact can be mentioned here. First, from its beginning it made contact with the World Council of Churches. The themes discussed by the theologians 'were those predominating in the World Council of Churches, especially in its Faith and Order Commission'.[29] Visser 't Hooft indicated that although this body had no official status, it was of great advantage for the WCC to be in conversation with a responsible body of Roman Catholic ecumenists.[30] The CCEQ would study and make contributions to the major themes the WCC was working on, even for assemblies, such as Evanston and New Delhi. Thus for Evanston (1954) the CCEQ asked Yves Congar to draft a paper presenting the Roman Catholic conception of the main theme 'Christ the Hope of the World'. The revised version of this paper was given to Visser 't Hooft, who made it available to Assembly delegates, and commented on it, telling the Assembly that it was a substantial and valuable contribution to its discussion.[31]

A second important aspect of the CCEQ was that its participants contributed to the origin and initial organization of the Secretariat for Promoting Christian

Unity (SPCU) established by Pope John XXIII in 1960.[32] Pope John appointed Willebrands as the first Secretary of the SPCU.[33] In fact all of those who served as SPCU Secretaries from 1960–1999 had participated in the CCEQ.[34]

It is not an exaggeration to say that because of their experience with the unofficial CCEQ in the 1950s, they could bring to the fledgling SPCU a 'sense of *commitment* to and support for this new official ecumenical initiative in the Catholic Church, a rich *experience* of study and struggle precisely with ecumenical issues, and in some cases, especially in the years and decades after the Second Vatican Council, a *perspective* on the dramatic ecumenical transition that the Catholic Church had been going through, since they participated in ecumenism both before the *Decree on Ecumenism Unitatis Redintegratio* (1964) and after.'[35]

The third period, 1962–2007: Vatican II to the present: A deep commitment to the modern ecumenical movement

The *Decree on Ecumenism* of the Second Vatican Council states:

> Concern for restoring unity pertains to the whole Church, faithful and clergy alike. It extends to everyone, according to the potential of each, whether it be exercised in daily Christian living or in theological and historical studies. This very concern already reveals to some extent the bond of brotherhood existing among all Christians, and it leads toward that full and perfect unity which God lovingly desires.[36]

With the Second Vatican Council the Catholic Church in the final third of the twentieth century moved to fully embrace the modern ecumenical movement. In many ways there was continuity with the Catholic concern for Christian unity which had been developing over previous decades. But starting with the Council, and in the decades that followed, the ecumenical concern and responsibility of the Catholic Church, 'the whole church, faithful and clergy alike', becomes structured into the life of the Church. This is sustained by four sources of authority.

Sources of authority for Catholic commitment to ecumenism

First, it is the *mandate of the Second Vatican Council*, approved by the Pope, thus representing the highest authority of the Church. The Council's mandate is articulated especially in the *Decree on Ecumenism* (*Unitatis Redintegratio*), but is referred to in all of the other fifteen conciliar documents. In the *Decree on Ecumenism*, one sees the two-fold approach to promoting Christian unity. First, to bring an ecumenical spirit within the Catholic Church. It calls the Catholic Church, as an institution, to internal renewal 'which has notable ecumenical importance'[37] and it calls individual Catholics to newness of attitudes towards other Christians.[38] Secondly, Christian unity is promoted externally, in partnership with other Christians. The *Decree on Ecumenism* speaks of 'dialogue between competent experts from different Churches and Communities', and cooperation with them on different projects for the common good, and common prayer. Since Vatican II the Catholic Church has opened a series of bilateral dialogues, and has participated in the multilateral dialogues opened by Faith and Order.

Second, there are *authoritative pastoral directives* to implement the Council's teachings. Thus, in 1967, after significant consultation with Bishops' conferences, the SPCU published Part One of an Ecumenical Directory. It proposed ways of structuring the ecumenical movement in the life of the Church. It urged, among many other things, that ecumenical commissions be set up by National episcopal conferences, and in each diocese, or at least that one person be delegated by the bishop for ecumenical matters. These commissions would implement the decisions of Vatican II on ecumenical affairs, promote cooperation and discussion with other Christians, and foster ecumenical formation. A revised version of the Ecumenical Directory was published in 1993.

A *third authoritative source* structuring ecumenism into the life of the Catholic Church is *Canon Law*. In 1983 a revision at the 1917 Code of Canon Law was published, taking into account the teaching of Vatican II. It includes an important ecumenical aspect. Canon 755 para 1 and 2 read:

> Para 1: It is within the special competence of the entire college of bishops and of the Apostolic See to promote and direct the participation of Catholics in the ecumenical movement, whose purpose is the restoration of unity among all Christians, which the Church is bound by the will of Christ to promote.
>
> Para 2: It is likewise within the competence of bishops and, in accord with the norm of law, of conferences of bishops to promote the same unity and to issue practical norms for the needs and opportunities presented by diverse circumstances in light of the prescriptions of the supreme church authority.

A *fourth authoritative source* promoting ecumenism in the Catholic Church is the *papal magisterium*, most particularly Pope John Paul II's encyclical *Ut Unum Sint* (on Commitment to Ecumenism). *Ut Unum Sint* calls Catholics to ecumenical commitment. 'Christ calls all his disciples to unity' the Pope says. 'My earnest desire is to renew this call today, to propose it once more with determination ...'.[39] 'At the Second Vatican Council, the Catholic Church committed herself *irrevocably* to following the path of the ecumenical venture.'[40] 'Ecumenism ... *is not just some sort of "appendix"*... added to the Church's traditional activity. Rather, ecumenism is an organic part of her life and work and consequently must pervade all that she is and does....'[41] (Emphasis original).

On numerous occasions John Paul II spoke of ecumenism as one of his pastoral priorities, including when he spoke of the need for a new evangelization, a theme of which he spoke frequently.[42] Pope Benedict XVI, in his first address on 20 April 2005, the day after being elected Pope, described 'as his primary task the duty to work tirelessly to rebuild the full and visible unity of all Christ's followers'.[43]

The Catholic Church in ecumenical contact and dialogue, 1965–2007

To illustrate its ecumenical commitment one can point to some of the ecumenical relationships and/or international dialogues, both bilateral and multilateral, in which the Catholic Church has been engaged since the Second Vatican Council.

Relations with the World Council of Churches

While the Catholic Church is not a member of the World Council of Churches, it has been involved in an important partnership with the WCC. For example, in 1961 even before Vatican II began, the Holy See accepted the invitation to send five official Catholic observers to the New Delhi General Assembly, which was a very helpful, even crucial sign of new ecumenical commitment. In turn, this encouraged the WCC and various churches, Orthodox, Anglican and Protestant to send observers to the Second Vatican Council.

Since 1965 there has been a Joint Working Group (JWG) between the World Council and the Catholic Church, which has met very year, with membership renewed after each General Assembly of the WCC. The JWG has overseen a variety of contacts between the WCC and various offices of the Holy See, and has produced many useful studies on a broad range of significant topics.

Since 1966 the WCC, through its Faith and Order Commission and the Secretariat/Pontifical Council for Promoting Christian Unity, have together produced materials for the Week of Prayer for Christian Unity. Churches around the world use these materials.

Since 1968, Catholic theologians have participated as full voting members of the WCC's Commission on Faith and Order, contributing to some of its great studies, such as the 1982 statement *Baptism, Eucharist and Ministry (BEM).*

From 1968–1978 the WCC and Catholic Church jointly sponsored the experiment called SODEPAX, fostering cooperation on matters of Society, Development and Peace.

Concerning ecumenical formation, since the 1960s Catholic theologians have lectured at the WCC Ecumenical Institute at Bossey. For almost 25 years a Catholic theologian, supported financially by the Catholic Church, has served as faculty member of Bossey. A number of theologians have served in that post over the years.

Since 1984 a Catholic Sister, or lay woman, involved in mission work, has been a member of the WCC's CWME staff, with the Pontifical Council for Promoting Christian Unity arranging for her salary.

There has been contact and collaboration between offices of the Roman Curia and comparable offices in the WCC, for example between the Pontifical

Council for Interreligious Dialogue and the WCC unit working on Interreligious Dialogue.

Two Popes have visited the WCC, Paul VI in 1969, and John Paul II in 1984. WCC General Secretaries have visited the Holy See.

Roman Catholic delegated observers have taken part in WCC Central Committee meetings each year, and Catholic delegations have taken part in all General Assemblies since 1961. Over the years the WCC has also been invited to send representatives to a variety of events sponsored by the Holy See. A true partnership has developed between the Catholic Church and the WCC.

Relations with churches and Christian world communions

Since Vatican II, the Catholic Church has been involved in a number of bilateral dialogues, which have produced some important results. We mention here only the international dialogues.

The goal of dialogue, for the Catholic Church, is the restoration of unity, of full communion in a common understanding of the Apostolic faith, sacramental life, and hierarchically ordered ministry; a unity in diversity. In some of the dialogues the Catholic Church and its partners are able to say that full communion is the goal of the dialogue. With others, at least at present, the goals are expressed as better mutual understanding, overcoming prejudices. The direction is not 'a return' to the past, but a movement forward in dialogue, hoping to reconcile the separated Christian communions by resolving the issues that have kept them apart. But some of the issues over which Christians have divided in the past are issues for dialogue today – such as the nature of the church, sacraments, episcopacy, and the role of the Bishop of Rome.

International bilateral dialogues began in 1967. The first was with the Lutheran World Federation, and in the same year, with the World Methodist Council. In each new decade new dialogues have begun, and earlier ones have continued. In 1970 dialogue began with the Anglican Communion and with the World Alliance of Reformed Churches, and then with Classical Pentecostals in 1972, with the Coptic Orthodox Church in 1976, with some Evangelicals in 1977, and, also in 1977, with the Christian Church (Disciples of Christ). In 1980 dialogue with the Orthodox Church began, then in 1984 with the Baptist World Alliance, and in 1989 with the Malankara Orthodox churches of India. In 1993 a phase of dialogue began with the World Evangelical Fellowship (Alliance). In 1996 dialogue was undertaken with the Assyrian Church of the East, and in 1998, with the Mennonite World Conference. In 2000, informal conversations began with the Seventh Day Adventists. In 2003, dialogue began with the Old Catholic Churches of the Union of Utrecht. In 2004, dialogue began with the family of Oriental Orthodox Churches all together.

Some significant results of dialogue

What are some of the major results of contacts and dialogue? We will list a few significant developments, from the perspective of the Catholic Church.

(a) The good and intense relations and partnership with the World Council of Churches for more than forty years.
(b) The Joint Declaration between Pope Paul VI and Ecumenical Patriarch Athanagoras I on December 7, 1965, regretting and wishing 'to erase from the memory and midst of the Church the (mutual) sentences of excommunication' that were made in 1054, and to establish a dialogue in search of full communion.[44]
(c) The Common Declarations on Christology between Popes and Patriarchs of Oriental Orthodox Churches, speaking together of the Divine and Human nature of Christ (true God and true Man), that virtually resolved the clashes that took place in reaction to the Council of Chalcedon (451).[45]
(d) The development of the Faith and Order text *Baptism, Eucharist and Ministry* (1982), in which the churches achieved a great deal of convergence on these three key issues.
(e) The Common Declaration (in 1994) between Pope John Paul II and Patriarch Mar Dinkha, of the Assyrian Church of the East, that expressed common Christological views, virtually resolving clashes that took place in reaction to the Council of Ephesus (431).
(f) The *Joint Declaration on the Doctrine of Justification*, signed together by the Lutheran World Federation and the Catholic Church in 1999, which presented mutual consensus on basic aspects of the doctrine of justification. This has virtually resolved the conflicts on the central theological issue over which Martin Luther clashed with Church authorities in the sixteenth century.
(g) Official responses affirm Anglican and Catholic consensus on the theology of eucharist and ministry as expressed in the Final Report of the Anglican Roman Catholic International commission.
(h) The important convergences concerning the nature of the Church found in various dialogues. For example the second phase of dialogue with the World Alliance of Reformed Churches (WARC) discovered *convergence* between the Reformed notion of the Church as *Creatura Verbi* and the Catholic notion of the Church as *Sacramentum Gratiae*. The third phase has gone further saying that an understanding of the nature of the Church *requires* both of these perspectives. Also convergence is found on the notion of the Church as koinonia, or communion in many dialogues: with the Orthodox and Anglicans, but also with Pentecostals, Baptists, and Disciples of Christ.
(i) The need for a healing of memory has become prominent, as in our dialogues with the Mennonite World Conference and with the WARC. There are also many other expressions of this, for example the action of the Church of Scotland Assembly in 1986 stating that candidates for the ministry would not be required to subscribe to

> particular anti-Catholic, anti-papal statements in the Westminster Confession. This contributes greatly to a healing of memory.

Thus, the ecumenical movement is an organic part of the life of the Catholic Church.

Part two: contemporary and future challenges

In some ways, the major challenge Christians face today is the same challenge faced by the World Missionary Conference at Edinburgh 1910. On the one hand, the modern ecumenical movement since Edinburgh has resulted in some great achievements. Many Christians have a new and deep conviction that, though still separated from other Christians, they share with them a real, though imperfect, communion. At the same time, serious division and discord still exists, the discord, which, 'openly contradicts the will of Christ, provides a stumbling block to the world, and inflicts damage on the most holy cause of proclaiming the good news to every creature'.[46]

Christians continue to separate from one another. David Barrett's *World Christian Encyclopedia*, (1982) counted 20,800 distinct Christian denominations around the world. That Encyclopedia's second edition (2001) counts 33,820 distinct Christian denominations. While many of these have some ecumenical relationships, for example within councils of churches or in federations and alliances of confessional families, the degree of unity existing in such bodies is often partial at best. And Christian communities today continue to divide. We need to understand why this happens and what to do about it.

In this situation, of both achievement and continuous problems, we would like to suggest, from Edinburgh 1910's Commission Eight report 'Cooperation and the Promotion of Unity', some challenges for us today. The report's seventh chapter, 'General Review of Conclusions', draws conclusions after reflecting on 130 pages of data sent from the missionaries. We would mention just three points made there that are still challenges for us today:

1) There is a call for visible unity.

> … throughout the mission field there is an earnest and growing desire for closer fellowship and for the healing of the broken unity of the Church of Christ. In this manifest evidence of the gracious working of the Holy Spirit we must … rejoice. While we may differ from one another in our conception of what unity involves and requires, we agree in believing that our Lord intended that we should be one in a visible fellowship…[47]

2) There is a call for repentance.

> The great issues which confront us in the modern situation are the concern of the whole Church of Christ; and the spiritual resources of the whole Church will be required to deal with them. The solution of problems so complex and difficult,

> and so vitally related to the advancement of the Kingdom of Christ, can be attempted *only in a spirit of penitence and of prayer*. Penitence is due for the arrogance of the past and for the lack of sympathy and of insight by which *all of us have helped to create and perpetuate a situation that retards so seriously the advancement of Christ's Kingdom*. Most of all do we need to lament that we carry about with us so small a sense of the harm that is wrought by our divisions, and so little pain for our lack of charity.[48] (Emphasis mine).

3) There is a call for mutual respect (re: against proselytism).

> … while the right of a convert to pass from one Christian body to another as a result of an honest change of conviction must be recognized, any attempt to proselytism among the Christians of another denomination is *fatal to effective and harmonious work.*[49] (Emphasis mine)

And perhaps one of the great lessons and challenges to us today from Edinburgh 1910 and Commission Eight concerns *continuation*. Edinburgh proposed a 'continuation committee', and the rest is ecumenical history. It inaugurated a pilgrimage toward unity that has continued for almost a century. Today, as we come up against difficult issues on the way towards visible unity, we need the patience to continue, realizing that the ecumenical movement is a work of the Holy Spirit.

Perhaps an immediate challenge to us will come in 2017, the fifth centenary of the Reformation. How, from an ecumenical perspective, should we observe that historic event? The pilgrimage toward unity which we have undertaken for a century should influence the way we observe that coming significant event.

Through ecumenical dialogue we have learned how much common ground we share on matters of faith. For example, on the great issue of justification, Lutherans and Catholics have today found reconciliation. The *Joint Declaration on the Doctrine of Justification*, signed in 1999, affirms consensus on basic truths of the doctrine of justification. Many of the different perspectives of Lutherans and Catholics, if properly understood, are not inherently divisive, but represent insights from which both can learn. The World Methodist Council formally adhered to this agreement in 2006. We believe other world communions could as well.

From the sixteenth century, the 'Reformation' and the 'Counter' or Catholic Reformation have occupied different sides of a great divide. But today, because of our century-long ecumenical pilgrimage together, many of the lines of division have been overcome.

Hopefully in 2017, the fifth centenary of the Reformation, we will able to commemorate together, first of all, *not* the divisions of the past, but *rather* the ecumenical pilgrimage all of us have undertaken since Edinburgh 1910 and the results it has produced. What has emerged is an awareness that we share a real, if still imperfect, communion. Though our divisions have not been completely healed, we know each other as brothers and sisters in Christ. We share a common pilgrimage toward Christ, in response to his prayer for his disciples 'that they may all be one' (John 17:21).

Endnotes

[1] It has been documented, for example, by George H. Tavard, *Two Centuries of Ecumenism: The Search for Unity*, New York: Mentor–Omega Books, 1962; Gregory Baum, *That They May Be One: A Study of Papal Doctrine (Leo XIII–Pius XII)*, London: Bloomsbury Publishing, 1958; Gregory Baum, *The Catholic Quest for Christian Unity*, Glen Rock, NJ: Paulist Press, 1965; Paul M. Minus, Jr., *The Catholic Rediscovery of Protestantism: A History of Roman Catholic Ecumenical Pioneering*, New York: Paulist Press, 1976; Oliver Stratford Tomkins, 'The Roman Catholic Church and the Ecumenical Movement, 1910–1948', in *A History of the Ecumenical Movement 1517–1948*, ed. Ruth Rouse and Stephen Charles Neill, 2nd edn, Philadelphia: Westminster Press, 1967, pp. 675–93.
[2] Pope Pius XI, *Mortalium Animos,* Encyclical on Religious Unity, *Acta Apostolicae Sedis (AAS),* vol. XX, 1928.
[3] Gregory Baum, *The Catholic Quest,* p. 37.
[4] Pope Leo XIII, *Praeclara Gratulationis Publicae*, Encyclical on the Reunion of Christendom, *Acta Leonis XIII,* vol. XIV, 1894.
[5] Pope Leo XIII, *Orientalium Dignitas,* Apostolic letter on the Churches of the East, *Acta Leonis XIII,* vol. XIV, 1894.
[6] Pope Leo XIII, *Praeclara Gratulationis Publicae*.
[7] Baum, *The Catholic Quest*, p. 44.
[8] Pope Leo XIII, in Minus, *The Catholic Rediscovery*, p. 34 (and note 11 and 12, p. 45).
[9] Pope Leo XIII, *Caritatis Studium*, Encyclical on the Church in Scotland, *Acta Leonis XIII,* vol. XVIII, 1898.
[10] Pope Leo XIII, *Caritatis Studium*, no. 9.
[11] Baum, *The Catholic Quest*, p. 45.
[12] Tavard, *Two Centuries*, pp. 73–4.
[13] Baum, *The Catholic Quest*, p. 41.
[14] Pope Pius XI, *Rerum Orientalium,* Encyclical on the Promotion of Oriental Studies, *AAS,* vol. XX, 1928.
[15] Cf. Baum, *The Catholic Quest,* p.43.
[16] Pope Pius XII in Baum, *The Catholic Quest,* p. 43.
[17] Minus, *The Catholic Rediscovery*, pp. 36–7.
[18] Minus, *The Catholic Rediscovery*, pp. 38–41.
[19] Tavard, *Two Centuries*, pp. 69–70.
[20] Minus, *The Catholic Rediscovery*, p. 55.
[21] Minus, *The Catholic Rediscovery*, pp. 60–61.
[22] See further in Minus, *The Catholic Rediscovery*.
[23] *On the Ecumenical Movement. An Instruction of the Holy Office*, 20 December 1949.
[24] *On the Ecumenical Movement.*
[25] W. A. Visser 't Hooft, *The Genesis and Formation of the World Council of Churches,* Geneva: World Council of Churches, 1982, pp. 74–5.
[26] Visser 't Hooft, *The Genesis and Formation of the World Council of Churches*, p. 76
[27] See '1951–1963, Johannes Willebrands and the Catholic Conference for Ecumenical Questions', in *Information Service* 101 (1999), Vatican City: Pontifical Council for

Promoting Christian Unity, pp. 62–9; This is a special issue of *IS*, 'A Tribute to Johannes Cardinal Willebrands on the Occasion of his Ninetieth Birthday'.
[28] W.A. Visser 't Hooft, *Memoirs*, 2nd edn, Geneva: WCC Publications, 1987, p. 323.
[29] Thomas F. Stransky, 'The Foundation of the Secretariat for Promoting Christian Unity', in *Vatican II By Those Who Were There*, ed. Alberic Stacpoole, London: Geoffrey Chapman, 1986, p.63.
[30] Visser 't Hooft, *Memoirs*, p. 323.
[31] Visser 't Hooft, *Memoirs*, p. 323.
[32] Its name was changed in 1988 to the Pontifical Council for Promoting Christian Unity.
[33] '1951–1963, Johannes Willebrands', p. 67.
[34] '1951–1963, Johannes Willebrands', p. 68; namely Willebrands (1960–68), Jerome Hamer (1969–73), Charles Moeller (1973–82), Pierre Duprey (1983–99).
[35] '1951–1963, Johannes Willebrands', p. 66.
[36] Second Vatican Council, *Unitatis Redintegratio*, Decree on Ecumenism, no. 5.
[37] *Unitatis Redintegratio*, 6.
[38] *Unitatis Redintegratio*, 7.
[39] Pope John Paul II, *Ut Unum Sint*, Encyclical on Commitment to Ecumenism, no. 1.
[40] *Ut Unum Sint*, no. 3.
[41] *Ut Unum Sint*, no. 20.
[42] On the relation of unity and mission, see Geoffrey Wainwright's interesting comparison of John Mott and John Paul II in 'Ut Unum Sint, Ut Mundus Credat: Classical Ecumenism from John R. Mott to John Paul II' in *Agapé: Études en l'honneur de Mgr Pierre Dupre, M.Afr.*, ed. Jean–Marie Roger Tillard, Chambésy–Geneve: Centre Orthodoxe du Patriarcat Oecuménique, 2000, p. 35.
[43] Pope Benedict XVI, in *Information Service*, 118 (2005), p. 27.
[44] 'The Common Declaration of Pope Paul VI and Patrarch Athenagoras I, 7 December 1965', in *Vatican Council II: The Conciliar and Post Conciliar Documents*, ed. Austin Flannery, Dublin: Dominican Publications, 1981, pp. 471–3.
[45] Examples are the Common Declarations of Pope Paul VI and Coptic Orthodox Pope Shenouda I (1973), Pope John Paul II and Syrian Orthodox Patriarch Zakka I Iwas (1984), and Pope John Paul II and Armenian Catholicos Karekin (1995).
[46] *Unitatis Redintegratio*, 1.
[47] World Missionary Conference, 1910, *Cooperation and the Promotion of Unity*, Report of Commission VIII, Edinburgh/London: Oliphant, Anderson & Ferrier; New York/Chicago/Toronto: Fleming H. Revell, 1910, p. 131.
[48] *Cooperation and the Promotion of Unity*, p. 138.
[49] *Cooperation and the Promotion of Unity*, p. 140.

Cooperation and the Promotion of Unity: A Pentecostal Perspective

Cecil M. Robeck, Jr.

Edinburgh and the Pentecostal Movement in 1910

It should come as no surprise to learn that when missionaries from around the world met in Edinburgh, Scotland, for the great World Missionary Conference of 1910 they would overlook the Pentecostal Movement completely. The Pentecostal Movement was no more than a decade old at the time, and most Christian leaders thought it was hardly worth noticing. Pentecostals had only begun to enter fulltime missionary service for the first time in 1906.[1] When invitations to the Conference went out, there were very few signs that Pentecostals were here to stay, and there were even fewer signs that they would make any substantive contribution to world missions. If the organizers did notice this tiny movement, they would surely have had little good to say about the Movement. What is more, they would have found it impossible to believe recent reports that spell out the impact that this Movement has had over the past century.

The earliest Pentecostal missionaries were frequently an irritating lot. They were not in the mood to listen to anyone who did not share the experience they called 'baptism in the Holy Spirit'. They publicly criticized all those with whom they disagreed, including veteran missionaries. They did not see any need for advanced theological training, or courses in cross-cultural immersion, or even the need for language study. They ignored most modern missionary wisdom, claiming instead that the Holy Spirit was leading them in a different and powerful way, and that they did not rely upon mere human wisdom. They openly proselytized. Furthermore they made outlandish claims!

It should come as no surprise, then, that when they made their appearance on various mission fields, they were criticized and ridiculed. Their unwillingness to cooperate with veteran missionaries except on their own terms, and their swaggering claims that they needed nothing more than the power of the Holy Spirit to spread the Gospel among the 'heathen', left them vulnerable to intense criticism. It is not surprising to realize, then, that they should not even have been invited to participate in such a gathering. It would be safe to say that neither the fledgling Pentecostal Movement nor the Edinburgh Missionary Conference were ready for one another.

Visible unity for the sake of mission

The care and balance with which the authors of the Commission's report approached their subject is obvious. While the Commission acknowledged in an even-handed way the strengths and weaknesses made explicit by differences in perception and thought that arose from regional differences, denominational concerns, and longstanding theological disputes, it did not push its readers into making any specific choice. It made itself quite clear, however, that while no one should be asked to relinquish his or her convictions of truth a way had to be found to reconcile these differences with the 'essential unity' that already existed between Christians of different traditions.[2] It confronted its delegates and readers to take the challenge of visible Christian unity seriously, and to act upon it. Moreover it concluded with the passage of a resolution that put into place a Continuation Committee of the World Missionary Conference that would be multi-national and multi-denominational, with power to follow up on unresolved issues.[3]

Even a cursory examination of the work of Commission Eight reveals that the participants were overwhelmingly representative of historic mainline Protestant and Anglican churches and their missionaries. Furthermore, the delegates were dominantly representative of North American, British and European churches and missionary agencies with missionary input from Asia (primarily China and India) and Africa (primarily from Anglophone countries). Notably absent from the conversation were the ancient Roman Catholic Church and the Orthodox churches. Thus, neither Latin America, which was dominantly Catholic and had been excluded from discussion because it was viewed as a 'Christian' region, nor Russia, which was Orthodox, were represented or formally discussed,[4] although some delegates expressed concern that the absence of the Roman Catholic and Orthodox churches might be highly significant for the successful implementation of Conference findings.[5] Thus, the Conference was limited by the realities of the East/West split of the eleventh century. It was further limited by the division between Catholic and Protestant/Anglican churches at the time of the sixteenth-century Reformation. In fact, the absence of any substantial voice from either Latin America or Russia was simply reflective of these same realities and not an unwitting omission on the part of Conference planners.

In the same way, there is no reference to the challenges that Pentecostals were already beginning to pose on the mission field. Clearly, the World Missionary Conference of 1910 was also limited either by its lack of knowledge and experience of Pentecostals on the mission field, or by the unwillingness of its organizers to pursue missionaries across the obvious doctrinal differences and class distinctions that separated the churches present at the Conference from Pentecostal missionaries. As a result, the potential contribution of this newest Christian movement was completely ignored or overlooked.[6]

What this meant was that the call to visible Christian unity was limited to those groups that were present at the Conference. It also meant that as important as the World Missionary Conference of 1910 was, and it was very important, it was actually a conference of what would become the representatives of the Christian minority among today's Church. If the Roman Catholic Church, the Orthodox Churches, and Pentecostals, none of whom were present at the World Missionary Conference of 1910, represent the vast majority of Christians around the world today, then by any accounting the churches that were present at the Conference are very much to be reckoned among the minority churches today. To take it one step further, it has been noted repeatedly in recent years that it is the churches that were not present at the Conference where the most substantial growth is taking place, while many of those groups that were present at the Conference now appear to be in rapid decline.[7]

Pentecostal responses

Given the fact that the emergence of Pentecostalism was not particularly welcomed by the historic churches it should come as no surprise that Pentecostals did not turn to them for acceptance. Though they held much in common with historic churches, acceptance by these churches was not easily found. Like other Christians in 1910, Pentecostals believed in the inspiration and authority of Scripture, the Trinity, and the person and work of Jesus Christ in classical terms. Like most Protestants, they taught the doctrine of justification by faith, they administered baptism, and they observed the Lord's Supper. Like most Methodists and Wesleyan-Holiness Christians, they were concerned about personal integrity, holiness, and what some called the 'Higher Christian Life'. Like those who convened the World Missionary Conference of 1910 and like most Evangelicals, they were committed to evangelization and missionary work among non-Christian people. And they did not invent any new polities; they simply adopted those of their forebears, Episcopal, Congregational, and Presbyterian.

What separated them from most Protestants were two things. The first was their approach to the Holy Spirit. They insisted that people could be 'baptized in the Holy Spirit' at a time subsequent to their regeneration, that this baptism equipped them with power for witnessing (Acts 1:8), and that it would be accompanied by some form of evidence such as speaking in tongues (Acts 2:4). They also insisted that the Holy Spirit continues to distribute charisms upon whomever He chooses (1 Corinthians 12:8–10) regardless of age, gender, race, ethnicity, color, class, or level of education. That many Protestants linked baptism in the Spirit with conversion and baptism, rejected any notion of evidence, and embraced a cessationist theory regarding certain charisms made things challenging at best. These differences led Protestants to reject Pentecostal claims, and because these differences went to the core of

Pentecostal identity, they led Pentecostals to distance themselves from many Protestants. This debate ultimately led Aimee Semple McPherson to preach a sermon titled, 'Is Jesus Christ the Great "I Am", or Is He the Great "I Was"?' Sister Aimee appealed to the dominant Pentecostal claim that mainline pastors were preaching a Christ who 'used to be', a distant and powerless Christ who had ceased to deal with the problems of the contemporary world in any meaningful way, while Pentecostals preached a Christ who was 'the same yesterday, today, and forever' (Hebrews 13:8), a Christ who was deeply involved in the everyday lives of ordinary people, just as He had been when he walked the roads of Palestine.[8]

The second issue that separated Pentecostals from most Protestants, indeed, from most Christians at that time, had to do with the fact that while most Christians viewed the contemporary Church as standing in continuity with the Church of all previous centuries, most Pentecostals viewed themselves as standing in discontinuity with much of that history. Pentecostals embraced a Restorationist reading of church history and that reading gave a particular spin to their eschatological views. God raised up the Pentecostal Movement at the end of the age when it was incumbent upon the Church to evangelize the world. The time would soon come when a universal religion would emerge and it would become the tool of the forces of antichrist. As a result, Pentecostals turned their backs on many discussions regarding visible forms of Christian unity. They feared that such discussions would ultimately lead to disaster. And they focused their attention on bringing all non-Christians to salvation and all believers into the fullness of the Holy Spirit.

That being said, Pentecostals were neither consistent nor generally militant in their treatment of all such discussions. This is because the issue of unity had deep roots in the foundations of the Movement. While they tended to emphasize the spiritual reality of their unity in Christ, and thus the invisible character of Christian unity, some early Pentecostals lifted up the challenge of visible unity. Charles F. Parham was troubled by the confusion of denominationalism at the beginning of the century. He came to believe that God had anointed him to be 'an apostle of unity'. Unity did not come through the establishment of denominations, which he described as 'concentration camps', but through the work of God among those who were '...baptized by the Holy Ghost into one Body, the gloriously redeemed Church...'. He viewed himself as the true Elijah who would lead this redeemed Church into fruitful evangelization in such a way as to result in a single, restored, visible, Pentecostal Church.[9]

The African American pastor of the famous Azusa Street Mission, William J. Seymour, articulated his stand in his publication *The Apostolic Faith*. In every issue of this newspaper he included these words: 'The Apostolic Faith Movement stands for the restoration of the faith once delivered unto the saints – the old time religion, camp meetings, revivals, missions, street and prison work and Christian Unity everywhere.'[10]

A decade later, Richard G. Spurling, founder of the Christian Union, the group that ultimately became the Church of God (Cleveland, TN), lamented frequently over the 'strife and confusion' he witnessed in denominational diversity. 'Above all this din of strife and confusion', he wrote, 'I hear Christ praying in John 17:21, that they may all be one.' He knew that some would argue that the answer to Jesus' prayer had already come. It could be found in the spiritual unity of all Christians. It was something that was essentially invisible. But he argued, '... our reason says not so', 'Christ said the world might believe, but there is not a unity that the world can see. No, it is not the unity which Christ wanted by any means, but a confusion that He does not want.'[11]

However in spite of the concern for Christian unity that had been articulated from the early days of the Pentecostal Movement, Pentecostals were slow to reach beyond themselves in any form of cooperative venture, even when it came to missionary work among non-Christians.

John R. Mott, the man who had so successfully chaired the 1910 Edinburgh Conference also chaired the 1925 Convention of the Foreign Missionary Conference of North America. The 1925 Convention was as close to the 1910 Conference that any Pentecostal would get. His plenary address, titled 'New Forces Released by Cooperation', echoed the theme of Commission Eight.[12] Throughout his message, Mott recalled the lessons learned and the challenges raised by the 1910 Edinburgh Conference, noting that the arguments that had been offered 'in favor of cooperation' then, were 'now accentuated tenfold'.[13] He lamented the divisions that continued to plague the Church and he pointed out the inconsistency of these divisions with Jesus' prayer in John 17:21 – unity *for the sake of mission*. He also drew from the visions of unity set forth in Ephesians 2 and again in Ephesians 4. Mott tied his vision for unity to the spiritual dimension that was so important to him personally and to the Holiness stream of Methodism of which he was a part.

The 1910 Conference had made it clear that there were times when differences in doctrine and polity needed to be set aside or bracketed in order to make progress in cooperation and the promotion of unity in missionary matters.[14] In 1925, Mott reiterated this point. He repeatedly called for the delegates to lead the way in setting aside their denominational distinctions in order to bring about unity. 'If we can forget that we are Americans, Canadians, British, Chinese, Dutch, French, Germans, Indians, Japanese, Scandinavians', he began,

> ... or that we are Baptists, Congregationalists, Disciples, Episcopalians, Friends, Methodists, Presbyterians, Lutherans; in the work of making Christ known to people in Asia, Africa, Latin America, or Europe, or of North America, we have gone a great way toward proving to unbelievers who are moved by facts, that the religion of Jesus Christ is the great solvent of the racial and national alienations of

> the world, and, therefore, is the mightiest force operating among men. The present is the time of times to present this apologetic.[15]

Upon his return from that meeting to the Assemblies of God headquarters in Springfield, Missouri, John W. Welch, the General Superintendent of the Assemblies of God, gave a report that was ultimately published in the denomination's periodical, *The Pentecostal Evangel*. Instead of affirming Mott's message, he made it clear that he did not agree with Mott at all.[16] Welch was clearly opposed to what he termed the 'get together' idea. 'Satan's superman is on the way', he warned, 'the modern church along with the nations, unconscious of what they are doing are leading their efforts directly to the establishment of conditions for the antichrist to take supreme control. This "get-together" idea is nothing other than that.'[17] He criticized the Conference for expecting denominations to set aside what he saw as their doctrinal commitments. 'When they lay aside all of the Methodist doctrine, and the Baptist and Presbyterian, etc., so that there will be no friction', he protested, 'there is nothing left much but a name.'[18]

John W. Welch was eight years older than Mott. Originally from Seneca, New York, he had worked with the American Sunday School Union for a number of years and had been a minister with the Christian and Missionary Alliance. After having a Pentecostal experience, joined the Assemblies of God, and pastored several congregations that stood on the margins of the larger Church.[19] Indeed he represented many people who stood on the margins of society. This location on the margins contributed substantially to his feeling that at this missionary conference he was out of place. He described the nearly 5000 delegates who had gathered in Washington D.C. as 'intelligent-looking, well-dressed, and sufficient in themselves'. He judged them as being delighted with their 'reputation of doing a great work in the ends of the world'. He complained that they were '...spending other people's money very lavishly'. 'I saw a lot of missionaries', he murmured, but 'none of them seemed to show any evidence that they were willing to sacrifice.'[20] Rubbing shoulders with so many international players, most of whom were educated far beyond him and supported and clothed beyond his means, must have been a challenging experience. Welch did not fit in and as a result, he was unable to hear what Mott was actually saying.

Understanding Pentecostal approaches to unity

In the years immediately following 1910, Pentecostals had four concerns. The first of these was its core concern for evangelization and world mission. From its beginning, it was clearly a missionary movement. As the Movement expanded and divided, it kept this concern at the forefront of its thinking. As new congregations were established, the number of evangelists who crossed the nations and the number of missionaries who went abroad increased. Soon, further organization would become necessary in order to accomplish with greater efficiency what Pentecostal missionaries were already doing.

Its second concern turned on how Pentecostalism would understand itself. The oldest groups with a Pentecostal self-understanding emerged in the first decade of the twentieth century. They held much in common with the Holiness Movement, though it was clear to both movements that they were different. In point of fact, they shared the identical milieu that had produced John R. Mott, for whom the language of holiness, entire sanctification, and being baptized in the Holy Spirit was quite normal.[21] They would have differed largely on the nature of baptism in the Spirit and the role of speaking in tongues.

In 1911, a different version of Pentecostalism emerged with the teaching of William H. Durham. Instead of viewing sanctification in terms of a crisis experience, Durham viewed it as part of the 'finished work' that Jesus had accomplished on the cross. Thus, sanctification began at conversion and continued as a process throughout the Christian life.[22]

Again, in 1913, a much more radical teaching began to emerge in part of the Pentecostal Movement. In their quest to be truly 'apostolic', some Pentecostals argued that new converts should be baptized 'in the name of Jesus Christ' rather than invoking the traditional Trinitarian Formula. That was the way it had been done by the Apostles throughout the book of Acts (cf. 2:38), they contended. This concern ultimately led to further reflection on the nature of the Godhead, the Name of God, and the place of baptism in the Spirit within the Christian life. Thus, by 1913, three major streams of Pentecostalism had developed.[23]

The third concern that the young Pentecostal Movement addressed revolved around its institutional makeup. As the revival spread, new churches sprang up and new missionary fields were opened. It soon became apparent that some form of organization was necessary. This led to the clear identification of some denominations as Pentecostal (e.g. Church of God in Christ, Church of God (Cleveland, TN), and the International Pentecostal Holiness Church) that had existed before the Pentecostal revivals in Topeka, Kansas (1900) and in Los Angeles, California (1906). It also led to the formation of new denominations such as the Assemblies of God, the Pentecostal Assemblies of the World, the International Church of the Foursquare Gospel, and the United Pentecostal Church. Within a century Pentecostalism would divide over virtually every issue that had caused division in the rest of the church during its 1900 years of history, producing a multiplicity of denominations worldwide.[24]

This led to the fourth concern, that of unity. As early as 1911, the Norwegian Pentecostal, Thomas Ball Barratt issued 'An Urgent Call for Charity and Unity'. He proposed an international Pentecostal Union. While the form of unity he sought was not accepted immediately, the following year a Consultative International Pentecostal Council was formed in order to provide advice to the growing movement. This council met in Amsterdam in December 1912, and again in Sunderland, England in May 1913 and 1914.[25] World War I put an end to these efforts until 1921, when once again the Council met in Amsterdam. Meanwhile, the question of whether or not Pentecostals stood in unity with one another and what constituted the basis for this unity was being resolved in other ways.

While relationships between the first two streams of Pentecostals, with their different perspectives on the doctrine of sanctification, were strained, they were not completely antagonistic to one another. At times their rhetoric was strong, but in the end, they recognized each other as legitimately sisters and brothers. That was not true for the understanding that developed between these Pentecostals and those who identified themselves as 'Apostolic' or 'Oneness' Pentecostals. Questions simmered for several years while Pentecostal leaders in each of these camps tried to find ways to coexist in fellowship with one another. In 1916, these efforts came to an end. The fact that 'Apostolics' insisted on the invocation of the 'name of Jesus Christ' for a baptism to be legitimate while the others insisted on the Trinitarian Formula might have been managed. But when the Apostolics adopted a modalist position on the Trinity, the older groups, which maintained a classic Trinitarian position, rejected them as legitimate Pentecostal partners.

Once these basic issues had been studied, the majority of Pentecostals sought partnerships with one another even as they opened themselves up to potential partnerships with other Christians. They remained fully committed to the invisible unity that exists between all believers through the Holy Spirit. But they were suspicious about entering into more broadly based partnerships if they suspected that these partnerships might mean that they would be asked to give up any of their own autonomy or authority.

Despite occasional collaboration with Evangelicals, it remains difficult to make a convincing case that the Pentecostal movement participated in efforts for Christian unity. Pentecostals continue to take part in various regional, national, and international associations of Evangelicals, but they have great fear of moving beyond what might be considered the safe space in which they understand many of the factors that are at play. To date, the most significant place where broader ecumenical engagement has taken place is at the bilateral level. An international dialogue between the Catholic Church and certain Pentecostal churches and leaders has existed since 1972, co-founded by David du Plessis and Fr. Kilian McDonnell, OSB. During its thirty-five years of existence it has made some important findings.

Other dialogues have begun as well. During the 1960s a series of dialogues took place between the Pentecostals and various Reformed denominations in the Netherlands,[26] while during the late 1980s, the Pentecostal Movement in Finland was engaged in discussions with the Finnish Lutheran Church.[27] Since that time, a bilateral dialogue between the World Alliance of Reformed Churches and Pentecostals has nearly completed two rounds of discussions,[28] and a conversation has been initiated between the Institute for Ecumenical

Research, in Strasbourg, France, on behalf of the Lutheran World Federation and Pentecostals.[29]

Lessons from Commission Eight

There is no question but that both in the Church's desire to support missionary service and cooperative witness among non-Christians, and in its quest for visible unity during the twentieth century and beyond, the World Missionary Conference that convened in Edinburgh in 1910 was a watershed. It definitively noted the need for some form of visible unity as a compelling force or apology for the reconciling message of the Gospel. Furthermore it repeatedly called for a clear, compelling, and singular vision and voice to declare Christ to the nations. It contributed substantially to the formation of both the Commission on Faith and Order and the International Missionary Council.

But Edinburgh proved also to be a moment marked by the finitude of human imagination. Those who convened the Conference did not envision the Church in 2010 as looking anything like it does today. They assumed, perhaps rather naively, that they held all the seeds of the answer to Jesus' prayer in their hands. A few participants in the Commission Eight discussions, especially those from the Anglican community, wanted to engage Catholics and the Orthodox more fully. Coming as it did a decade later, the call of the Ecumenical Patriarch which was developed independently of the Conference, could be interpreted in some way as being fruit borne from his reflection on the subject subsequent to the Edinburgh Conference *and* at it should be viewed as coming at the prodding of the Holy Spirit.[30] Since that time, it has become equally clear that something was also happening among Roman Catholics at the time. It is doubtful that any of those who attended the Conference in 1910 anticipated the changes brought about by the Second Vatican Council, but its ecumenical fruit is now a well-established fact. Still, notably absent from the Edinburgh Conference, and from any deliberation that took place in conjunction with Commission Eight, was even a single representative of the Pentecostal Movement. What seems to be the case is that the Holy Spirit was at work within historic Protestantism, among the Orthodox, within the Catholic Church, and in the latest Christian movement – the Pentecostals.[31]

Those on Commission Eight who envisioned the future of world mission were fully aware of the limitations of comity agreements. Even as they encouraged further use of these treaties, they recognized that they were not ultimate solutions to real problems.[32] These limitations would only grow when groups such as the Pentecostals, who had not been part of the implementation process, simply ignored them and crossed lines without regard for those who were already present. They believed that there was no need to respect these agreements when they had not been part of putting them in place, and they sometimes viewed them as standing in the way of the will of the Holy Spirit.

The Commission was also very much aware of the fact that the so-called 'Sleeping Giants' of the world were beginning to stir and at one level they knew that the end of Western Colonialism was at hand. But while recognizing that in light of emerging events the time for action was limited, the commissioners were unable to think beyond the present form of 'Christendom' to which they had grown accustomed. Their vision was still highly dependent on the *status quo*. In far too many cases they had failed to educate indigenous clergy to adequate levels to take leadership positions. Indeed, in many cases the neglect was intentional. In some cases, they established schools only to certain levels of attainment to ensure this limitation. They seem to have expected to be in positions of authority even when the financial and political support from colonizing governments and the home offices that frequently oversaw their work began to dry up. As new nations under indigenous leadership began to emerge, many churches seemed to lose their will or ability to proclaim the Gospel through the historic means of evangelization, preaching, and teaching. They increasingly withdrew or they turned their funds toward other enterprises, projects associated with health, education, and general welfare. Even so, many churches have withdrawn in the name of cleaning up paternalism.

In a sense, what Edinburgh also demonstrates is that, in the words of the Scottish bard, Robert Burns, 'The best laid plans of mice and men often go astray.' The Pentecostal and related movements that began to emerge about the time of the Edinburgh Conference were not yet part of the Conference vision. And while their vision of the world and the challenges they would face began to increase, the vision of those who had been so committed to unity for the sake of mission seem to have lost the second part of that vision. For too many, perhaps, unity became an end in itself.[33] As a result, Pentecostals now frequently wonder why they need a relationship with historic churches. They wonder what these churches can bring to the table that they might find of value. Perhaps it can be said that the vision of Edinburgh for the unity of the Church was a large one, just as the missionary vision of contemporary Pentecostals could be said to be large. But in neither case has it been as large as the vision that God has for the Church. God's perspective calls for visionaries who can see beyond themselves. In addition to the many contributions of historic Protestant, Catholic, and Orthodox churches, that vision *must* include a role for the witness of Pentecostal, Charismatic, and related types of groups to the ongoing power of the Holy Spirit through signs, wonders, and witness. In the end, that may even call into question long held understandings of the marks of the Church.

Commission Eight called the churches to listen to the voices of the churches on the mission field. 'The Churches in the mission field may lead the way to unity', they observed, 'but they cannot move far and move safely without the co-operation of the Church at home.'[34] This possibility was undoubtedly raised in light of the progress that had been made, even by 1910, in the development of what would later be called the united and uniting churches. But more than that, it seems to have been a recognition that the key to the unity of the Church for the sake of mission might rest in the hands of Christians in the South. 'We are only beginning to understand that the beliefs and customs and capacities of the coloured races are in future to be regarded as worthy of attention', they noted.

> These coloured races have their own future, and mean to work out their own political, religious and social history; and they will no longer do so apart from, and with negligible influence on, the community of the civilized nations. We are beginning to see that the Church is again facing a mighty conflict, like that which arose when the living forces of the Gospel contended with the forces of the pagan world in the early centuries.[35]

Over the past half-century or so, we have seen the rise of indigenous Christianity around the world. It looks more like Pentecostalism than it does many of the historic churches. Even many of the historic churches, especially on the African continent, have become part of movements for renewal that are viewed as grounded in the Holy Spirit. The question is whether or not the historic churches have a vision for reaching beyond their time worn traditions, whether they have the ability to think dramatically new thoughts, and whether they are willing to learn from the newer, younger, vibrant, 'southern' churches. The question must also be raised in the other direction. Do many of these newer Pentecostal, charismatic, third wave, new apostolic, independent, and prosperity driven, 'southern' churches have the patience to learn from the long and valuable experience of the older churches. The option to dismiss one another is not now open. If the conditions that called for the World Missionary Conference were serious in 1910, they are infinitely more serious today. As John R. Mott summarized the issue in 1925,

> The missionary message will be wonderfully enriched through the most intimate cooperation of all true believers. In fact, is not genuine cooperation and unity absolutely essential to ensure the giving of full orbed expression to the message of the Church of Christ? Christ has not revealed himself solely or fully through any one nation, race, or communion. No part of [hu]mankind has a monopoly of His unsearchable riches. Every national and denominational tradition has a contribution to make which can enrich the whole Body of Christ. The help of all who bear His name and who have had experience of Him is necessary adequately to reveal His excellencies and to communicate His power.[36]

The call of Commission Eight for visionary people and the call that John R. Mott reiterated fifteen years later is still a call that is waiting to be answered. The question is, 'When are the churches going to heed the call and rely both on the Lord and on one another instead of on their own strength and wisdom?'

Endnotes

[1] Cecil M. Robeck, Jr., 'Pentecostalism and Mission: From Azusa Street to the Ends of the Earth', *Missiology: An International Review* 35, no. 1 (January 2007), pp. 75–92, especially pp. 81–3; See also, Allan Anderson, *Spreading Fires: The Missionary Nature of Early Pentecostalism*, London, UK: SCM Press, 2007.
[2] World Missionary Conference, 1910, *Cooperation and the Promotion of Unity*, Report of Commission VIII, Edinburgh & London: Oliphant, Anderson & Ferrier; New York, Chicago and Toronto: Fleming H. Revell, 1910, p. 134.
[3] For a useful summary of the week and the debate surrounding this resolution see, W. H. T. Gairdner, *'Edinburgh 1910': An Account and Interpretation of the World Missionary Conference*, Edinburgh & London: Oliphant, Anderson & Ferrier; New York, Chicago and Toronto: Fleming H. Revell, 1910, pp. 178–214.
[4] It had been agreed beforehand that missions to and among Roman Catholics would be excluded because the focus of the conference was to be on missions to 'non-Christians' and 'non-Christian countries'. See, Kenneth Scott Latourette, 'Ecumenical Bearings of he Missionary Movement and the International Missionary Conference', in Ruth Rouse and Stephen Charles Neill, eds., *A History of the Ecumenical Movement*, vol. 1, Geneva: WCC, 1993 [1954], p. 396.
[5] See the comments made in *Cooperation and the Promotion of Unity* by the Right Reverend Bishop Brandt (American Episcopal Church), pp. 198–9, the Right Reverend E. S. Talbot, Bishop of Southwark (Anglican), pp. 201–2, and pp. 233–4, and the Reverend R. Wardlaw Thompson (London Missionary Society), p. 216.
[6] Donald W. Dayton, 'Yet Another Layer of the Onion or Opening the Ecumenical Door to Let the Riffraff in', *The Ecumenical Review* 40 (1988), pp. 87–110.
[7] See, Philip Jenkins, *The Next Christendom: The Coming of Global Christianity*, New York, NY: Oxford University Press, 2002; Konrad Raiser, *To Be the Church: Challenges and Hopes for a New Millennium*, Geneva: Risk Books/WCC Publications, 1997, p. 101. Here Raiser writes 'We have noted earlier that the ecumenical scope of the WCC is limited because its member churches include only a minority – and probably a shrinking one – of world Christianity. This is the case because the Roman Catholic Church on the one hand and most evangelical and Pentecostal churches on the other have not so far seen the possibility of joining the WCC'.
[8] Aimee Semple McPherson, *Divine Healing Sermons*, privately published, ca. 1923, pp. 11–22.
[9] Charles F. Parham, *A Voice Crying in the Wilderness*, Baxter Springs, KS: Apostolic Faith Bible College, 1902, pp. 61–5.
[10] William J. Seymour, *The Apostolic Faith*, [Los Angeles, CA] 1.1, September 1906, p. 2.
[11] R. G. Spurling, *The Lost Link*, Turtletown, TN: Farner Church of God, 1920; reprint, 1971, p. 20.
[12] John R. Mott, 'New Forces Released by Cooperation', in Fennell P. Turner and Frank Knight Sanders, eds., *The Foreign Missions Convention at Washington 1925*, New York, NY: Foreign Missions Conference of North America, 1925; New York, NY: Fleming H. Revell Company, 1925, pp. 209–22.
[13] Mott, 'New Forces', p. 209.
[14] *Cooperation and the Promotion of Unity*, p. 50.
[15] Mott, 'New Forces', p. 218.
[16] J. W. Welch, 'The Present Great World Crisis', *The Pentecostal Evangel* 590 (March 28, 1925), pp. 2–3, pp. 8–9; Gary B. McGee, *The Gospel Shall Be Preached: A History*

and Theology of Assemblies of God Foreign Missions to 1959, Springfield, MO: Gospel Publishing House, 1986, 1: pp. 120–21.

[17] Welch, 'The Present Great World Crisis', p. 2.

[18] Welch, 'The Present Great World Crisis', p. 3.

[19] C. E. Jones, 'Welch, John William', in Stanley M. Burgess and Eduard M. van der Maas, eds., *The New International Dictionary of Pentecostal and Charismatic Movements*, revised and expanded ed., Grand Rapids, MI: Zondervan, 2002, p. 1187.

[20] Welch, 'The Present Great World Crisis', p. 9.

[21] Mott was reared within and remained loyal to the Holiness tradition within the Methodist Church. See, C. Howard Hopkins, *John R. Mott: 1865–1955: A Biography* (Grand Rapids, MI: William B. Eerdmans Publishing Company, 1979, pp. 9–46.

[22] William H. Durham, 'The Great Revival at Azusa Street Mission – How It Began and How It Ended', *Pentecostal Testimony* 1, no. 8 (ca. July/August 1911), p. 3.

[23] On the early years of this movement see James L. Tyson, *The Early Pentecostal Revival: History of Twentieth-Century Pentecostals and the Pentecostal Assemblies of the World 1901–30*, Hazelwood, MO: Word Aflame Press, 1992, pp. 169–76.

[24] Cecil M. Robeck Jr., 'Pentecostals and Ecumenism in a Pluralistic World', in Murray W. Dempster, Byron Klaus, and Douglas Peterson, eds., *The Globalization of Pentecostalism: A Religion Made to Travel*, Oxford, UK: Regnum Press, 1999, pp. 340–41.

[25] Cornelis van der Laan, 'The Proceedings of the Leaders' Meetings (1908-1911) and of the International Pentecostal Council (1912-1914)', *EPTA Bulletin* 6, no. 3 (1987): pp.76–96; see also *Pneuma: The Journal of the Society for Pentecostal Studies* 10 (1988): pp. 36–49.

[26] See, *De Kerk en de Pinkster Groepen*, S-Gravenhage, Netherlands: Boekencentrum N.V., 1960.

[27] 'The Official Discussions between the Evangelical Lutheran Church of Finland and the Pentecostal Movement of Finland 1987–1989', in *Dialogues with The Evangelical Free Church of Finland and the Finnish Pentecostal Movement,* Documents of the Evangelical Lutheran Church of Finland 2, Helsinki, Finland: Church Council for Foreign Affairs, Ecclesiastical Board, 1990, pp. 33–56.

[28] See 'Word and Spirit, Church and World: The Final Report of the International Dialogue between Representatives of the World Alliance of Reformed Churches and Some Classical Pentecostal Churches and Leaders', *Pneuma: The Journal of the Society for Pentecostal Studies* 23, no. 1 (Spring 2001), pp. 9–43.

[29] Ken Appold, 'Institute Begins Lutheran-Pentecostal Study Group', *Building Bridges: Newsletter of the Institute for Ecumenical Research 6* (Summer 2005), pp. 2–3.

[30] 'Unto the Churches of Christ Everywhere, Encyclical of the Ecumenical Patriarch, 1920', in Michael Kinnamon and Brian E. Cope, eds., *The Ecumenical Movement: An Anthology of Key Texts and Voices*, Grand Rapids, MI: William B. Eerdmans Publishing Company; Geneva, Switzerland: WCC Publications, 1997, pp. 11–14.

[31] Huibert van Beek, 'Pentecostals-Ecumenicals Dialogue', ed. André Droogers, Cornelis van der Laan, and Wout van Laar, *Fruitful in This Land: Pluralism, Dialogue and Healing in Migrant Pentecostalism*, Zoetermeer, Netherlands: Boekencentrum Publishing House, 2006, pp. 81–92.

[32] 'The delimitation of territory, as we have seen, can be carried out only under certain limitations, and cannot provide an ultimate solution of the problems of the mission field. But for the present, it has been found to work well, and might be considerably extended in many fields'. *Cooperation and the Promotion of Unity*, p. 139.

[33] In his address to the Convention at Washington, D.C. John R. Mott reminded his audience of precisely this concern. 'The unity or oneness among His followers down the

generations, for which Christ prayed, was not to be regarded as an end in itself, but rather as a means to ensure the great central end of Christian missions, namely, "that the world may believe".' Mott, 'New Forces', p. 217. This admonition bears repeating in 2010.

[34] *Cooperation and the Promotion of Unity*, p. 138.

[35] *Cooperation and the Promotion of Unity*, pp. 5–6.

[36] Mott, 'New Forces', p. 216.

CONCLUSION

THE COMMISSIONS AFTER A CENTURY

Kenneth R. Ross and David A. Kerr

'The World Missionary Conference held at Edinburgh in June, 1910, has been described', wrote William Richey Hogg, 'as a turning point, a lens, a landmark, and a watershed.'[1] Study of the Commissions which reported to the Conference, in the light of a subsequent century of experience, reveals why it proved to be such a decisive and historic moment. Edinburgh 1910, more than any other occasion, gave expression to a concentrated distillation of the wisdom and experience of the modern missionary movement. Despite that movement's many limitations, it proved effective in re-shaping the religious demography of the world, with many of its most cherished dreams being fulfilled. Hence the concerted attempt to enunciate its leading principles and to strengthen its methodology, represented by the Edinburgh Conference, is one which continues to repay careful study and reflection, both by those concerned with the missionary task today and by those who, from a variety of perspectives, seek to understand the dynamics at play in the drama of human history. Without substantial reference to the work of the Commissions, it is not possible to appreciate the inner genius or central concerns of the Conference. The research and reports of the eight Commissions gave the Conference its substance. Across the range of issues which confronted the missionary project, delegates were provided with substantial texts reflecting both extensive primary research and incisive analysis of its results. This level of engagement set a standard which remains challenging today.

Yet by and large, even where the Edinburgh 1910 Commission Reports have survived, they have received little attention with only the occasional specialist blowing off the dust to consult the contents. It is only as the approaching centenary has provoked a fresh engagement with these texts, that the enduring value of the work they represent has shone through. Of course, the framework of thought, the categories of analysis and the forms of language are evidently outdated. The post-modern and post-colonial critique offered by many of the contributors to this volume has exposed the essentially modern and Eurocentric mental landscape of Edinburgh 1910. The great changes of the twentieth century and the new perspectives that have been developed provide us with new eyes to see the work of the conference and its limitations are clearly revealed. Nonetheless, many of the themes which the Commissions address remain of great relevance, even in the vastly altered conditions of today. The authors of the essays in this volume have, time and again, been surprised by the freshness and relevance of the material found in the 1910 Reports. The successive chapters have shown that the issues raised by the Commission Reports continue to be highly relevant to anyone attempting to discern the meaning and direction of Christian mission.[2]

Commission One put the focus on the church's evangelistic mandate. While the prevailing definition of the 'non-Christian world' may no longer be applicable and while 'carrying' may no longer be the verb which is most readily applied to the gospel, a century of analysis of the missionary task has underlined the primary place of evangelism. To be sure, responsible evangelism today has a far greater sensitivity to the integrity of the faith and outlook of those to whom the Christian message is addressed. Yet it remains fundamental that the gospel is a message to be shared. Indeed, as Andrew Walls makes plain, it has been shared to such great effect that the demographic and cultural make-up of the Christian Church has been completely transformed in the course of a century.[3] A huge reversal of the position in 1910 has taken place as large parts of the 'Non-Christian World' have become predominantly Christian while the churches in the 'Christian World' of Western Europe have undergone an unprecedented recession. Indeed, no world missionary conference being held today would be able to escape the question of whether the West can be re-evangelized.

Where perhaps the most searching questions must be asked concerns the dualistic outlook that underlies the work of Commission One: the territorial duality of Christendom confronting the so-called 'non-Christian world;' the cultural duality of Christian civilization *versus* regions of the world that were judged to be valuable only insofar as they could be construed as preparations for Christianity; and a theological duality that replicated St Augustine's dialectic between the heavenly City of God (Jerusalem) and the earthly city of humankind (Babylon). These were dualities that the conference resolved in its robustly masculine confidence in the evolutionary superiority of Christianity and Christendom. The subsequent century, however, would reveal all too vividly the violent and destructive potential inherent in such a dualistic outlook on the world. The territorial understanding of Christian expansion was allied with an activist mentality and a military metaphor. This mood unfortunately was often expressed in the vocabulary of aggression, attack, conquest and crusade. Participants saw nothing incongruous in using the language of violent military campaigns to describe their missionary engagement and aspirations. The enthusiasm and drive which marked the Conference drew much more than it realized on the optimistic self-confidence of imperial expansion, technological advance and military power. The sobering reflections of Kosuke Koyama on the century of violence which followed the Conference call for a different paradigm and a different metaphor from one that is predicated on conquest of an enemy.[4] In light of his experience of the US atomic bombing of Hiroshima and Nagasaki, Koyama points to the imperative of reconstructing the missionary message on the premise of the political powerlessness of the Cross, and moral-spiritual powerfulness of non-violence.

Commission Two heralded the emergence of what William Temple would describe as 'the great new fact of our time' – a truly worldwide Christian Church.[5] It also laid the ground for growing awareness that 'missions' are not a semi-autonomous adjunct to the life of the church but that mission, at root, is an essential expression of the being of the church. It was this Commission which brought into focus a question which greatly exercised the conference. Was the most urgent task of mission to preach the Gospel to the millions of non-Christians who had yet to be evangelized – as John Mott tended to argue, at least at this point in his career; or was it – as Gustav Warneck expressed in a letter to the conference – to strengthen 'native congregations' for their role in the missionary task?[6] The first proposition was preferred by those for whom mission was functionally independent of ecclesiology, and accentuated methodological and quantitative issues pertaining to the transmission of the Christian message; the second proposition saw mission as essentially and inseparably related to the church, and therefore gave greater attention to the adaptation of the Christian message to churches that were already established in the global South. In the context of Edinburgh 1910 both approaches were steeped in the European colonialism of the day. However, the tension between these two propositions can be seen to anticipate the fragmentation of the Protestant missionary movement in the later twentieth century.

A century of experience has brought to light something that Edinburgh 1910 was unable to anticipate. The 'church in the mission field' has brought a fundamental epistemological challenge to the entire understanding of the Christian faith. To be fair, in the context of its time, Edinburgh 1910 was remarkably radical in recognising that the faith would find very different forms of expression as it was received in different cultural contexts. Nonetheless, when Teresa Okure reads the Report today she is forcibly struck by how much the Commissioners were in thrall to a colonial caricature of Africa as a savage, barbaric and uncultured continent.[7] A process of inculturation has seen the churches of Africa and elsewhere engage with the gospel in terms of their own culture. Still more influentially, churches of the global South have engaged with Christian faith from a social location of powerlessness and suffering. Liberation theology has read the Bible not as the revelation of transcendent truths that are then applied in action, but as the narrative of Israel's struggle for justice and truth, the story being told from the perspective of the poor and oppressed. By re-setting itself on the same course, mission no longer begins with a transcendent truth that demands action, but with Biblically-modelled action that discovers God's truth in the actual contexts of human communities. Far from being an *a priori* propositional truth, the missionary message discovers its truth in the contextual dialectic between action and theory. Assessing Edinburgh 1910 from a Korean perspective, Kyo Seong Ahn proposes a further step to move beyond either orthodoxy or orthopraxis to what he terms 'orthopathy' – proclaiming the truth not merely from the head, nor from the hand, but from the heart. Drawing on the Korean experience of suffering as *han,* Ahn suggests that the 'church in the mission field' has developed a pathos-oriented approach to mission.[8]

Commission Three, with its focus on the educational work of the missionary movement, demonstrated that mission is not concerned only with narrowly religious concerns but aims to shape the whole life of society. This remains pertinent today as progressive theologians in all traditions seek to articulate the holistic character of Christian mission. However, Ogbu Kalu argues that the missionary project too readily stopped at *training* and did not go further to provide an *education.*[9] Moreover, the massive concentration on Western-style school education meant that missionaries often had little awareness of the forces which proved to be decisive in shaping African Christianity, such as the indigenising movement, Ethiopianism and the rising tide of charismatic revivals. MP Joseph contends that missionary education was marked by an uncritical absolutism that provided legitimation for totalitarianism, and stimulated, by way of reaction, a fundamentalist and equally totalitarian approach in other religions.[10] Again the implicit alliance of the missionary movement with Western power caused it to be compromised in ways of which the Edinburgh 1910 delegates showed little awareness. The post-colonial age has seen a sharpening understanding of the power dynamics at play. Indigenization and contextualization have become key concerns of the missionary movement, largely under the influence of a new generation of mission scholars from the global South. This will remain a contested arena, however, so long as Western power seeks to entrench its dominance.

Commission Four provided what was perhaps the most strikingly original of all the Reports and the one which attracts the greatest interest today, described by Kenneth Cracknell as '... one of the great turning points in the Christian theology of religion'.[11]It is remarkable for the degree to which it scotches the idea that Western missionaries were iconoclasts bent on the eradication of existing religions in order to impose their own understanding of Christianity. On the contrary, the Report concludes by noting 'the practically universal testimony that the true attitude of the Christian missionary to the non-Christian religions should be one of true understanding and, as far as possible, of sympathy'.[12] Consensus formed around the notion of 'fulfilment', based on St Matthew's statement that Jesus came not to abolish but to fulfil the law (*Matt.*5:17). This was coupled with the application of social Darwinism to the history of religions, on the basis of which it was asserted that whatsoever is good in other religions is evolving in the direction of the Gospel. However, the fulfilment theology was heavily based on the contemporary missionary understanding of Hinduism. Guli Francis-Dehqani points out that Islam did not fit the mould. Developments in the twentieth century have underlined the inadequacy of fulfilment theology in regard to the inter-relation of Christianity and Islam. Nonetheless, the Report's combination of confidence in the Christian faith with sympathetic appreciation of other religious traditions provides a basis for sensitive witness and responsible dialogue. In his critique of the Report, the Sri Lankan Evangelical theologian, Vinoth Ramachandra, offers a concise analysis of recent theologies of religion, with particular reference to South Asian contributions. Drawing his own conclusions, he recommends the current emphasis on the history of the Spirit, while insisting on both a firm identification of the Spirit with Jesus Christ, and an open-ended faithfulness to Jesus that allows for deeper insights that the Spirit affords. Inter-religious dialogue thus becomes the way of responsible and responsive Gospel witness: *responsible* in that dialogue challenges Christians to tell the Gospel story in eschatological hope rather than depending on theories of religion; and *responsive* in that dialogue challenges Christians to engage beliefs that may be profoundly different from their own, with the confidence that 'we are not moving into a void, but that we go expecting to meet the God who has preceded us'.[13]

Commission Five took up the question of formation for missionary service. While today the missionaries may be very different from those envizaged by the 1910 Report and while their missionary assignments may differ markedly, yet many of the principles laid out in the Report are readily applicable today – as Anne-Marie Kool has demonstrated.[14] The 'home base' of mission has changed out of all recognition in the course of a century. Yet Commission Six's passionate insistence on the dependence of missionary initiative on the spiritual life of the church continues to have resonance with those nurturing a vision for mission today. Underlying both of these Commissions was the assumption that the initiative and the authority in Christianity's expansion would lie with the Western churches for generations to come. The new churches emerging in the mission fields were regarded as 'infant' churches and it was expected that they would require the care and direction of their 'parents' for many years to come. With the move in mid-century to a 'partnership' understanding of the relationship between the Western churches and the new churches which resulted from missionary work, it may be thought that this issue has been happily resolved. Yet, with Western dominance still well entrenched today at the economic and political level, it cannot be taken for granted that relations between churches will not still be infected with the condescension and paternalism which was so evident in 1910. There is need for clear recognition that initiative in Christian mission is not the exclusive prerogative of the West. Mission, as Samuel Escobar makes plain, is 'from everywhere to everyone'.[15] Indeed increasingly it is to the churches of the non-Western world that responsibility is falling. Any worthy celebration of the centenary of Edinburgh 1910 has to recognize that the Western sense of ownership of the missionary enterprise must give way to an appreciation of the worldwide church as the base for Christian mission.

The attention paid to the relationship between missions and government, an innovative move represented by the work of Commission Seven, opened up an area of analysis which has grown in importance as the years have passed. With a recognition today of the salience of religion in international relations and a new emphasis on the interaction of Government and faith-based organizations in development work, Commission Seven's work remains topical. But as Adolfo Ham from Cuba argues in his assessment of this commission, it perpetuated an essentially Constantinian model of church-state relations.[16] It relegated indigenous nationalist movements to the periphery of its vision, and failed to foresee the potential of Christianity as an agent of democratic change. With the rise of liberation theologies in the mid twentieth century, this Constantinian worldview was radically revised as Biblical hermeneutics, ecclesiology and mission engagement re-centered themselves in the existential realities of peoples who are marginalized from structures of power, and oppressed and impoverished by them. Today we are faced by the globalization of free-trade capitalism. As Tinyiko Maluleke from South Africa argues in his assessment of 'Missions and Governments,' this intensifies the need of a radical missiological engagement with inequalities of political power: 'the real mega question for mission today is how we conceive of Christian Mission in the light of globalization as driven by WTO, G7 nations and the rampant USA – which also happens to be Christian'.[17]

Perhaps Commission Eight has been the most often invoked of them all. Though its approach to the question of cooperation and unity was hedged around by limitations, particularly in regard to doctrinal and ecclesial questions, nonetheless a vision of the unity of the church broke surface at Edinburgh and remained a guiding light for many in the century which followed. Within its limitations, it succeeded in bringing together Protestants who were not accustomed to cooperating in any sphere of Christian activity, and lifted the eyes of Western churches to the emerging significance of churches and Christian communities outside Europe and North America. Samuel Kobia reminds us of the enormous challenges that this relationship has had to overcome in the continuing struggle for equal partnership and shared power.[18] It may nonetheless be said in favour of Edinburgh 1910 and the International Missionary Council that they succeeded in upholding an internationalist vision of ecumenism that contrasted the Eurocentric preoccupations of mainstream ecumenical movement of the first half of the twentieth century. It was not until 1961, when the IMC integrated with the WCC, that these two dimensions of ecumenism were reconciled.

Reconciliation came at a cost. The WCC's holistic approach to mission as inherently part of the vocation of the church was feared by others to mean the subordination of mission to the confessional and social agendas of liberal ecumenism. In 1974 the Lausanne Movement sought to redress this perceived imbalance by re-claiming Edinburgh 1910's priority of 'world evangelisation'. The tension in Edinburgh 1910 between the ecclesiological and para-church conceptions of mission – loosely identified with Gustav Warneck and John Mott respectively – ripped the Protestant missionary movement apart in the second half of the twentieth century. In his assessment of post-Edinburgh 1910 mission, however, Samuel Escobar argues that Lausanne 1974 should not be understood as a rejection of holistic mission, but as the beginning of a movement that curbed the excesses of especially North American evangelical missionaries who confused WCC ecumenism with Cold-War communism. The Lausanne movement thus served to broaden dialogue among evangelical mission groups, and to prepare the ground on which post-Cold War dialogue between evangelical and ecumenical concepts of mission has begun. Rosemary Dowsett offers frank and incisive criticism of both evangelical and ecumenical approaches and anticipates that entirely new initiatives in ecumenism are necessary to embrace the Pentecostal and charismatic movements.[19]

Addressing this same issue, Samuel Kobia points to the Global Christian Forum, to meet for the first time in Nairobi in late 2007, as evidence of a new approach to ecumenism that includes Orthodox, Roman Catholic, Anglican, Reformation Protestant, Pentecostal and Evangelical churches as well as Christian networks and para-church organizations.[20] The five contributors who focus on Commission VIII form, in a sense, a microcosm of the Global Christian Forum. Joining the discussion among Protestants are John Radano and Viorel Ionita who offer thoughtful and engaging analyses of, respectively, Roman Catholic and Orthodox approaches to questions of cooperation and unity since 1910. The extent of the differences is apparent but in each tradition there are points which invite conversation and stimulate the thirst for unity. No such discussion would be complete today without a Pentecostal voice being raised. Though unrecognized by Edinburgh 1910, the Pentecostal movement which was beginning around the same time has grown into perhaps the most dynamic missionary movement in the world today. Cecil Robeck, while recognising that the Pentecostal movement has proceeded independently of other Christian missionary traditions and in turn been eschewed by them, argues that there are significant elements in Pentecostalism which make for cooperation and hold the promise of greater unity. The five assessments of Commission Eight all recognize that missionary engagement invariably raises the question of unity. A century after Edinburgh, this remains a primary challenge for the churches.

In this and in many other important respects, Edinburgh 1910 raised questions which remain seminal for any serious discussion of church and mission today. In retrospect, after a century, the limitations of the Conference's conceptual landscape are plain to see. The systematic examination of the Commissions has demonstrated the extent to which Christian mission has been re-thought and re-cast in the space of one hundred years. Yet it has been equally apparent that the Commissions were grappling with profound questions of perennial importance to Christian mission.

The width of their primary research and the depth of their analysis will ensure that they continue to merit study for many years to come. Edinburgh 1910 did much to stimulate the development of the science of mission, often termed 'missiology', as a distinct academic discipline. In his analysis of the work of Commission Six, Samuel Escobar demonstrates how much the practice of mission is governed by the conceptual categories underlying it.[21] To the extent that the vision of Edinburgh 1910 rested on the worldview of modernity, it was destined to look ever more inadequate as the very different worldview of post-modernity took hold in the West and beyond. Nonetheless, despite their many mistakes and limitations, the delegates who gathered in Edinburgh in 1910 did something which proved to be truly historic. They caught a vision of something which did not then exist: a 'world church' with deep roots and vigorous expression widely apparent on every continent. The fact that this is a manifest reality today indicates that their vision has been realized: something to be celebrated.

Admittedly, the celebration must be tempered by recognition that, in many respects, the Edinburgh conference was over-heated and over-ambitious. It was carried away by the self-confidence of the Western powers at the height of the age of empire. Its slogans proved to be hollow. The world was not evangelized in that generation. The gospel was not carried to the entire non-Christian world. Within a few years of the Conference, the energies of the Western 'missionized' nations would be consumed by a war more destructive than any experienced hitherto and a great deal of the worldwide evangelistic effort would be put on hold. Nor was this to prove to be a temporary interruption. Edinburgh 1910 which understood itself to be on the brink of a great new surge of missionary advance was, in fact, the high point of the movement. Never again would the Western missionary movement occupy centre-stage in the way that it felt it did at Edinburgh. For most of the mission boards and societies represented, the twentieth century would be one of remorseless decline in their operations.

Nonetheless, the twentieth century has witnessed a vindication of a fundamental conviction of Edinburgh 1910: that the good news of Jesus Christ can take root in every culture across the world and produce fruit in church and society everywhere. The great drama of the coming century, in terms of church history, would be the growth of Christian faith in Asia, Africa, Oceania and Latin America. In some respects it has surpassed even the most sanguine expectations of 1910. The extraordinary growth of Christianity in Africa, for example, was not foreseen by any of the Edinburgh delegates. Nor had they anticipated how Latin America would become the theatre of a powerful renewal of Christian faith. This worldwide flourishing of the faith stands as a demonstration of the validity of their missionary vision that the gospel could be received and find expression in completely new contexts. Without the missionary impetus represented by Edinburgh 1910, the prospects for Christianity as a world religion might well be doubtful today, particularly as its long-time European homeland is proving inhospitable. Largely as a result of the seeds planted by missionary endeavour, vigorous and numerous expressions of Christian faith are to be found on all six continents today. Inasmuch as Edinburgh 1910 was the occasion on which the vision of the modern missionary movement found its most concentrated articulation, it calls for celebration as a vision fulfilled.

In institutional terms, the direct outcome of Edinburgh 1910 was the International Missionary Council, constituted in 1921.[22] For forty years it ran in parallel with the 'Faith and Order' and 'Life and Work' streams of ecumenical engagement which flowed together to form the World Council of Churches in 1948.[23] Though these movements had themselves been galvanized by Edinburgh 1910, it was not apparent to everyone that a single ecumenical organization should be formed. Debates on 'integration' raged for many years in the mid twentieth century before the IMC was finally integrated into the WCC in 1961.[24] Those with a strong mission agenda and/or a conservative theological position feared that the 'churchy' concerns of the World Council of Churches would lead to mission being sidelined, despite the formation of a Division of World Mission and Evangelism which was intended to carry forward the life and action of the International Missionary Council within the life of the WCC.

It has to be acknowledged that these tensions were never fully resolved. Indeed the formation of the Lausanne Committee for World Evangelization in 1974 proved to be a rallying point for those who feared that the WCC was failing to deliver an explicit and convincing commitment to evangelism.[25] Though in strictly institutional terms it is the World Council of Churches which is the heir of Edinburgh 1910, in terms of promoting the agenda of world evangelization the Lausanne movement might be seen as standing in direct continuity. Could the centenary provide an opportunity for both streams to re-engage with the Edinburgh 1910 heritage and with each other? As Andrew Walls suggests: 'both "ecumenical" and "evangelical" today have their roots in Edinburgh 1910. If each will go back to the pit whence both were dug, each may understand both themselves and the other better.'[26] Anne-Marie Kool suggests that there has been an amnesia in relation to the work represented by the 1910 Conference.[27] Retrieving the work of the Commissions and engaging afresh with their Reports in light of the context of the twenty-first century is an opportunity to recover shared memory and to work with it in new and creative ways.

The historical perspective opened up by the centenary also creates the possibility, for both traditions, to recognize how much they represent a mid-twentieth-century response to world affairs and theological trends. Major new movements lay down the challenge that it may be in new paradigms that Christian mission discovers the cutting edge it needs for the very different world of the twenty-first century. While there are traditions arising from the 1910 conference which deserve all due respect, it may be that their renewal will come from reconnecting fragments which have broken apart and making new connections among contemporary movements of Christian mission. A process taking its inspiration from the 1910 Conference but thoroughly contemporary and forward-looking would give an opportunity for connections to be made which will be fruitful in shaping Christian mission for a new century. Indeed the world of the early twenty-first century provides greater opportunity for listening attentively to one another within the world church than anything the Edinburgh delegates could have dreamed of in 1910. Now more than then we can realize the hope which James Barton expressed, in presenting the Report of Commission Six on 'The Home Base', when he concluded with these words: 'We can never understand our own Holy Scriptures until they are interpreted to us through the language of every nation under heaven. We can never know our Lord Jesus Christ in fullness and in the length and breadth of His love until He is revealed to the world in the redeemed life and character of men [*sic*] out of every race for which He died.'[28]

Endnotes

[1] William Richey Hogg, 'Edinburgh, 1910 – Ecumenical Keystone', *Religion in Life* 29 (1959–60), pp. 339–51, p. 339.
[2] See further David A. Kerr, 'Missiological Developments from Edinburgh 1910 to Today,' *Swedish Missiological Themes*, forthcoming 2008.
[3] Andrew F. Walls, pp.27ff.
[4] Kosuke Koyama, pp.41ff.
[5] William Temple, *The Church Looks Forward*, London: MacMillan & Co., 1944, pp. 2–3.
[6] World Missionary Conference, 1910, *Carrying the Gospel to all the Non-Christian World*, Report of Commission I, Edinburgh & London: Oliphant, Anderson & Ferrier; New York, Chicago and Toronto: Fleming H. Revell, 1910, pp. 434–6.
[7] Teresa Okure, pp.59ff.
[8] Kyo-Seong Ahn, pp.74ff.
[9] Ogbu Kalu, pp.91ff.
[10] M. P. Joseph, pp.105ff.
[11] Kenneth Cracknell, *Justice, Courtesy and Love: Theologians and Missionaries Encountering World Religions 1846-1914*, London: Epworth Press, 1995, p. xi.
[12] World Missionary Conference, 1910, *Report of Commission IV: The Missionary Message in Relation to Non-Christian Religions*, Edinburgh & London: Oliphant, Anderson & Ferrier; New York, Chicago and Toronto: Fleming H. Revell, 1910, p.267.
[13] Vinoth Ramachandra, pp.139ff.
[14] Anne Marie Kool, pp.158ff.
[15] Samuel Escobar, pp.185ff.
[16] Adolfo Ham, pp.217ff.
[17] Tinyiko Malulekepp.204ff.
[18] Samuel Kobia, pp.237ff.
[19] Rosemary Dowsett, pp.250ff.
[20] Samuel Kobia, pp.237ff. For the official communiqué of the Global Christian Forum, see 'Cooperation and Promotion of Unity: An Orthodox Perspective', 2007, http://www.towards2010.org.uk/papers.htm accessed 7 August 2007.
[21] Samuel Escobar, pp.185ff.
[22] See Tom Stransky, 'International Missionary Council', in Nicholas Lossky et al., eds., *Dictionary of the Ecumenical Movement*, Geneva and Grand Rapids: World Council of

Churches and Eerdmans, 1991, pp. 526–9; W. R. Hogg, *Ecumenical Foundations: A History of the IMC*, New York: Harper, 1952.

[23] See Gunther Gassmann, 'Faith and Order', in Lossky et al., *Dictionary of the Ecumenical Movement*, pp. 411–13; Paul Abrecht, 'Life and Work', in ibid., pp. 612–14.

[24] See Timothy Yates, *Christian Mission in the Twentieth Century*, Cambridge: Cambridge University Press, 1994, pp. 155–8.

[25] See Robert T. Coote, 'Lausanne Committee for World Evangelization', in Nicholas Lossky et al., eds., *Dictionary of the Ecumenical Movement*, Geneva and Grand Rapids: World Council of Churches and Eerdmans, 1991, pp. 594–5.

[26] Andrew F. Walls, *The Cross-Cultural Process in Christian History: Studies in the Transmission and Appropriation of Faith*, New York and Edinburgh: Orbis and T. & T. Clark, 2002, p. 62.

[27] Anne-Marie Kool, pp.158ff.

[28] World Missionary Conference, 1910, *The Home Base of Missions*, Report of Commission VI, Edinburgh & London: Oliphant, Anderson & Ferrier; New York, Chicago and Toronto: Fleming H. Revell, 1910, p. 296.

Bibliography

Records of the World Missionary Conference, Edinburgh 1910

World Missionary Conference, 1910. *Carrying the Gospel into all the Non-Christian World*. Report of Commission I. Edinburgh & London: Oliphant, Anderson & Ferrier; New York, Chicago and Toronto: Fleming H. Revell, 1910.

World Missionary Conference, 1910. *The Church in the Mission Field*. Report of Commission II. Edinburgh & London: Oliphant, Anderson & Ferrier; New York, Chicago and Toronto: Fleming H. Revell, 1910.

World Missionary Conference, 1910. *Education in Relation to the Christianisation of National Life*. Report of Commission III. Edinburgh & London: Oliphant, Anderson & Ferrier; New York, Chicago and Toronto: Fleming H. Revell, 1910.

World Missionary Conference, 1910. *The Missionary Message in Relation to Non-Christian Religions*. Report of Commission IV. Edinburgh & London: Oliphant, Anderson & Ferrier; New York, Chicago and Toronto: Fleming H. Revell, 1910.

World Missionary Conference, 1910. *The Training of Teachers: with Supplement*. Report of Commission V. Edinburgh & London: Oliphant, Anderson & Ferrier; New York, Chicago and Toronto: Fleming H. Revell, 1910.

World Missionary Conference, 1910. *The Home Base of Missions*. Report of Commission VI. Edinburgh & London: Oliphant, Anderson & Ferrier; New York, Chicago. and Toronto: Fleming H. Revell, 1910.

World Missionary Conference, 1910. *Missions and Governments*. Report of Commission VII. Edinburgh & London: Oliphant, Anderson & Ferrier; New York, Chicago and Toronto: Fleming H. Revell, 1910.

World Missionary Conference, 1910. *Cooperation and the Promotion of Unity*. Report of Commission VIII. Edinburgh & London: Oliphant, Anderson & Ferrier; New York, Chicago and Toronto: Fleming H. Revell, 1910.

World Missionary Conference, 1910. *The History and Records of the Conference*. Edinburgh & London: Oliphant, Anderson & Ferrier; New York, Chicago and Toronto: Fleming H. Revell, 1910.

Gairdner, W. H. Temple. *"Edinburgh 1910": An Account and Interpretation of the World Missionary Conference*. Edinburgh & London: Oliphant, Anderson & Ferrier; New York, Chicago and Toronto: Fleming H. Revell, 1910.

Gairdner, W. H. Temple and John Raleigh Mott. *Echoes from Edinburgh, 1910: an Account and Interpretation of the World Missionary Conference*. New York, Chicago [etc.]: Fleming H. Revell, 1910.

Secondary Sources

Abrecht, Paul. "Life and Work." In *Dictionary of the Ecumenical Movement*. ed. Nicholas Lossky, et al. Geneva: World Council of Churches; Grand Rapids: Eerdmans, 1991.

Amaladoss, Michael. "Mission in a Post-Modern World. A Call to be Counter-Cultural." *Mission Studies* 8, no. 1 & 2 (1996).

Amanze, James. "Some Large Ecumenical Organisations on the African Continent." In *Essays and Exercises in Ecumenism*. ed. Christo Lombard. Pietermaritzburg: Cluster Publications, 1999.

Anastasios of Androussa. "Orthodox Mission: Past, Present, Future." In *Your Will be Done: Orthodoxy in Mission*. ed. George Lemopoulos. Geneva: WCC Publications, 1989.

Anderson, Allan. *Spreading Fires: The Missionary Nature of Early Pentecostalism*. London. UK: SCM Press, 2007.

Aquinas, Thomas. *Summa Theologiae*. London: Eyre & Spottiswoode; New York: McGraw-Hill, 1975.

Ayandele, E. A. *The Missionary Impact on Modern Nigeria, 1842-1914*. London: Longmans, 1966.

Barclay, O. R. and R. Horn. *From Cambridge to the World*. Leicester: Intervarsity Press, 2002.

Barrett, David B. *Schism and Renewal in Africa: An Analysis of Six Thousand Contemporary Religious Movements*. London and Nairobi: Oxford University Press, 1968.

Barrett, David B., Todd M. Johnson, and Peter F. Crossing. "Table on the Status of Global Mission, Presence and Activities, AD 1800 – 2025." *International Bulletin of Missionary Research* 31. no. 1 (January 2007).

Barrett, David. *World Christian Encyclopaedia*. Oxford: Oxford University Press, 2001.

Bate, Stewart C. *Human Life is Cultural: Introducing Anthropology*. Pietermaritzburg: Cluster Publications, 2002.

Bauckham, Richard. *Bible and Mission: Christian Witness in a Postmodern World*. Grand Rapids: Baker Academic, 2003.

Bauerochse, Lothar. *Learning to Live Together: Interchurch Partnerships as Ecumenical Communities of Learning*. Geneva: WCC Publications, 2001.

Baum, Gregory, *The Catholic Quest for Christian Unity*. Glen Rock, NJ: Paulist Press, 1965.

Baum, Gregory, *That They May Be One: A Study of Papal Doctrine (Leo XIII-Pius XII)*. London: Bloomsbury Publishing, 1958.

Bebbington, David. *Evangelicalism in Modern Britain: A History from the 1730s to the 1980s*. London: Routledge, 1989.

Bediako, Kwame. *Christianity in Africa: The Renewal of a Non-Western Religion*. Edinburgh: Edinburgh University Press, 1995.

Bediako, Kwame. *Theology and Identity: The Impact of Culture upon Christian Thought in the Second Century and Modern Africa*. Oxford: Regnum Books, 1992.

Bentley-Taylor, David. *My Love Must Wait*. London: Intervarsity Press, 1975.

Bonino, Jose Míguez. "The Condition and Prospects of Christianity in Latin America." In *New Face of the Church in Latin America: Between Tradition and Change*. ed. Guillermo Cook. Maryknoll, NY: Orbis, 1994.

Bonk, Jonathan J. *The Theory and Practice of Missionary Identification 1860-1920*. Lewiston, NY: The Edwin Mellen Press, 1989.

Bosch, David J. *A Spirituality of the Road*. Pretoria: IMER, 1994.

Bosch, David J. "Theological Education in Missionary Perspective." *Missiology: An International Review* 10, no. 1 (1982).

Bosch, David. *Transforming Mission: Paradigm Shifts in Theology of Mission*. Maryknoll, NY: Orbis, 1991.

Boyd, A. J. *Christian Encounter*. Edinburgh: Saint Andrew Press, 1961.

Boyd, Robin H. S. *An Introduction to Indian Christian Theology*. Delhi: ITL, 1969.

Bria, Ion. *Liturgy after the Liturgy: Mission and Witness from an Orthodox Perspective*. Geneva: WCC Publications, 1996.

Broomhall, A. J. *Hudson Taylor and China's Open Century*. 7 vols. London: Hodder & Stoughton, 1981-1990.

Brown, Lindsay. *Shining Like Stars*. Nottingham: Intervarsity Press, 2006.

Bünker, Michael, and Martin Friedrich, eds. *Evangelising: Protestant Perspectives for the Churches in Europe*. Wien, Community of Protestant Churches in Europe, 2007.

Caldarola, Carlo. *Christianity: the Japanese Way*. Leiden: Brill, 1979.

Candler, W. A. "The peculiar appeal made to us by our Cuba Mission." *The Cuban Evangelist* (16 October 1907).

Carpenter, Joel A. "The Christian Scholar in an Age of Global Christianity." *Minds in the Making* 1. no. 2 (2004).

Carpenter, Joel A. and Wilbert R. Shenk. eds. *Earthen Vessels: American Evangelicals and Foreign Missions, 1880-1980*. Grand Rapids: Eerdmans, 1990.

Cepeda, Rafael. *José Martí: Perspectyivas Éticas de la Fe Cristiana*. S. José: DEI, 1991.

Chapman, Colin. "An Agenda for Dialogue." In *A Faithful Presence: Essays for Kenneth Cragg*. ed. David Thomas. London: Melisende, 2003.

Chau, Jonathan Tien-en. "The Nature of the Unity of the Local and Universal Church in Evangelism and Church Growth." In James Dixon Douglas. *Let the Earth Hear His Voice: Official Reference Volume, Papers and Responses*. Minneapolis: World Wide Publications, 1975.

Christian Community Within Human Community. Bangkok: East Asia Council of Churches, 1964.

Ciobotea, Daniel. *Confessing the Truth in Love: Orthodox Prespectives on Life, Mission and Unity*. Iasi: Trinitas, 2001.

Clapsis, Emmanuel. "The Eucharist as Missionary Event in a Suffering World." In *Your Will be Done: Orthodoxy in Mission*. ed. George Lemopoulos. Geneva: WCC Publications, 1989.

Clements, Keith. *Faith on the Frontier: A Life of J. H. Oldham*. Edinburgh: T. & T. Clark; Geneva: World Council of Churches, 1999.

Coote, Robert T. Coote. "Lausanne Committee for World Evangelization." In *Dictionary of the Ecumenical Movement*. ed. Nicholas Lossky, et al. Geneva: World Council of Churches; Grand Rapids: Eerdmans, 1991.

Cotterell, Peter. *Mission and Meaninglessness: The Good News in a World of Suffering and Disorder*. London: SPCK, 1990.

Cracknell, Kenneth. *Justice. Courtesy and Love: Theologians and Missionaries Encountering World Religions 1846-1914*. London: Epworth Press, 1995.

Cracknell, Kenneth. To Guli E. Francis-Dehqani. Personal emails, (18 - 19 November 1996).

Cragg, Kenneth. *The Call of the Minaret.* 2nd ed. London: SPCK, 1985.

Cragg, Kenneth. *The Christ and the Faiths*. London: SPCK, 1986.

Cragg, Kenneth. "Editor's Postscript. " In Hassan Dehqani-Tafti. *The Unfolding Design of my World: A Pilgrim in Exile.* Norwich: Canterbury Press, 2000.

Cuthbertson, Greg. "Protestant Paradigms of Mission. Review of *Transforming Mission: Paradigm Shifts in Theology of Mission* by David J. Bosch." *Journal of Theology for Southern Africa* 81 (1992).

D'Costa, Gavin. *Theology and Religious Pluralism.* Oxford: Blackwell, 1986.

Dalton, Eira M. *Fellow Workers With God.* Kottayam: CMS Press, 1966.

Daneel, Inus. *Quest for Belonging*. Gueru. Zimbabwe: Mambu, 1982.

Davie, Grace. *Europe – the Exceptional Case: Parameters of Faith in the Modern World*. London: Darton, Longman & Todd, 2002.

Davie, Grace. *Religion in Britain Since 1945: Believing without Belonging.* Oxford: Blackwell, 1995.

Dayton, Donald W. "Yet Another Layer of the Onion or Opening the Ecumenical Door to Let the Riffraff in." *The Ecumenical Review* 40 (1988).

De Certeau, Michel. *The Practice of Everyday Life.* Translated by Steven Rendall. Berkeley: University of California Press, 1984.

De Kerk en de Pinkster Groepen. S-Gravenhage, Netherlands: Boekencentrum N.V, 1960.

De las Casas, Bartolomé. *Obras Completas*. Vol. 2. Madrid: Alianza Editorial, 1990.

Declaration on the Relation of the Church to Non-Christian Religions. *Nostra Aetate. The Documents of Vatican II*. Vol. 2. London: Geoffrey Chapman, 1966.

Dehqani-Tafti, Hassan. & Guli Francis-Dehqani. "By Their Fruits Shall You Know Them." In *A Faithful Presence: Essays for Kenneth Cragg.* ed. David Thomas. London: Melisende, 2003.

Dehqani-Tafti, Hassan. *The Hard Awakening.* London: Triangle. SPCK, 1981.

Dharmaraj, Jacob S. *Colonialism and Christian Mission: Postcolonial Reflections.* Delhi: ISPCK, 1999.

Dickson, Kwesi and Paul Ellingworth. eds. *Biblical Revelation and African Beliefs*. Maryknoll, NY: Orbis, 1969.

Douglas, James Dixon. *Let the Earth Hear His Voice: Official Reference Volume. Papers and Responses*. Minneapolis: World Wide Publications, 1975.

Dube, Musa W. and Musimbi R. A. Kanyoro. eds. *Talitha Qum!: Theologies of African Women*. Pietermaritzburg: Cluster Publications, 2001.

Dube, Musa W., ed. *Other Ways of Reading: African Women and the Bible*. Atlanta, GA: Society of Biblical Literature; Geneva: WCC Publications, 2001.

Dube, Musa W. *Post-Colonial Feminist Interpretations of the Bible*. St. Louis, MO: Chalice, 2000.

Dussel, Enrique. *Beyond Philosophy: Ethics, History, Marxism and Liberation Theology.* New York: Ronman & Littlefield Publishers, 2003.

Engelsviken, Tormod. "Convergence or Divergence? The Relationship between Recent Ecumenical and Evangelical Mission Documents." *Swedish Missiological Themes* 89, no. 2 (2001).

Escobar, Samuel. "A Missiological Approach to Latin American Protestantism." *International Review of Mission* 87, no. 345 (April 1998).

Escobar, Samuel. "New Patterns for Interdependence in Mission." In *The Urban Face of Mission: Ministering the Gospel in a Diverse and Changing World.* ed. Manuel Ortiz and Susan S. Baker. Phillipsburg: Presbyterian and Reformed, 2002.

Exley, Richard and Helen. *The Missionary Myth: An Agnostic View of Contemporary Missionaries*. Guildford: Lutterworth Press, 1973.

Fidel y la Religión: Conversaciones con Frei Betto. La Habana: Oficina de Publicaciones del Consejo de Estado, 1985.

Fiorenza, Elizabeth Schüssler. In *Memory of Her: A Feminist Reconstruction of Christian Origins*. New York: Crossroad, 1983.

Flannery, Austin, ed. *Vatican Council II*. Vol. 2. *More Post Conciliar Documents*. New York: Costello, 1982.

Forward, Martin. "'Is Thine Heart Right, As My Heart is with Thy Heart?' A Christian Spiritual Theology for Dialogue with Muslims." In *A Faithful Presence: Essays for Kenneth Cragg.* ed. David Thomas. London: Melisende, 2003.

Francis-Dehqani, Guli. "Religious Feminism in an Age of Empire: CMS Women Missionaries in Iran, 1869-1934." Ph.D. thesis, University of Bristol, 1999.

Francis-Dehqani, Guli. *Religious Feminism in an Age of Empire: CMS Women Missionaries in Iran, 1869-1934.* Bristol: CCSRG University of Bristol, 2000.

Freire, Paulo. *Pedagogy of the Oppressed*. New York: Continuum, 1970.

Freston, Paul. “The Transnationalization of Brazilian Pentecostalism: The Universal Church of the Kingdom of God.” In *Between Babel and Pentecost: Transnational Pentecostalism in Africa and Latin America*. ed. André Corten and Ruth Marshall-Fratani. Bloomington: Indiana University Press, 2001.

Friesen, J. Stanley. *Missionary Responses to Tribal Religions at Edinburgh 1910*. New York: Peter Lang, 1996.

Gassmann, Gunther. “Faith and Order.” In *Dictionary of the Ecumenical Movement*. ed. Nicholas Lossky, et al. Geneva: World Council of Churches; Grand Rapids: Eerdmans, 1991.

Geoffrion, Timothy C. *The Spirit-Led Leader: Nine Leadership Practices and Soul Principles*. Herndon. Va.: Alban Institute, 2005.

George, Timothy. *Faithful Witness: The Life and Mission of William Carey*. Leicester: Intervarsity Press, 1991.

Gerloff, Roswith. “Introduction.” In *Mission Is Crossing Frontiers: Essays in Honour of Bongani Mazibuko*. ed. Roswith Gerloff. Pietermaritzburg: Cluster Publications, 2003.

Goheen, Michael W. *"As the Father Has Sent Me. I Am Sending You": J. E. Lesslie Newbigin's Missionary Ecclesiology*. Zoetermeer Netherlands: Boekencentrum, 2000.

Goldingay, John E. and Christopher J. H. Wright. “‘Yahweh our God Yahweh One’: The Old Testament and Religious Pluralism.” In *One God. One Lord in a World of Religious Pluralism*. ed. A. D. Clark and B. W. Winter. Cambridge: Tyndale House, 1991.

Guder, Darrell L. *The Continuing Conversion of the Church*. ed. Craig van Gelder. The Gospel and Our Culture Series. Grand Rapids. MI: Eerdmans, 2000.

Guder, Darrell L., ed. *Missional Church: A Vision for the Sending of the Church in North America*. ed. Craig van Gelder. The Gospel and Our Culture Series. Grand Rapids. MI: Eerdmans, 1998.

“Guidelines for Sharing. WCC World Consultation on Koinonia. El Escorial, 1987.” In *The Ecumenical Movement. An Anthology of Key Texts and Voices*. ed. Michael Kinnamon and Brian E. Cope. Grand Rapids. MI: Eerdmans; Geneva: WCC Publications, 1997.

Gunter, W. Stephen and Elaine Robinson, eds. *Considering the Great Commission: Evangelism and Mission in the Wesleyan Spirit.* Nashville: Abingdon Press, 2005.

Günther, Wolfgang. *Von Edinburgh Nach Mexico City: Die Ekklesiologischen Bemühungen Der Weltmissionskonferenzen (1910-1963)*. Stuttgart: Evang. Missionsverlag: 1970.

Haliburton, Gordon M. *The Prophet Harris.* London: Oxford University Press, 1973.

Hastings, Adrian. *The Church in Africa. 1450-1950*. Oxford: Clarendon Press, 1994.

Heisenberg, Werner. *Physics and Philosophy*. London: Allen and Unwin, 1958.

Heschel, Abraham Joshua. *The Sabbath.* New York: Farrer, Strauss and Giroux, 1951.

Hick, John and Paul Knitter, eds. *The Myth of Christian Uniqueness*. London: SCM, 1987.

Hiebert, Paul G. *Anthropological Reflection on Missiological Issues*. Grand Rapids: Baker Books, 1994.

Hobsbawn, Eric. *The Age of Extremes.* London: Michael Joseph, 1994.

Hoffet, Frederick. *El Imperialismo Protestante*. Buenos Aires: La Aurora, 1951.

Hoffet, Frederick. *L'Impérialisme Protestant*. Paris: Flammarion, 1948.

Hogg, W. R. *Ecumenical Foundations: A History of the International Missionary Council and its Nineteenth Century Background.* New York: Harper, 1952.

Hogg, W. Richey. "Edinburgh 1910 – Perspective 1980." *Occasional Bulletin of Missionary Research* 4, no. 4 (Oct./1980).

Hogg, William Richey. "Edinburgh, 1910 – Ecumenical Keystone." *Religion in Life* 29 (1959-60).

Hoke, Stephen T. and Jim Roché. "The Missionary Training Assessment: A Best Practices Case Study in Missionary Training." *Common Ground Journal* 4, no. 2 (2007).

Hoke, Stephen T. "Paradigm Shifts and Trends in Missions Training -- a Call to Servant-Teaching, a Ministry of Humility." *Evangelical Review of Theology* 23 (1999).

Hopkins, C. Howard. *John R. Mott 1865-1955: A Biography*. Geneva: WCC Publications; Grand Rapids: Eerdmans, 1979.

Hunt, Keith and Gladys. *For Christ and the University*. Downers Grove, Illinois: Intervarsity Press, 1991.

Huntington, Samuel. *The Clash of Civilizations and the Remaking of the World Order.* New York: Simon & Schuster, 1998.

Hutchison, William H. *Errand to the World: American Protestant Thought and Foreign Mission.* Chicago: The University of Chicago Press, 1987.

Ingleby, J. C. *Missionaries. Education and India: Issues in Protestant Missionary Education in the Long Nineteenth Century.* Delhi: ISPCK, 2000.

Jaffarian, Michael. "Are There More Non-Western Missionaries than Western Missionaries?" *International Bulletin of Missionary Research* 28, no. 3 (July 2004).

Jenkins, Phillip. *The Next Christendom: The Coming of Global Christianity.* Oxford: Oxford University Press, 2002.

John Paul II. *Post-Synodal Apostolic Exhortation of John Paul II. Ecclesia in Africa. on the Church in Africa and its Evangelising Mission Towards the Year 2000*. Vatican City: Editrice Vaticana, 1995.

Johnstone, Patrick and Jason Mandryk. *Operation World, 21st Century Edition.* Carlisle: Paternoster, 2001.

Jones, C. E. "Welch. John William." In *The New International Dictionary of Pentecostal and Charismatic Movements*. Revised and expanded edition. ed. Stanley M. Burgess and Eduard M. van der Maas. Grand Rapids. MI: Zondervan, 2002.

Jones, Rufus M. "Secular Civilization and the Christian Task." *Report of the Jerusalem Meeting of the International Missionary Council, 1928.* Vol. 1. London: Oxford University Press, 1928.

Joseph, M. P. "Suttee: A Critique from an Ethical Perspective." *The Sathri Journal* 1 (1993).

Kalu, Ogbu U. "Ethiopianism in African Christianity." In *African Christianity: An African Story*. ed. Ogbu U. Kalu. Pretoria: University of Pretoria Department of Church History, 2005.

Kanyoro, Musimbi R. A. and Nyambura J. Nyoroge, eds. *Groaning in Faith: African Women in the Household of God.* Nairobi: Acton Publishers, 1996.

Keshishian, Aram. *Orthodox Perspectives on Mission*. Oxford: Regnum, 1992.

Khodre, George. "The Church as the Privileged Witness of God." In *Martyria/ Mission: The Witness of the Orthodox Church Today*. ed. Ion Bria. Geneva: WCC Publications, 1980.

Kings, Graham. "Mission and the Meeting of Faiths: The Theologies of Max Warren and John V. Taylor" in *The Church Mission Society and World Christianity, 1799-1999.* ed. Kevin Ward & Brian Stanley. Grand Rapids & Cambridge: Eerdmans, 2000.

Kinnamon, Michael and Brian E. Cope, eds. *The Ecumenical Movement: An Anthology of Key Texts and Voices.* Geneva: WCC Publications; Grand Rapids: Eerdmans, 1997.

Kitamori, Kazo. *Theology of the Pain of God.* Richmond, Virginia: John Knox Press, 1965.

Knitter, Paul. *No Other Name?: A Critical Survey of Christian Attitudes Towards the World Religions.* Maryknoll, NY: Orbis, 1985.

Kraemer, Hendrik. *The Christian Message in a Non-Christian World.* London: The Edinburgh House Press, 1938.

Kritzinger, J. J. (Dons). "Training for Mission." *Missionalia* 30, no. 1 (2002).

Kubi, Kofi Appia and Sergio Torres. eds. *African Theology en Route*. Mayknoll. NY: Orbis, 1988.

Küng, Hans. "Christianity and World Religions: Dialogue with Islam." In *Toward a Universal Theology of Religion.* ed. Leonard Swidler. Maryknoll, NY: Orbis, 1987.

Lagerwerf, Leny. "African Women Doing Theology: Survey." *Exchange* 19, no. 1 (1990).

Lamb, Christopher. *The Call to Retrieval: Kenneth Cragg's Christian Vocation to Islam.* London: Grey Seal, 1997.

Latourette, Kenneth Scott. "Carnahan Lectures 1956." In *Desafio a los Protestantes*. Buenos Aires: La Aurora, 1957.

Latourette, Kenneth Scott. "Ecumenical Bearings of the Missionary Movement and the International Missionary Conference." In *A History of the*

Ecumenical Movement. Vol. 1. ed. Ruth Rouse and Stephen Charles Neill. Geneva: WCC Publications, 1993 [1954].

Latourette, Kenneth Scott. *A History of the Expansion of Christianity*. Vol. 7. Grand Rapids: Zondervan, 1971.

"Lausanne Covenant." In *Making Christ Known: Historic Mission Documents from the Lausanne Movement 1974-1989*. ed. John Stott. Grand Rapids: Eerdmans, 1996.

Lee, Yon Ok. *Daehanyesugyojangrohoe Yeojeondohoe Baeknyeonsa [Centennial History of the National Organisation of the Korean Presbyterian Women]*. Seoul: The Editorial Committee of the NOKPW, 1998.

Lemarquand, Grant. "A Bibliography of the Bible in Africa." In *The Bible in Africa: Transactions, Trajectories, and Trends*. ed. Gerald West & Musa W. Dube. Leiden: E. J. Brill, 2001.

Lemopoulos, George, ed. *Your Will be Done: Orthodoxy in Mission*. Geneva: WCC Publications, 1989.

Leo XIII. *Caritatis Studium*, Encyclical on the Church in Scotland. *Acta Leonis XIII*. Vol. 18. 1898.

Leo XIII. *Orientalium Dignitas,* Apostolic Letter on the Churches of the East. *Acta Leonis XIII*. Vol. XIV. 1894.

Leo XIII. In Paul M. Minus, Jr. *The Catholic Rediscovery of Protestantism: A History of Roman Catholic Ecumenical Pioneering*. New York: Paulist Press, 1976.

Leo XIII. *Praeclara Gratulationis Publicae*, Encyclical on the Reunion of Christendom. *Acta Leonis XIII*. Vol. 14. 1894.

Lowman, Pete. *The Day of His Power*. Leicester: Intervarsity Press, 1983.

Magesa, Laurenti. *African Religion: The Moral Traditions of Abundant Life*. Maryknoll, NY: Orbis, 1991.

Makubu, Paulus. *Who are the Independent Churches?*. Johannesburg: Skotville, 1988.

Maluleke, Tinyiko S., and Sarojini Nadar. "Alien Fraudsters in the White Academy: Agency in Gendered Colour." *Journal of Theology for Southern Africa* 120 (2004).

Maluleke, Tinyiko S. "Black and African Theologies in the New World Order: A Time to Drink from Our Own Wells." *Journal of Theology for Southern Africa* 96 (1996).

Maluleke, Tinyiko S. Half a Century of African Christian Theologies: Elements of the Emerging Agenda for the Twenty-First Century." *Journal of Theology for Southern Africa* 99 (1997).

Maluleke, Tinyiko S. "In Search of 'The True Character of African Christian Identity'. A Review of the Theology of Kwame Bediako." *Missionalia* 25, no. 2, (1997).

Maluleke, Tinyiko S. "The Quest for Muted Black Voices in History: Some Pertinent Issues in (South) African Mission Historiography." *Missionalia* 28, no. 1 (2000).

Maluleke, Tinyiko S. “Recent Developments in the Christian Theologies of Africa: Towards the Twenty-First Century.” *Journal of Constructive Theology* 2, no. 2 (1996).

Maluleke, Tinyiko S. “The Rediscovery of the Agency of Africans: An Emerging Paradigm of Post-cold War and Post-apartheid Black and African Theology.” *Journal of Theology for Southern Africa* 108 (2000).

Maluleke, Tinyiko S. “Review of *From Liberation to Reconstruction: African Christian Theology after the Cold War, From Liberation to Reconstruction: African Christian Theology after the Cold War,* by J. N. K. Mugambi.” *Missionalia* 34, no. 3 (1996).

Martey, Emmanuel. “African Women and Theology in Africa and the Third World.” *Voices from the Third World* 13, no. 2 (1990).

Mattam, J. “Evangelism in a Dialogical Context from a Third World Perspective.” *Mission Studies* 9, no. 2 (1992).

Mbiti, John. *African Religions and Philosophy*. London: Heinemann, 1969.

Mbiti, John. *Concepts of God in Africa*. London: SPCK, 1970.

Mbiti, John. In Kwame Bediako. *Christianity in Africa: The Renewal of a Non-Western Religion.* Edinburgh: Edinburgh University Press, 1995.

McClung, L. Grant. In Stephen T. Hoke. "Paradigm Shifts and Trends in Missions Training -- a Call to Servant-Teaching, a Ministry of Humility." *Evangelical Review of Theology* 23 (1999).

McGee, Gary B. *The Gospel Shall Be Preached: A History and Theology of Assemblies of God Foreign Missions to 1959*. Springfield, MO: Gospel Publishing House, 1986.

McPherson, Aimee Semple. *Divine Healing Sermons*. Privately published. ca, 1923.

Meeks, M. Douglas. *God the Economist.* Minneapolis: Fortress Press, 1989.

Millar, A. A. *Alexander Duff of India*. Edinburgh: Canongate Press, 1992.

Miller, J. Michael. *The Encyclicals of John Paul II*. Huntington, IN: Our Sunday Visitor, 1996.

Minus, Paul M., Jr. *The Catholic Rediscovery of Protestantism: A History of Roman Catholic Ecumenical Pioneering.* New York: Paulist Press, 1976.

“Mission and Evangelism in Unity Today.” In *“You are the Light of the World”: Statements on Mission by the World Council of Churches 1980-2005*. Geneva: WCC Publications, 2005.

“Mission and Evangelism: An Ecumenical Affirmation.” In *“You are the Light of the World”: Statements on Mission by the World Council of Churches 1980-2005*. Geneva: WCC Publications, 2005.

Moon, Steve C. “The Recent Korean Missionary Movement: A Record of Growth. and More Growth Needed.” *International Bulletin of Missionary Research* 27, no. 1 (Jan 2003).

Mott, John R. *Addresses and Papers of John R. Mott.* Vol. V. New York: Association Press, 1947.

Mott, John R. *The Decisive Hour of Christian Missions*. New York: Student Volunteer Movement for Foreign Missions, 1912.

Mott, John R. *The Evangelization of the World in This Generation*. London: Student Volunteer Missionary Union, 1900.

Mott, John R. "New Forces Released by Cooperation." In *The Foreign Missions Convention at Washington 1925*. ed. Fennell P. Turner and Frank Knight Sanders. New York: Foreign Missions Conference of North America; New York: Fleming H. Revell Company, 1925.

Mugambi, Jesse N. K. *From Liberation to Reconstruction: African Christian Theology after the Cold War*. Nairobi: East African Educational Publishers, 1995.

Mukenge, André Kabasele. "Les manifestations de l'identité chrétienne au Congo-Kinshasa: De l'affirmation aux derives." *Christian Identity, Forum Mission* 3 (2007).

Nandy, Ashis. "Introduction: Science as a Reason of State." In *Science, Hegemony and Violence*. ed. Ashis Nandy. New Delhi: OUP, 1990.

The Nature and Mission of the Church: A Stage on the Way to a Common Statement. "Faith and Order Paper, no. 198." Geneva: WCC Publications, 2005.

Newbigin, J. E. Lesslie. "Bringing Our Missionary Methods under the Word of God." *Occasional Bulletin from the Missionary Research Library* 13, no. 11 (1962).

Newbigin, J. E. Lesslie. "The Future of Missions and Missionaries." *Review and Expositor* 74, no. 2 (1977).

Newbigin, J. E. Lesslie. *The Gospel in a Pluralist Society*. Grand Rapids: Eerdmans, 1989.

Newbigin, J. E. Lesslie. *In* Michael W. Goheen. *"As the Father Has Sent Me. I Am Sending You": J. E. Lesslie Newbigin's Missionary Ecclesiology*. Zoetermeer, Netherlands: Boekencentrum, 2000.

Newbigin, J. E. Lesslie. *One Body. One Gospel. One World: The Christian Mission Today*. London and New York: International Missionary Council, 1958.

Newbigin, J. E. Lesslie. *The Open Secret: Sketches for a Missionary Theology*. London: SPCK, 1978.

Newbigin, J. E. Lesslie. *Unfinished Agenda: An Updated Autobiography*. Edinburgh: St. Andrew Press. 1993.

Niebuhr, Reinhold. *The Kingdom of God in America*. Chicago & New York: Willet. Clark & Co, 1937.

Nielsen, Jorgen. "Is there an Escape from the History of Christian-Muslim Relations?" in *A Faithful Presence: Essays for Kenneth Cragg*. ed. David Thomas. London: Melisende, 2003.

O'Donnell, Kelly. *Doing Member Care Well*. Pasadena: William Carey Library, 2002.

Oduyoye, Mercy A. and Musimbi R. A. Kanyoro. *Introducing African Women's Theology*. Sheffield: Academic Press, 2001.

Oduyoye, Mercy A. and Musimbi R. A. Kanyoro, eds. *Talitha Qumi: The Proceedings of the Convocation of African Women Theologians.* Ibadan: Daystar, 1990.

Oduyoye, Mercy A. and Musimbi R. A. Kanyoro, eds. *The Will to Arise: Women, Tradition and Church in Africa.* Maryknoll: Orbis, 1992.

Okure, Teresa. "Africa: A Refugee Camp Experience." In *Migrants and Refugees.* ed. Dietmar Mieth and Lisa Sowle Cahill. *Concilium* 1993/4. London: SCM Press; Maryknoll, NY: Orbis, 1993.

Okure, Teresa. "Africa: Globalisation and the Loss of Cultural Identity." In *Globalisation and Its Victims.* ed. Jon Sobrino and Felix Wilfred. *Concilium* 2001/5. London: SCM Press, 2001.

Okure, Teresa. "The Beatitudes in African Context: A Bible Study of Matt 3:3-22." Nairobi: Joint Africa Theological Conference, 14-18 August 2000.

Okure, Teresa. "The Bible in Africa: A Select Literary Survey." In *Yearbook of Contextual Theologies. MWI* Missio Aachen; Frankfurt and London: IKO-Verlag für kontextuelle Theologen, 2002.

Okure, Teresa. "Christian Identity and the Challenge of Authenticity: A View from Africa." *Christian Identity, Forum Mission* 3 (2007).

Okure, Teresa. "I will Open my Mouth in Parables: Matt 13:35. A Case for a Gospel Based Biblical Hermeneutics." *New Testament Studies* 46 (2000).

Okure, Teresa. "Invitation to African Women's Hermeneutical Concerns." In *Interpreting the New Testament in Africa.* ed. Mary Getui, Tinyiko Maluleke and Justin Ukpong. Nairobi: Acton Publishers, 2001.

Okure, Teresa. "Martyred Africa: Seed for a New Humanity." In *Martyrdom Reconsidered.* ed. Teresa Okure, Jon Sobrino and Felix Wilfred. Concilium 2003/1. London: SCM Press, 2003.

Oldham, J. H. "Reflections on Edinburgh 1910." *Religion in Life* 29 (1959-60).

Osthathios, Geevarghese Mar. "Mission and the Uniqueness of Jesus Christ." *Mission Studies* 12, no. 1 (1995).

Pagán, Luis Rivera. *Entre el Oro y la Fe.* San Juan: University of Puerto Rico, 1995.

Panikkar, Raimundo. "Christians And So-Called 'Non-Christians.'" In *What Asian Christians are Thinking.* ed. Douglas J. Elwood. Quezon City: New Day Publishers, 1976.

Parham, Charles F. *A Voice Crying in the Wilderness.* Baxter Springs, KS: Apostolic Faith Bible College, 1902.

Pate, Larry. *From Every People.* Monrovia: MARC, 1989.

Patelos, Constantin G., ed. *The Orthodox Church in the Ecumenical Movement: Documents and Statements 1902-1975.* Geneva: WCC Publications, 1978.

Patten, John. *These Remarkable Men.* London. Lutterworth Press, 1945.

Philip, T.V. *Edinburgh to Salvador: Twentieth Century Ecumenical Missiology.* Delhi: CSS & ISPCK, 1999.

Phiri, Isabel Apawo, et al., eds. *Her-Stories: Hidden Histories of Women of Faith in Africa.* Pietermaritzburg: Cluster 2002.

Pieris, Aloysius. "Towards an Asian Theology of Liberation." In *Asia's Struggle for Full Humanity.* ed. Virginia Fabella. New York: Orbis, 1980.

Pierson, Arthur T. *The Modern Mission Century Viewed as a Cycle of Divine Working*. London: James Nisbet & Co., 1901.

Piper, John F. *Robert E. Speer: Prophet of the American Church.* Louisville. KY: Geneva Press, 2000.

Pius XI. *Mortalium Animos,* Encyclical on Religious Unity. *Acta Apostolicae Sedis.* Vol. 20. 1928.

Pius XI. *Rerum Orientalium,* Encyclical on the Promotion of Oriental Studies. *Acta Apostolicae Sedis.* Vol. 20. 1928.

Pobee, John S. and B. von Wartenberg-Potter, eds. *New Eyes for Reading: Biblical and Theological Reflections by Women from the Third World.* Geneva: WCC Publications, 1986.

Pobee, John S. and Gabriel Ositelu II. *African Initiatives in Christianity: The Growth, Gifts and Diversities of African Churches: A Challenge to the Ecumenical Movement.* Geneva: WCC Publications, 1998.

Pollock, John. *Wilberforce* London: Lion, 1977.

Popescu, Dumitru. "Theology, Culture, Church: The Relation between Theology and Culture in Orthodoxy and in the Present Day Romanian Society." In *European Forum on Gospel and Culture(s).* ed. Viorel Ionita and Dietrich Werner. Hamburg: *EMW Informationen*, no. 113 (December 1996).

Pratt, Douglas. "Pluralism and Interreligious Engagement: The Contexts of Dialogue." In *A Faithful Presence: Essays for Kenneth Cragg.* ed. David Thomas. London: Melisende, 2003.

Priest, Robert J., Terry Dischinger, Steve Rasmussen, and C. M. Brown. "Researching the Short-Term Mission Movement." *Missiology: an International Review* 34, no. 4 (October 2006).

Race, Alan. *Christians and Religious Pluralism: Patterns in the Christian Theology of Religions.* London: SCM, 1983.

Rahner, Karl. *Theological Investigations*. Vol. 5. *Later Writings*. Translated by Karl-H. Kruger. London: Darton, Longman and Todd, 1966.

Raiser, Konrad. *To Be the Church: Challenges and Hopes for a New Millennium*. Geneva: Risk Books/WCC Publications, 1997.

Randall, Ian. and David Hilborn. *One Body in Christ: The History & Significance of the Evangelical Alliance*. Carlisle: Paternoster Publishing, 2001.

Rayan, Samuel. "Religions, Salvation, Mission." In *Christian Mission and Inter-Religious Dialogue*. ed. Paul Mojzes and Leonard Swidler. Lewiston, USA & Lampeter, UK: Edwin Mellor Press, 1990.

Richter, Julius. In

Robeck, Cecil M., Jr. "Pentecostals and Ecumenism in a Pluralistic World." In *The Globalization of Pentecostalism: A Religion Made to Travel*. ed. Murray W. Dempster. Byron Klaus. and Douglas Peterson. Oxford, UK: Regnum Press, 1999.

Robeck, Cecil M., Jr. “Pentecostalism and Mission: From Azusa Street to the Ends of the Earth.” *Missiology: An International Review* 35, no. 1 (January 2007).

Robert, Dana L. "From Missions to Mission to Beyond Mission: the Historiography of American Protestant Foreign Missions since World War II." *International Bulletin of Missionary Research* 18, no. 4 (1994).

Rodinson, Maxime. *Europe and the Mystique of Islam.* Seatle & London: University of Washington Press, 1991.

Rosales, Gaudencio, and C. G. Arevalo, eds. *For All the Peoples of Asia: Federation of Asian Bishops' Conferences. Documents from 1970-1991.* Quezon City, Philippines: Claretian; New York: Orbis, 1992.

Ross, Kenneth R. “The Centenary of Edinburgh 1910: Its Possibilities.” *International Bulletin of Missionary Research* 30, no. 4 (Oct./2006).

Rouse, Ruth. “William Carey's ‘Pleasing Dream’.” *International Review of Mission* 38 (April 1949).

Said, Edward. *Orientalism: Western Conceptions of the Orient.* London: Penguin, 1987; reprint 1995.

Salt, Henry. In Adrian Hastings. *The Church in Africa. 1450-1950*. Oxford: Clarendon Press, 1994.

Sanneh, Lamin. *Abolitionists Abroad: American Blacks and the Making of Modern West Africa.* Cambridge, MA: Harvard University Press, 1999.

Sarkar, Sumit. *Modern India: 1885-1947.* Delhi: Macmillan, 2000.

Sarpong, P. K. *Ghana in Retrospect: Some Aspects of Ghanaian Culture*. 2nd ed. Accra-Tema: Ghana Publishing Cooperation; Ostfildern, Germany: Schwabenverlag, 1974.

Sauca, Ioan, ed. *Orthodoxy and Cultures: Inter-Orthodox Consultation on Gospel and Cultures*. Geneva: WCC Publications, 1996.

Scherer, James A. *Gospel, Church and Kingdom: Comparative Studies in World Mission Theology*. Minneapolis: Augsburg, 1987.

Scherer, James A. "The Preparation of Missionaries in an Ecumenical Era." *Occasional Bulletin from the Missionary Research Library* 15, no. 2 (1964).

Schoen, Ulrich. “Dialogue.” In *Dictionary of Mission: Theology, History, Perspectives*. ed. Karl Műller, et al. Maryknoll, NY: Orbis, 1997.

Senior, Donald, and Carroll Stuhlmueller. *The Biblical Foundations for Mission.* London: SCM, 1983.

Seymour, William J. *The Apostolic Faith* 1, no. 1 (September 1906).

Sharpe, Eric J. *Not to Destroy but to Fulfil: The Contribution of J.N. Farquhar to Protestant Missionary Thought in India before 1914*. Uppsala: Swedish Institute of Missionary Research, 1965.

Shenk, Wilbert R. "Training Missiologists for Western Culture." In *Changing Frontiers of Mission. American Society of Missiology Series.* no. 28. Maryknoll, NY: Orbis, 1999.

Slessor, Mary. “Letter from Miss Slessor.” *The Missionary Record of the United Free Church of Scotland* 11 (1911).

Snyder, Howard. *Signs of the Spirit*. Grand Rapids: Baker, 1999.

Spurling, R. G. *The Lost Link*. Turtletown, TN: Farner Church of God, 1920; reprint, 1971.

Stanley, Brian. "Church, State, and the Hierarchy of 'Civilization': The Making of the 'Missions and Governments' Report at the World Missionary Conference, Edinburgh 1910." In *The Imperial Horizons of British Protestant Missions, 1880-1914*. ed. Andrew Porter. Grand Rapids: Eerdmans, 2003.

Steer, Roger. *J. Hudson Taylor: A Man in Christ*. Singapore: OMF, 1990.

Stransky, Thomas F. "The Foundation of the Secretariat for Promoting Christian Unity." In *Vatican II, By Those Who Were There*. ed. Alberic Stacpoole. London: Geoffrey Chapman, 1986.

Stransky, Tom. "International Missionary Council." In *Dictionary of the Ecumenical Movement*. ed. Nicholas Lossky, et al. Geneva: World Council of Churches; Grand Rapids: Eerdmans, 1991.

John Stott ed. *Making Christ Known: Historic Mission Documents from the Lausanne Movement 1974-1989*. Grand Rapids: Eerdmans, 1996.

Suh, David Kwang-sun. *The Korean Minjung in Christ*. Singapore: Christian Conference of Asia, 1991.

Talbot, E. S. In World Missionary Conference, 1910. *Cooperation and the Promotion of Unity*. Report of Commission VIII. Edinburgh & London: Oliphant, Anderson & Ferrier; New York, Chicago and Toronto: Fleming H. Revell, 1910.

Tavard, George H. *Two Centuries of Ecumenism. The Search for Unity*. New York: Mentor-Omega Books, 1962.

Taylor, J. Hudson. "Anniversary Meetings at the Conference Hall, Mildmay Park, 30 May 1889." *China's Millions* (July 1889).

Taylor, William D. *Global Missiology for the 21st Century: The Iguassu Dialogue*. Grand Rapids, MI: Baker Academic, 2000.

Taylor, William D., ed. *Internationalizing Missionary Training: A Global Perspective*. Exeter: Paternoster Press; Grand Rapids: Baker Book House, 1991.

Taylor, William D. ed. *Too Valuable to Lose: Exploring the Causes and Cures of Missionary Attrition*. Pasadena: William Carey, 1997.

Temple, William. *The Church Looks Forward*. London: MacMillan & Co, 1944.

Thomas, M. M. "The Absoluteness of Jesus Christ and Christ-Centred Syncretism." *Ecumenical Review* 37 (October 1985).

Thomas, M. M. *The Christian Response to the Asian Revolution*. London: SCM Press, 1966.

Thomkins, Oliver Stratford. "The Roman Catholic Church and the Ecumenical Movement, 1910-1948."□ In *A History of the Ecumenical Movement 1517-1948*. 2nd edition. ed. Ruth Rouse and Stephen Charles Neill. Philadelphia: Westminster Press, 1967.

Thorogood, Bernard, ed. *Gales of Change: Responding to a Shifting Missionary Context*. Geneva: WCC Publications, 1994.

Tillich, Paul. *Systematic Theology*. Vol. I. London: Nisbet, 1953.

Tisdall, William St. Clair. *Christianity and Other Faiths*. London: SPCK, 1912.
Tisdall, William St. Clair. *The Religion of the Crescent*. London: SPCK, 1910.
Tisdall, William St. Clair. *The Sources of Islam: A Persian Treatise*. Translated & abridged by William Muir. Edinburgh: T & T Clark 1901.
Turner, Harold W. "Historical Support for Pluralism? The 'Copernican Revolution' Revisited." *Mission Studies* 8, no. 1 (1991).
Tweedale, Marquis of. In J. C. Ingleby. *Missionaries. Education and India: Issues in Protestant Missionary Education in the Long Nineteenth Century*. Delhi: ISPCK, 2000.
The Two-Party System and the Missionary Enterprise." In *Reforming the Center: American Protestantism, 1900 to the Present*. ed. Douglas Jacobsen and William Vance Trollinger Jr. Grand Rapids: Eerdmans, 1998.
Tyson, James L. *The Early Pentecostal Revival: History of Twentieth-Century Pentecostals and the Pentecostal Assemblies of the World 1901-30*. Hazelwood, MO: Word Aflame Press, 1992.
"Unto the Churches of Christ Everywhere. Encyclical of the Ecumenical Patriarch, 1920." In *The Ecumenical Movement: An Anthology of Key Texts and Voices*. ed. Michael Kinnamon and Brian E. Cope. Grand Rapids: Eerdmans; Geneva: WCC Publications, 1997.
Van Beek, Huibert. "Pentecostals-Ecumenicals Dialogue." In *Fruitful in This Land: Pluralism. Dialogue and Healing in Migrant Pentecostalism*. ed. André Droogers, Cornelis van der Laan and Wout van Laar. Zoetermeer, Netherlands: Boekencentrum Publishing House, 2006.
Van der Laan, Cornelis. "The Proceedings of the Leaders' Meetings (1908-1911) and of the International Pentecostal Council (1912-1914)." *EPTA Bulletin* 6, no. 3 (1987).
Visser't Hooft, W. A. *The Genesis and Formation of the World Council of Churches*. Geneva: World Council of Churches, 1982.
Visser't Hooft, W. A. *Memoirs*. 2nd ed. Geneva: WCC Publications, 1987.
Wainwright, Geoffrey. "Ut Unum Sint, Ut Mundus Credat: Classical Ecumenism from John R. Mott to John Paul II." In *Agapé: Études en l'honneur de Mgr Pierre Dupre, M.Afr.* ed. Jean–Marie Roger Tillard. Chambésy–Geneve: Centre Orthodoxe du Patriarcat Oecuménique, 2000.
Walls, Andrew F. *The Cross-Cultural Process in Christian History: Studies in the Transmission and Appropriation of Faith*. Maryknoll, NY: Orbis; Edinburgh: T. & T. Clark, 2002.
Walls, Andrew F. "Mission and Migration: the Diaspora in Christian History." *Journal of African Christian Thought* 5, no. 2 (2002).
Walls, Andrew F. *The Missionary Movement in Christian History: Studies in the Transmission of Faith*. Maryknoll, NY: Orbis, 1996.
Welbourne, E. and B. M. Ogot. *A Place to Feel at Home*. London & Nairobi: Oxford University Press, 1962.
Welch, J. W. "The Present Great World Crisis." *The Pentecostal Evangel* 590 (28 March 1925).

"Word and Spirit, Church and World: The Final Report of the International Dialogue between Representatives of the World Alliance of Reformed Churches and Some Classical Pentecostal Churches and Leaders." *Pneuma: The Journal of the Society for Pentecostal Studies* 23, no. 1 (Spring 2001).

Wuthnow, Robert. *After Heaven: Spirituality in America Since the 1950s*. Berkeley: University of California Press, 1998.

Yamamoto, Sumiko. *History of Protestantism in China: The Indigenization of Christianity*. Tokyo: The Institute of Eastern Culture, 2000.

Yates, Timothy. *Christian Mission in the Twentieth Century*. Cambridge: Cambridge University Press, 1994.

Zizioulas, John D. *Being as Communion*. London: Darton, Longman and Todd, 1993.

Index

Notes on Contributors

Kyo Seong Ahn is a minister of the Presbyterian Church of Korea who worked as a missionary to Mongolia and then as Executive Secretary of the World Mission Department of the PCK. He was founding Director of the Union Bible Training Center in Mongolia and acting General Secretary of the Mongolian Bible Society. He recently completed his doctoral studies at the University of Cambridge.

Rose Dowsett, a serving member of OMF International since 1969, lived in Asia for eight years, training staff workers for the International Federation of Evangelical Students. Based in Scotland since 1978, she is an international speaker, author, and missiologist. She is Vice-Chairman of the Mission Commission of the World Evangelical Alliance.

Samuel Escobar is from Peru and worked with his wife Lilly as a missionary to universities under the International Fellowship of Evangelical Students, in several Latin American countries and Canada. From 1985 to 2005 he was Professor of Missiology at Eastern Baptist Theological Seminary (now Palmer Theological Seminary) in the United States. Presently he teaches at the Baptist Seminary in Madrid.

Gulnar (Guli) Francis-Dehqani was born and raised in Iran and moved to England following the Islamic Revolution. She is an Anglican priest with experience of both parish and chaplaincy work, with particular interest in religious feminism and interfaith studies. She is currently engaged in a project to improve the multi-faith dimension of the chaplaincy at Northampton University.

Adolfo Ham has served as Chairperson and Executive Secretary of the Cuban Council of Churches. He also chaired the Cuban Anti-Apartheid Committee and served on several World Council of Churches committees. Presently he is Professor of Philosophy and Patristics at the Evangelical Seminary, Matanzas, Cuba; and Principal of ISEBIT. His main interests are ecumenics and inter-religious dialogue.

Viorel Ionita is Professor at the Orthodox Theological Faculty of the University of Bucharest, Romania, and Director of the Churches in Dialogue Commission of the Conference of European Churches in Geneva. An ordained Orthodox priest, he is the author and editor of numerous studies on Church History and Ecumenism.

M.P. Joseph is currently Professor of Ethics at the School of Theology, Chang Jung Christian University, Taiwan. His work is done at the interface between people's movements and academic/theological reflection. His current research focuses on the impact of globalization from the perspective of the marginalized. He serves as the chief editor of the bi-annual journal *Theologies and Cultures*.

Ogbu U. Kalu was, until his death in January 2009, Henry Winters Luce Professor of World Christianity and Mission at McCormick Theological Seminary, Chicago and Director of the Chicago Center for Global Ministries, an ecumenical, collaborative mission project of several schools in Chicago. He is the editor of the Center's contribution to Edinburgh 2010 - *After the Christendom: Emergent Themes in Contemporary Mission* to be published by Westminster John Knox in 2009.

David A. Kerr served, until his death in April 2008, as Professor of Missiology and Ecumenics at the University of Lund. Prior to this, from 1996 to 2005, he was Director of the Centre for the Study of Christianity in the Non-Western World at the University of Edinburgh. He played a key role in the inception and development of the Towards 2010 conference series on which this book is based.

Samuel Kobia, of the Methodist Church in Kenya, is general secretary of the World Council of Churches. He served from 1987 to1993 as general secretary of Kenya's National Council of Churches. In recognition of his position within the ecumenical family in Kenya and beyond, Kobia was awarded the country's National Ecumenical Award and appointed chancellor of St. Paul's University, Limuru, Kenya, in 2007.

Anne-Marie Kool is from the Netherlands, and has lived and worked in Hungary since 1987. From 1995-2005 she served as the director of the Protestant Institute for Mission Studies in Budapest. In 2006 she was appointed as professor of Missiology at the Károli Gaspar University in the Reformed Church in Hungary and as director of the Central and Eastern European Institute for Mission Studies.

Kosuke Koyama was born in 1929 in Tokyo where he survived the carpet bombings of 1945. He served as a Japanese missionary to Thailand (1960-68), Dean of the South East Asia Graduate School of Theology (1968-74), Senior Lecturer in Religious Studies, Otago University, New Zealand (1974-79), and Professor of World Christianity at Union Theological Seminary, New York (1980-96).

Tinyiko Sam Maluleke is a trained missiologist appointed as Professor of African Theology at the University of South Africa in Pretoria, South Africa.

He currently works as the Executive Director for Research at that University. He has published more than fifty articles in the areas of missiology, African Theology and Black Theology. He is the current president of the South African Council of Churches.

Teresa Okure is Professor of New Testament and Gender Hermeneutics and Academic Dean at the Catholic Institute of West Africa, Port Harcourt, Nigeria. A Roman Catholic Sister, she is currently President of the Catholic Biblical Association of Nigeria. She has written many scholarly works, lectured extensively worldwide and held executive posts in international associations.

Vinoth Ramachandra lives and works in Colombo, Sri Lanka, with his Danish wife Karin. He is on the senior leadership team of the International Fellowship of Evangelical Students (IFES) as the Secretary for Dialogue and Social Engagement. His most recent book is *Subverting Global Myths : Theology and the Public Issues Shaping Our World* (2008).

John A. Radano, a priest in the Roman Catholic Archdiocese of Newark, New Jersey, is a serving member of the Pontifical Council for Promoting Christian Union. He has extensive experience of international bilateral dialogues and is the Pontifical Council's liaison to the Faith and Order Commission of the World Council of Churches. He co-chairs the dialogue between the Roman Catholic Church and the Classical Pentecostals.

Cecil M. Robeck, Jr., an ordained minister with the Assemblies of God, currently serves as Professor of Church History and Ecumenics and Director of the David du Plessis Center for Christian Spirituality at Fuller Theological Seminary. He currently co-chairs the International Catholic – Pentecostal Dialogue, as well as the Joint Consultative Group with the World Council of Churches. He was founding co-chair of the WARC – Pentecostal Dialogue, and the Lutheran – Pentecostal Conversation.

Kenneth R. Ross, formerly Professor of Theology at the University of Malawi, is Council Secretary of the Church of Scotland World Mission Council. Since 2001 he has chaired the Towards 2010 Council which has coordinated Scottish reflection on the centenary of Edinburgh 1910 and acted as a catalyst for the broad-based international movement finding expression in "Edinburgh 2010".

Andrew F. Walls, after missionary service in Sierra Leone and Nigeria, directed the Centre for the Study of Christianity in the Non-Western World, first at the University of Aberdeen and later at the University of Edinburgh where he remains Honorary Professor. He is also Professor of the History of Mission at Liverpool Hope University and Professor of Mission Studies at the Akrofi Christaller Institute in Akropong-Akuapem, Ghana.

REGNUM EDINBURGH CENTENARY SERIES

David A. Kerr, Kenneth R. Ross (Eds)
Mission Then and Now
2009 / 978-1-870345-73-6 / 343pp (paperback)
2009 / 978-1-870345-76-7 / 343pp (hardback)

No one can hope to fully understand the modern Christian missionary movement without engaging substantially with the World Missionary Conference, held at Edinburgh in 1910. This book is the first to systematically examine the eight Commissions which reported to Edinburgh 1910 and gave the conference much of its substance and enduring value. It will deepen and extend the reflection being stimulated by the upcoming centenary and will kindle the missionary imagination for 2010 and beyond.

Daryl M. Balia, Kirsteen Kim (Eds)
Witnessing to Christ Today
2010 / 978-1-870345-77-4 / 301pp (hardback)

This volume, the second in the Edinburgh 2010 series, includes reports of the nine main study groups working on different themes for the celebration of the centenary of the World Missionary Conference, Edinburgh 1910. Their collaborative work brings together perspectives that are as inclusive as possible of contemporary world Christianity and helps readers to grasp what it means in different contexts to be 'witnessing to Christ today'.

Claudia Währisch-Oblau, Fidon Mwombeki (Eds)
Mission Continues
Global Impulses for the 21st Century
2010 / 978-1-870345-82-8 / 271pp (hardback)

In May 2009, 35 theologians from Asia, Africa and Europe met in Wuppertal, Germany, for a consultation on mission theology organized by the United Evangelical Mission: Communion of 35 Churches in Three Continents. The aim was to participate in the 100th anniversary of the Edinburgh conference through a study process and reflect on the challenges for mission in the 21st century. This book brings together these papers written by experienced practitioners from around the world.

Brian Woolnough and Wonsuk Ma (Eds)
Holistic Mission
God's Plan for God's People
2010 / 978-1-870345-85-9 / 268pp (hardback)

Holistic mission, or integral mission, implies God is concerned with the whole person, the whole community, body, mind and spirit. This book discusses the meaning of the holistic gospel, how it has developed, and implications for the church. It takes a global, eclectic approach, with 19 writers, all of whom have much experience in, and commitment to, holistic mission. It addresses critically and honestly one of the most exciting, and challenging, issues facing the church today. To be part of God's plan for God's people, the church must take holistic mission to the world.

Kirsteen Kim and Andrew Anderson (Eds)
Mission Today and Tomorrow
2010 / 978-1-870345-91-0 / 450pp (hardback)

There are moments in our lives when we come to realise that we are participating in the triune God's mission. If we believe the church to be as sign and symbol of the reign of God in the world, then we are called to witness to Christ today by sharing in God's mission of love through the transforming power of the Holy Spirit. We can all participate in God's transforming and reconciling mission of love to the whole creation.

Tormod Engelsviken, Erling Lundeby and Dagfinn Solheim (Eds)
The Church Going Glocal
Mission and Globalisation
2011 / 978-1-870345-93-4 / 262pp (hardback)

The New Testament church is… universal and local at the same time. The universal, one and holy apostolic church appears in local manifestations. Missiologically speaking… the church can take courage as she faces the increasing impact of globalisation on local communities today. Being universal and concrete, the church is geared for the simultaneous challenges of the glocal and local.

Marina Ngurusangzeli Behera (Ed)
Interfaith Relations after One Hundred Years
Christian Mission among Other Faiths
2011 / 978-1-870345-96-5 / 338pp (hardback)

The essays of this book reflect not only the acceptance and celebration of pluralism within India but also by extension an acceptance as well as a need for unity among Indian Christians of different denominations. The essays were presented and studied at a preparatory consultation on Study Theme II: Christian Mission Among Other Faiths at the United Theological College, India July 2009.

Lalsangkima Pachuau and Knud Jørgensen (Eds)
Witnessing to Christ in a Pluralistic Age
Christian Mission among Other Faiths
2011 / 978-1-870345-95-8 / 277pp (hardback)

In a world where plurality of faiths is increasingly becoming a norm of life, insights on the theology of religious plurality are needed to strengthen our understanding of our own faith and the faith of others. Even though religious diversity is not new, we are seeing an upsurge in interest on the theologies of religion among all Christian confessional traditions. It can be claimed that no other issue in Christian mission is more important and more difficult than the theologies of religions.

Beth Snodderly and A Scott Moreau (Eds)
Evangelical Frontier Mission
Perspectives on the Global Progress of the Gospel
2011 / 978-1-870345-98-9 / 312pp (hardback)

This important volume demonstrates that 100 years after the World Missionary Conference in Edinburgh, Evangelism has become truly global. Twenty-first-century Evangelism continues to focus on frontier mission, but significantly, and in the spirit of Edinburgh 1910, it also has re-engaged social action.

Rolv Olsen (Ed)
Mission and Postmodernities
2011 / 978-1-870345-97-2 / 279pp (hardback)

This volume takes on meaning because its authors honestly struggle with and debate how we should relate to postmodernities. Should our response be accommodation, relativizing or counter-culture? How do we strike a balance between listening and understanding, and at the same time exploring how postmodernities influence the interpretation and application of the Bible as the normative story of God's mission in the world?

Cathy Ross (Ed)
Life-Widening Mission
2012 / 978-1-908355-00-3 / 163pp (hardback)

It is clear from the essays collected here that the experience of the 2010 World Mission Conference in Edinburgh was both affirming and frustrating for those taking part - affirming because of its recognition of how the centre of gravity has moved in global Christianity; frustrating because of the relative slowness of so many global Christian bodies to catch up with this and to embody it in the way they do business and in the way they represent themselves. These reflections will - or should - provide plenty of food for thought in the various councils of the Communion in the coming years.

Beate Fagerli, Knud Jørgensen, Rolv Olsen, Kari Storstein Haug and Knut Tveitereid (Eds)
A Learning Missional Church
Reflections from Young Missiologists
2012 / 978-1-908355-01-0 / 218pp (hardback)

Cross-cultural mission has always been a primary learning experience for the church. It pulls us out of a mono-cultural understanding and helps us discover a legitimate theological pluralism which opens up for new perspectives in the Gospel. Translating the Gospel into new languages and cultures is a human and divine means of making us learn new 'incarnations' of the Good News.

Emma Wild-Wood & Peniel Rajkumar (Eds)
Foundations for Mission
2012 / 978-1-908355-12-6 / 309pp (hardback)

This volume provides an important resource for those wishing to gain an overview of significant issues in contemporary missiology whilst understanding how they are applied in particular contexts.

Wonsuk Ma & Kenneth R Ross (Eds)
Mission Spirituality and Authentic Discipleship
2013 / 978-1-908355-24-9 / 248pp (hardback)

This book argues for the primacy of spirituality in the practice of mission. Since God is the primary agent of mission and God works through the power of the Holy Spirit, it is through openness to the Spirit that mission finds its true character and has its authentic impact.

Stephen B Bevans (Ed)
A Century of Catholic Mission
2013 / 978-1-908355-14-0 / 337pp (hardback)

A Century of Catholic Mission surveys the complex and rich history and theology of Roman Catholic Mission in the one hundred years since the 1910 Edinburgh World Mission Conference. Essays written by an international team of Catholic mission scholars focus on Catholic Mission in every region of the world, summarize church teaching on mission before and after the watershed event of the Second Vatican Council, and reflect on a wide variety of theological issues.

Robert Schreiter & Knud Jørgensen (Eds)
Mission as Ministry of Reconcilation
2013 / 978-1-908355-26-3 / 382pp (hardback)

There is hope – even if it is "Hope in a Fragile World", as the concluding chapter of Mission as Ministry of Reconciliation puts it. At the very heart of the gospel of Jesus Christ is a message of hope and reconciliation. Nothing could be more relevant and more necessary in a broken world than this Christian message of hope and reconciliation. ... I would like to congratulate the editors of Mission as Ministry of Reconciliation, for they listened carefully and planned with farsightedness. ... This rich book offers a valuable elucidation of the importance and the understanding of mission as ministry of reconciliation.

Petros Vassiliadis, Editor
Orthodox Perspectives on Mission
2013 / 978-1908355-25-6 / 262pp (hardback)

Orthodox Perspectives on Mission is both a humble tribute to some great Orthodox theologians, who in the past have provided substantial contribution to contemporary missiological and ecumenical discussions, and an Orthodox input to the upcoming 2013 Busan WCC General Assembly. The collected volume is divided into two parts: Part I: The Orthodox Heritage consists of Orthodox missiological contributions of the past, whereas Part II includes all the papers presented in the Plenary of the recent Edinburgh 2010 conference, as well as the short studies and contributions prepared, during the Edinburgh 2010 on going study process.

Pauline Hoggarth, Fergus MacDonald,
Bill Mitchell & Knud Jørgensen, Editors
Bible in Mission
2013 / 978-1908355-42-3 / 317pp (hardback)

To the authors of Bible in Mission, the Bible is the book of life, and mission is life in the Word. This core reality cuts across the diversity of contexts and hermeneutical strategies represented in these essays. The authors are committed to the boundary-crossings that characterize contemporary mission – and each sees the Bible as foundational to the missio Dei, to God's work in the world.

Wonsuk Ma, Veli-Matti Kärkkäinnen
& J Kwabena Asamoah
Pentecostal Mission and Global Christianity
2014 / 978-1908355-43-0 / 397pp (hardback)

Although Pentecostalism worldwide represent the most rapidly growing missionary movement in Christian history, only recently scholars from within and outside the movement have begun academic reflection on the mission. This volume represents the coming of age of emerging scholarship of various aspects of the Pentecostal mission, including theological, historical, strategic, and practical aspects.

Afe Adogame, Janice McLean & Anderson Jeremiah, Editors
Engaging the World
Christian Communities in Contemporary Global Societies
2014 / 978-1908355-21-8 / 235pp (hardback)

Engaging the World deals with the lived experiences and expressions of Christians in diverse communities across the globe. Christian communities do not live in a vacuum but in complex, diverse social-cultural contexts; within wider communities of different faith and social realities. Power, identity and community are key issues in considering Christian communities in contemporary contexts.

Peniel Jesudason Rufus Rajkumar, Joseph Prabhakar Dayam
& IP Asheervadham, Editors
Mission At and From the Margins
Patterns, Protagonists and Perspectives
2014 / 978-1908355-13-3 / 283pp (hardback)

Mission At and From the Margins: Patterns, Protagonists and Perspectives revisits the 'hi-stories' of Mission from the 'bottom up' paying critical attention to people, perspectives and patterns that have often been elided in the construction of mission history. Focusing on the mission story of Christian churches in the South Indian state of Abdhra Pradesh this collection of essays ushers its readers to re-shape their understanding of the landscape of mission history by drawing their attention to the silences and absences within pre-dominant historical accounts.

REGNUM STUDIES IN GLOBAL CHRISTIANITY

David Emmanuel Singh (Ed)
Jesus and the Cross
Reflections of Christians from Islamic Contexts
2008 / 978-1-870345-65-1 / 226pp

The Cross reminds us that the sins of the world are not borne through the exercise of power but through Jesus Christ's submission to the will of the Father. The papers in this volume are organised in three parts: scriptural, contextual and theological. The central question being addressed is: how do Christians living in contexts, where Islam is a majority or minority religion, experience, express or think of the Cross?

Sung-wook Hong
Naming God in Korea
The Case of Protestant Christianity
2008 / 978-1-870345-66-8 / 170pp (hardback)

Since Christianity was introduced to Korea more than a century ago, one of the most controversial issues has been the Korean term for the Christian 'God'. This issue is not merely about naming the Christian God in Korean language, but it relates to the question of theological contextualization - the relationship between the gospel and culture - and the question of Korean Christian identity. This book demonstrates the nature of the gospel in relation to cultures, i.e., the universality of the gospel expressed in all human cultures.

Hubert van Beek (Ed)
Revisioning Christian Unity
The Global Christian Forum
2009 / 978-1-870345-74-3 / 288pp (hardback)

This book contains the records of the Global Christian Forum gathering held in Limuru near Nairobi, Kenya, on 6 – 9 November 2007 as well as the papers presented at that historic event. Also included are a summary of the Global Christian Forum process from its inception until the 2007 gathering and the reports of the evaluation of the process that was carried out in 2008.

Young-hoon Lee

The Holy Spirit Movement in Korea

Its Historical and Theological Development

2009 / 978-1-870345-67-5 / 174pp (hardback)

This book traces the historical and theological development of the Holy Spirit Movement in Korea through six successive periods (from 1900 to the present time). These periods are characterized by repentance and revival (1900-20), persecution and suffering under Japanese occupation (1920-40), confusion and division (1940-60), explosive revival in which the Pentecostal movement played a major role in the rapid growth of Korean churches (1960-80), the movement reaching out to all denominations (1980-2000), and the new context demanding the Holy Spirit movement to open new horizons in its mission engagement (2000-).

Paul Hang-Sik Cho

Eschatology and Ecology

Experiences of the Korean Church

2010 / 978-1-870345-75-0 / 260pp (hardback)

This book raises the question of why Korean people, and Korean Protestant Christians in particular, pay so little attention to ecological issues. The author argues that there is an important connection (or elective affinity) between this lack of attention and the other-worldly eschatology that is so dominant within Korean Protestant Christianity.

Dietrich Werner, David Esterline, Namsoon Kang, Joshva Raja (Eds)

The Handbook of Theological Education in World Christianity

Theological Perspectives, Ecumenical Trends, Regional Surveys

2010 / 978-1-870345-80-0 / 759pp

This major reference work is the first ever comprehensive study of Theological Education in Christianity of its kind. With contributions from over 90 international scholars and church leaders, it aims to be easily accessible across denominational, cultural, educational, and geographic boundaries. The Handbook will aid international dialogue and networking among theological educators, institutions, and agencies.

David Emmanuel Singh & Bernard C Farr (Eds)

Christianity and Education

Shaping of Christian Context in Thinking

2010 / 978-1-870345-81-1 / 374pp

Christianity and Education is a collection of papers published in *Transformation: An International Journal of Holistic Mission Studies* over a period of 15 years. The articles represent a spectrum of Christian thinking addressing issues of institutional development for theological education, theological studies in the context of global mission, contextually aware/informed education, and academies which deliver such education, methodologies and personal reflections.

J.Andrew Kirk

Civilisations in Conflict?

Islam, the West and Christian Faith

2011 / 978-1-870345-87-3 / 205pp

Samuel Huntington's thesis, which argues that there appear to be aspects of Islam that could be on a collision course with the politics and values of Western societies, has provoked much controversy. The purpose of this study is to offer a particular response to Huntington's thesis by making a comparison between the origins of Islam and Christianity.

David Emmanuel Singh (Ed)

Jesus and the Incarnation

Reflections of Christians from Islamic Contexts

2011 / 978-1-870345-90-3 / 245pp

In the dialogues of Christians with Muslims nothing is more fundamental than the Cross, the Incarnation and the Resurrection of Jesus. Building on the *Jesus and the Cross*, this book contains voices of Christians living in various 'Islamic contexts' and reflecting on the Incarnation of Jesus. The aim and hope of these reflections is that the papers weaved around the notion of 'the Word' will not only promote dialogue among Christians on the roles of the Person and the Book but, also, create a positive environment for their conversations with Muslim neighbours.

Ivan M Satyavrata

God Has Not left Himself Without Witness

2011 / 978-1-870345-79-8 / 264pp

Since its earliest inception the Christian Church has had to address the question of what common ground exits between Christian faiths and other religions. This issue is not merely of academic interest but one with critical existential and socio-political consequences. This study presents a case for the revitalization of the fulfillment tradition based on a recovery and assessment of the fulfillment approaches of Indian Christian converts in the pre-independence period.

Bal Krishna Sharma

From this World to the Next

Christian Identity and Funerary Rites in Nepal

2013 / 978-1-908355-08-9 / 238pp

This book explores and analyses funerary rite struggles in a nation where Christianity is a comparatively recent phenomenon, and many families have multi-faith, who go through traumatic experiences at the death of their family members. The author has used an applied theological approach to explore and analyse the findings in order to address the issue of funerary rites with which the Nepalese church is struggling.

J Kwabena Asamoah-Gyada

Contemporary Pentecostal Christianity

Interpretations from an African Context

2013 / 978-1-908355-07-2 / 194pp

Pentecostalism is the fastest growing stream of Christianity in the world. The real evidence for the significance of Pentecostalism lies in the actual churches they have built and the numbers they attract. This work interprets key theological and missiological themes in African Pentecostalism by using material from the live experiences of the movement itself.

David Emmanuel Singh and Bernard C Farr (Eds)

The Bible and Christian Ethics

2013 / 978-1-908355-20-1 / 217pp

This book contains papers from the Oxford Centre for Mission Studies' quarterly journal, Transformation, on the topic of Christian Ethics. Here, Mission Studies is understood in its widest sense to also encompass Christian Ethics. At the very hearts of it lies the Family as the basic unit of society. All the papers together seek to contribute to understanding how Christian thought is shaped in contexts each of which poses its own challenge to Christian living in family and in broader society.

Martin Allaby

Inequality, Corruption and the Church

Challenges & Opportunities in the Global Church

2013 / 978-1-908355-16-4 / 228pp

Why are economic inequalities greatest in the southern countries where most people are Christians? This book teases out the influences that have created this situation, and concludes that Christians could help reduce economic inequalities by opposing corruption. Interviews in the Philippines, Kenya, Zambia and Peru reveal opportunities and challenges for Christians as they face up to corruption.

Paul Alexander and Al Tizon (Eds)

Following Jesus

Journeys in Radical Discipleship – Essays in Honor of Ronald J Sider

2013 / 978-1-908355-27-0 / 228pp

Ronald J. Sider and the organization that he founded, *Evangelicals for Social Action*, are most respected for their pioneering work in the area of evangelical social concern. However, Sider's great contribution to social justice is but a part of a larger vision – namely, biblical discipleship. His works, which span more than four decades, have guided the faithful to be authentic gospel-bearers in ecclesial, cultural and political arenas. This book honors Ron Sider, by bringing together a group of scholar-activists, old and young, to reflect upon the gospel and its radical implications for the 21st century.

Cawley Bolt

Reluctant or Radical Revolutionaries?

Evangelical Missionaries and Afro-Jamaican Character, 1834-1870

2013 / 978-1-908355-18-8 / 287pp

This study is based on extensive research that challenges traditional ways of understanding some evangelical missionaries of nineteenth century Jamaica and calls for revision of those views. It highlights the strength and character of persons facing various challenges of life in their effort to be faithful to the guiding principles of their existence.

Isabel Apawo Phiri & Dietrich Werner (Eds)

Handbook of Theological Education in Africa

2013 / 978-1-908355-45-4 / 1110pp

The *Handbook of Theological Education in Africa* is a wake-up call for African churches to give proper prominence to theological education institutions and their programmes which serve them. It is unique, comprehensive and ambitious in its aim and scope.

Hope Antone, Wati Longchar, Hyunju Bae, Huang Po Ho, Dietrich Werner (Eds)

Asian Handbook for Theological Education and Ecumenism

2013 / 978-1-908355-30-0 / 675pp (hardback)

This impressive and comprehensive book focuses on key resources for teaching Christian unity and common witness in Asian contexts. It is a collection of articles that reflects the ongoing 'double wrestle' with the texts of biblical tradition as well as with contemporary contexts. It signals an investment towards the future of the ecumenical movement in Asia.

Bernhard Reitsma

The God of My Enemy

The Middle East and the Nature of God

2014 / 978-1-908355-50-8 / 206pp

The establishment of the State of Israel in 1948 for the Church in the West has been the starting point of a rediscovery of its own roots. In the Middle East the effect has been exactly the opposite: Christians have become estranged from their Old Testament roots, because they have been expelled from their land exactly because of an appeal to the Old Testament. The concept of Israel changed from a nation in the Bible, with which they could associate, to an economic, political and military power that was against them

REGNUM STUDIES IN MISSION

Kwame Bediako
Theology and Identity
The Impact of Culture upon Christian Thought in the Second Century and in Modern Africa
1992 / 978-1870345-10-1 / 507pp

The author examines the question of Christian identity in the context of the Graeco–Roman culture of the early Roman Empire. He then addresses the modern African predicament of quests for identity and integration.

Christopher Sugden
Seeking the Asian Face of Jesus
The Practice and Theology of Christian Social Witness in Indonesia and India 1974–1996
1997 / 1-870345-26-6 / 496pp

This study focuses on contemporary holistic mission with the poor in India and Indonesia combined with the call to transformation of all life in Christ with micro-credit enterprise schemes. 'The literature on contextual theology now has a new standard to rise to' – Lamin Sanneh (Yale University, USA).

Hwa Yung
Mangoes or Bananas?
The Quest for an Authentic Asian Christian Theology
1997 / 1-870345-25-5 / 274pp

Asian Christian thought remains largely captive to Greek dualism and Enlightenment rationalism because of the overwhelming dominance of Western culture. Authentic contextual Christian theologies will emerge within Asian Christianity with a dual recovery of confidence in culture and the gospel.

Keith E. Eitel
Paradigm Wars
The Southern Baptist International Mission Board Faces the Third Millennium
1999 / 1-870345-12-6 / 140pp

The International Mission Board of the Southern Baptist Convention is the largest denominational mission agency in North America. This volume chronicles the historic and contemporary forces that led to the IMB's recent extensive reorganization, providing the most comprehensive case study to date of a historic mission agency restructuring to continue its mission purpose into the twenty-first century more effectively.

Samuel Jayakumar
Dalit Consciousness and Christian Conversion
Historical Resources for a Contemporary Debate
1999 / 81-7214-497-0 / 434pp
(Published jointly with ISPCK)

The main focus of this historical study is social change and transformation among the Dalit Christian communities in India. Historiography tests the evidence in the light of the conclusions of the modern Dalit liberation theologians.

Vinay Samuel and Christopher Sugden (Eds)
Mission as Transformation
A Theology of the Whole Gospel
1999 / 978-18703455-13-2 / 522pp

This book brings together in one volume twenty five years of biblical reflection on mission practice with the poor from around the world. This volume helps anyone understand how evangelicals, struggling to unite evangelism and social action, found their way in the last twenty five years to the biblical view of mission in which God calls all human beings to love God and their neighbour; never creating a separation between the two.

Christopher Sugden
Gospel, Culture and Transformation
2000 / 1-870345-32-3 / 152pp
A Reprint, with a New Introduction,
of Part Two of Seeking the Asian Face of Jesus

Gospel, Culture and Transformation explores the practice of mission especially in relation to transforming cultures and communities. - 'Transformation is to enable God's vision of society to be actualised in all relationships: social, economic and spiritual, so that God's will may be reflected in human society and his love experienced by all communities, especially the poor.'

Bernhard Ott
Beyond Fragmentation: Integrating Mission and Theological Education
A Critical Assessment of some Recent Developments
in Evangelical Theological Education
2001 / 1-870345-14-9 / 382pp

Beyond Fragmentation is an enquiry into the development of Mission Studies in evangelical theological education in Germany and German-speaking Switzerland between 1960 and 1995. The author undertakes a detailed examination of the paradigm shifts which have taken place in recent years in both the theology of mission and the understanding of theological education.

Gideon Githiga
The Church as the Bulwark against Authoritarianism
Development of Church and State Relations in Kenya, with Particular Reference to the Years after Political Independence 1963-1992
2002 / 1-870345-38-x / 218pp

'All who care for love, peace and unity in Kenyan society will want to read this careful history by Bishop Githiga of how Kenyan Christians, drawing on the Bible, have sought to share the love of God, bring his peace and build up the unity of the nation, often in the face of great difficulties and opposition.' Canon Dr Chris Sugden, Oxford Centre for Mission Studies.

Myung Sung-Hoon, Hong Young-Gi (Eds)

Charis and Charisma

David Yonggi Cho and the Growth of Yoido Full Gospel Church

2003 / 978-1870345-45-3 / 218pp

This book discusses the factors responsible for the growth of the world's largest church. It expounds the role of the Holy Spirit, the leadership, prayer, preaching, cell groups and creativity in promoting church growth. It focuses on God's grace (charis) and inspiring leadership (charisma) as the two essential factors and the book's purpose is to present a model for church growth worldwide.

Samuel Jayakumar

Mission Reader

Historical Models for Wholistic Mission in the Indian Context

2003 / 1-870345-42-8 / 250pp

(Published jointly with ISPCK)

This book is written from an evangelical point of view revalidating and reaffirming the Christian commitment to wholistic mission. The roots of the 'wholistic mission' combining 'evangelism and social concerns' are to be located in the history and tradition of Christian evangelism in the past; and the civilizing purpose of evangelism is compatible with modernity as an instrument in nation building.

Bob Robinson

Christians Meeting Hindus

An Analysis and Theological Critique of the Hindu-Christian Encounter in India

2004 / 987-1870345-39-2 / 392pp

This book focuses on the Hindu-Christian encounter, especially the intentional meeting called dialogue, mainly during the last four decades of the twentieth century, and specifically in India itself.

Gene Early

Leadership Expectations

How Executive Expectations are Created and Used in a Non-Profit Setting

2005 / 1-870345-30-9 / 276pp

The author creates an Expectation Enactment Analysis to study the role of the Chancellor of the University of the Nations-Kona, Hawaii. This study is grounded in the field of managerial work, jobs, and behaviour and draws on symbolic interactionism, role theory, role identity theory and enactment theory. The result is a conceptual framework for developing an understanding of managerial roles.

Tharcisse Gatwa

The Churches and Ethnic Ideology in the Rwandan Crises 1900-1994

2005 / 978-1870345-24-8 / 300pp

(Reprinted 2011)

Since the early years of the twentieth century Christianity has become a new factor in Rwandan society. This book investigates the role Christian churches played in the formulation and development of the racial ideology that culminated in the 1994 genocide.

Julie Ma

Mission Possible

Biblical Strategies for Reaching the Lost

2005 / 978-1870345-37-8 / 142pp

This is a missiology book for the church which liberates missiology from the specialists for the benefit of every believer. It also serves as a textbook that is simple and friendly, and yet solid in biblical interpretation. This book links the biblical teaching to the actual and contemporary missiological settings with examples, making the Bible come alive to the reader.

I. Mark Beaumont

Christology in Dialogue with Muslims

A Critical Analysis of Christian Presentations of Christ for Muslims from the Ninth and Twentieth Centuries

2005 / 978-1870345-46-0 / 227pp

This book analyses Christian presentations of Christ for Muslims in the most creative periods of Christian-Muslim dialogue, the first half of the ninth century and the second half of the twentieth century. In these two periods, Christians made serious attempts to present their faith in Christ in terms that take into account Muslim perceptions of him, with a view to bridging the gap between Muslim and Christian convictions.

Thomas Czövek,

Three Seasons of Charismatic Leadership

A Literary-Critical and Theological Interpretation of the Narrative of Saul, David and Solomon

2006 / 978-1870345-48-4 / 272pp

This book investigates the charismatic leadership of Saul, David and Solomon. It suggests that charismatic leaders emerge in crisis situations in order to resolve the crisis by the charisma granted by God. Czovek argues that Saul proved himself as a charismatic leader as long as he acted resolutely and independently from his mentor Samuel. In the author's eyes, Saul's failure to establish himself as a charismatic leader is caused by his inability to step out from Samuel's shadow.

Richard Burgess

Nigeria's Christian Revolution

The Civil War Revival and Its Pentecostal Progeny (1967-2006)

2008 / 978-1-870345-63-7 / 347pp

This book describes the revival that occurred among the Igbo people of Eastern Nigeria and the new Pentecostal churches it generated, and documents the changes that have occurred as the movement has responded to global flows and local demands. As such, it explores the nature of revivalist and Pentecostal experience, but does so against the backdrop of local socio-political and economic developments, such as decolonisation and civil war, as well as broader processes, such as modernisation and globalisation.

David Emmanuel Singh & Bernard C Farr (Eds)

Christianity and Cultures

Shaping Christian Thinking in Context

2008 / 978-1-870345-69-9 / 271pp

This volume marks an important milestone, the 25th anniversary of the Oxford Centre for Mission Studies (OCMS). The papers here have been exclusively sourced from Transformation, a quarterly journal of OCMS, and seek to provide a tripartite view of

Christianity's engagement with cultures by focusing on the question: how is Christian thinking being formed or reformed through its interaction with the varied contexts it encounters? The subject matters include different strands of theological-missiological thinking, socio-political engagements and forms of family relationships in interaction with the host cultures.

Tormod Engelsviken, Ernst Harbakk, Rolv Olsen, Thor Strandenæs (Eds)
Mission to the World
Communicating the Gospel in the 21st Century:
Essays in Honour of Knud Jørgensen
2008 / 978-1-870345-64-4 / 472pp (hardback)

Knud Jørgensen is Director of Areopagos and Associate Professor of Missiology at MF Norwegian School of Theology. This book reflects on the main areas of Jørgensen's commitment to mission. At the same time it focuses on the main frontier of mission, the world, the content of mission, the Gospel, the fact that the Gospel has to be communicated, and the context of contemporary mission in the 21st century.

Al Tizon
Transformation after Lausanne
Radical Evangelical Mission in Global-Local Perspective
2008 / 978-1-870345-68-2 / 281pp

After Lausanne '74, a worldwide network of radical evangelical mission theologians and practitioners use the notion of "Mission as Transformation" to integrate evangelism and social concern together, thus lifting theological voices from the Two Thirds World to places of prominence. This book documents the definitive gatherings, theological tensions, and social forces within and without evangelicalism that led up to Mission as Transformation. And it does so through a global-local grid that points the way toward greater holistic mission in the 21st century.

Bambang Budijanto
Values and Participation
Development in Rural Indonesia
2009 / 978-1-870345-70-4 / 237pp

Socio-religious values and socio-economic development are inter-dependant, inter-related and are constantly changing in the context of macro political structures, economic policy, religious organizations and globalization; and micro influences such as local affinities, identity, politics, leadership and beliefs. The book argues that the comprehensive approach in understanding the socio-religious values of each of the three local Lopait communities in Central Java is essential to accurately describing their respective identity.

Alan R. Johnson
Leadership in a Slum
A Bangkok Case Study
2009 / 978-1-870345-71-2 / 238pp

This book looks at leadership in the social context of a slum in Bangkok from a different perspective than traditional studies which measure well educated Thais on leadership scales derived in the West. Using both systematic data collection and participant observation, it develops a culturally preferred model as well as a set of models based in Thai concepts that reflect on-the-ground realities. It concludes by looking at the implications of the anthropological approach for those who are involved in leadership training in Thai settings and beyond.

Titre Ande

Leadership and Authority

Bula Matari and Life - Community Ecclesiology in Congo

2010 / 978-1-870345-72-9 / 189pp

Christian theology in Africa can make significant development if a critical understanding of the socio-political context in contemporary Africa is taken seriously, particularly as Africa's post-colonial Christian leadership based its understanding and use of authority on the Bula Matari model. This has caused many problems and Titre proposes a Life-Community ecclesiology for liberating authority, here leadership is a function, not a status, and 'apostolic succession' belongs to all people of God.

Frank Kwesi Adams

Odwira and the Gospel

A Study of the Asante Odwira Festival and its Significance for Christianity in Ghana

2010 /978-1-870345-59-0 / 232pp

The study of the Odwira festival is the key to the understanding of Asante religious and political life in Ghana. The book explores the nature of the Odwira festival longitudinally - in pre-colonial, colonial and post-independence Ghana - and examines the Odwira ideology and its implications for understanding the Asante self-identity. Also discussed is how some elements of faith portrayed in the Odwira festival can provide a framework for Christianity to engage with Asante culture at a greater depth.

Bruce Carlton

Strategy Coordinator

Changing the Course of Southern Baptist Missions

2010 / 978-1-870345-78-1 / 273pp

This is an outstanding, one-of-a-kind work addressing the influence of the non-residential missionary/strategy coordinator's role in Southern Baptist missions. This scholarly text examines the twentieth century global missiological currents that influenced the leadership of the International Mission Board, resulting in a new paradigm to assist in taking the gospel to the nations.

Julie Ma & Wonsuk Ma

Mission in the Spirit:

Towards a Pentecostal/Charismatic Missiology

2010 / 978-1-870345-84-2 / 312pp

The book explores the unique contribution of Pentecostal/Charismatic mission from the beginning of the twentieth century. The first part considers the theological basis of Pentecostal/Charismatic mission thinking and practice. Special attention is paid to the Old Testament, which has been regularly overlooked by the modern Pentecostal/Charismatic movements. The second part discusses major mission topics with contributions and challenges unique to Pentecostal/Charismatic mission. The book concludes with a reflection on the future of this powerful missionary movement. As the authors served as Korean missionaries in Asia, often their missionary experiences in Asia are reflected in their discussions.

Allan Anderson, Edmond Tang (Eds)

Asian and Pentecostal

The Charismatic Face of Christianity in Asia

2011 / 978-1870345-94-1 / 500pp

(Revised Edition)

This book provides a thematic discussion and pioneering case studies on the history and development of Pentecostal and Charismatic churches in the countries of South Asia, South East Asia and East Asia.

S. Hun Kim & Wonsuk Ma (Eds)
Korean Diaspora and Christian Mission
2011 / 978-1-870345-89-7 / 301pp (hardback)

As a 'divine conspiracy' for Missio Dei, the global phenomenon of people on the move has shown itself to be invaluable. In 2004 two significant documents concerning Diaspora were introduced, one by the Filipino International Network and the other by the Lausanne Committee for World Evangelization. These have created awareness of the importance of people on the move for Christian mission. Since then, Korean Diaspora has conducted similar research among Korean missions, resulting in this book

Jin Huat Tan
Planting an Indigenous Church
The Case of the Borneo Evangelical Mission
2011 / 978-1-870345-99-6 / 343pp

Dr Jin Huat Tan has written a pioneering study of the origins and development of Malaysia's most significant indigenous church. This is an amazing story of revival, renewal and transformation of the entire region chronicling the powerful effect of it evident to date! What can we learn from this extensive and careful study of the Borneo Revival, so the global Christianity will become ever more dynamic?

Bill Prevette
Child, Church and Compassion
Towards Child Theology in Romania
2012 / 978-1-908355-03-4 / 382pp

Bill Prevett comments that "children are like 'canaries in a mine shaft'; they provide a focal point for discovery and encounter of perilous aspects of our world that are often ignored." True, but miners also carried a lamp to see into the subterranean darkness. This book is such a lamp. It lights up the subterranean world of children and youth in danger of exploitation, and as it does so travels deep into their lives and also into the activities of those who seek to help them.

Samuel Cyuma
Picking up the Pieces
The Church and Conflict Resolution in South Africa and Rwanda
2012 / 978-1-908355-02-7 / 373pp

In the last ten years of the 20th century, the world was twice confronted with unbelievable news from Africa. First, there was the end of Apartheid in South Africa, without bloodshed, due to responsible political and Church leaders. The second was the mass killings in Rwanda, which soon escalated into real genocide. Political and Church leaders had been unable to prevents this crime against humanity. In this book, the question is raised: can we compare the situation in South Africa with that in Rwanda? Can Rwandan leaders draw lessons from the peace process in South Africa?

Peter Rowan
Proclaiming the Peacemaker
The Malaysian Church as an Agent of Reconciliation in a Multicultural Society
2012 / 978-1-908355-05-8 / 268pp

With a history of racial violence and in recent years, low-level ethnic tensions, the themes of peaceful coexistence and social harmony are recurring ones in the discourse of Malaysian society. In such a context, this book looks at the role of the church as a reconciling agent, arguing that a reconciling presence within a divided society necessitates an ethos of peacemaking.

Edward Ontita

Resources and Opportunity

The Architecture of Livelihoods in Rural Kenya

2012 / 978-1-908355-04-1 / 328pp

Poor people in most rural areas of developing countries often improvise resources in unique ways to enable them make a living. Resources and Opportunity takes the view that resources are dynamic and fluid, arguing that villagers co-produce them through redefinition and renaming in everyday practice and use them in diverse ways. The book focuses on ordinary social activities to bring out people's creativity in locating, redesigning and embracing livelihood opportunities in processes.

Kathryn Kraft

Searching for Heaven in the Real World

A Sociological Discussion of Conversion in the Arab World

2012 / 978-1-908355-15-7 / 142pp

Kathryn Kraft explores the breadth of psychological and social issues faced by Arab Muslims after making a decision to adopt a faith in Christ or Christianity, investigating some of the most surprising and significant challenges new believers face.

Wessley Lukose

Contextual Missiology of the Spirit

Pentecostalism in Rajasthan, India

2013 / 978-1-908355-09-6 / 256pp

This book explores the identity, context and features of Pentecostalism in Rajasthan, India as well as the internal and external issues facing Pentecostals. It aims to suggest 'a contextual missiology of the Spirit,' as a new model of contextual missiology from a Pentecostal perspective. It is presented as a glocal, ecumenical, transformational, and public missiology.

Paul M Miller

Evangelical Mission in Co-operation with Catholics

A Study of Evangelical Tensions

2013 / 978-1-908355-17-1 / 291pp

This book brings the first thorough examination of the discussions going on within Evangelicalism about the viability of a good conscience dialogue with Roman Catholics. Those who are interested in evangelical world missions and Roman Catholic views of world missions will find this informative.

Alemayehu Mekonnen

Culture Change in Ethiopia

An Evangelical Perspective

2013 / 978-1-908355-39-3 / 199pp

This book addresses the causes and consequences of culture change in Ethiopia, from Haile Selassie to the present, based on thorough academic research. Although written from an evangelical perspective, this book invites Ethiopians from all religions, ideological, and ethnic backgrounds to reflect on their past, to analyse their present and to engage in unity with diversity to face the future.

Godwin Lekundayo

The Cosmic Christ

Towards Effective Mission Among the Maasai

2013 / 978-1-908355-28- 7 / 259 pp

This book reveals a complex interaction between the Christian gospel brought by western missionaries and the nomadic Massai culture of Tanzania … an important insider's voice courageously questioning the approach to condemn some critical Maasai practices, particularly polygamy, and its missionary consequences. This is a rare study from a Maasai Christian leader.

Philippe Ouedraogo

Female Education and Mission

A Burkina Faso Experience

2014 / 978-1-908355-11-9 / 263pp

This volume is the result of six years research in 'Overcoming Obstacles to Female Education in Burkina Faso'. It narrates how Christians and religious groups can speed up female education and contribute to the socio-economic growth of Burkina Faso. Religious culture and traditions were seen as a problem to female education. However, the evidence from this research shows that Christianity is also part of the solution to a quality female education, thus a key factor of socio economic growth of the country.

Haw Yung

Mangoes or Bananas?

The Quest for an Authentic Asian Christian Theology (Second Edition)

2014 / 978-1-908355-47-8 / 232pp

Over the past few decades there has been a growing awareness of the need for contextual theologies throughout Asia. But how genuinely contextual are these? Based on the premise that theology and mission are inseparable, the author applies four missiological criteria to representative examples of Protestant Asian writings to assess their adequacy or otherwise as contextual theologies.

Daniel Taichoul Yang

Called Out for Witness

The Missionary Journey of Grace Korean Church

2014 / 978-1-908355-49-2 / 167pp

This book investigates the theological motivation for GKC's missions: Reformed theology, Presbyterian theology, and mission theology. The book also shows the extent of the church's mission engagement by continents. Finally, the book turns its attention to the future with an evaluation of the church's missionary journey.

REGNUM RESOURCES FOR MISSION

Knud Jørgensen

Equipping for Service

Christian Leadership in Church and Society

2012 / 978-1-908355-06-5 / 150pp

This book is written out of decades of experience of leading churches and missions in Ethiopia, Geneva, Norway and Hong Kong. Combining the teaching of Scripture with the insights of contemporary management philosophy, Jørgensen writes in a way which is practical and applicable to anyone in Christian service. "The intention has been to challenge towards a leadership relevant for work in church and mission, and in public and civil society, with special attention to leadership in Church and organisation."

Mary Miller
What does Love have to do with Leadership?
2013 / 978-1-908355-10-2 / 100pp

Leadership is a performing art, not a science. It is the art of influencing others, not just to accomplish something together, but to want to accomplish great things together. Mary Miller captures the art of servant leadership in her powerful book. She understands that servant leaders challenge existing processes without manipulating or overpowering people.

Mary Miller (Ed)
Faces of Holistic Mission
Stories of the OCMS Family
2013 / 978-1-908355-32-4 / 104pp

There is a popular worship song that begins with the refrain, 'look what the Lord has done, look what the Lord has done'. This book does exactly that; it seeks to show what the Lord has done. Fifteen authors from five different continents identify what the Lord has indeed been doing, and continues to do, in their lives. These are their stories.

David Cranston and Ruth Padilla DeBorst (Eds)
Mission as Transformation
Learning from Catalysts
2013 / 978-1-908355-34-8 / 77pp

This book is the product of the first Stott-Bediako Forum, held in 2012 with the title *Portraits of Catalysts*. Its aim was to learn from the stories of Christian leaders whose lives and work have served as catalysts for transformation as each, in his or her particular way, facilitated the intersection between the Good News of Jesus Christ and the context in which they lived, in particular amongst people who are suffering.

Brian Woolnough (Ed)
Good News from Africa
Community Transformation Through the Church
2013 / 978-1-908355-33-1 / 123pp

This book discusses how sustainable, holistic, community development can be, and is being, achieved through the work of the local church. Leading African development practitioners describe different aspects of development through their own experience.

Makonen Getu (Ed)
Transforming Microfinance
A Christian Approach
2013 / 978-1-908355-31-7 / 264pp

"This book highlights the important role that Christian-based organisations bring to the delivery of financial services for the poor. It is times, significant and important and deserves a wide circulation".

Lord Carey of Clifton, former Archbishop of Canterbury

Jonathan Ingleby, Tan Kand San, Tan Loun Ling, (Eds)
Contextualisation & Mission Training
Engaging Asia's Religious Worlds
2013 / 978-1-908355-40-9 / 109pp

Contextualisation & Mission Training, offers "contextual frameworks" and "explorations" in order to enhance deeper engagement with the complexity of Asian social, cultural and religious systems.

On Eagle's Wings
Models in Mentoring
2013 / 978-1-908355-46-1 / 105pp

David Cranston writes unashamedly as a Christian for whom no account of mentoring would be complete without placing it in the biggest context of all – that of the relationship between humans and God.

John Lennox, Professor of Mathematics, University of Oxford
Fellow in Mathematics and Philosophy of Science

GENERAL REGNUM TITLES

Vinay Samuel, Chris Sugden (Eds)
The Church in Response to Human Need
1987 / 1870345045 / xii+268pp

Philip Sampson, Vinay Samuel, Chris Sugden (Eds)
Faith and Modernity
Essays in modernity and post-modernity
1994 / 1870345177 / 352pp

Klaus Fiedler
The Story of Faith Missions
1994 / 0745926878 / 428pp

Douglas Peterson
Not by Might nor by Power
A Pentecostal Theology of Social Concern in Latin America
1996 / 1870345207 / xvi+260pp

David Gitari
In Season and Out of Season
Sermons to a Nation
1996 / 1870345118 / 155pp

David. W. Virtue
A Vision of Hope
The Story of Samuel Habib
1996 / 1870345169 / xiv+137pp

Everett A Wilson
Strategy of the Spirit

J.Philip Hogan and the Growth of the Assemblies of God Worldwide, 1960 - 1990
1997 /1870345231/214

Murray Dempster, Byron Klaus, Douglas Petersen (Eds)
The Globalization of Pentecostalism
A Religion Made to Travel
1999 / 1870345290 / xvii+406pp

Peter Johnson, Chris Sugden (Eds)
Markets, Fair Trade and the Kingdom of God
Essays to Celebrate Traidcraft's 21st Birthday
2001 / 1870345193 / xii+155pp

Robert Hillman, Coral Chamberlain, Linda Harding
Healing & Wholeness
Reflections on the Healing Ministry
2002 / 978-1- 870345-35- 4 / xvii+283pp

David Bussau, Russell Mask
Christian Microenterprise Development
An Introduction
2003 / 1870345282 / xiii–142pp

David Singh
Sainthood and Revelatory Discourse
An Examination of the Basis for the Authority of Bayan in Mahdawi Islam
2003 / 8172147285 / xxiv+485pp

REGNUM AFRICA TITLES

Kwame Bediako
Jesus in Africa, The Christian Gospel in African History and Experience
(2000) (Theological Reflections from the South series)
SECOND EDITION FORTHCOMING 2013

Mercy Amba Oduyoye
Beads and Strands, Reflections of an African Woman on Christianity in Africa
(Theological Reflections from the South series)
2002 / 1-870345-41-X / 114pp

Kä Mana
Christians and Churches of Africa Envisioning the Future, Salvation in Christ and the Building of a new African Society
(Theological Reflections from the South series)
2002 / 1-870345-27-4 / 119pp

Ype Schaaf
On Their Way Rejoicing, The History and Role of the Bible in Africa
2002 / 1-870345-35-9 / 252pp

E.A.W. Engmann
Kpawo-Kpawo Toi Kpawo – Vol. 1, Adesai, Oboade, Lalai, Ajenui ke Shwemoi
(Folklore of the Ga People)
(Gbotsui Series - Indigenous Sources of Knowledge in Ghanaian Languages)
2009 / 978-9988-1-2296-6 / 70pp

Philip Tetteh Laryea
Yesu Homowo Nuntso (Jesus, Lord of Homowo)
(Nyamedua series in Mother-tongue Theology)
(reprinted 2011) / 1-870345-54-1 / 176pp

E.A.W. Engmann
Kpawo-Kpawo Toi Kpawo – Vol. 2, Kusumii (Folklore of the Ga People)
(Gbotsui Series - Indigenous Sources of Knowledge in Ghanaian Languages)
2012 / 978-9988-1-2294-2, 186pp

Philip T. Laryea
Ephraim Amu: Nationalist, Poet and Theologian (1899–1995)
2012 / 978-9988-1-2293-5, 425pp

Jon P. Kirby
The Power and the Glory, Popular Christianity in Northern Ghana
(Trends in African Christianity Series)
2012 / 978-9988-1-2295-9, 350pp

For the up-to-date listing of the Regnum books visit www.ocms.ac.uk/regnum

Regnum Books International
Regnum is an Imprint of The Oxford Centre for Mission Studies
St. Philip and St. James Church
Woodstock Road
Oxford, OX2 6HR

regnum